C000319200

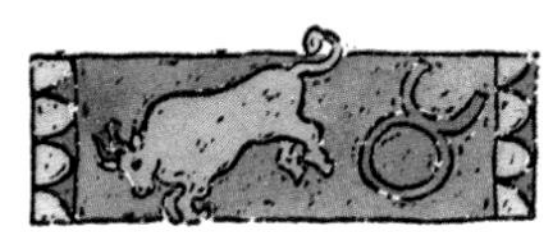

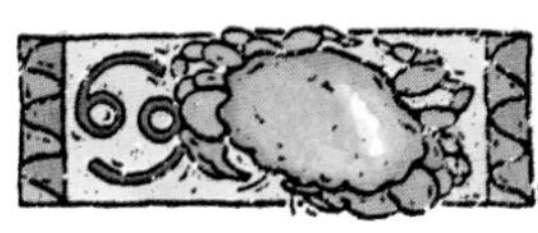
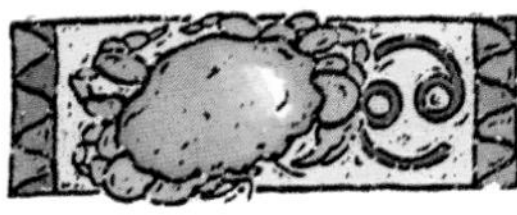

ASTROLOGY
FOR THE AGE OF AQUARIUS

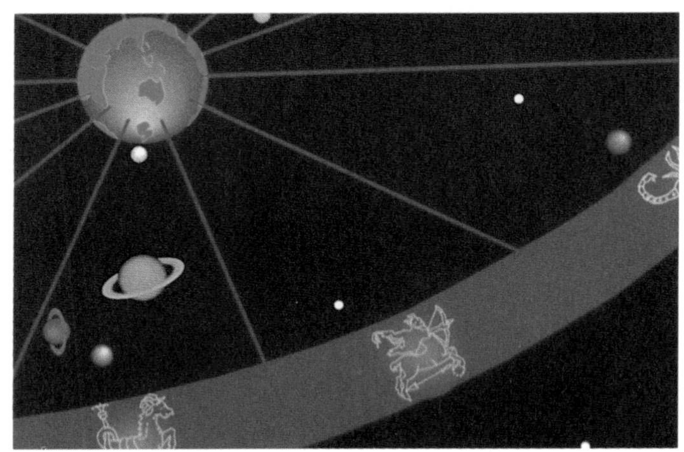

ASTROLOGY
FOR THE AGE OF AQUARIUS

Jan Kurrels

ANAYA PUBLISHERS LTD, LONDON

First published in Great Britain 1990
by Anaya Publishers Ltd,
49 Neal Street, London WC2H 9PJ

British Library Cataloguing in Publication Data
Kurrels, Jan
Astrology for the Age of Aquarius
1. Astrology
I. Title
133.5

ISBN 1-85470-041-3

SPECIAL CONTRIBUTOR: *The Story of Astrology* by James R. Clark

MANAGING EDITOR: Barbara Horn
EDITOR: Viv Croot
ART DIRECTOR: Terry Jeavons
DESIGNER: Sara Nunan
ARTWORK: Jenny Millington
ILLUSTRATORS: Tony Masero, Lorraine Harrison
Computer Graphics by TBS, Brighton
JACKET ILLUSTRATION: front jacket, *Aquarius* by Carolyn Scrace; back jacket, *Earth and the Zodiac* by TBS Brighton
PICTURE RESEARCHER: Andrea Stern
INDEXER: Kathy Gill

Typeset in Goudy Old Style by Central Southern Typesetters, Eastbourne

Colour reproduction by Columbia Offset, Singapore

Printed in England by Clays Ltd, St Ives plc

Contents

Introduction

THE AGE OF AQUARIUS HAS FINALLY DAWNED; THIS IS AN ASTRONOMICAL FACT.

About 2000 years before Jesus Christ was born, the zodiacal constellation behind the Sun at the time of the spring equinox or vernal point was Aries, and it coincided with the zodiac sign Aries. By the time Christ was born, this vernal point had shifted into the constellation Pisces, and the world was enveloped in the Piscean Age, which has just drawn to a close. Now, the zodiacal constellation forming the background for the Sun at the time of the spring equinox is Aquarius, and for the next 2000 years or so, the influence of this constellation will be paramount.

Even so, in spite of the fact that Pisces has shifted into second place, and Aries, still known as the first sign of the zodiac, is now in third place, some modern astrologers seem curiously disinclined to address this fact, or to explore the exciting possibilities that new astronomical research is opening up.

And yet, there is a general resurgence of interest in astrology and a new perception of its status. The interest shown and the new theories discussed by eminent scientists and astronomers, such as Dr Percy Seymour in his book *Astrology: the Evidence of Science*, suggest that astrology and astronomy may well work hand in hand again, as they did originally. The time has come for astrologers throughout the world to work out a formula to establish astrology on a more scientific footing, even to recognize it as a true science in its own right. It is certainly time to work out just what effect the Aquarian Age will have on astrology and our lives for the next 2000 years or so.

Astrology for the Age of Aquarius is a preliminary exploration of the implications of this New Age. It is conceived both as a primer for those coming new to the science of the stars and an introductory evaluation of the effects of the Age of Aquarius. An historical essay sets modern astrology in context; the mechanics of the zodiac and the workings of the horoscope are explained; astronomical, astrological and historical terms are defined in a dictionary for astrologers; and a review of the twelve Sun-sign outlines the possible effects the shift into the new Age may have on traditional characteristics.

In January 1996, Uranus, ruler of Aquarius, enters its own sign. In January 1997, Jupiter, ruler of Sagittarius, enters Aquarius and moves into conjunction with Uranus. In the same year, on 22 December, Venus and Mars will be in absolute conjunction in Aquarius. This amazing alignment of planets in Aquarius reaches a high peak when in February 1998 the planet Neptune, ruler of Pisces, also moves into Aquarius, a most important placing at the start of the Aquarian Age. The new positions of the major planets seem to act as pointers, signposts in the sky that indicate the astrological trends for the new Age of Aquarius. This is only the beginning.

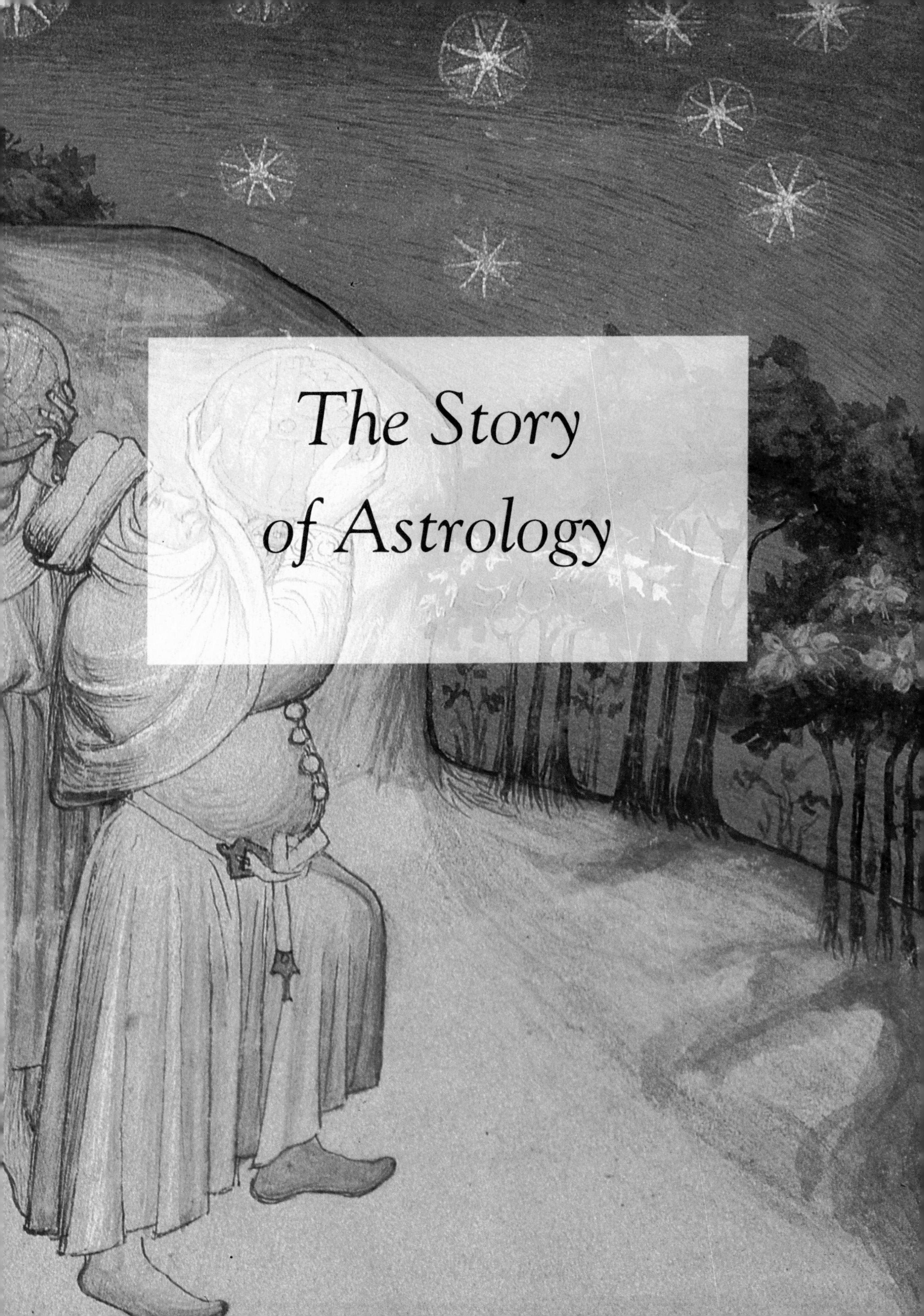
The Story
of Astrology

Star-Lore in Prehistory

Looking up on a clear night, it is not difficult to let oneself feel, as our Stone Age ancestors might have done, that what looks like the dome of heaven swinging slowly over the Earth is just a huge apparatus of lights. In primitive cultures, people do not feel that this apparatus is different in quality from the Earth around them. Their universe is all one: trees and rivers and stars with a life of their own, and able to do good or harm to people. We, too, could accept (if we did not know otherwise) that the Earth we are standing on is fixed eternally in its place at the centre of the grand and stately spectacle of the sky.

In the simple 'with-our-own-eyes' view, we would notice for example that two of the moving points of light – the ones named Mercury and Venus – stay fairly close to the Sun. Sometimes we would see that they moved slowly in a west-to-east direction between us and the Sun, while at other times we would see them moving in an east-to-west direction on the far side of the Sun.

If we steadily tracked the course of the Sun itself we would discover that the speed of its motion in the middle of winter seems to be slightly faster that in the height of summer. These are the sort of observations, 'obvious, direct and immediate', which, as Professor Percy Seymour has pointed out, constitute 'the basic facts that any geometrical picture of the universe had to explain'. What was a Stone Age star-gazer to make of what he saw?

TOUCHING THE SKY

We have no direct way of knowing what the earliest people who we would recognize as fully human like us – they seem to have begun spreading out over the empty spaces of the continents between 200000 and 100000 years ago – thought about the sky and the things they could see in it. But we can guess that they wanted answers to such questions as 'Where do the stars go in the daytime, and where does the sun go at night?' 'How close to us are the stars?' 'Are they alive, and how did they get there?'

We can be fairly sure that people a hundred thousand years ago had room in their minds for thoughts about the significance of everything for their survival – from what a stream is saying to the messages signalled from the stars.

We can also reasonably guess that those early questioners came up with two different sets of answers. We know that in the history of ideas there have always been, as far back as we can see, some who could be called the 'measurers' and others who could be called the 'imaginers'. The measurers would have looked up and said, 'those lights in the sky are at least so many times further away from us than those hills over there' (wrong, of course, but trying their best to be factual). When the imaginers looked up they would have said, 'that bright one over there looks new – I wonder whether it's the soul of some great hero?' (wrong, too, but looking for a message from nature to humanity.)

Closely tied up with their most urgent strategies for staying alive – above all, hunting game and keeping out of trouble – was the need to *know more*: the need to look into what is going to happen, to find out whether what you undertake is going to succeed, whether 'fate' holds out a prosperous future for you, and, on a wider scale, whether the invisible powers who keep the world going will give safety to your own tribe or community or nation among its competitors.. This is where we can look for the deep roots of magic, of religion, of prophecy, of myths – and of astrology.

TAMING THE LAND

Not far inland from the eastern Mediterranean, in hilly country where the climate was pleasant, lived some Stone Age people whose name we do not know. All we do know – from the archaeological study of their camp-sites – is that they hunted gazelles for meat to cook and skins to wear. Also that they gathered wild grass seeds which they ground up in a paste to be baked into flat cakes, or to be stirred in hand-formed clay pots as a sort of porridge for their children to eat.

We also have evidence that at some time between about 8000 and 7000 BC these people made a hugely significant discovery; it was a discovery that they were to share, as time went on, with many of their neighbours – and eventually, with the whole world. They began to sow some of the wild grass seeds themselves; some of these seeds were the result of naturally hybridized (mixed strain) grasses and when they grew, they produced a better quality of grain: the ears of the mixed strain did not shatter and so the grains were not lost as they dropped and blew away. It was the first step on the road to organized cereal farming.

No longer was the people's survival going to depend on constant moving on – after having exhausted one area – until they found a new supply of the wild plants and grains. Camp-sites could become permanent homes, and small groups of families began to shape a new way of life. Goats – and later sheep – readily provided milk, meat, skins and wool. It was a far more reliable arrangement than going to hunt the herds of gazelles on the plains. A settled existence had arrived. Archaeologists call it the Agricultural Revolution.

Sumerian Daybreak

The earliest farming communities began to establish themselves in the lowlands and the inland plains that stretched away towards the great desert of Arabia. Many little settlements came into being in northern Syria, where the upper Euphrates flows through dry steppes. The people living there realized that they could exploit the great river's regular seasonal floods to water their gardens.

It became vitally important to know exactly when the flooding would occur so that crops could be sown beforehand. The necessity of timing their crops properly gave the farmers a sharper awareness of the cyclic movements they could see in the sky. It was obvious from watching the progress of the star patterns (constellations) that the huge bowl overhead made one complete turn, corresponding closely to the seasons.

The trick was to count the exact number of days between the regular reappearances. The idea of the calendar was born. Keeping track of 365 days in a row had, however, its problems for pre-literate people: their numbering systems were not up to it. It seemed best to count the new Moons – the most obvious and often repeated event in the night sky – but then the sequence never came out the same as the seasons of the year.

The search was on for some other regular appearances in the night sky on which people could anchor their heavenly calendar. Here in Mesopotamia they were to find them in the rising and setting of individual stars, such as Arcturus (Alpha Boötis) the brightest star in the northern hemisphere, or distinctive constellations such as the Pleiades or Seven Sisters.

IRRIGATION AND ORGANIZATION

By about 6000 BC, people living in the lower-lying regions of the Middle East started to find ways of bringing water to their plots instead of sitting around fatalistically waiting for either the rains or the floods to come. The management of water in ditches and ponds – in other words, irrigation – was an enormous step forward.

Around 4000 BC, with populations increasing, social changes took place. Sharing work and produce forced people to organize themselves in a new way. People who had been used to family or village units found themselves becoming members of larger groups. Questions of power within these groups led to the rise of dominant personalities or clans. Competition for resources between groups led to conflicts and what can legitimately be called the beginning of history, as the tales of struggle and adventure were handed down in songs and oral poetry.

RIGHT ***The 4000-year-old inlaid panel in the British Museum, London, called the 'Standard of Ur', shows the Sumerian priests, scribes and astrologers at the top of the social hierarchy, while farmers and nomads are seen in the lower bands bringing in produce to them for registration.***

CITY-STATES AND CIVILIZATION

The archaeological evidence of change now begins to be measured in hundreds instead of thousands of years. Right round the 'fertile crescent' that arches from the Persian Gulf in the east to Gaza on the Mediterranean in the west, seeds of city life had been planted. They were to flourish first in the area then known as Sumer, the rich plains bordering the lower Euphrates in modern Iraq. Their names are known: Kish, Nippur, Umma, Lagash, Erech, Ur and Eridu.

Evidence for the organization of production and property is already found from about 6000 BC. At this archaeological level the oldest shrines have been excavated – buried under stepped pyramids known as *ziggurats*. The Sumerians had an urge to build higher and higher shrines to the gods, piling newer temples on top of older ones, raising the summit and broadening the base. Their shrines, supporting a bureaucracy of priests and scribes, were the focus of community life.

Not long after 3500 BC, a system of writing, using some 1500 pictographic signs, was invented. It probably evolved from 'writing in the dust', devised long before for impermanent purposes such as apportioning work and sharing out produce when the first villages came into being. A numerical system – constructed on a base of tens and sixties, and good for quite elaborate arithmetical functions – was also in use. By the beginning of the Early Dynastic period, about 3000 BC, the temple bureaucrats were managing the civil administration of the prosperous city-states.

It was the duty of the temple scribes to make lists of everything, writing with a sharp stylus on pads of soft clay. The tablets recorded how produce was to be stored and distributed, and there was a well developed system of indicating ownership by the use of seal impressions on clay. King-lists were produced, hymns and legends written down, and correspondence with other cities filed away. For the priests and sky-watchers (generally the same class of person), tablets were kept with lists of stars and constellations. The Sumerians thought of the stars in the sky as a mirror image of their own flocks of sheep grazing on the plains of the Euphrates, and referred to them as the 'flock of heaven'. Their leader was the Sun, called therefore Old Tup (Tup being the boss ram of a flock), and the moving stars (the Moon and five planets) were called 'Old Tup's Ewes'. The brightest of the fixed stars were the 'Shepherds'. Arcturus (Alpha Boötis) was the 'Star of the Shepherds'.

WRITTEN IN THE STARS

Eclipses and comets were also noted, and from the recorded risings and phases of the Moon the length of the months and the divisions of the calendar were computed. As well as heavenly happenings, any major storm or flood or drought had to be recorded.

Every phenomenon was important because people felt they were all interconnected aspects of the universe. If a halo surrounded the sun, or the moon was a strange colour, or rain fell out of season, it must mean something. Anything unusual in one part of the cosmos suggested disorder in another part. It was up to the priests and wise men to interpret what the event held for the community.

We can see from their tablets that astrology as understood by the Sumerians – and their Babylonian successors down to about the middle of the fifth century BC – was really a star-omen technique, bundling together 'darkening of the heavens' (dust storms?) and flash floods with eclipses, comets and other astronomical observations. Here is a Babylonian example from the seventh century BC:

When on the first of the month of Nisan the rising sun appears red like a torch, white clouds rise from it, and the wind blows from the east, then there will be a solar eclipse on the 28th or 29th day of the month, the king will die that very month, and his son will ascend the throne.

This is a prescription: there is no escaping the effects of the omens described. If those things should happen, the king *will* die.

We see here a specimen of the fatalistic type of divination which was to make such an impression on the educated classes of the Graeco-Roman world many centuries later. The underlying conflict between the champions of free will (for whom reading the message of the stars could alert you to dangers in something you proposed to do) and those of 'scientific' or fatalist astrology (for whom the fate revealed in the stars is a rigorous law) is still with us.

ABOVE ***A star map or 'astrolabe' drawn on a clay tablet found in the Assyrian capital, Nineveh. The fixed stars are mapped radially in twelve segments.***

RIGHT ***Clay teaching models of animal's livers were ruled off into sections showing where omens could be interpreted by Babylonian diviners. On this sham sheep's liver of the nineteenth to sixteenth century BC there are peg-holes for the instructor's use.***

LEFT ***The Sumerians invented the world's earliest form of writing – the basis for all civilized order. Signs like these on seals of the Early Dynastic period (from 3000 BC) stood for separate sounds or numbers. They made it possible to record the names, times and positions of the heavenly bodies.***

The Valley of the Nile

Even more, perhaps, than Mesopotamia, the valley of the Nile was a location ideally marked out for the growth of early human settlements. Like a tube of fertility running through the desert of northern Africa, it could be entered at both ends. It seems that people moved up from the south to populate the river banks, while the enormous delta on the Mediterranean was the home of groups open to influences (and possibly also to immigration) from western Asia. The Nile delta seems to have the route by which the practice of farming – the Agricultural Revolution in the Middle East – was introduced to the Egyptians.

Once the people of the valley had ceased to rely on hunting and gathering for survival, and had taken up the new life-style of farming, the rhythm of their lives was set by the great annual flooding of the Nile, depositing the rich silt on which all growth depended. It meant careful timing when planting, and they themselves had to be ready to get out of the way before the water rose. A reliable signal was necessary: and the early Egyptians found the marker they needed in the sky.

They noticed that one of the brightest stars they could see, which they called Sothis (our Sirius), would reappear once a year just before sunrise, after having been blotted out for a period previously by the closeness of the Sun itself. This event was followed very soon by the beginning of the Nile flood. The star's heliacal rising (heliacal means 'with the Sun') became the first day of the Egyptian calendar: but that was where the problems began.

EGYPT'S SOTHIC YEAR

Like everybody else in prehistoric ages, the Egyptians used the Moon to mark a unit of time. However, they were unable to divide the year that ran from one 'Sothis-day' to the next into equal 'Moons'. So they made a calendar of twelve nominal months of thirty days each, and threw in five bonus days at the end of the year to make up the full number of 365. The problem with this calendar was that – as the Egyptians must have noticed – Sirius rises a day later every four years.

The calendar soon began to slip 'out of synch' with the Sun and with the seasons, not to mention with the Nile flood. The result was that it took 1460 (four times 365) years for Sothis-day to come back to its proper coincidence with the star's heliacal rising. Roman records indicate Sothis-day fell on the right day in AD 139, and we can work back to possible dates for the launch of the original calendar: 1321 – 2781 – 4241 – 5701 BC. Since texts found in the Pyramids of the Fifth and Sixth Dynasties (between c2494 and 2181 BC) mention a calendar with the five bonus days, either 2781 or 4241 BC present themselves as good candidates for having been, by our reckoning, the actual year when the first Sothic era was instituted in Egypt.

Curiously, the priests did nothing about correcting their calendar until quite a late period. This was probably due to the Egyptians' intensely traditional way of thinking, and may give us some idea of the reason why Egyptian astrologers and diviners enjoyed such prestige in the Greek-speaking world. Their wisdom appeared to come directly from sources in the remotest possible past, and their occult skills seemed to be unchanged by the passing of time.

STAR WARS: EGYPT V. BABYLON

The pragmatic Romans tried to get to the bottom of the question. The Egyptians assured them that records of astral influences had been kept for over 400,000 years in the Nile valley – possibly even for 630,000 years. On behalf of the Babylonians it was claimed, on the other hand, that their tablets of observations went back 730,000 years – a figure that was later improved to 1,440,000 years! These astonishing computations cannot be reconciled with our knowledge of human prehistory. Rather, they may be regarded as being symbolic of how long ago 'long ago' seemed to people.

Archaeological study of the Babylonian tablets tells us that in fact more solid observational work on the stars was done in ancient Mesopotamia than can be found in Egyptian texts. Yet even after Egypt had been absorbed into the Greek-speaking culture by the conquests of Alexander the Great late in the third century BC, it was still, in the eyes of the Greeks and Romans, the birthplace of star-lore. Since the new city of Alexandria in Egypt was by then host to the world's foremost school of observers of, and theorists about, the stars, we should not begrudge the Egyptians their otherwise not fully deserved reputation for having started it all.

THE DECANS: EGYPT'S ZODIAC

The origin of the system of thirty-six star-gods, called in Greek the 'Decans', is without question Egyptian. Long before the Egyptians had heard of the Babylonian scheme of the zodiac divided into twelve houses they had noticed that a different constellation rose up over the horizon behind the Sun at regular ten-day intervals throughout the year. (Hippopotamus was their name for Cassiopeia, but most of the patterns of the stars were in Egyptian eyes different from the Babylonian and Greek constellations.) They assigned a god's name and immense powers over human fates to each of the thirty-six segments into which they divided the Sun's path. The Decans were the basis on which the Egyptians erected their horoscopes.

The Hellenistic astrologers assimilated both traditions into their own system, and from then on the Decans would often be found transformed into a 360-degree subdivision of the zodiac. Consequently, the original divinatory values given to the Decans by the Egyptian priests gradually faded away.

BELOW ***The fertile silt deposited by the flooding of the Nile made a garden in the desert. The ancient Egyptians felt this was an annual miracle they owed to a god named Hapi – pictured on this papyrus of the eighteenth Dynasty (1567–1320 BC).***

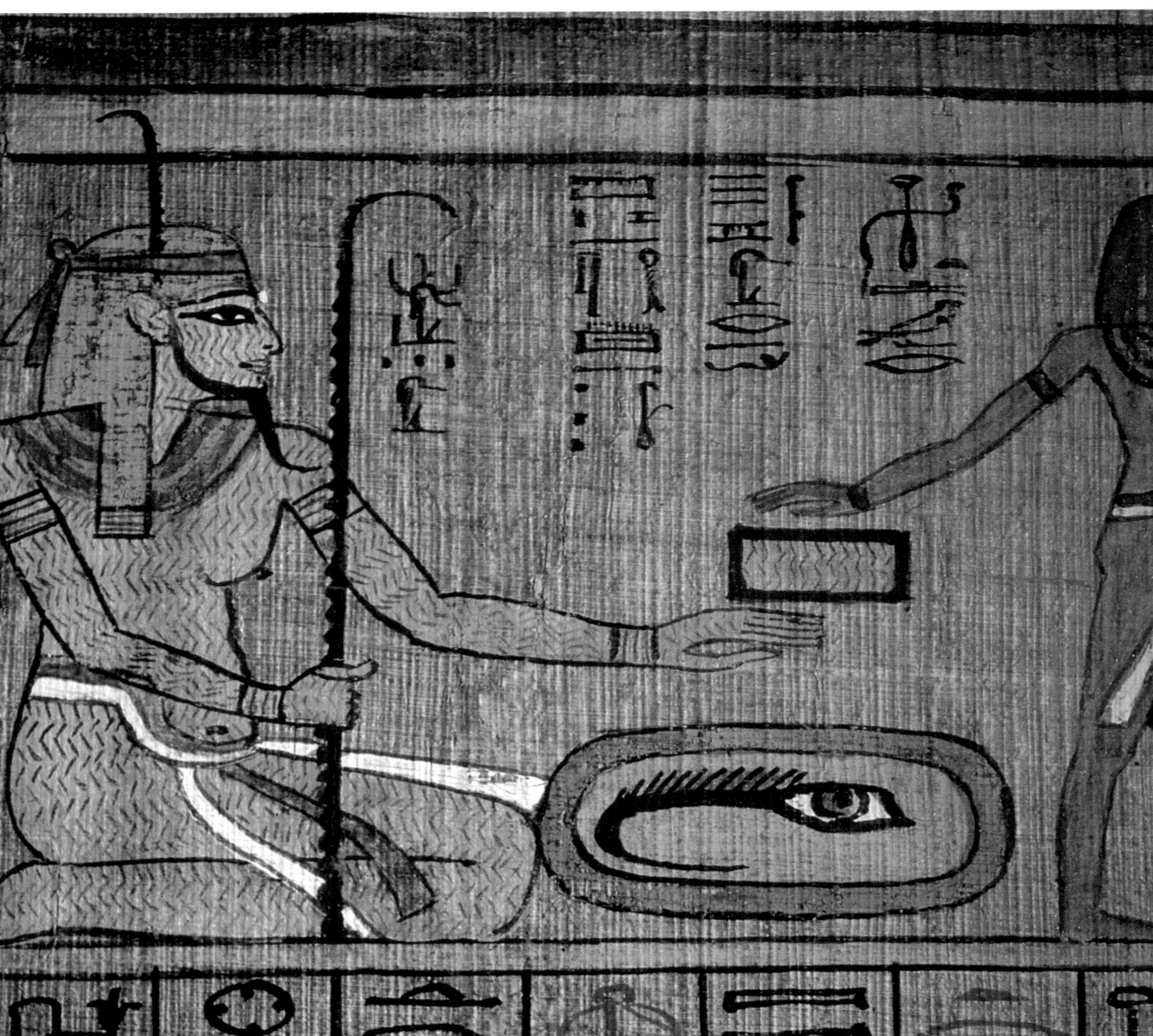

RIGHT *Stonehenge in its final form as seen from the air. The original Heel Stone stands in the entrance gap (left of photograph), facing the sunrise on midsummer's morn.*

The Stonehenge Sun-Moon Reckoner

While the Sumerians were wrestling with the meaning of the cosmos , in a remote north-west corner of Europe, the builders of Stonehenge were trying to contruct a three-dimensional device to help them measure, record and predict the bewildering activities of the celestial bodies.

The most exciting result of recent research into the enigmas of Stonehenge is the realization that its layout is Sun and Moon oriented in great and subtly realized detail. Gerald S. Hawkins of the Smithsonian Astrophysical Observatory has demonstrated the prehistoric solar and – especially – lunar calculations that must have been based on accurate observations made over many centuries before the first Stonehenge building.

Hawkins' special achievement was, in the 1960s, to have been the first researcher who put a computer to work on the question. From co-ordinates of pairs of stones, the computer was asked which Sun and Moon events in the sixteenth century BC they would have been aligned towards. The answer indicated that the Stonehenge people had laid out a sanctuary (marked with posts, wooden at first, boulders later) which gave them crucial sightings of the Sun and Moon. Using these, they were able to do two – for them – very important things: find a reliable recurrent starter for the year and its seasons, and predict the otherwise terrifying eclipses.

EARLY ALIGNMENTS

The Stone Age in Britain was nearing its end about 4 000 years ago. The farming revolution had by then reached western Europe. People lived by herding and growing simple crops. The agricultural year dominated their lives in a way that would have depressed their hunting and gathering ancestors of many thousands of years. Food may have been in better supply now, but work was hard labour when you had to dig with a deer antler, plough with a sharpened stick and shape a stone with another stone. The survival of the community might depend on getting the time right for sowing. As for the Nile valley people, finding a firm date for the start of the year had become an economic necessity.

The task for the calendar-makers, therefore, was to set out accurately the major stations of the Sun and Moon and mark them with the alignment of two posts. Then there could be no arguments among the people. In this way, the builders of the first version of Stonehenge opened the way – as Hawkins discovered – to developments which in less than a hundred years made this site an observatory and ready-reckoner of astonishing ingenuity.

STONEHENGE MARK I

The first Stonehenge, as it took shape between about 2500 and 1900 BC, was like an open corral surrounded by a big ditch. The one way in and out faced northeast – the direction of sunrise on midsummer's day. Inside the corral, and forming a rectangle within the ditch, were four upright stones. A fifth one – the great 'heel stone' which is a feature of the place to this day – stood in the entrance. By looking along an alignment of any two of them, at the right times, you would have been able, weather permitting, to see the winter sun rise at its most southerly, or the summer sun at its most northerly. (It has long been obvious, of course, that from the centre of the ring you could on midsummer's morn watch the sun come up over the heel stone.)

The Moon's summer and winter extremes of rising or setting could be viewed along different combinations of the same stones on different dates. Some other alignments were possible for both Sun and Moon by taking in a few additional stones. All alignments that were to be added later, such as the equinoxes, seem to be refinements of these original markers.

The other major function of Stonehenge was to predict eclipses. This was Hawkins' most brilliant deduction, and although strictly speaking unproven, it is a highly persuasive thesis. It is based on the otherwise inexplicable 'Aubrey holes'.

THE ECLIPSE CALCULATOR

The Aubrey holes get their name from the English antiquary, John Aubrey (1626-1697), who first reported their existence. They consist of a ring of fifty-six small pits dug just inside the inner bank of the surrounding ditch and date from the first phase, about 1900 BC. Not only do they appear never to have had stones standing in them, but they were filled and refilled several times and finally left looking rather conspicuous and enigmatic with their crushed chalk tops. What were they for?

Hawkins reasoned that since, *firstly* the builders of Stonehenge needed a means of predicting eclipses of the Moon (always a fear-making event in early societies); and *secondly* there was a hint by an ancient Greek geographer, that a nineteen-year Moon cycle was inaugurated with important rituals in a far northern island; and *thirdly* the Moon cycle in question lasts not nineteen but almost exactly 18.61 years – it seemed possible that some mathematical way of correcting the start of each new cycle might have been devised.

It struck Hawkins that if you adjusted the Moon cycles to run for 19/19/18 years repetitively the error would be overcome. He already knew from records that Moon phenomena repeated at Stonehenge fairly uniformly every fifty-six years. Now 19+19+18 is fifty-six, and there are fifty-six Aubrey holes. Was this a clue to be followed up? Hawkins decided that it was, and his calculations showed that a simple scheme of moving six stones – spaced 9/9/10/9/9/10 holes apart – once a year on to the next hole in the Aubrey ring will correctly predict possible eclipses over hundreds of years.

STONEHENGE MARK II

This fascinating suggestion may explain the immense prestige Stonehenge obviously retained for several centuries and under three successive cultures in the Wessex region. Quite soon after the initial phase, during which the Late Stone Age people had laid down all the basic alignments, and positioned the Aubrey holes, the first cultural change occurred. A new population, who worked copper and gold, and are referred to by archaeologists as the Beaker People, took over in Salisbury Plain around 1750 BC. For about a hundred years Stonehenge seems to have gone through a period of trial and error. New boulders, known as the 'bluestones', seem to have been brought, somehow, from the Prescelly Mountains in Wales and introduced into the circle in two concentric rings. They were uprooted, placed somewhere else and again moved. In the end, whatever the Beaker People were trying to do was aborted abruptly, and nothing remains of their version of Stonehenge. The next group to move in are called the Wessex People.

THE FINAL GLORY OF STONEHENGE

With their Bronze Age culture, the Wessex People were the architects of the splendid Stonehenge, unique in north-western Europe, the remains of which we can admire today. The layout was changed to allow for enhanced alignments and 'surprise' views. More than eighty-one huge sarsen stones or monoliths were transported from the Marlborough Downs to the site, and set up as an imposing outer circle of thirty uprights joined by lintels, and enclosing an inner horseshoe layout of five trilithons (a trilithon is a group of two uprights and a lintel). This must have been about 1650 BC. More short-term schemes affected the smaller bluestones dating from the Beaker People phase, possibly in the course of similar astronomic experiments. At this period, too, two concentric rings of thirty and twenty-nine holes were dug outside the great ditch. These might have been another try for better predictive observations. Finally, and probably before 1600 BC, the remaining bluestones were placed in their present positions (a horseshoe within the trilithons, and a circle between the trilithons and the outer circle). And that is the last we know of Stonehenge's history.

Babylon the Great

In the eighteenth century BC, the famous city of Babylon makes its first major appearance in history. Under its ruler Hammurabi the Law-giver (c1792-1750 BC), Sumerian was still in use as the literary, legal and religious language of educated people, just as Latin continued to be used in Europe for a thousand years after the Roman empire had broken up. The Sumerian empire of city-states had bequeathed its great invention, cuneiform or wedge shaped writing to the coming Babylonians. Later dynasties continued to foster the Sumerian-Babylonian tradition, right up to the tenth century BC.

THE MONTHLY PROGNOSTICATORS

Astrologers had a respected and well-defined role in Babylonian culture and in the administration of the various states and empires that succeeded each other in Mesopotamia. It was their particular responsibility to give advance notice of the final day of each month, which fluctuated from the twenty-ninth to the thirtieth, and was dependent on observations of the Sun and Moon around the fourteenth of each month. A calendar of lunar months was used, with the familiar problem of adjusting this to the solar year. The astrologers were also required to determine how many days would be needed to be added in order to keep them in step.

When reporting their observations, the astrologers took care to describe the appearance of the Moon. Were its horns equal or unequal? Did it stay close to the horizon? All could be interpreted. 'If the horns are pointed, the king will triumph over whomever he gores.' 'If the Moon is low when it appears, the submission of a distant nation will be brought to the king.' The halo of the Moon was an area that interested them greatly. Any star, constellation or planet visible inside the halo was considered a significant omen.

The divinatory work of the scribes and clergy of the sun-baked cities of Mesopotamia attracted the disapproval, however, of the prophets of Israel. Isaiah seems to have known them well when he thundered (xlvii, 12, 13):

> *Stand now [Babylon] with thine enchantments, and with the multitude of thy sorceries, wherein thou hast laboured from thy youth . . . Let now the astrologers, the stargazers, the monthly prognosticators, stand up, and save thee from these things that shall come upon thee.*

THE IDEA OF THE ZODIAC

It must eventually have struck someone that since there is one band of sky through which all the planets (including the Sun and Moon) have their courses and that this band lies over at least a segment of twelve separate constellations, these could be used to identify twelve equal compartments of the band. The number twelve being divisible by the Babylonian base of sixtieths, a convenient calibration was to hand. Moreover, the twelve constellations had already been assigned qualities. The zodiac had been discovered.

The earliest known horoscope using the zodiac is on a clay tablet inscribed in cuneiform writing and dated, by modern calculations from the planetary longitudes provided, to 29 April 410 BC. Thus, after 3 000 years of practice, astrology reached its full development for personal horoscopes scarcely a hundred years before Alexander the Great's conquests brought the tide of Hellenistic culture swirling into the Middle East.

RIGHT ***This diagram on a clay tablet of c600 BC locates Babylon in relation to the known world. The Euphrates is marked as two vertical lines, with cities and neighbouring countries listed. Outside Mesopotamia, which is encircled by the 'bitter ocean', lie fabulous lands infested by monsters and visited only by heroes.***

LEFT ***Hammurabi (2067–25 BC), who first made Babylon great, offering his laws to the seated figure of Shamash the sun-god and patron of justice. Babylon's rulers relied on regular reports from star-watchers for keeping the lunar and solar parts of the official calendar in step.***

THE BABYLONIAN BLIND SPOT

The Babylonians appear to have had a blind spot for the precession of the equinoxes – the slow movement westwards along the ecliptic (the apparent path of the Sun) of the point where the Sun appears to cross the celestial equator. Although it has been claimed that around 343 BC, in the last decade before Alexander the Great, the Babylonian astronomer Kidin-ni (Cidenas) discovered the slippage which had taken place along the ecliptic, the tablets which have been discovered so far show that the Babylonians had been unaware of it.

The Greeks and the Wisdom of the East

There is a familiar quotation from the historian Herodotus (c484-425 BC) which is regarded as summing up the first contact between Greek and Mesopotamian science: 'From the Babylonians the Greeks learned *polos* (the Pole Star) and *gnomon* (the finger of the sun-dial) and the twelve parts of the day.' Initially, the likely intermediaries between the two cultures were Phoenician sea traders.

Before this contact with the cities of the east had been made, the ancient Greek perception of astronomical matters was largely concerned with weather forecasting. Where the poetical farmer's almanac composed by Hesiod (c700 BC) pays any attention to them, it is of the 'red sky at morning, shepherd's warning' variety. The Greeks did not even learn to distinguish planets from fixed stars until under Babylonian influence in the fifth century BC.

LEFT ***A Babylonian boundary stone of about 11200 BC. Below the divine symbols of the sun, moon and Venus, the inscription records a gift of land, and invokes the curse of the gods on anyone who moves it. Among the animal emblems of minor deities is a scorpion which may prefigure the zodiacal sign.***

IONIAN GENIUS

Thales of Miletus (c625-547 BC), the fountainhead of the great stream of Greek scientists and philosophers, was seen in his day as an 'importer' of eastern knowledge. He seems to have travelled in Egypt and he was also allegedly of half-Phoenician ancestry. (He passed on a Phoenician tip to Greek sailors: steer by the Little Bear rather than the Great Bear.) His astronomy and mathematics were exact enough for him to predict successfully an eclipse in 585 BC. His astronomical work was continued by his followers in Miletus, one of whom, Anaximenes (died c500 BC) theorized that the stars were glittering studs fixed to a transparent rotating sphere.

HEAVENLY SPHERES

The concept of Earth as a motionless sphere around which the Sun and stars revolve in a stately and regular manner was well established by now; by the fifth century BC, the Greeks had resolved the anomalies of the seasons and it was agreed that the Sun moved round the Earth in a perfectly circular orbit. Perfect circular motion was so satisfying philosophically to Plato (427-348 BC) that he encouraged his students to develop the theory to account for the motion of the other heavenly bodies. His challenge was taken up by Eudoxus of Cnidus (c408-c353 BC), the greatest mathematician of his time. Eudoxus' put forward the idea of cosmic spheres. He proposed that the Sun, Moon and planets were each mounted on one of a sequence of twenty-six separate, transparent spheres, one inside another. The independent revolution of each sphere on its own axis would therefore account for the movements that one saw in the sky. Eudoxus' major work, incidentally, the *Phainomena*, was based on borrowed and unadjusted Egyptian data so traditional that it has been calculated that they refer to conditions in the sky from 1600 years earlier: that is to say, about 1950 BC!

THE PYTHAGOREANS

A 'brotherhood' that was both moralistic and scientific arose in the later part of the sixth century BC; its members were to give currency to many of the ideas that are familiar in astrology. Founded by the philosopher Pythagoras (c580-c500 BC), their organization had political aims as well as being concerned with propagating a variety of novel theories (and theorems) in music, mathematics, numerology, ethics and philosophy. A distinctively eastern element in their teaching was the idea that souls migrated from one life to another until they finally achieved bliss and consummation as fiery stars in the sky.

The ideas of the Pythagoreans underline the emotional and mystical aspects of the Greeks' developing knowledge of the stars. Greek astrologers now rounded off the Mesopotamian star list by giving each one of the planets the name and attributes of a god or goddess – something the eastern astrologers had not found it necessary to do in every case. The Sun and the Moon, the planets, constellations and stars were coming to be seen both as signals to the human race and as divine in themselves. Through them, astrologers could interpret the will of the gods to humanity. Astrologers were informers in a heavenly mechanism of fate.

ASTROLOGIA AND ASTRONOMIA

There was a popular anecdote among the Greeks that made fun of Thales the philosopher Miletus. They said that when he was out one night 'astronomizing', with his head in the air, he fell into a well . . . We are not told what exactly people originally meant by 'astronomizing': in the great age of Greek philosophers, the fifth century BC, debate raged about what was *astrologia* and what was *astronomia*, and what was the difference, if any, between them.

The matter was not decisively settled. In the fourth century BC, the great classifier of knowledge, Aristotle, taught that there was a practical application of star-lore in, for example, navigation at sea, and that there was a field of theoretical investigation that was concerned with the measurement and calculation of the positions and relative motions of planets and stars. What *he* referred to as 'astrology' was what we call geometry and mathematics.

BELOW ***Notes and diagrams in an astronomical papyrus from Egypt, written during the Greek period (332–30 BC).***

NEW EXPLANATIONS

Heracleides Ponticus (mid-fourth century BC), another of Plato's students, had already postulated that Mercury and Venus might be satellites of the Sun, with the whole group moving round the Earth. Now, the Alexandrian geometrician Apollonius of Perga (c262-c200 BC) was of the opinion that if the planets really revolved round the Earth then their paths could not be circular, but would have to describe epicycles and eccentric circles. The Earth itself could not be at the centre of their observed orbits.

Only one Greek astronomer of the third century BC, Aristarchus of Samos (c310-230 BC), came to the conclusion publicly that the Earth turned on its own axis and must revolve round

LEFT ***Detail of carving on a sarcophagus from Sidon, showing Alexander the Great in battle against the Persians at Issus.***

BELOW ***Anaximander (sixth century BC), here seen on a Roman mosaic from the Rhineland, was popularly credited with 'inventing' the sundial.***

The root meaning of the word mathematics has to do with learning, and as the Pythagoreans, for example, associated the idea of learning supremely with the science of numbers (for them, the metaphysical key to everything), they felt mathematicians belonged to their inner circle. So when later on (especially among the Romans) the name *mathematikoi* was applied to the so-called Chaldeans or oriental astrologers, it had a hint of 'learned doctor' about it, as well as meaning someone who 'calculated' horoscopes.

Hellenistic Astrology

The fusion of the western and eastern cultures that Alexander the Great had tried to enforce when he was living certainly came about after his death – in the sense that the Middle East became thoroughly Hellenized. From the time of Alexander's death until the explosion of Islam, a period of 960 years, Greek was the common language and Greek forms of thought, art and religion prevailed.

Alexandria in Egypt, founded by Alexander himself, became the greatest Greek city in the world, and Seleucia on the Tigris soon eclipsed nearby Babylon. Closer acquaintance with the records and calculations of the old Babylonian masters enhanced the star sciences of the Greeks. Refinements on the astronomical theories of the age of Aristotle were proposed, as observers struggled to fit the observable facts into the generally approved theory.

the Sun – a view which was denounced as 'irreligious', since it diminished the received idea of the Sun God, Apollo, driving his chariot in glory across the heavens!

While the philosopher-scientists laboured to construct theories of the universe that would bear out their direct observations, the professional astrologers were refining their methods reading a person's fate from zodiacal horoscopes. A learned priest named Berossus from the temple of Bel Marduk in Babylon settled on the island of Kos (with its school of medicine) where he carried out the self-imposed task of making the knowledge of the Babylonian priesthood available to the Hellenistic world in the Greek language. This compendium of Babylonian star-lore, finished in about 280 BC, became a standard work for Greek and Latin readers.

FATALISTIC ATTRACTION

Within thirty years of the death of Alexander the Great, a new intellectual movement arrived in the Hellenistic world. Its adherents came largely from the ruling classes. They were nicknamed 'Stoics', and the movement itself called Stoicism, from a *stoa* (or open gallery) on the market place of Athens where its founder, Zeno, talked and taught. His and his successors' teachings gave a widely accepted basis for the fatalism that underlies the individual, birth-hour contingent horoscope, newly made possible by that oriental invention, the zodiac.

If everything in the universe moves according to the unchanging laws of nature, as the Stoics held, it follows that the events of a person's life are pre-determined. This greatly strengthens the acceptance of a method of forecasting that is calculated, as the horoscope is, from concrete mathematical data (however interpreted). It is a state of mind that was to smooth the way for the acceptance of the astrologer's role in the civilization which was to comprise the Roman empire.

CATARCHICS AND CATASTERISMS

Two distinct trends became apparent among the consumers of Hellenistic astrology, and these have persisted in one guise or another until the present day. On the one hand, the sterner doctrine of the two, which appealed primarily to the ruling classes, among whom the austere Stoic philosophy of the Stiff Upper Lip had a hold, accepted that the constellation prevailing at birth put a pre-determined stamp on the whole character and destiny of a person. This is called 'fatalistic' astrology, meaning that your fate is fixed without escape. For some, the implacable character of this kind of horoscope might be softened by the belief, popularized by the Pythagoreans, that the soul remained free after death and could return again and again for a new and perhaps better life.

On the other hand, you might, especially if you belonged to the poor and mainly illiterate mass of society, choose to consult a 'catarchic' astrologer – one more like a modern funfair's Madame Stella. This kind of astrologer would answer questions about favourable and unfavourable influences at certain times or for certain actions. The set questions listed by one such practitioner have been preserved in a Latin manuscript. Here are a few examples: 'Will someone return from abroad?', 'Which boxer will win?', 'Is he jealous?', 'Will someone get back what he is owed?', 'Has he made someone pregnant?', and so on.

Beyond these different approaches loomed another and newer perception of the stars. It was to gain an increasingly strong a hold over people's imaginations as the Hellenistic turned into the Roman centuries. In fact, it was new only in the sense that astrology was now reaching a much wider audience: it was a perception that had always been dimly present, since the days when primitive humans first wondered about the night sky. Astrologers call it the belief in catasterism or 'becoming a star'.

It was felt by many that the souls of the dead, instead of shuffling and whispering unhappily in a dark underworld (as the early Greeks and other peoples thought), would leave their bodies and float upwards. Where would they go then? They would become immortal and be transformed into stars.

EXPLAINING THE EQUINOXES

In the late second century BC, the great mathematician, geographer and astronomer Hipparchus made a discovery that had apparently eluded the Babylonian astrologers: the precession of the equinoxes.

Hipparchus made his own direct observations between 146 and 127 BC both from his home country, Bithynia (east of the sea of Marmara, Turkey), and from Rhodes.

Hipparchus would not have been able to make the precise calculations which led to his discovery if he had been limited to reliable Greek data accumulated over a mere two centuries or so. Earlier Babylonian data had already begun to relate the position of stars to the ecliptic (the apparent path of the Sun). Correlating the current longitude of low-latitude stars such as Spica (Alpha Virginis) with their longitudes recorded in Alexandria 150 years earlier, he found that the older Babylonian data confirmed that the longitude was increasing. Hipparchus therefore concluded, correctly, that the equinoxes must be slipping westward along the ecliptic by at least a degree every century.

LEFT *Like most of his family, Soter, son of Cornelius Pollios of West Thebes, wished to be buried under the gaze of the benign sky-goddess Nút. Inside the lid of the wooden coffins in which their mummified bodies lay Nút was painted between two rows of the signs of the Graeco-Babylonian zodiac. This custom – in the second century AD – would have seemed as foreign to ancient Egyptian embalmers as the Greek-origin family itself.*

Astral Secrets of the Pharaohs

The ordinary people of Hellenized Egypt, packed into crowded towns and villages – and above all in the shanty-towns of the brand-new capital city, Alexandria – had little use for scientific and philosophical novelties. They simply needed help with their lives. Tracts on astrological medicine and recipes for charms and amulets sold well. Although written mostly in Greek, now the language common to eastern Mediterranean society, they drew on, or were clothed in, concepts straight out of the 3 000-year old culture of ancient Egypt.

It was normal practice to attribute the authorship of these Hellenistic 'revelation books' to someone from times past – the more distant the better. One of the best known seems to have been written between 200 and 150 BC, but the author claimed to be a sixth-century BC priest named Petosiris who had been inspired by the ghost of the Pharaoh Nechepso (Twenty-sixth Dynasty, 663-522 BC). The most famous of all, however, claimed to have as its author no less an authority than the Egyptian god of learning, Thoth.

HERMES THE GREATEST!

The title of the famous collection of occult writings known as the *Hermes Trismegistus* is in fact the Greek version of the title of the god himself who was supposed to have written (or dictated) them. The ibis-headed god Thoth was among other things the patron of writing and of book-learning. In the pictures of the weighing of souls for their place in the after-life, Thoth was shown as keeping the records.

RIGHT ***During the Italian Renaissance, enthusiastic revivers of esoteric philosophy (astrology, alchemy and magic) revered the figure of Hermes Trismegistus – pictured here as an elderly sage in an inlaid pavement in Siena cathedral, Italy – as the transmitter of 'ancient wisdom' from Greece and Egypt.***

When the Greeks became acquainted with the Nile valley civilization, they approximated the local gods, as far as they could, to their own gods of Olympus. In the case of Thoth, they thought they saw similarities between his role and that of the 'messenger of the gods', Hermes (or Mercury, as the Romans called him). In Greek popular religion, Hermes – whose symbol was originally a phallus – evoked a more powerful image than the rather light-weight and devious character we think of as wing-heeled Mercury. 'Trismegistus' or 'thrice-greatest' is simply the translation of Thoth's Egyptian title.

The writings grouped together as the *Hermes*, and which give the name 'hermetic' to this kind of literature, cover not only astrological but also deeply spiritual treatises, and magical remedies for the sick as well. ('Hermetically sealed' once meant, of course, 'concealed as closely as the mysteries revealed in *Hermes Trismegistus*'; now it just means 'airtight'!) Centuries after they had ceased to circulate, interest in their mystical contents revived strongly in the Renaissance, and later again under the influence of Theosophy, as we shall see.

Republican Rome

Until their final defeat of Hannibal (204 BC) conferred Great Power status on them, the Romans were an agrarian republic run by an aristocratic clique, with the culture you would expect of one: earthy, unimaginative, conservative. They had their time-honoured ways of predicting the weather and, as in other peasant societies, they were to a high degree superstitious over omens such as comets, earthquakes, the flight of birds and the markings on the entrails of sacrificial animals.

After the curtain had been rung down on the war against Carthage, however, the Romans' involvement with the cultivated Greek cities of southern Italy and Sicily which they now ruled – such as Naples, Taranto, Syracuse, Messina, Agrigento – as well as diplomatic contacts with (and military intervention in) Greece itself led to a gradual change of attitude in the Roman upper classes. Signs of this can be seen in the pioneering Latin writers early in the second century BC.

Plautus (c253-184 BC), the pioneer comic playwright in Rome, gave the prologue of his comedy *Rudens* (c192 BC) to be spoken by 'Arcturus', the name of the bright star in Boötes the Herdsman. He comes on as the spy for the gods, declaring:

Night times I glitter up there in the army of gods;
daytimes I slip around among the humans on Earth. Nor
am I the only star to come down here.

The poet Ennius (c239-169 BC), born in the Greek-speaking south, seems to have been the first Latin writer to mention astrologers as such . . . selling tips for winning horses at the circus!

A THREAT TO SOCIETY

In their at first rather provincial way, Roman gentlemen began to lap up the varied riches of Greek civilization. Rubbing shoulders with educated Greeks in Rome itself, they were drawn into fundamental arguments about fate and free will. If they inclined to the Stoics' point of view, they were the more ready to pay attention to the Hellenistic astrologers arriving in Rome, now the capital city of the whole Mediterranean. If they were sceptical of astrology, there were always others among the Greek intellectuals who, with their love of argument, were ready to demolish its claims.

In Rome, the conservatives in the Senate still had the upper hand. On the whole, even the 'humanists' who had absorbed Greek ideas had little sympathy for the discontents of the non-noble classes who were ready to claim their share of the republic's growing political power. The principle taught by some of the Stoics that everyone was equal had been taken up by the astrologers: since the stars at one's birth were the determining factor in everyone's life, one's class, wealth or upbringing could only be of secondary importance. The conservatives struck hard to eradicate this destabilizing notion: in 139 BC, all 'foreign astrologers' were banned and expelled from the city.

CICERO AND CO.

Flinging out the astrologers was not enough to preserve the old order of things. Bitter civil wars undermined it and a new generation brought in leaders sympathetic to Hellenistic astrology. Although Cicero (106-43 BC) wrote what he intended as a critical treatise entitled *On Divination*, his grasp of the techniques he describes is shaky. Cicero's friend, the scholar Publius Nigidius Figulus (c99-45 BC), and their slightly older contemporary, Marcus Terentius Varro (116-27 BC), were both devotees of the astrological world-view.

Nigidius embraced the whole Hellenistic system, and wrote and lived in accordance with his mystical concept of it. As a member of the Roman Establishment (he was clerk to the Senate) he was well placed to form a 'brotherhood' of like-minded neo-Pythagoreans. These goings-on, combined with the employment of boy mediums, gave them a rather lurid reputation among ordinary people. The scholarly Varro was author of Europe's first collection of illustrated biographies (700 notable Greeks and Romans, in fifteen books). Sceptical at first, it was when Varro decided to include horoscopes of his subjects, and commissioned some from Lucius Tarutius, that he became seriously involved with astrology. Cicero, Nigidius and Varro all knew Tarutius. He was a practising astrologer in Rome, and what has survived of his work throws a light on changes that were taking place.

The idea of mathematical reversibility – that is to say, if you know someone's biographical details, you can deduce the moment of their birth from them, as you derive the solution to a geometrical problem from the given facts – is traceable to the revived school of neo-Pythagoreans at Athens. Likewise, Tarutius' use of the Egyptian names of the months in his horoscopes shows an obvious deference to his sources.

The Stars of the Caesars

In the spring of 44 BC, the body of the assassinated dictator Julius Caesar had been cremated in the Forum of Rome and, soon after, the dead man's adopted son, Octavius, arrived in the city to perform the funeral ceremonies. By custom, these included a day of free public sports at the deceased's expense. In the late afternoon, a comet of unusual brightness was noticed in the northern sky above the stadium. Romans habitually read meanings into such events, and young Octavius, aged eighteen, saw his chance. 'It's my father's soul!' he shouted with excitement to the awed spectators.

The comet of 44 BC was visible for seven evenings and nights. Octavius' exclamation had been entirely in tune with popular feeling, and he was able to get a decree adopted to the effect that the comet signified the gods' acceptance of Julius Caesar's soul. In the streets they went further: the comet *was* Caesar's soul, and it had become a star, shining down on them from the sky for ever. On the strength of all this, Octavius ordered a gilt star to be fixed over the head of Caesar's statue on the Capitol.

The political opponents of the pro-Caesar faction could hardly let him get away with it. They hauled out an elderly Etruscan soothsayer called Vulcatius, who addressed a public meeting on the real and gloomy meaning of the comet – it heralded the Tenth Age of Mankind and all sorts of dismal things could be expected: whereupon Vulcatius fell dead of a stroke on the platform. So Caesar's soul continued to glitter among the stars, and in 29 BC, after a long struggle, Octavius became sole ruler of the Roman empire. He received the title 'Augustus' ('the increase bringer') in 27 BC.

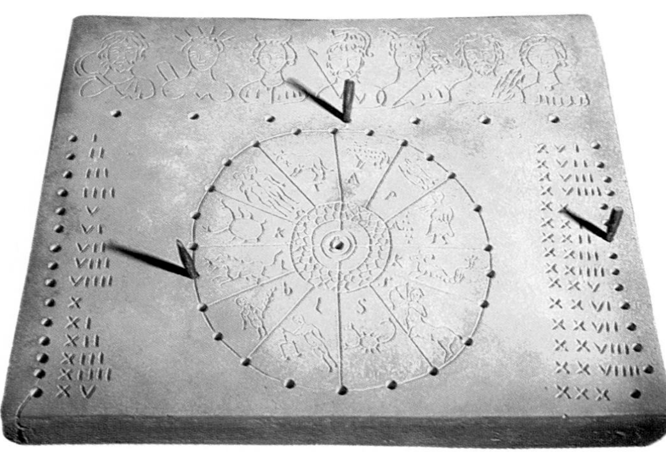

ABOVE ***Pegs placed in the right holes in this incised Roman calendar tell the day, week and month. The twelve segments which represent the months within the circle are marked with the zodiacal signs, but it is not clear how these were assimilated to the traditional months of the old Roman year.***

UNIVERSAL ACCEPTANCE

From the expulsion order of 139 BC to the start of the imperial regime under Augustus in 29 BC, social attitudes to astrology and the political implications of divination had gone through several changes. For upper-class Romans of that first couple of generations who were still taking on board the thought and arts of the Greeks, the tone was set by the Stoic philosophers. Among these, the prevailing school had no time for the fatalism which went hand in hand with oriental astrology. Well-bred scepticism was *à la mode*, and if the masses tended to whole-hearted acceptance, then the foreign charlatans should be sent packing.

When the Syrian-born philosopher Posidonius (c135-c50 BC) brought the Stoics back to their earlier rigid fatalism, the Roman aristocracy's resistance weakened. As we have seen, leading members such as Figulus and Varro were convinced and active believers. For the appeal of astrology to educated minds had two sides: on the one hand, the rationally minded saw the astrologers' observations as a sort of bridge between the cosmic laws that governed the universe and day-to-day life on Earth; on the other hand, to the religiously inclined, astrology offered insights into a cosmic wholeness of a different kind. In circles where the mystical ideas of the Pythagoreans were cultivated, scientific astrology had less appeal than the 'hermetic' astrological writings, with their direct personal revelations of the mysteries of existence. The *Nechepso-Petosiris* manual was one of the most widely circulated.

THE PURGE OF 33 BC

Both rational and religious trends in the Roman élite were thus halfway to acknowledging the force of Octavius Augustus's salute to Caesar's comet in front of the cheering crowd in 44 BC. Eleven years on, however, when the civil war between Octavius and the Mark Antony-Cleopatra alliance was coming to a head, he was politician enough to sense the danger of popular enthusiasm being swayed against him by eastern diviners. Middle-East-based, his enemies had sympathizers among the masses in Rome, particularly Greeks or orientals.

This time Octavius decided to give the boot to the politically unreliable astrologers (together with assorted practitioners of eastern magical cults), and got the expulsion order through by appointing an ally, Agrippa, to the city government. However, once Mark Antony and Cleopatra were dead, and his own position was secure, Augustus (as he now was) could afford to be clement, and the astrologers drifted back to the metropolis. (It was Agrippa, incidentally, who commissioned the circular Pantheon which still stands in Rome; its shallow dome, resembling the sky, and the seven niches – perhaps for the gods of the seven planets – suggest a receptiveness to astrological ideas.)

LITERARY TREASON

By trading their privileges for the benign absolutism of Augustus, the Romans found they had lost any means of political change except by conspiracy and assassination. Finding out the emperor's date of birth, and inquiring from his horoscope when he was going to die, was made a crime that ruined many – plotter and *mantis* alike. Augustus passed a law in AD 8, under which books offending the emperor were to be burned and, in serious cases, their authors exiled; the death sentence for 'Literary Treason' was added by edict in AD 11. Executions followed in the reign of Tiberius (AD 14-37).

In AD 16, the trial and suicide of Scribonius Libo, an ambitious young nobleman who had collected any number of predictions about his own glorious future, prompted further anti-astrologer measures . In AD 52, under Claudius AD 41-54, diviners were expelled from the whole of Italy – this time following evidence given at a treason trial. (Claudius, however, kept a 'court astrologer' Balbillus for his own purposes – see below). In AD 66, under Nero (AD 54-68), two distinguished Romans were condemned to death for even consulting the exiled Egyptian astrologer Pammenes by post.

ABOVE ***Plundered from Egypt in 13 BC, this obelisk was set up by the emperor Augustus on the Field of Mars in Rome as the gnomon of a gigantic sundial and calendar, full of references to his own horoscope. At sunset on his birthday, under Libra, the shadow pointed to the 'Altar of Peace' he built, while his conception day, under Capricorn, fell on the winter solstice, initiating a new year.***

A DYNASTY OF ASTROLOGERS

Thrasyllus of Alexandria, the Greek literary editor and astrologer, was working and teaching in Rhodes when he first met his future friend and patron, Tiberius, who in 6 BC chose its academic atmosphere for his self-exile. He followed Tiberius back to Rome (after AD 2) and remained his personal astrologer for the rest of his life. In Rome, Thrasyllus belonged to an intellectual circle with mystical leanings, and made a socially advantageous marriage. Right up to his (self-predicted) death in AD 36, he had a hand in the secret political machinations of Tiberius's court.

Thrasyllus' son Balbillus carried on his father's astrological practice. When Tiberius died in AD 37, Balbillus retired to Alexandria, leaving his relatives in Rome to play a fatal part in the murderous manoeuvrings of Caligula's reign (AD 37-41). The 41-year-old Claudius, who to everyone's surprise was made the next emperor, was an old friend of the Thrasyllus family, and Balbillus was able to return to Rome to a warm welcome. He held the post of court astrologer to Claudius (AD 41-54) and, with Ptolemy Seleucus, performed the same service for Nero (AD 54-68), and managed to end up in the good books of Vespasian (AD 70-79).

DOMITIAN AND THE DOGS OF DEATH

Domitian (AD 81-96) shared the popular trust in horoscopes to the point – so it was rumoured – of obtaining the birth details of prominent people in public life and systematically eliminating those whose signs indicated that they would be dangerous to him. Through his informers, Domitian kept a close watch on the activities of diviners who were patronized by much of Roman society.

There is a tale that a foreign astrologer called Ascletarius, charged with treasonable slander, pleaded guilty before the emperor, and then announced that Domitian would be killed the very next day, and named the hour. When asked by the emperor to forecast his own death, Ascletarius replied that he would shortly be eaten by dogs. To prove him wrong about everything, Ascletarius was immediately sentenced to be burned at the stake.

Later, Domitian discovered that after Ascletarius had been shackled to the stake and the fire lit, a violent squall had blown down the pyre, putting out the flames, and driving the soldiers to take shelter. As the astrologer's body was still smouldering, stray dogs had come up and torn it to pieces. That same day, the emperor Domitian was stabbed to death in his bedroom by conspirators.

ASTROLOGY AS EVIDENCE IN COURT

A showpiece exercise in legal pleading written by the Spanish-born teacher of public speaking, Quintilian (AD c35-95), is spun from the supposition that a boy's horoscope, taken at his birth, predicts not only his sex and a military career correctly, but also that he will kill his father. Is it therefore a crime for the son to commit suicide, if it were done in order to prevent the prediction of a murder from coming true? Discuss.

It is also clear from other writings of Quintilian's that Roman courts were prepared to receive 'oracles' – including astrology – in evidence and to hear pleadings for and against the credibility of both the predictions themselves and the practitioners who made them.

JUVENAL'S GIBES

For bitchy Juvenal, the satirical poet (AD c60-140), 'Chaldeans' offered an easy target. 'People receive their every word like something from the Egyptian sun god's holy fountain,' he sighs. In Juvenal's day, persecution of the astrologers by several mid-century emperors had accorded heroic glamour to those who survived and returned to Rome. He tells us that 'one simply had to know one who'd been sent in chains to Serifos' – or some other prison island in the Cyclades – 'and nearly died from the brutality, otherwise his horoscopes could not be taken seriously'.

PTOLEMY , THE GREAT AUTHORITY

Without doubt, the greatest astronomer of the Graeco-Roman world since Hipparchus was Claudius Ptolemy (AD c100-c170). He lived and worked at Canopus near Alexandria in Egypt, in an observatory provided by the *Mouseion* or university of Alexandria. He was a far more scientific observer and compiler of natural data than anyone before him. Although he lived in the middle of the second century , his encyclopaedia of astronomy – generally known by its Arabic title *Almagest* – remained unaltered and unchallenged as the standard work of reference for nearly one and a half thousand years.

At first called the *Mathematike Syntaxis*, it became known later as the *Megale* (or 'Greater') *Syntaxis*, to distinguish it from Ptolemy's other scientific writings. This became *Megiste* or 'The Greatest', which the Arabs took over for their ninth-century translation as *al-Magest*. Ironically, it was the translation of this from Arabic into Latin, produced in 1138, that re-introduced Ptolemy to the West.

Ptolemy followed this work with his handbook of astrology, known, since it was in four parts, as the *Tetrabiblos* (or *Quadri-*

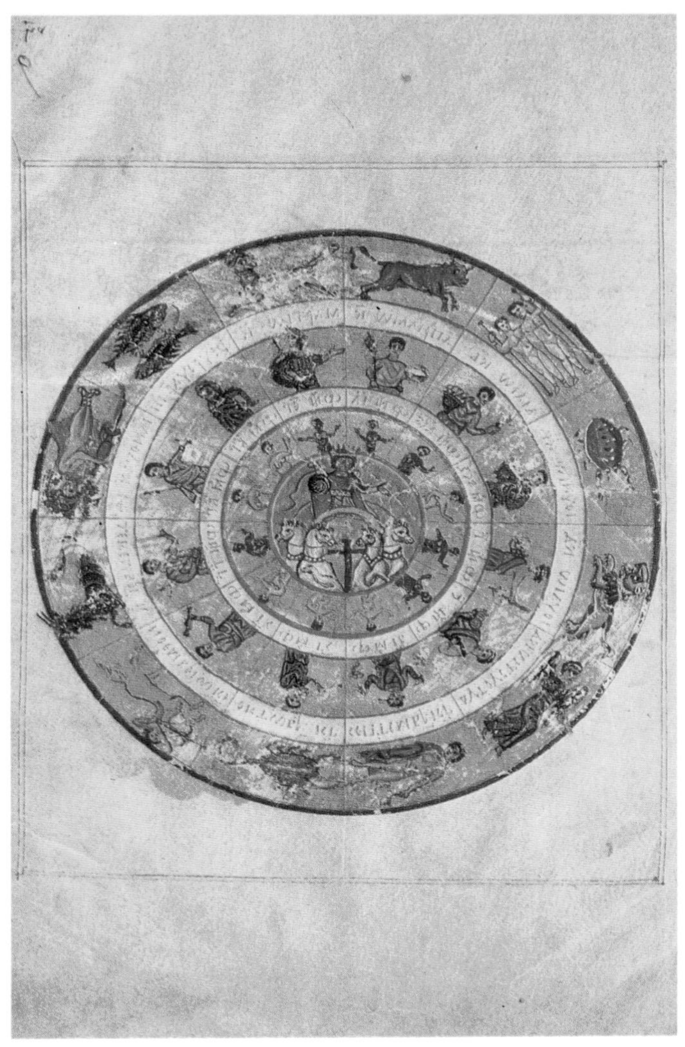

ABOVE *This page from a Byzantine codex (AD 820) of Ptolemy's* Tetrabiblos *shows the sun-god Helios in his chariot at the centre, in the guise of a conquering emperor. Radiating outward are figures representing hours and days, enclosed by the zodiac.*

partitus). Acknowledged as the scientist who knew more about the structure of the universe than anyone else in his period, Ptolemy's authorship, and the calm and reasonable style in which he wrote, ensured that in this book he gave astrology the supreme seal of scientific approval.

Ptolemy's stand was moderate: he argued that since we know the Sun and Moon influence life on Earth, and since (as he accepted) the weather is influenced by the stars, it might be possible, if one had all the necessary facts, to forecast their influence on our lives. He discussed the free will *versus* fatalism issue and settled for a mixture of chance and fate, and made allowance for the effects of our upbringing and environment on what has already been imprinted by influences from the universe around us.

Learning transmitted by Islam

The pursuit of scientific knowledge and the exercise of speculative thought seemed at the turn of the second and third centuries to be firmly established in civilized Europe. Unnoticed except by a few pessimists, the universal culture that had welded the seven-centuries-long heritage of classical Greece and the Hellenistic world to the iron framework of Roman administration was growing weary. Disintegration and rebirth faced all the peoples ruled from imperial Rome.

When society in the Roman empire collapsed in the fifth century, education collapsed with it. Bands of Germanic migrants were on the move; whole provinces were falling under their control. Established ideas were under challenge by a completely new way of thinking that could not tolerate deviation or dissent: the Christian Church had come out of the underground. And in the Church's eyes, astrology was compromised by its long association with the 'pagan' way of life. It might even be a diabolical superstition.

At a time when not even England, France or Germany existed as united countries, events in the eastern Mediterranean suddenly turned the world upside down. Inside less than fifty years – 636 to 711 – the entire southern shore of the Graeco-Roman world disappeared under a new religion (Islam), a new empire (the Caliphate) and a new common language (Arabic). It was as if the tables had been turned – as Alexander the Great had done in his day – in reverse. The supremacy of an oriental empire based on Mesopotamia had been restored.

MUSLIM SCIENCE

Islam, when it was first heard of in Arabia, was a fiercely expansionist religion with no time for any human prying into the will of God. All knowledge was manifested in the Koran. But after supplanting the Byzantine rulers of the Middle East, the Arabs eagerly naturalized as their own the rich and ancient culture they found there. The writings of the Greek scientists and philosophers were translated into Arabic and made available to the schools and the courts of Muslim kingdoms from Central Asia to Spain. As it had among the Greeks, the study of geometry, mathematics, medicine and astronomy went hand in hand with the practice of astrology.

RIGHT *These mobile discs divided and inscribed in Hebrew were a gadget made by Jewish scholars in Christian Castile around 1300 for use as a perpetual calendar of the Jewish year by rotating the inner and outer discs according to a code inscribed in the bands round the edges.*

Alongside this Classical heritage, the Muslims encountered the tenaciously preserved and partly Hellenized culture of the Jews in Mesopotamia, Palestine and Egypt. With their skills as astrologers the Jews seemed to outsiders to be the heirs of the 'Chaldaeans'. When Caliph al-Mansur founded his new capital, Baghdad, in 764, he called in the Jewish astrologer Jacob ibn Tariq (who was believed to have obtained star tables from India) to help him set up a school of astronomy. Al-Mansur (754-775) and Caliph Ma'mun (813-833), himself an enthusiastic astronomer, employed another Jew, named Mashallah (in Latin, Messahala), as court astrologer.

The Baghdad school became famous. Abu Ma'shur (better known as Albumazar, 805-885) from Balkh in Afghanistan, studied there. At Baghdad he was also a pupil of the first major Muslim philosopher, al-Kindi, who followed Greek examples in treating astrology as a branch of the sciences. Albumazar's astrological writings, in Latin translations, became standard works in Europe.

THE JEWISH GOLDEN AGE IN SPAIN

So, when Arab and Berber conquerors from north Africa swung Spain and Portugal into the Islamic orbit – now unbroken between the Atlantic and northern India – they brought with them well-grown seedlings of a brilliant civilization. As long as the local Christians (those, that is to say, who did not take up the offer of immediate conversion to Islam) paid their taxes, they were left alone. The aggravated persecution of the Jews under the Gothic kings of Spain since the 620s was replaced by toleration. Jews from as far afield as Iraq made their way to the prosperous and gracious cities of al-Andalus (as Muslim Spain was known) – Toledo, Cordova, Granada.

Contests on the battlefield of ideas between thinkers who preferred to follow a rationalist path, basing their arguments on the writings of Aristotle, and their more mystical opponents, who took their inspiration from Plato and his later exponents, raged as fruitfully among the Jews of Spain as among the

Muslims. With the major exception of the outstanding philosopher of the Spanish Golden Age, Moses Maimonides (1135–1204), the majority of Jewish scholars accepted the reality of astrology in greater or lesser degree.

Abenezra (Abraham ibn Ezra, c1092-1167) – neo-Platonist, poet, biblical commentator and scientist – and Abraham bar Hiyya ha-Nasi (known as 'Savasorda' in Latin, active about 1130) – mathematician and astronomer – practised as astrologers for patrons both Muslim and Christian. Judah ha-Levi the Hebrew poet from Toledo (c1085-c1140) – known in Arabic as Abu Hassan al-Lawi – did not question the dominion of the stars. Abraham ben David (ibn Daoud) from Toledo (c1110-c1180) and his namesake, Abraham ben David of Posquières (c1125-1198), were scholars and philosophers whose wide interests included the debate over free will and determinism in astrology.

THE KABBALAH AND THE ZOHAR

Jews in the Muslim world could not avoid discussing the implications for Judaism in the new Islamic philosophy fashioned, from the ninth century onwards, out of Greek and Koranic materials. One response, which had long-lasting repercussions, was a deepening of the mystical and occult tradition in Judaism. Enriched with ideas derived from the teachings of the Pythagoreans and other sects concerned with the nature and destination of the human soul, such as the Gnostics, this tradition found expression in the writings – which are difficult to date precisely – put together and known as the *Kabbalah*, meaning 'Things Received'.

In Spain, Abenezra fostered the 'sublime science' of the Kabbalah with enthusiasm. Moses ben Nahman (Nahmanides, 1194-1270) trod the path of mysticism with his biblical commentaries, a path that culminated about 1290 in the esoteric discourses of the *Zohar* (*Sefer ha-Zohar*, 'Book of Splendour'), compiled by Moses de León (c1250–1305). Astrological concepts pervaded all these writings, since elements of both astrology and Kabbalism drew on shared roots in the Hermetic tradition of the Graeco-Roman world.

Consequently, when Jews began to flee the intolerance of new fundamentalist Muslim sects (and of the Christian reconquerors), astrological ideas found their way back to Europe. The reawakening of intellectual life in Europe was stimulated by the translation of Greek classics, via Arabic versions, into Latin. Along with the classics, Muslim and Jewish astrological texts became available for translation. They found receptive readers among Christian scholars and churchmen. Light glimmered in the Dark Ages.

THE ALPHONSINE TABLES

The bigoted rule of sects from north Africa ushered in the twilight of Muslim Spain. Between about 1150 and 1250, all of the emirates, from Saragossa to Seville, were lost, leaving only Granada to Islam. Among the victorious Christian rulers, one – Alphonso X of Castile and León – earned the title of The Learned for raising the cultural level of his enlarged kingdom. Among his achievements was the compilation of a revised version of the Arabic tables of planetary motion.

Fifty astronomers, including Muslims and Jews (Isaac ibn Sid of Toledo among them), were put to work, and in about 1252 what became known as the Alphonsine Tables were completed. They remained in use by astronomers, astrologers and navigators throughout Europe almost until the time of Copernicus (1473-1543).

The Middle Ages in Europe

In its earliest period, the Christian church saw astrology as part and parcel of the pagan system of ideas. St Paul insisted that no 'angels' or 'powers' (by which he meant the gods of the planets) stood between God and the faithful. Potential converts with a pagan background, most of

BELOW ***Fourth-century AD Roman mosaic, showing the Sun god Helios ringed by the zodiac, from Hammath near Tiberias in Israel.***

ABOVE ***The macrocosm of the universe fused with nature and human life on earth is symbolized in a vision of the medieval mystic, St Hildegard of Bingen (1098–1179). She sits at the bottom left, expounding in Christian terms a fundamental insight which is shared by astrologers.***

whom had accepted astrology, were told – from about the end of the first century – that astrologers received their predictions from demons. One Christian writer (Tatian, c150) thought that people believed the old gods were carried up into the sky and lived on as planets and constellations because they had been tricked by demons in disguise as gods.

Not long after, another Christian writer (Tertullian, c155-c222) proposed that God had permitted astrology and all kinds of divination *before* the Incarnation, but that since the coming of Christ, the demons' hold on the world was abolished and the subject was now forbidden to Christians. This idea was picked up in an encyclopaedia compiled by Isidore of Seville (c560-636) and repeated by other writers and canonists until at least the twelfth century.

St Augustine of Hippo (354-430) came down heavily on astrologers, but he too put their successes down to inspiration by spirits. He argued that demons – who were higher intelligences – obtained their knowledge of the future by permission of God, but that humans were banned from sharing such esoteric knowledge. While Augustine was writing (in what is now Algeria), a sect known as the Priscillianists (over in Spain) was mixing Christianity with Hermetic concepts. Priscillianists identified the signs of the zodiac with the Old Testament patriarchs, and gave the planets the names of angels.

The astrology attacked by the Church was, of course, the Hellenistic kind, left over from the Graeco-Roman world and by now for the most part only encountered in polemics by the earlier Christian writers. In the newly converted northern parts of Europe, especially beyond the old Roman frontiers, it was in any case unknown. In English, French and German monasteries, scholars as learned as Bede (c673–735) mechanically copied the verdicts of Tertullian and Isidore.

ASTROLOGY RESURFACES

The Dark Ages of Europe – roughly 400 to 900 – were times marred by clan warfare, invasion by the Huns, Viking raids and the loss of Spain to the new faith of Islam. Cultural and living standards sank, especially in the west. By the year 1000 the worst seemed to be over, and with the beginning of the period we call the feudal Middle Ages, and the rise of western monasticism, centres of learning were appearing. One of the most famous of these was at Chartres in France, and there the study of Latin literature revived in earnest. One of the results of reading classical Latin manuscripts was the rediscovery of pagan texts referring to astrology.

Old questions of fatalism *versus* free will engaged the interest of monkish commentators, and the debate on reconciling astrology with the Church's teaching was re-opened. Some of the most original minds of the school of Paris were interested: Peter Abelard (1079-1142), his pupil, John of Salisbury (c1120-c1180), and Hugh of St Victor (1096-1141).

Just then, when astrology was no more than an abstract problem for logical and doctrinal discussion by intellectual priests, and remote from the concerns of ordinary people, a cultural change began to take place. The classical works of Greek science and philosophy – 'lost' in western Europe for some five hundred years – appeared on the market in the Arabic versions long since in use by Muslim scholars, introduced to the wider world by the Jews fleeing from Islamic Spain. The translation of these books into Latin was undertaken with enthusiasm, but many years passed before Aristotle and Plato, Euclid and Ptolemy had been assimilated by the Latin west. When they were, Aristotle seemed unchallengeable for as long as the Middle Ages lasted. Aristotle's ideas endorsed astrology as one of the sciences and consequently his authority was stamped on the study of this subject. This authority was to remain until halfway through the seventeenth century, when Copernicus changed the view of the cosmos for ever.

THE BAPTISM OF ASTROLOGY

All that astrology needed now was for its principles of correspondences with the stars and planets to be Christianized. This task of compromise was accomplished principally by three famous and scientifically inclined scholars: Robert Grosseteste, bishop of Lincoln (c1175-1253), Albertus Magnus of Cologne (c1200-1280) and Roger Bacon of Oxford (c1220-c1292). In 1255, the whole works of Aristotle in Latin were licenced for study at the University of Paris.

St Thomas Aquinas (1225-1274), who codified in its most complete form the theology of the medieval Church, gave astrology a clean bill of health as far as it could be regarded as a science – but he stopped short at judicial astrology, in other words, forecasting future events with certainty from the stars. For Aquinas, this was unacceptable to a Christian, and had to be classed with prophesying by demons.

BELOW *This panel – one of a series on astronomical observations painted by Donato Creti (1671–1749) – celebrates the benefits of a telescope for Moon-watchers.*

ASTROLOGY ESTABLISHED

With Muslim Spain's decline during the thirteenth century, Italy became the great centre for astrology. Padua and Milan universities had chairs of astrology early in the century – Bologna's chair is even believed to date from 1125. As king of Sicily, the Emperor Frederick II (1194-1250) kept a cosmopolitan and liberal court, employing Muslim and Jewish astrologers from Spain, and the Scottish occultist and translator of books from Arabic, Michael Scot (c1175-c1232).

Guido Bonatti, of uncertain dates, was famous all over Europe for recommending propitious times for the battles of several thirteenth-century Italian warlords whom he served. In the next century, however, Bologna's professor of astrology, Cecco d'Ascoli, fell foul of the Inquisition, and was executed as a heretic at Florence in 1327.

With the increasing wealth and complexity of society in the later Middle Ages, astrology itself became divided between a role in the market-places and another kind in the works of philosophers and theologians. So long as the cosmos was understood through the systems of Aristotle and Ptolemy, the scientific respectability of astrology – as part and parcel of the scientific heritage of classical astronomy – was unassailable.

The only issues debated were technical: did the stars rule a person's fate absolutely (fatalism), or were the predictions of astrology open to modification by human choice (free will) – or, indeed, by God's intervention? And should astrology be restricted solely to forecasting the weather? But people who scoffed at astrology's claims in any area were growing louder, even though they did not challenge the official cosmology of the Sun orbiting the Earth that supported it. Petrarch (1304-1374), the poet of the dawn of humanism and the Renaissance, led the scoffers, yet it was the Renaissance, ironically, that was to give astrology its greatest scope since the reign of the Caesars.

Chaucer (c1340–1400) weaves astrological ideas or images into the *Franklin's, Man of Law's* and the *Knight's Tale*, and elsewhere. For example, the magician hero of the *Franklin's Tale* is a law graduate from the University of Orleans, a noted centre of astrological lore, who chooses the propitious moment to make his magic effective by means of astrology. Chaucer also wrote a practical handbook on the astrolabe which makes no distinction between astronomical and astrological uses of the instrument. He does warn, in the chapter on ascendants and aspects: 'naytheless, these been . . . rites of pagans, in which my spirit nay hath no faith . . .'. His caution, apparently, is on the grounds of Christian faith rather than of scepticism.

From the Renaissance to Rationalism

The rediscovery of Aristotle and other Greek thinkers through their Arabic translations in the twelfth century was surpassed in effect by the recovery of the whole range of the classics in their original Latin and Greek texts after 1400. Partly unearthed in monastery libraries, and partly brought by Byzantine refugees from the Turks, these works filled the new humanist scholars with enthusiasm for every aspect of the lost Graeco-Roman civilization.

RIGHT ***Court astrologer 'Dr' Dee inscribed this gold disc as a memento of his friend Edward Kelly, the medium. It records Kelly's vision at Cracow in 1584 when the pair were free-loading around the continent of Europe.***

The chorus of voices from the past included, of course, those of the occultists, mystics and gnostics whose teachings had been one of the ingredients of that civilization. The scholar Poggio of Florence found the unknown *Astronomica* by Manilius in 1410. The platonist Marsilio Ficino (1433-1499), also of Florence, translated 'Hermetic' writings from Greek into Latin in 1463. Regiomontanus (Johann Mueller 'of Koenigsberg', 1436-1476) the corrector of the translation of the *Almagest* and of astronomical data in the Alphonsine Tables, published an astrological manual (*Tabulae Directionum*) in 1475.

The traffic of accessible texts carried an interest in Hellenistic astrology along the scholarly circuits of European humanism, provoking a reasoned attack, on religious grounds, from the philosopher Pico della Mirandola (1463-1494), answered by the Aristotelian Pietro Pomponazzi (1462-1525). These rarefied arguments could only enhance the standing of astrology in the eyes of the élite.

The German physician and courtier Cornelius Agrippa (1486-1535) was drawn to the mysticism of the cabbala, and took up astrology. He pleaded in the defence of a woman accused of witchcraft, and got into trouble with the Inquisition. Paracelsus (c1490-1541), the medical experimenter from Switzerland, taught that a good physician needed to be trained in astronomy and astrology. He believed, with all the classical astrologers, that the stars influence disease and that everyone is 'penetrated by the astral spirit'.

THE COPERNICAN REVOLUTION

It was, in the event, not argument, nor religious bigotry, that pushed astrology off its Renaissance pedestal. It was, instead, the collapse of Aristotelian cosmology, and with it, the Ptolomaic system, that removed astrology from the company of astronomy and other sciences. This collapse was in its way as painful for devout Christians as it was for scholars, who had been taught to regard astrology as a science securely based on an accurate view of the universe that had – on the authority of the classical scientists – the Earth at its centre.

Nicolas Copernicus (1473-1543) died after a busy life as a cleric and physician in Poland and Prussia, knowing that the most important work of his life had just been completed. On his bed, as he lay dying, the printer's advance copy of his book *De Revolutionibus Orbium Coelestium* was placed too late for him to be able to open it. Written without the benefit of observation by telescope (and not without a few flaws of computation), his book set out to show that Ptolemy's system could not be the true picture of the universe.

Copernicus did not make a scientific discovery. All he did was to demonstrate rationally to the reading public that what we see of the movements of the planets and the rising and setting of the fixed stars could be explained in a far more satisfactory way than Ptolemy had done. He postulated that if the planets, including the Earth, orbited round the Sun at the centre, and if the Earth was turning on its axis, the problems created by the old view could be solved.

STOPPING THE SUN

Three men born within twenty years of the death of Copernicus drew the main outlines of the modern understanding of the cosmos. They were Tycho Brahe (1546-1601) in Denmark, his German assistant Johannes Kepler (1571-1630) and Galileo Galilei (1564-1642) in Florence – the first astronomer to observe by telescope. They all belonged to a generation in which the majority's faith in the old Earth-centred system was still strong. Neither Brahe nor Kepler saw anything wrong with producing horoscopes under their terms of employment.

Although Copernicus had deduced what we know is the true nature of the solar system, and Galileo had verified his deductions with evidence observed through his telescope, the new view of the cosmos was upsetting to most people brought up in the old beliefs.

ABOVE ***The famous 1660 engraving of the Copernican solar system in a two-dimensional view was published to popularize the sun-centred alternative proposed by the 'new' astronomy. The zodiac still retained its place of honour round the circumference.***

TURBULENT PRIESTS

Three more or less contemporary rebels against orthodoxy were Bernardino Telesio (1508-1588), Giordano Bruno (1548-1600) and Tommaso Campanella (1568-1639). All came from southern Italy – the homeland of the Pythagoreans – and championed individual responsibility against inherited authority. Telesio was the pioneer of scientific method and, through the other two, his influence reached into the next century. Like the scientist Galileo, Campanella was persecuted by intolerant scholastics, and Bruno was burnt at the stake as one of the great martyrs to freedom of the intellect.

In 1629 Campanella published *Astrologia*, at a time when he was working as astrologer for Pope Urban VIII (1623-1644), and performing zodiacal rites in the pontifical palace to ward off the effects of the eclipses of 1628-1630.

Bruno (like Campanella, a Dominican friar of unorthodox opinions) had the distinction of being excommunicated by the Catholic Church, the Lutherans and the Calvinists in turn. Bruno's execution for heresy was the fate held over Galileo during his examination, and in 1633 Galileo denied his own conclusions about the solar system, although secretly he must have known he would be proved right in the end. The reigning pope was the same Urban VIII who had been Campanella's patron in astrology.

DOCTOR DEE

Queen Elizabeth I had a soft spot for John Dee. In the course of a long life (1527-1608), 'Doctor' Dee enjoyed patronage at court, but he belonged to an endangered species: the official court astrologer.

Dee's son presented his father's papers, and his occult equipment, to Elias Ashmole (1617-1692), the English antiquary. Ashmole studied science, including astrology, at Oxford during the Civil War, wrote horoscopes, and in 1650 was elected Steward of the Astrologers Society in London – enjoying, in that first year of the Commonwealth, Parliamentary patronage. When Ashmole gave his own collections – including the Dee material – to Oxford university in 1682 it formed the conerstone of the Ashmolean Museum, the earliest science museum to be founded in Britain, and named after him.

LEFT

This very finely worked example of an astrolabe – faithful to the Ptolemaic concept of the universe – was made in 1548 by Georg Hartmann of Nurnberg.

The Seventeenth Century

It seems almost symbolic for the beginning of the age of science and enlightenment that Isaac Newton was born in 1642, the year in which Galileo died: between them, Galileo and Newton set out the basic propositions of motion and mechanics in the cosmos which guided researchers until Einstein. In his writings, Newton (1642-1727) was deeply concerned with theological implications arising from his own discoveries, and familiar with the classical principles of astrology that had been part of pre-Copernican astronomy.

All through the seventeenth century, men of learning endeavoured to adapt the heritage of astrology to the new scientific climate. It is not hard to understand why. Since the beginning of the Renaissance period, answering astrological inquiries with the aid of tables and instruments was, for many educated men, the only serious opportunity for working out problems of computation from first principles. The only other intellectual challenge that could be compared with it – navigation at sea – was necessarily restricted. Now, abandoning the centuries-old and hitherto respectable practice of astrology meant for many a loss for which the broadening of scientific knowledge and experiment had not yet provided a substitute.

ROUNDHEAD ASTROLOGY

At the start of the English Civil War in 1642, Parliament appointed an astrologer, John Booker, in place of the bishops as 'licencer' (that is to say, censor) of astrological books. Almanacs flourished: it has been estimated that forty thousand copies of various titles were sold every year. Astrologers were kept busy as propagandists by all parties, from Charles II in exile to the Levellers and Ranters on the far left of the Parliament side. William Lilly (1602–1681) England's senior astrologer at the time, was firmly parliamentarian.

When the monarchy returned in 1660, astrologers like Lilly suffered from loss of patronage. In the second half of the century, the rise of the mercantile middle class with its bias towards the new scientific discoveries put astrologers (whatever their political leanings) increasingly on the defensive.

REARGUARD ACTIONS

English astrologers became, in one way or another, involved in the last major creative movement in their subject before the late nineteenth-century revival. This was a variety of attempts to 'reform' astrology. Undertaken by John Goad (1616-89), Joshua Childrey (1625-1670) and John Gadbury (1628-1704) of the High Church and royalist persuasion on one side, and by the successor to Lilly's title as leading astrologer of his day, John Partridge (1644-1715), of the other – Whig and Dissenting – side, an immense amount of printer's ink was used up. It all came too late to sustain the old high standing of astrology, and in 1707 the merciless satire of Jonathan Swift made a laughing stock of poor Partridge.

Swift's squib was the bogus *Bickerstaff's Almanack*, in which he used apparently authentic astrological calculations to announce the imminent death of Partridge – to the minute. The day after the predicted demise, Swift published a second pamphlet describing the supposed death-bed scene, but criticizing 'Bickerstaff' for getting the time wrong by nearly four hours. Superior readers hooted, but at least Partridge's almanac had a faithful readership until his actual death ten years later.

The first Astronomer Royal, appointed in 1675, was John Flamsteed (1646-1719), whose serious study of astrology as a young man caused him much embarrassment as Britain's official astronomer at Greenwich in later life. The original 'Old Moore' of *Old Moore's Almanac*, Francis Moore (c1657-1715), was his close contemporary. Flamsteed is a link with the past, when astrology was the sister-science of astronomy. Moore is a link forward to the popular almanac-astrology of the nineteenth century and the media-astrology of this century.

Vox Stellarum, 'the Voice of the Stars', was the title of the original *Old Moore's Almanac*, which, after a rather convoluted publishing history, is still a regular favourite. In the middle of the eighteenth century, it was selling over 100 000 copies a year, when Partridge had slid from the 30 000 copies of the 1650s to 5600. By 1803, *Old Moore's* was past 390 000 copies, and reached its peak of 560 000 copies in 1839. A connection can be made between the decline that followed and the growing pace of the industrial revolution in Britain. The old rural population was the reliable market for almanacs. However, the tradition of publishing popular predictive astrology seems to have survived in Britain as it did nowhere else in Europe.

The Revival

The years of survival – roughly from the 1830s to the 1880s – do not lack interest. They were, after all, the era of the almost legendary astrologers 'Zadkiel' and the three 'Raphaels'. Their 'angelic' *noms-de-plume* seem to harken back to the ideas of the Hermetic astrologers in the Greco-Roman world. In the USA the earliest astrological journalism is traced to *The Horoscope*, published in Philadelphia between 1840 and 1844 by Thomas Hague. Philadelphia was also the base for the English-born astrological family of the Broughtons, who emigrated from Leeds in the 1850s. *Broughton's Monthly Planet Reader* came out in 1860, and continued from New York City in 1863.

THEOSOPHY: MIDDLE CLASS MYSTICISM

Before a revival of an activity as basically mathematical as astrology can take place and flourish, there have to be tables, ephemerides and classical texts for study. Thanks to cheap Victorian printing and the efforts of a few, sometimes rather eccentric, enthusiasts the ground for revival was well prepared. The event which gave the revival its initial impetus is remarkably clear: the appearance in English-speaking countries of Theosophy in the decade 1874–1885. This system of esoteric philosophy was the creation of the Russian-born medium known as Madame Blavatsky, and drew some of its ideas from Hinduism and Slavic mysticism.

One can see a parallel between the Theosophical Society nurturing the revival of interest in astrology, and the way Hellenistic astrology interacted with the Hermetic tradition. Theosophy was a social success, bringing a variety of previously ignored or derided occult subjects to the notice of educated circles in the late Victorian world. An occult 'Order of the Golden Dawn' was founded and it attracted experimenters in magic from among a 'superior' class of person – one of them was the poet W.B. Yeats. Initiates were required to take an examination in 'the true system of Astrological Divination'.

Credit for raising astrology not merely out of banal prediction to an adjunct of Theosophy, but also into a rewarding business activity, goes to two among Madame Blavatsky's loyal helpers – W.F. Allen ('Alan Leo', 1860–1917) and W.R. Old ('Seraphial', 1864–1929). Leo was the first astrological publicist of the twentieth century. Charles Carter was instrumental in popularizing Leo's work. One way or another, most early students of modern astrology owe a debt to Leo's series of textbooks – especially in Germany.

FRENCH REVIVAL

The practice of astrology seems to have died out in France almost at the same time as the appearance in 1661 of a landmark volume in Latin – the posthumous and often quoted *Astrologia Gallica* by Morinus (Jean-Baptiste Morin de Villefranche, 1591-1659). Between that date and the nineteenth-century seekers for 'hidden knowledge', inspired by the writings of the Abbé Louis Constant ('Eliphas Levi', 1810-1878), we do not hear anything of mainstream astrology from France.

If it was Theosophy's high-minded esoteric philosophy that raised the status of astrology in Britain and America, it was the Romantic excitement of flirting with cabbalism, black magic and 'decadence' that restored it in France. French occultism of the 1890s was very much a movement of poets and painters, and harked back not only to ancient Egypt but to specifically French traditions, such as the manichaean Cathars (or Albigenses) of Languedoc.

Another contrast with the English-speaking experience is that as late as 1891, the occultist Gérard Encausse ('Papus' 1865-1916) could write: 'astrology is one of the ancient divinatory sciences the rules of which have been completely lost today.' Before long, Morinus had been rediscovered by Henri Selva (1861-?) and with access to the traditional techniques, French astrology left cabbalist ideas behind, and the number of practitioners multiplied in the 1920s.

ASTROLOGY AND STATISTICS

Probably the most interesting figure in France today is not an astrologer at all, but a scientist. He is Michel Gauquelin (b. 1928), a statistician at the Centre National de Recherche Scientifique with a doctorate in psychology. He set out to test the claims of astrology by painstaking statistical analysis of groups of real people for their character categories according to the planets at their birth. Gauquelin's work does not offer much support to Sun sign astrology, but his work on 'planetary heredity' is significant. There is statistical evidence that planetary positions in a parent's birth chart are more than likely to be repeated in their child's chart. He has gone on to search for clues in the natural sciences to explain correspondences that seemed statistically valid – for example, by checking birth dates against disturbances in the Earth's magnetosphere.

Gauquelin's work, and his book *Cosmic Influences on Human Behaviour* (English edition, 1976) have been so influential that no present-day discussion about the validity of astrology can afford to ignore them. He has reduced the gap between sceptical science and astrology as it is practised today.

GERMAN REVIVAL

As might perhaps be expected, astrology was taken up in the German-speaking lands more systematically and its history examined with more scholarly thoroughness than elsewhere. It is in Germany, moreover, that one of the more surprising excesses of astrological speculation has been proposed: eight hypothetical planets beyond the orbit of Neptune for which the Hamburg School of Alfred Witte (1878-1941) prepared its own special tables in 1928.

The Renaissance tradition of astrology is thought to have died out in Germany with its last exponent, Julius Pfaff (1774-1835), professor of mathematics at Erlangen university from 1818. The revival seems to have stemmed from a marriage of influences – Theosophy with French magic – in 1884. Madame Blavatsky made the acquaintance of Irish-born Frau Gebhard (herself in correspondence with Eliphas Levi) in that year, and the German section of the Theosophical Society was founded in the Gebhard home at Elberfeld in the Ruhr.

The significant outcome of this foundation was that Dr Franz Hartmann (1838-1912) became involved in its work. Hartmann had given up his medical studies to sail for America (where he qualified as a doctor and became an American citizen), and later travelled *via* Japan to meet Madame Blavatsky at her headquarters in India. He was a prolific writer and had a serious and deep understanding of Hindu and Buddhist beliefs, and was thus instrumental in giving German Theosophy a suitably solid theoretical frame of reference.

In turn, Hartmann engaged a student, Hugo Vollrath (1877-194?), as his personal assistant in about 1899, and through Vollrath initiated the complex and often somewhat absurd feuding that bedevilled the astrological community in Germany right into the Hitler era. In 1907 and 1908, one such squabble involving Vollrath led to Rudolf Steiner's split from the Theosophical Society in 1912 to found his own movement, the Anthroposophical Society, which is still in existence worldwide. Apart from the regular (and sometimes acrimonious) conferences, the German astrological revival was accompanied by vigorous publishing.

Probably the most valuable distillation of the German astrological ferment – certainly the one with the most cultural resonance – is enshrined in the Warburg Institute. The brainchild of Aby Warburg (1866-1929), and carried on by his disciple Fritz Saxl (1890-1948), it is the unique centre for the study of astrological and occult symbolism and influence in the art and literature of the Renaissance humanists, in their search for alternative authorities outside the orthodox Christian tradition. Set up in Hamburg, it slipped away to Britain to escape Hitler, and now forms part of London University.

Astrology Beyond Europe

Although the European system of astrology (perhaps more realistically defined as the 'Graeco-Egyptian-Babylonian' system) dominates the westernized parts of the world, it certainly does not represent the sum total of humanity's achievement in the field – it does not even display its most sophisticated developments.

Two great systems grew up in Asia: one in India, the other in China. Both spring from the common prehistoric experience of all cultures – the attempt to understand the significance of the patterns in the sky. Both have followed courses shaped by their own particular cultural experience.

Of the two, Hindu astrology is rather closer to western ideas than the Chinese system; this is partly thanks to a two-way traffic in mathematical ideas and astronomical data that accompanied the general trade through the Persian Gulf between the Sumerians and the cities of the Indus Valley two or three thousand years BC and culminated in the period following Alexander the Great's invasion of the Punjab in 327 BC.

HINDU ASTROLOGY

We have no record of the star lore of the people of the Indus Valley civilization before it was overwhelmed by the invasions of northern Aryans around 2000 BC. Possibly, elements from an older way of thinking survived subconsciously and crept into the developing system of Hinduism at a later stage. This may have happened when the Yoga-inspired 'Tantrik astrology' – a system for calculating auspicious and inauspicious times – made its appearance almost three thousand years later in the eighth century AD.

At any rate, the gods of the Aryans, as portrayed in their earliest literature (known as 'Vedic'), followed their personal whims in much the same way as did the Olympian gods of the ancient Greeks. Day and night, and a few stars, were identified with various gods, and there were references to omens and portents and methods of divination quite similar to those in Hesiod and Homer. However, only the Sun and Moon were mentioned specifically, and of these, the Moon as a measurement of the seasons was considered more important. These forerunners of full-blown Hinduism seem to have had a non-

BELOW ***An Indian court astrologer, surrounded by the instruments of his craft, is depicted in this marginal painting in an album made by command of the Moghul emperor Jahangir (1605–27).***

ABOVE ***Europeans bringing Western instruments as a gift to the emperor at the Winter Palace, Peking. The huge celestial and armillary spheres depicted in this silk-and-metal-thread tapestry were copied from the Jesuits' observatory at Peking.***

fatalistic outlook, and this suggests that true astrology had yet to emerge.

When it did emerge, and was given its more or less final form in the writings attributed to a learned astrologer, Varahamihira, in the fifth century, its system came to be seen as being as venerable as the holy books of the long-ago Vedic age. Nothing in those might be tampered with, and the same applied to Varahamihira's astrology, which was a mixture of ancient Moon-based data (Hindus continued to believe that the Moon was further away than the Sun from Earth until late in the first century) and the new Alexandrian zodiac signs (called *drekkanas* by the Hindus). Hindu astrology plots the constellations seen behind the Moon rather than the Sun; twenty-seven of these were described, each eventually allocated 13° 20″ of arc on the circle; an optional twenty-eighth (actually constellation number twenty-two, Abhijit) is occasionally interpolated as a kind of 'intercalary' division (this is always necessary when attempts are made to match lunar and solar years, which only coincide every nineteen years). These lunar divisions are called *nakshatras* and are by far the most important aspect of Hindu astrology. When the Sun-based zodiac signs from Alexandria were introduced, they sat awkwardly on the native system: each sign was associated with two *nakshatras* and a fraction of the remaining three (or four).

For Hindu astrologers, the zodiac signs never assumed as much importance as the *nakshatras*, each one of which is significant for a different aspect of a person's life. Planets are considered to be the messengers of God, and their positions in the *nakshatras* are interpreted accordingly. Although Hindu astrology ignores Uranus, Neptune and Pluto (they were not mentioned by Varahamihira), it does incorporate the influence of the Moon's nodes (the two points where the Moon's orbit crosses the Sun's apparent path), which they call *Rahu* and *Ketu*.

However, one specifically Hindu concept had to be incorporated into the system in order to meet the expectations of Hindu inquirers: reincarnation. Reincarnation is Hinduism's unique contribution to the theory of astrology. The idea of the soul progressing through a series of lives, from the lowest form to human, on its way to ultimate release from the bonds of the material world through moral perfection, naturally complicates the drawing of a horoscope. How much of a person's previous existences, and how far into future existences, could an astrologer read in the stars? In the Hindu world view, astrology should be more than a method of seeking out one's fate – important though that may be – in modern everyday life. It should serve the quest for self-knowledge.

CHINA: THE RED PATH AND THE YELLOW PATH

The Chinese, too, have their own scheme for plotting the sky unrelated to the zodiac as we know it: the ecliptic is divided into twenty-four segments, associated with a Solar year likewise divided into twenty-four periods, each of fifteen or sixteen days. These are equal to one half of a zodiac sign, but the western zodiac has no place in the Chinese world view. Similar to the importance of *nakshatras* for Hindu astrologers are the Chinese 'Lunar Mansions' – meaning the twenty-eight constellations which the Moon traverses, or the twenty-eight segments of the sky containing these constellations.

Broad similarities such as those that link Indian and western astrology fade the more closely one looks at Chinese astronomy and astrology. The first significant difference is that from the earliest known records, the Chinese, grouped constellations on an entirely different basis from the Sumerians and Egyptians.

There may be a straightforward geographical explanation for this. While western astronomers map the sky by reference to the ecliptic (the apparent path of the Sun and Moon across the sky, known to the Chinese as the Yellow Path), the Chinese use the celestial equator (which they call the Red Path) as a base line and fix stellar positions from it relative to the Pole Star. They therefore classify heavenly bodies at their highest points in the sky.

This fact suggests that the Chinese system was devised by a people who did not have that clear view of constellations, stars and planets rising straight up over the horizon enjoyed by the inhabitants of Mesopotamia and Egypt. We know that the earliest distinctively Chinese culture was nurtured in the region of the upper Yellow River, among the northern mountains, where the cultivation of millet began some six thousand years ago. The primitive home of these people may possibly have been even further north, in the forests of eastern Siberia. It seems reasonable to deduce that the Chinese system originated among valley-dwellers in northern regions, where long twilights concealed the rise of the fainter stars and the horizon was blocked by a hilly skyline.

Another major difference is that the constellation pictures that took shape early in the minds of Chinese observers are made up in almost entirely different combinations of stars from the patterns which evolved in the west. A traditional Chinese star map is scarcely recognizable to a western observer, and where constellations are shared they are accorded different importance. For example, Ursa Major, a very potent star group to Chinese astrologers, is of no account in the West.

The overriding philosophy of Chinese culture calls for the maintenance of harmony between Heaven and Earth. If that harmony is disturbed, the reproof to humanity will be conveyed by the 'heavenly messengers' (planets) and recorded by the astrologers, whose attitude to celestial phenomena is very like that in the Babylonian astrologers' reports to the rulers of the country: everything seen in the sky is a message from the supernatural powers. The Chinese read meanings into the colour or brightness of planets, even though the changes may be due to weather conditions. Chinese planetary symbolism also differs, most noticeable in their interpretation of Venus as a masculine planet and Jupiter as a feminine.

There is no western equivalent for Chinese interpretations based on *direction* and *number* which reinforce the omens of the stars. The rules combining the 'five cardinal points' (east, west, north, south and centre), the 'five elements' (water, earth, metal, fire, wood) and the symbolism of the *I Ching* (The Book of Changes) show how closely Chinese astrology is woven together with geomancy, or Earth Omens. Geomancy, like astrology, goes back to the most primitive human consciousness, but nowhere has it survived and flourished as it has among the Chinese.

The twelve-year cycle of animals, probably the best known aspect of Chinese astrology in the west, where it is erroneously called the 'Chinese zodiac', is not mentioned in astrological classics as late as the mid-seventh century. It may have been introduced into China by the Turks of central Asia, who were invading the empire after the 670s. By the late tenth century it was already well established. Some authorities maintain that it is an oriental expression of the twelve-year Jupiter cycle (Jupiter takes twelve years to complete its orbit); others that it is an expansion of the Twelve Branches (that is the twelve 'double hours' into which the Chinese, along with other oriental civilizations, divided the twenty-four-hour day). In any event, it seems that the animals of the 'Chinese zodiac' were not an original part of the complicated calculations of Chinese astrology. Although they had a popular following, and gave rise to many homely proverbs, serious astrologers rather despised them.

However, they form part of the popular Chinese astrology called Suan Ming, or Fate Divination, a method of predicting the future based entirely on the calendar. This 'Lesser Astrology' was specifically designed to foretell the fates of the ordinary people (Great Astrology concerned itself with enlightening the Imperial Court). Fate Divination is drawn up entirely from calendrical data, a task made complex by meshing two number systems, one based on tens, the other on twelves. Established late in the Han dynasty (206 BC–AD 220), it was codified during the T'ang period (AD 618–907), and is today what most Chinese mean when they refer to astrology.

AZTECS AND INCAS

A purely calendrical method of predicting a person's fate was also practised by the Aztecs and their predecessors in central America for many centuries before the Spanish conquest in the sixteenth century. As in Chinese Fate Calculation, two different calendar systems needed to be computed before an answer could be found. Most of the Central American civilizations combined two calendars: the 365-day solar year, divided into eighteen weeks of twenty days each plus five odd 'unlucky' days'; and a ceremonial 260 day calendar, known to the Aztecs as *Tonalhualli* and the Maya as *tzolkin*, which was a series of 13 'months' of twenty days. Both calendars were used as reference, and it took 52 years for the systems to synchronize.

Under the Aztecs as rulers of what is now Mexico, and in the Incas' huge empire stretching from Ecuador through Peru to parts of Chile, both cultures built impressive 'ceremonial' cities, laid out to accommodate pyramids, temples and observatories. The movements of the Sun, Moon and five visible planets were tracked by astronomer priests, to help keep track of the regular, and sometimes bloodthirsty, ceremonies that punctuated the agricultural year.

In the Inca strongholds, smooth pillars were shaped from the living rock and used to predict the solstices from the angle and length of the Sun's shadow. There is some evidence that the position of the stars and planets at the time of birth was considered significant, but no evidence of a zodiac as the west knows it. The days of the Sacred Calendar had names (as did the months) and special glyphs, and the sacred day and month of a birth or special event may have been considered significant, but evidence is lacking. This is a consequence of the Spanish Conquest of 1521, which effectively destroyed these ancient Central American civilizations forever.

BELOW ***The great 'Sun Stone' that survived the destruction of the Aztec temples of Mexico City. It forms a complex cosmological calendar, from the 'five ages of humanity' in the centre, through the symbols of the days and the stars, to the encircling sky bound round by fiery serpents.***

Any more planets to come?

Since 1781, when William Herschel in England identified a new planet, now known as Uranus, two more members of the Solar family have been located still further out. Uranus had been seen (but at first mistaken for a fixed star) by astronomers using rapidly improved telescopes evolved from the instruments used by Galileo in the previous century. The other two 'new' planets, Neptune (1846) and Pluto (1930), were, on the other hand, tracked down by calculation from irregularities in the orbit of each predecessor.

Astronomers constantly revise their ideas as they take in new data through ever more powerful and sophisticated procedures. But how about astrologers? Does the existence of three extra planets, which nobody, from the Sumerians to Ptolemy, could possibly have noticed with the naked eye, make nonsense of the basic tenets of astrology?

Logically, it does not. It means that until now astrologers have had to do their work with, presumably, only seventy-five per cent of the planetary data – unless the influences of the most distant planets are considered to be proportionately weaker than those of visible ones. The present-day astrologers' real problem is that of course the traditions handed down could not enlighten them about the kind of influences they should attribute to Uranus, Neptune and Pluto when interpreting their relative positions in a person's horoscope. Once there is agreement on this, it could be expected that astrology will be in a stronger position to 'get it right' than in any previous age.

The new age

We are now moving into the first degree of the Age of Aquarius. This is an exciting turning point in astrology; the last time Earth moved into a new Age was 2000 years ago, when the Age of Pisces began and Christianity was born. With the same awe as our

LEFT *Voyager 2's 1989 shot of Neptune – processed in false-colour by NASA scientists – reveals for the first time the planet's Great Dark Spot and the haze that crowns its methane atmosphere.*

distant ancestors, but with truer understanding, we get ready to cast a glance into the New Age ahead.

In the 1960s people had no hesitation in proclaiming that the New Age was dawning. We may still have to wait a little longer to find out what it is like living in it. But we do know what we expect from it. An age of technology, of humanity, of freedom – an age of care for the planet; an age of intuition coupled with the most sensitive knowledge of the natural world. And for practitioners of astrology, an age in which cosmic exploration coincides with a reappraisal of traditional methods.

Who, for example, is assessing the astrological impact of the newly discovered moons of Neptune? There is so much to look forward to in everything new that future space programmes will bring back – not to mention *Hubble*, the optical space telescope orbiting the Earth, and the Earth-based *radio-telescope*. Work on the electromagnetic fields of all the planets may bring vindication to the astrological ideas of planetary influence. Astrologers' present knowledge is not finite. The New Age may not be over-kind to astrologers who are too timid, or too conservative, or just too lazy, to study and adjust.

When Jack Lindsay, in his *Origins of Astrology*, discusses the theory of correspondences between things vast and very far away in the cosmos and things human and very small on Earth he quotes a profound scientific thinker, the late Sir Peter Medawar, writing in *The Art of the Soluble* (1967), on the closeness of living and inanimate matter at the microscopic level:

> *. . . there is no dividing line between structures in the molecular and in the anatomical sense: macro-molecules have structures in a sense intelligible to the anatomist, and small atomical structures are molecular in a sense intelligible to the chemist . . .*

Sceptics are inclined to put the question: 'How can the planets, stars and galaxies possibly have anything to do with our daily lives?' As we saw at the beginning of this article, people who lived before history are more likely to have asked, 'How can they possibly *not* be influencing us?'

Some Scientific Evidence
by Dr Percy Seymour

When we talk about astrology in the Western world, we usually have in mind natal astrology, which links the personality and destiny of the individual with the positions of the planets at birth and the subsequent motions of the planets with respect to the birth chart. When this type of astrology began in the ancient world, it was closely related to astronomy; since then the relationship has changed considerably, to the point of total schism.

THE PARTING OF THE WAYS

What shattered the interdependence of astrology and astronomy was the acceptance of the revolutionary theory put forward by Nicolas Copernicus late in the sixteenth century. Copernicus placed the Sun at the centre of the Solar System and recognized that the Earth was just another orbiting planet. Of course, this completely changed the unique position of the Earth as centre of our System, a position vital to the long-accepted cosmology of Aristotle, the system of planetary spheres put forward by Ptolemy and the theoretical basis of astrology. A second blow came from the work of Sir Isaac Newton: Newton's laws of motion and gravitation showed that, although every particle in the universe attracts every other particle, gravitation is greatly weakened by distance. Therefore, it was reasoned, the Sun, Moon, planets and stars could not conceivably affect life on Earth in the direct ways astrologers seemed to believe they could.

MODERN OBJECTIONS

In our own age, a variety of reasons have been put forward to back the orthodox scientific view that astrology just cannot work. It is pointed out that the gravitational pull of the midwife on the child at birth is greater than that of the Sun, Moon or any of the planets. It is shown that the lights in a delivery room are stronger than radiation we receive from the planets. In other words, many scientists set up a simple single-link theory, shoot it down and from this conclude that no scientific theory can be constructed to explain any part of astrology. Such a dismissal takes no account of the enormous effect of the solar wind, first recognized in 1958, my own work on the complex jigsaw of the vast magnetic fields which thread their way between the stars, the development of instruments that can monitor hitherto unrecognized sections of the spectrum of electromagnetic radiation and the growing work from biologists tracking the effects of activity in the cosmos on life-forms on Earth. We cannot separate ourselves from the rest of the cosmos; there are a wide variety of forces, fields and particles which link our Earth to the rest of the universe. Science has been aware of this for a long time.

SOME STATISTICAL EVIDENCE

The modern scientific approach to astrology really started with the work of Dr Michel Gauquelin in the 1950s. While Gauquelin showed that many of the claims made by astrology, particularly those of Sun-sign astrology, were not really valid, he did make some important and statistically significant discoveries. His first findings showed that people who had achieved success in particular professions tended to be born with specific planets in certain parts of the sky. These findings could be criticized because they depend on one's definition of 'success', but a more important aspect of his work is not open to such criticism. This concerns planetary heredity.

Gauquelin showed that if a child is born with a particular planet in a specific area of the sky, then it is more than likely that at least one of the parents would have been born with the same planet in a similar part of the sky. This effect obeyed the established laws of heredity, did not hold when birth was medically induced, and was enhanced by disturbances of the geomagnetic field. My own work set out to provide a theory that would explain this planetary heredity effect.

A MAGNETIC THEORY OF ASTROLOGY

In recent years, biologists have shown that many life-forms such as bacteria, birds and fish can use the magnetic field of Earth to find direction; there is evidence that some human beings can also, to a limited extent, find direction using only the magnetic field. Biologists have shown that vibrations in the Earth's field do have an effect on the central nervous systems of many life-forms, including humans. The building block of the nervous system is the neuron, containing a 'message transmitter' called an axon. This is usually stimulated by electrical activity generated within the neuron, but it can also be activated by electrical stimulus from outside. Since a changing magnetic field generates an associated electrical field, it can also act as a stimulus to the central nervous system. It is as if the nervous system can act as an aerial through which we can detect some of the vibrations of the Earth's field.

There is growing evidence that the magnetic behaviour of the Sun is linked to the relative positions and motion of the planets. The magnetic field of the Earth is linked to the magnetic fluctuations of the Sun through the agency of the solar wind. The solar wind is a constant stream of sub-atomic particles flowing from the Sun's corona, 'gusting' and 'squalling' much like a real wind. It has also already been established that the magnetic field of the Earth varies in a manner linked to the motions and phases of the Moon. This means that the whole Solar System is playing a 'symphony' on the magnetic field of Earth.

BELOW *An interpretation of the Jupiter's magnetosphere, the area of the planet's magnetic field containing high energy particles of various intensities. The solar wind, a constant stream of atomic particles which flows from the Sun in all directions, determines the shape of the magnetosphere and replenishes it with particles. Jupiter's magnetic field is the strongest yet discovered in the Solar System. Of the inner planets, only Earth has an extensive magnetosphere (first explored in 1958).*

THE MAGNETIC MUSIC OF THE SPHERES

According to my theory, we are all genetically 'tuned' to receive a different set of 'melodies' from this symphony. While in the womb, the organs of our familiar five senses are still developing, so they are less effective in receiving information than they are once we are born. However, the womb is no hiding place from the all-pervading and constantly fluctuating magnetic field of Earth, so the symphonic tunes which we pick up can become part of our earliest memories. It is here that some of the magnetic music of the spheres becomes etched on our brains. The first role of our particular response to this music is to provide the cue for our entry on to the stage of the world. At later stages in life, when the Solar System 'plays our tune' again on the magnetic field of Earth, it evokes these memories and our response may influence the way we react in a given situation. This gives some weight to a very old astrological saying: 'The stars incline, they do not command.'

When the complexity of the cosmic forces acting on Earth is taken into account it is surely possible that further relationships, not yet recognized, might well exist. As we move into the Age of Aquarius, we make further progress towards a more fully developed theory of astrology. As Karl Popper, philosopher of science, states, 'Connections which are not far to seek may easily be overlooked if it is often repeated that the search for such connections is meaningless.'

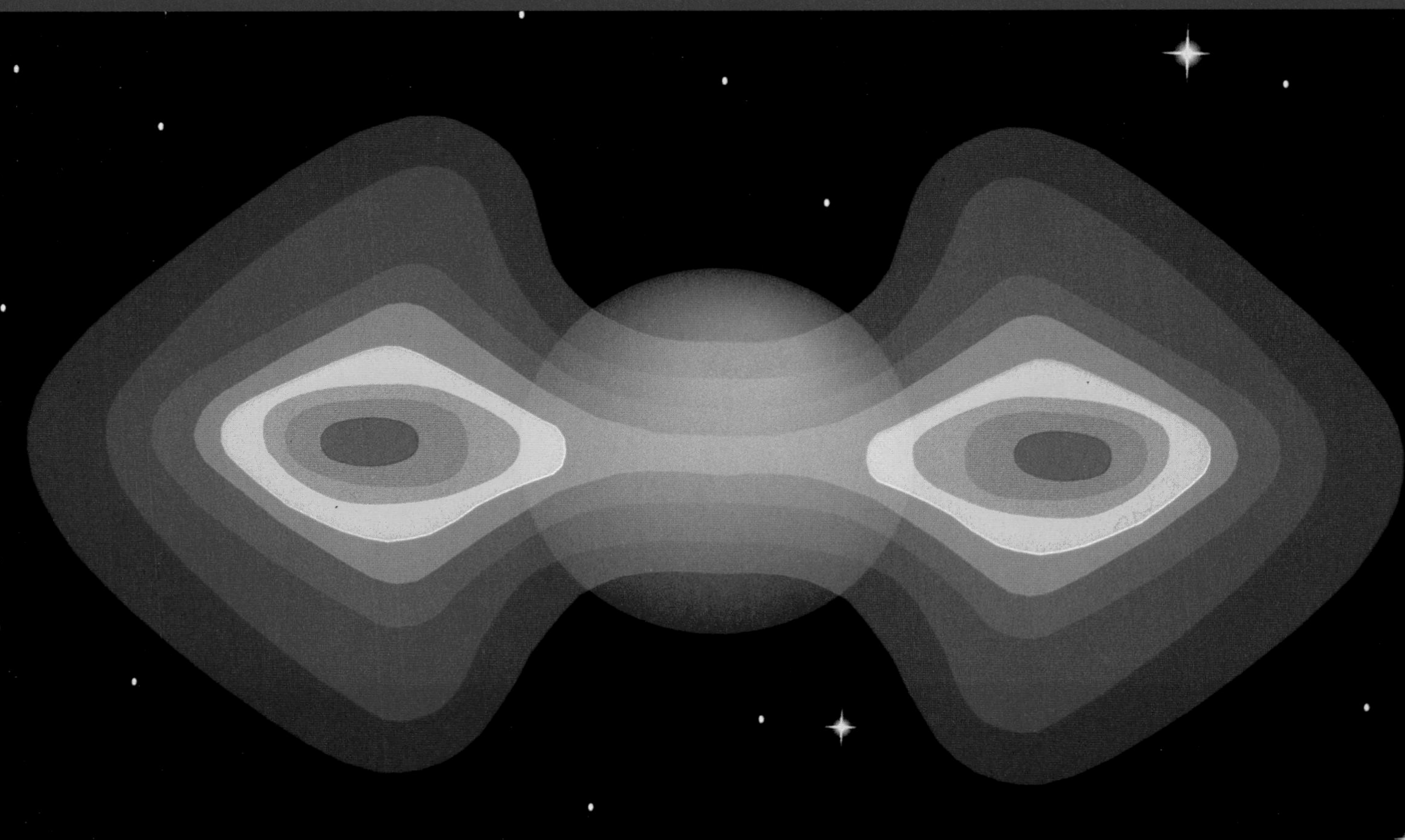

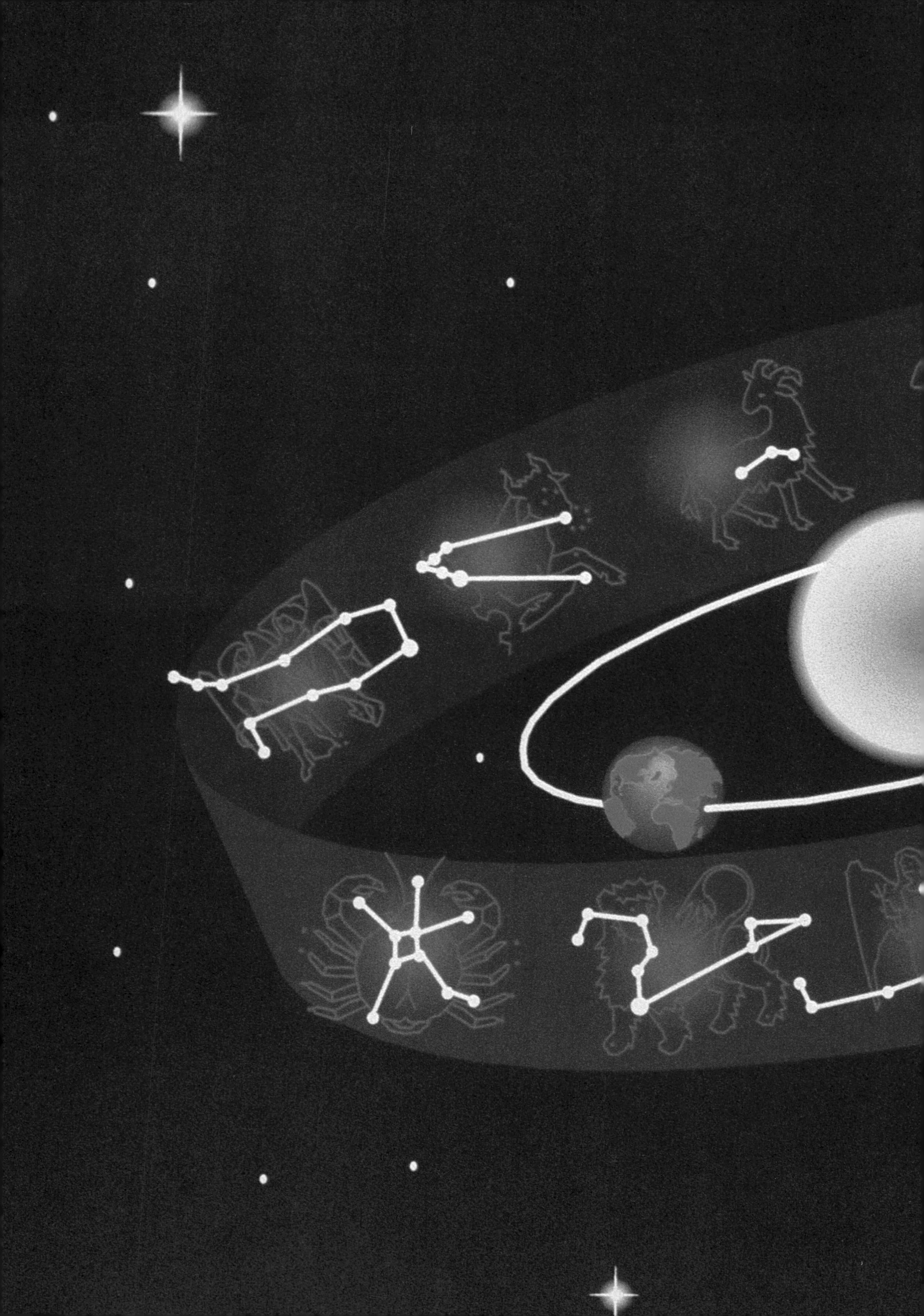

Understanding the Zodiac

THE CONCEPT OF THE ZODIAC

The zodiac is a belt of sky around the celestial sphere about 18 degrees in width, tilted at an angle of 23.5 degrees relative to the Earth's equator. It is centred on the ecliptic (so called because eclipses occur along it), which is the projection of the Earth's orbit on to the celestial sphere. It passes through the twelve zodiac constellations, and is the pathway along which the Sun, Moon and planets appear to move, apart from Pluto, whose orbit is eccentric. Every twenty-four hours, the zodiac appears to pass clockwise overhead, carrying the Sun, Moon and planets with it; this of course is an illusion created by the anticlockwise rotation of the Earth. Of course, the zodiac is invisible, and its position can only be detected by observing the positions of the planets at night-time, just as one can trace the night flightpath of an aircraft by watching its navigation lights tracing a pathway in the sky.

THE ASTRONOMY OF THE ZODIAC

To understand why the zodiac is limited to this particular narrow band of sky, we need to know a little about astronomy and the Solar System. As the Sun moves relentlessly on its journey along one of the spiral arms of our Galaxy, the Milky Way, it carries with it its family of orbiting planets, of which Earth is one, and the asteroids, some of which are minor planets, lying between the orbits of Mars and Jupiter. As the planets' orbital planes coincide to a large extent, they appear to an observer on Earth all in the same ribbon of sky.

When the ancient astronomer-priests who first conceived the zodiac studied the sky at night, they of course tracked the motion and changing shape of the Moon, but noted two other phenomena: the frosty grandeur of the fixed stars and the different movements of the five observable planets. The fixed stars are not, of course, really stationary, but are so remote – the nearest being some 30 million million kilometres/18 million million miles away – that their movement is undetectable to

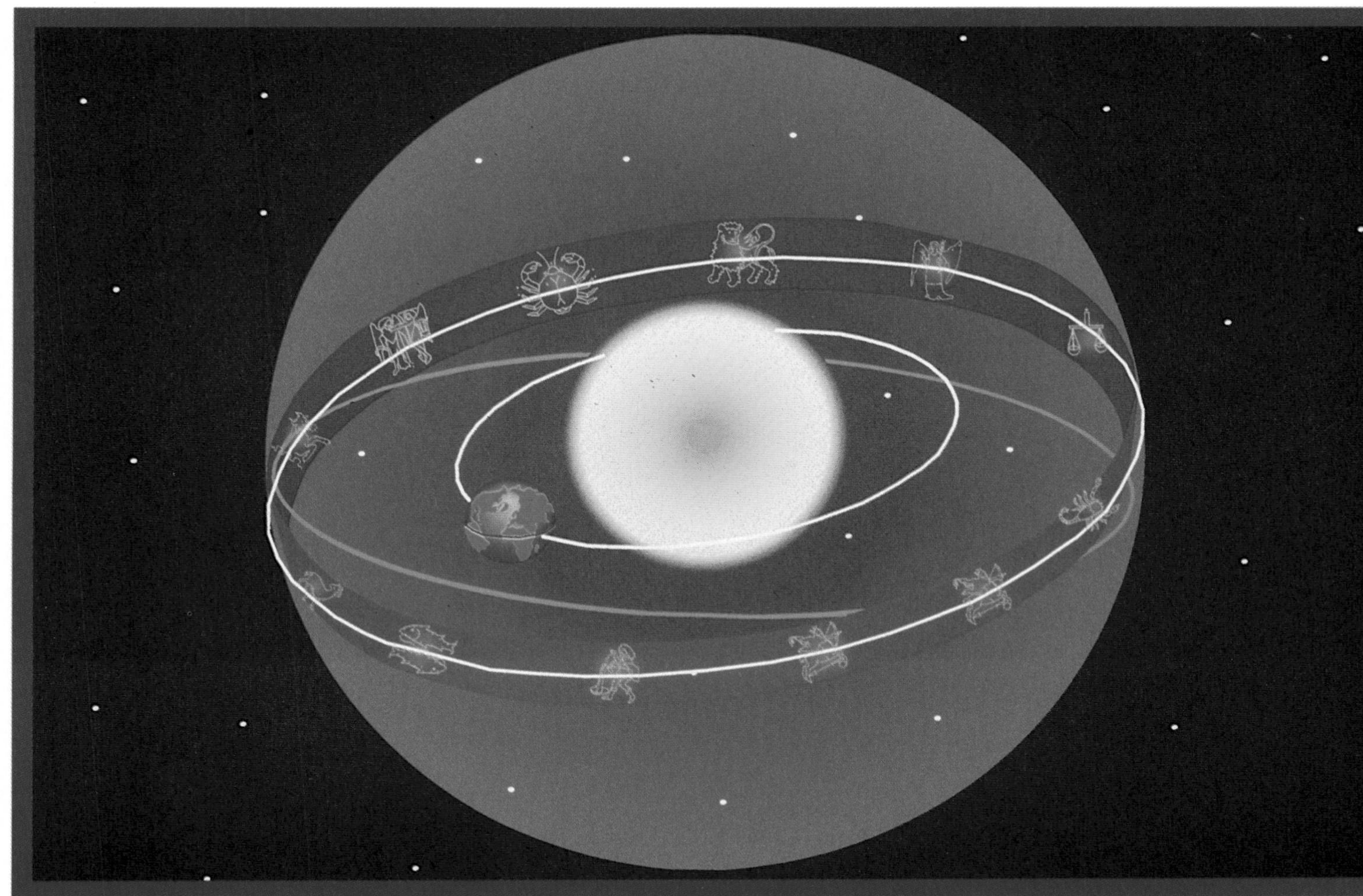

LEFT *The Solar System comprises the Sun and its attendant planets; in order from the Sun, they are Mercury, Venus, Earth with its Moon, Mars, Jupiter, Saturn, Uranus, Neptune and Pluto. Surrounding the Solar System like a transparent bubble is the celestial sphere, a purely imaginary concept, but invaluable to astronomers and astrologers alike for measuring and plotting the positions of the stars and celestial bodies.*

ABOVE *The Sun and the Earth within the celestial sphere (the other planets have been omitted for clarity). The light blue circle is the celestial equator, the projection of Earth's equator on to the celestial sphere; the white circle is the Earth's orbit, inclined to an angle of 23.5°, the angle of the Earth's axial tilt. The projection of this orbit on to the celestial sphere marks the ecliptic, which forms the central pathway of the zodiac. Astrologers divide the zodiac into twelve equal segments, not always coincidental with the zodiacal constellations.*

the naked eye. The five planets known at the time, however, were a different matter. Mercury, Venus, Mars, Jupiter and Saturn moved and weaved about the night sky in repeating patterns always within the same 18-degree width of sky.

To an observer, therefore, it appeared that most of the action, celestially speaking, took place in a restricted heavenly corridor. Astronomers and astrologers therefore gave this strip of sky priority, and noted what else appeared in it. Sharing the strip were twelve constellations, known from ancient times and listed by Ptolemy in his Star Catalogue of AD 150. They were Aries the Ram, Taurus the Bull, Gemini the Twins, Cancer the Crab, Leo the Lion, Virgo the Virgin, Libra the Balance, Scorpius the Scorpion, Sagittarius the Archer, Capricornus the Goat, Aquarius the Water Carrier and Pisces the Fishes. Certain other constellations border on the zodiac, and partly intrude. The ecliptic passes through part of the constellation Ophiuchus, and the zodiac also includes portions of Cetus, Orion and Sextans. Astrologically these facts are not taken into consideration, yet some astrologers consider they should be.

LEFT *The zodiac is confined to a narrow band of sky 18° wide and centred on the ecliptic, the projection of the Earth's orbit on to the celestial sphere. Most of the planets in the Solar System have orbital paths whose planes almost coincide with the ecliptic, and so appear to us to follow a pathway along the zodiac. The exceptions are Mercury, the planet nearest the Sun, which deviates by 7° from the ecliptic, and Pluto, the outermost known planet, which deviates up to 17° 10″ from the ecliptic. Venus (second planet from the Sun) inclines by 3° 24″, Mars (fourth planet) by 1° 51″, Jupiter (fifth planet) by 1° 18″, Saturn (sixth planet) by 2° 29″, Uranus (seventh planet) by 0° 46″ and Neptune (eighth planet) by 1° 46″. Mercury and Pluto also have the most eccentric orbits. Although the planes of the planetary orbits are similar, the time they take to make one revolution round the Sun differs greatly. Mercury makes a revolution in a brisk 87.9 days, Venus takes 224.7 days, Mars takes 1.88 years, Jupiter 1.86 years. Saturn 29.46 years, Uranus 84.01 years, Neptune 164.79 years and Pluto 247.7 years. Mercury has been round the Sun more than ninety-one times in the time it takes Pluto to make one revolution.*

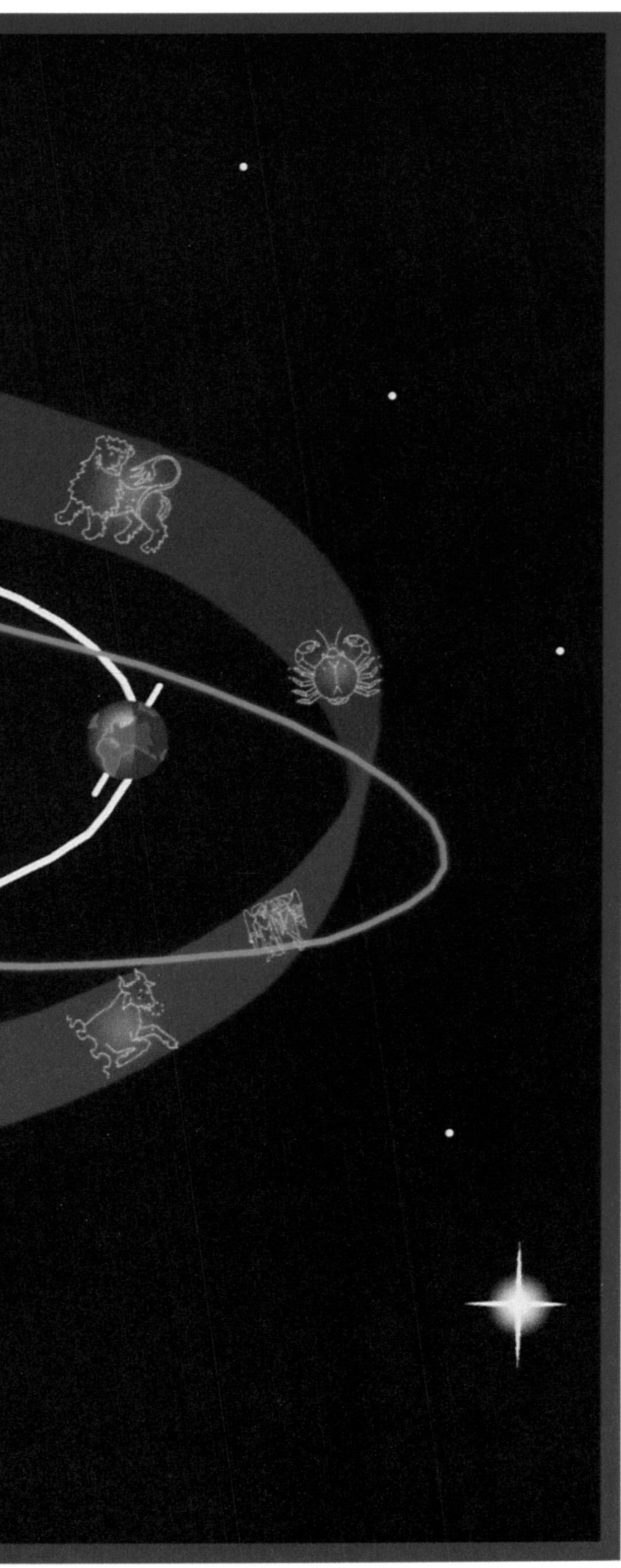

SOLSTICES AND EQUINOXES

We now come to one important point. As the zodiacal circle had no beginning, it was necessary to invent one and the best suggestion offered was the point where the planes of the two great circles – the ecliptic and the equator – intersect: at the spring equinox in the northern hemisphere (autumnal equinox in the southern hemisphere), the time when the Sun on its journey along the ecliptic is poised ready to cross the equator and its declination is zero. (Declination is measured north and south from the equator.) When this point was agreed, the Sun appeared to cross the equator at 0 degrees Aries, and so the beginning of the zodiac became the First Point of Aries (the name is retained even though the precession of the equinoxes has moved the vernal point to 0 degrees Aquarius.). This is the first cardinal point. There are three others: the First Point of Libra (0 degrees Libra), which marks the autumnal equinox in the northern hemisphere (spring equinox in the southern hemisphere); the First Point of Cancer (0 degrees Cancer) which in the northern hemisphere marks the summer solstice, when the Sun is at its highest declination; and the First Point of Capricorn (0 degrees Capricorn), which in the northern hemisphere marks the winter solstice, when the Sun is at its lowest declination. The equinoxes are so called because days and nights are equal; the solstices are so called because they are the two points when the Sun appears to 'stand still' at its lowest or highest point in the sky before continuing on its journey towards the opposite solstice.

LEFT *In this representation of the solsticial and equinoctial points, Earth's orbit (the white circle) is shown horizontal and the ecliptic (blue circle) at an angle of 23.5°. The solstices and equinoxes are the four most significant points on the Earth's annual orbit. The equinoxes are the two points each year when the ecliptic cuts the celestial equator, days and nights are equal in length and the Sun is at zero declination. The spring equinox occurs around 21 March and the autumnal equinox around the 22 September; in the southern hemisphere, the seasons are reversed. The solstices occur when the Sun appears to 'stand still' at its highest or lowest declination in the sky, producing the longest day and shortest night (in the summer) and shortest day and longest night (in the winter). At the summer solstice, (around 21 June in northern hemisphere) the Sun appears at its highest declination in the sky because the Earth is at the lowest point in its orbit; at the winter solstice, (around 22 December in the northern hemisphere) the Sun appears at its lowest declination in the sky because the Earth is at the highest point in its orbit.*

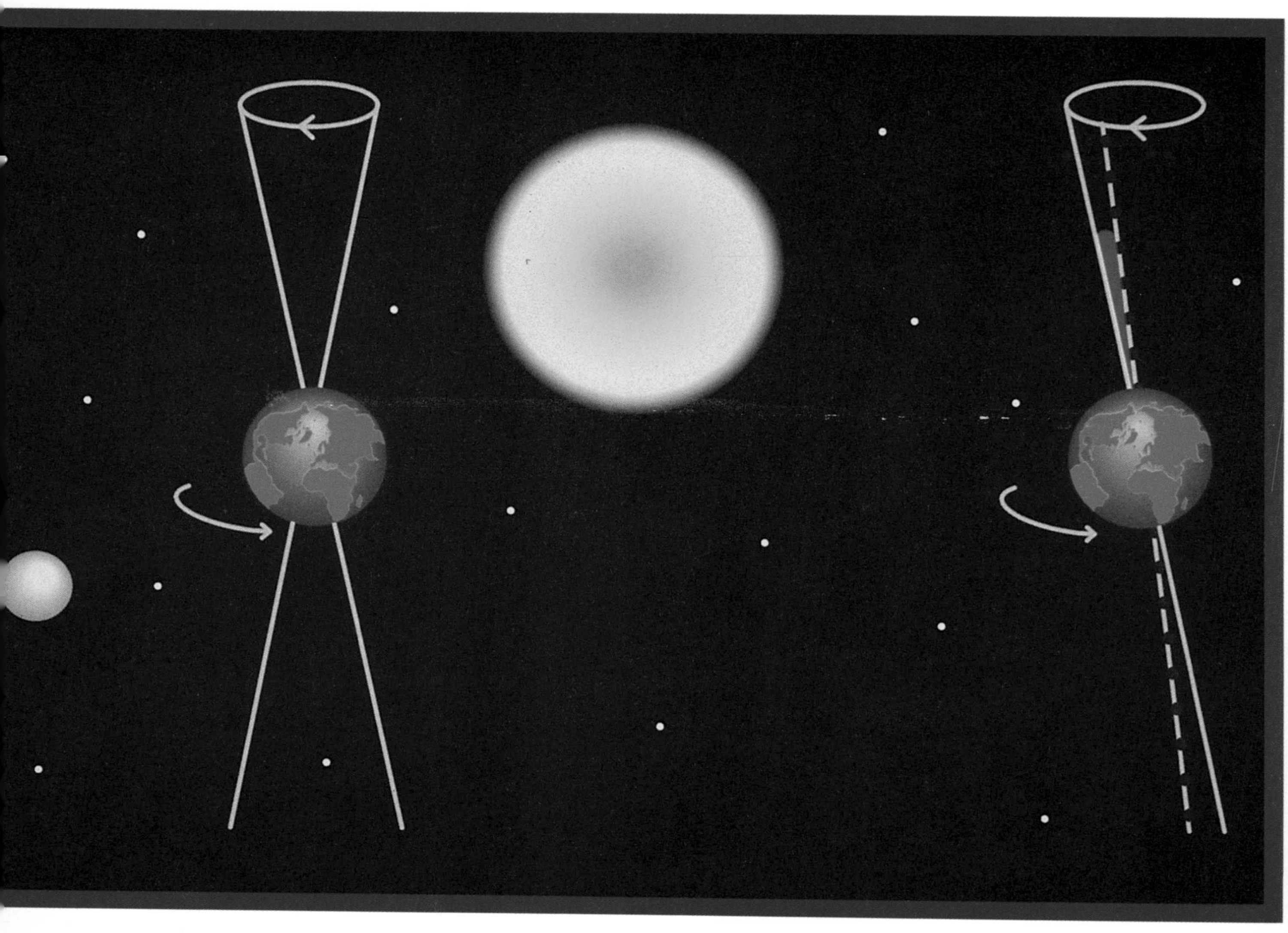

THE PRECESSION OF THE EQUINOXES

When the first zodiacs were drawn up over 2 000 years ago, the first constellation (Aries) and the first zodiac sign coincided, but due to the precession of the equinoxes, this is no longer so. The spring equinox, or vernal point, is the point where the equator and the ecliptic intersect around 21 March. Over a period of a year, when the Sun once again reaches the vernal point, it is fifty seconds of arc behind its last position; therefore, the vernal point recedes by about fifty seconds of arc each year, equal to about one degree of arc every seventy-two years; it is receding backwards around the zodiac and in about 26 000 years, it will return to the same point it occupies today. Over 2 000 years ago, the constellation observed behind the Sun at the vernal point was Aries; today, because of the vernal point's 'slippage' it is Aquarius.

ABOVE *Because the Earth is not a perfect sphere – the gravitational pull of the Sun and Moon make it bulge around the equator – it wobbles on its axis like a spinning top. Over a period of 26 000 years, the celestial north pole, the projection of the North Pole on to the celestial sphere, describes a huge circle in the sky, covering about one degree of the circumference every seventy-two years.*

RIGHT *Associated with the Earth's 'wobble' is the precession of the equinoxes. Every seventy-two years, the point where the ecliptic cuts the celestial equator at the spring equinox slips backward by about one degree. Over 2 000 years ago, the constellation behind the Sun at the time of the spring equinox was Aries (indicated by the faint Earth on the green orbit); today, because of the precession, the constellation is Aquarius, indicated by the Earth shown on the white orbit.*

THE CHANGING POLE STAR

This Earth is not a perfect sphere, but slightly flattened at both poles. The gravitational pull exerted by the Sun and Moon on the Earth's equatorial bulge causes the Earth's axis to wobble, rather like a slowly spinning top. As the Earth's axis precesses, the north celestial pole (which is a projection of the Earth's North Pole on to the celestial sphere) describes a huge circle in the sky, in a period of about 26 000 years. In 2500 BC the Pole Star was Thuban, in the constellation Draco the Dragon. The Great Pyramid of Cheops was built with a main passageway aligned to observe Thuban. Our Pole Star at present is Polaris, in the constellation Ursa Minor. In the year 4000 it will be Alrai (Gamma Cephei) in the constellation Cepheus.

TYPES OF ZODIAC

The origin of the term 'zodiac' is derived from the Greek *zodiacus*, which means little animals or creatures. The Chaldeans of Mesopotamia wove magical mythological pictures around the various star clusters, and these myths were adopted and transformed by the Babylonians, Egyptians and ultimately the Greeks, each of whom made their own contributions.

Although many different zodiacs have been invented, all have a common idea in mind, to measure the positions of the celestial bodies in the heavens. Astrologically, these are measured along the ecliptic, but with astronomy and navigation, measurements are made on the celestial equator.

One of the important differences between the modern Western and Indian astrology is the different ways of measuring the zodiac. Indian astrology uses the sidereal or fixed zodiac, which observes the passage of the celestial bodies against the background of the constellations. This makes calculation of the planetary positions, for example, very complicated as the constellations vary greatly in size and the sidereal zodiac has no fixed, agreed starting point. Most Western astrologers use the tropical or moving zodiac, which plots the positions of the celestial bodies along the ecliptic.

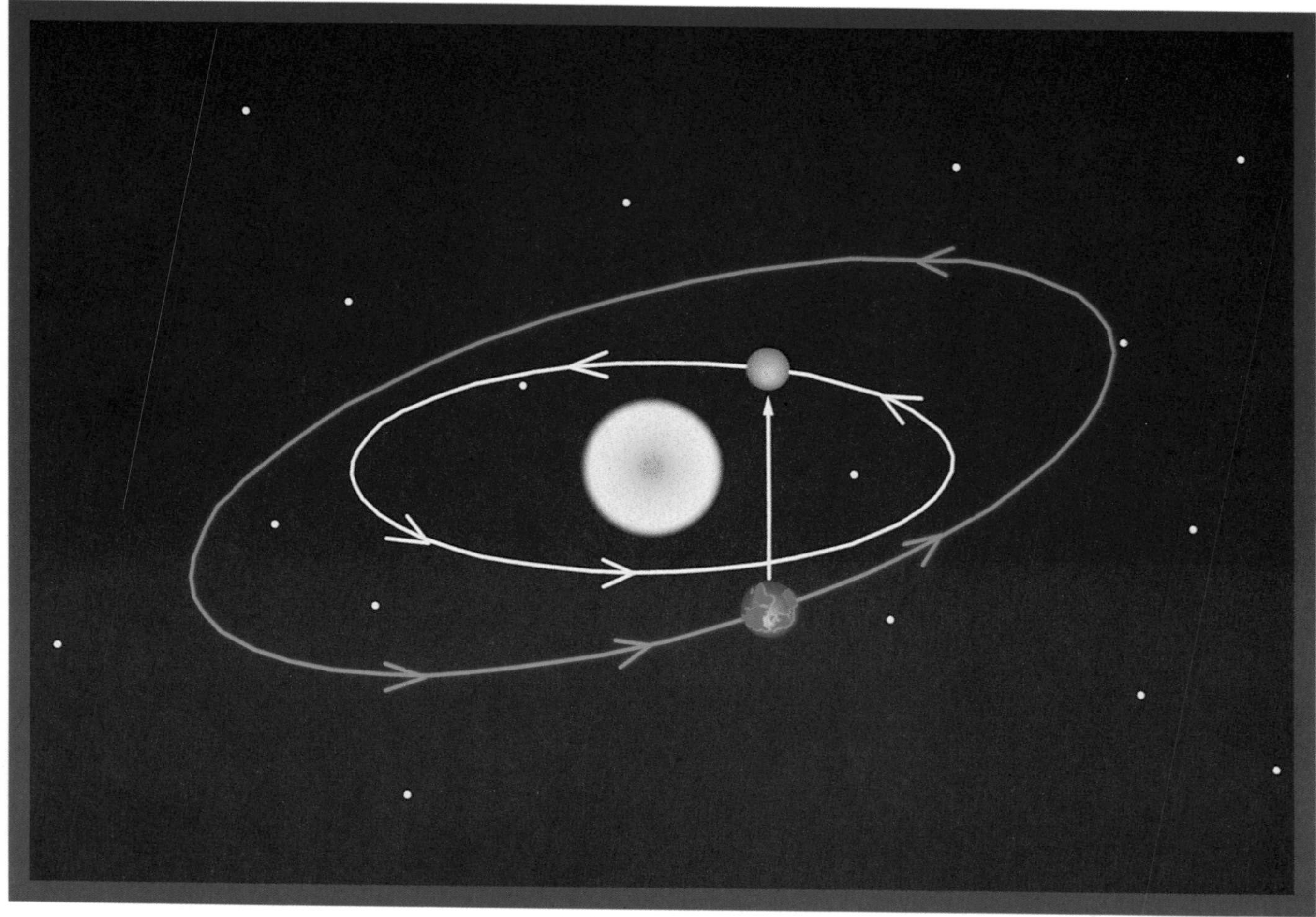

ABOVE *All planets, including Earth, move anticlockwise round the Sun. Occasionally, however, planets appear to move backwards; this is known as retrograde motion, and is an illusion caused by relative orbital speeds. Mercury and Venus, the planets between the Earth and the Sun, sometimes appear retrograde because they move faster than Earth, and are on their return journey while the Earth is still on the first lap.*

THE STARS AND THE ZODIAC

It is important to understand the difference between the constellations and the zodiac signs, which bear the same names. Whereas the zodiacal constellations differ greatly in size and shape, the twelve signs occupy 30 degrees each, measured along the ecliptic.

The fixed stars are not limited to the zodiac constellations, which is clearly seen as they are scattered over the whole dome of the sky. However, some very important ones do lie in the zodiac, as for instance Antares – Alpha Scorpii; Aldebaran – Alpha Tauri, the red giant star situated in the 'eye' of the Bull; and Regulus – Alpha Leonis in the constellation Leo.

FROM ZODIAC TO HOROSCOPE

Astrology is Earth-centred; astronomy is Sun-centred. Much of the confusion that exists springs from this difference in starting point. From our position on Earth, the constellations and planets appear to move in a clockwise direction but this is an illusion due to the anticlockwise rotation of the Earth itself. The planets' proper motion is anticlockwise. The Earth moves around the Sun at a mean distance of 150 million kilometres/93 million miles, the actual distance changing a little throughout the year due to variations in the Earth's orbit. Yet from our position on Earth, the Sun appears to travel round the zodiac in one year, spending roughly a month in each sign. Few people understand the true meaning of the statement that the Sun is 'in' a sign. This in effect is an illusion, caused by our view of the Sun from our position on Earth. For example, when we on Earth are moving through Virgo, and we look at the Sun, it will appear to be 'in' Pisces.

Apart from the position of the observer, the astronomical and astrological zodiac is the same; astrologically, however, the Earth is the focal point in the centre. Instead of consulting the sky directly, astrologers draw up charts to represent the heavens at the time of birth or other event, and plot the positions of the planets from ephemerides, prepared from the known movements of the celestial bodies.

If you could hover in a spacecraft over the north celestial pole and look down to the Earth, you would see our planet moving in a direct or anticlockwise motion. You would also see the whole panorama of the Solar System, with the Sun, Moon and planets moving along the pathway of the ecliptic. The Earth would appear to be directly below and therefore in the centre of your picture. The picture you see would be identical for a child born at that moment in time on planet Earth, and a copy of this picture on paper would be the same as the child's natal chart. This is a simple example of how astrologers transpose the celestial panorama on to paper, how a birth chart relates directly to the heavens.

BELOW *Superior planets (those beyond the Earth's orbit) can also appear to be retrograde. In this case, it is the Earth that moves the fastest, and is on the return journey when the superior planet is still on the outward leg of its orbit. It therefore appears to an observer on Earth that the superior planet is moving backwards.*

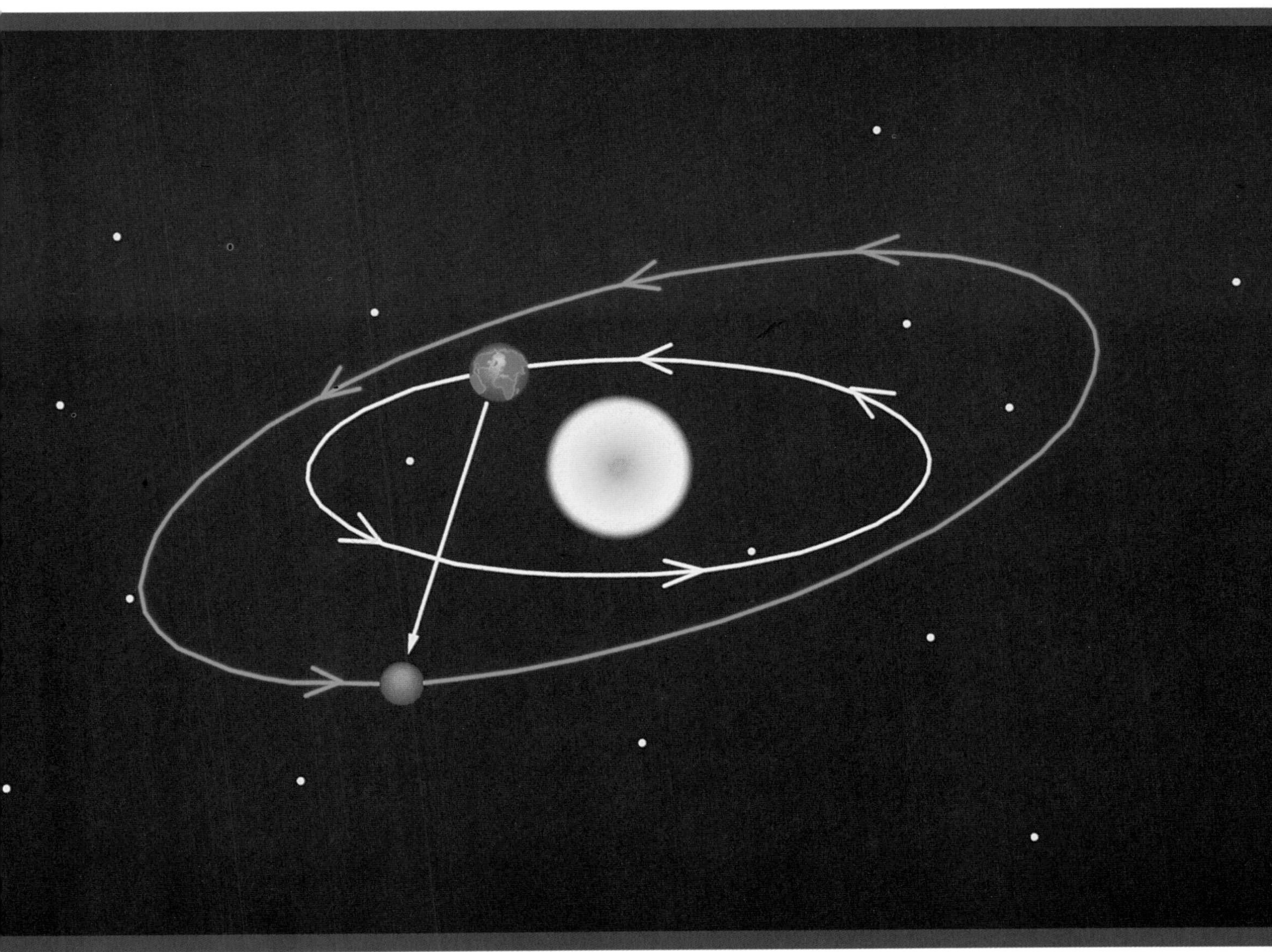

ABOVE *A picture of the heavens on 4 August 1990 from the Sun-centred viewpoint, showing the position of the planets relative to the zodiac. The Sun is not 'in' any sign, but sits at the centre of the Solar System; Mercury (yellow) is 18° in Scorpio; Venus (blue) is 10° in Gemini; Earth (blue and green) and its Moon (white) are 12° in Aquarius; Mars (orange) is 26° in Pisces; Jupiter (green) is 24° in Cancer; Saturn (yellow, ringed) is 22° in Capricorn; Uranus (blue, ringed) is 8° in Capricorn; Neptune (mauve) is 13° in Capricorn; and Pluto (purple) is 17° in Scorpio.*

ABOVE *The heavens on the same date from an Earth-centred viewpoint. The Earth is not 'in' a sign, but sits in the centre; the Sun and the faster moving planets have shifted, relatively speaking. The Sun (large, yellow) is 12° in Leo, the Moon (white) is 17° in Capricorn, Mercury (small, yellow) is 8° in Virgo, Venus (blue) is 19° in Cancer, Mars (orange) is 15° in Taurus, Jupiter (green) is 27° in Cancer, Saturn (yellow, ringed) is 21° in Capricorn, Uranus (blue, ringed) is 6° in Capricorn, Neptune (mauve) is 12° 5″ in Capricorn and Pluto (purple) is 15° in Scorpio.*

RIGHT *The transformation of the celestial layout into an astrological chart represents a four-dimensional event in two-dimensional terms. The zodiac is represented by the outer circle of the birth chart; the chart itself is a map of the heavens as if seen from a point above Earth, taking Earth as the centre of the Solar System with the Sun, Moon and planets revolving round it. Their positions at the moment of birth are indicated by pinpointing the degree they have reached in whatever zodiac sign they are in at the time in question. Once this 'snapshot' of the heavens has been expressed as a birth chart, an astrologer can begin to interpret the influence and effects of the planets.*

The Horoscope

Derived from the Greek *horoscopos* – *hora* an hour and *skopos* observer – a horoscope is a map of the heavens compiled for any time or place, for astrological purposes and study. A horoscope drawn up for a birth time is called a birth chart, a natus, nativity or geniture. A birth chart is a map of the heavens erected for the time of birth and is a blueprint of its subject's life.

THE IMPORTANCE OF TIMING

Before a birth chart can be drawn up, the date, time and place of birth have to be established. This birth data is necessary as a basis for the calculation of the local sidereal time at the place of birth, for the time of birth. (Sidereal time is time measured by the stars, not by an ordinary clock.) This is a complicated procedure for which you need to consult an ephemeris: adjustments have to be made to take account of the operation of summer time, and for the longitude of the place of birth (east of Greenwich adds four minutes per degree of longitude, west subtracts the same.) For a birth in southern latitudes, a further adjustment is needed: twelve hours must be added to the final answer.

BUILDING THE CHART

Charts are usually drawn up on a circular grid; in astrology, the eastern side of a chart is on the left, and corresponds to the eastern horizon. The sidereal time at the place of birth will yield the degree of the rising sign (from the table of houses) which dictates the order of the whole chart. It establishes the chart's horizon. Once this is done, the houses can be numbered (anticlockwise), the glyphs of the signs filled in (clockwise), and the degree of the midheaven, or Medium Coeli, calculated (again from tables). Once again, adjustments have to be made for births in the southern latitudes. The houses are the same, but the signs must be reversed before filling them in on the chart. So if Capricorn was rising in the northern hemisphere, Cancer would be rising in the south. The degree of the midheaven is calculated in a similar way.

The chart is now ready for the addition of the positions of the Sun, Moon and planets, which have to be calculated relative to the time of birth. This information can also be found in an ephemeris. The positions of the planets can be calculated either from their midday or midnight positions, according to the ephemeris being used. The mean motions of the planets are also listed in the ephemeris. The planets appear to be carried round with the signs each day in a clockwise motion, due to the Earth spinning anticlockwise on its axis, but the proper motion of the planets is anticlockwise. A planet may be retrograde (appear to be moving backwards); this will be indicated in the ephemeris and adjustments will have to be made to its position before its motion is calculated.

INTERPRETING THE CHART

It is not difficult to learn how to draw up a birth chart, but when it is complete, the question is what to do with it, and how to begin to understand it. Gradually, with time and concentrated effort, all the little pieces of the jigsaw start to fall into place, and create a picture of a person's life and circumstances. Interpreting a chart needs knowledge, experience and skill, plus a blending of astrological art, a unique gift which gives an understanding of the chart as a whole.

There is another important factor to be considered, when judging horoscopes, which concerns astrology from a feminine point of view. When the zodiac was devised by the Chaldeans and Babylonians, no thought was conceived that a woman could ever wish to create an independent way of life for herself, the idea would have been quite unthinkable. She was not expected to have a mind of her own, but was considered to be a part of the household, like a piece of furniture. However, nowadays less importance might be placed on a woman's domestic involvements, and more on her ability and potential to live a fuller life, broaden her mind, consider developing her talents and expand her interests.

Before approaching interpretation, some knowledge of astrological terms is necessary. Understanding of the ascendant, the astrological houses, the planets, the aspects and the astrological elements and qualities will help.

THE ASCENDANT AND MIDHEAVEN

The ascendant is the cusp or starting point of the First House. The sign in which it appears is called the rising or ascending sign. This is very important, as it modifies the power of the Sun sign and may explain characteristics that are not covered by the more familiar Sun sign list. It is interesting to note that when a birth takes place at around 6 am GMT, the Sun sign and rising sign are usually the same, making the native of the chart a strong representative of the sign concerned. Planets placed in the rising sign also need careful interpretation.

The midheaven marks the place on a birth chart where the Sun is at midday on the day of birth, the point where the ecliptic crosses the subject's meridian. It is usually interpreted

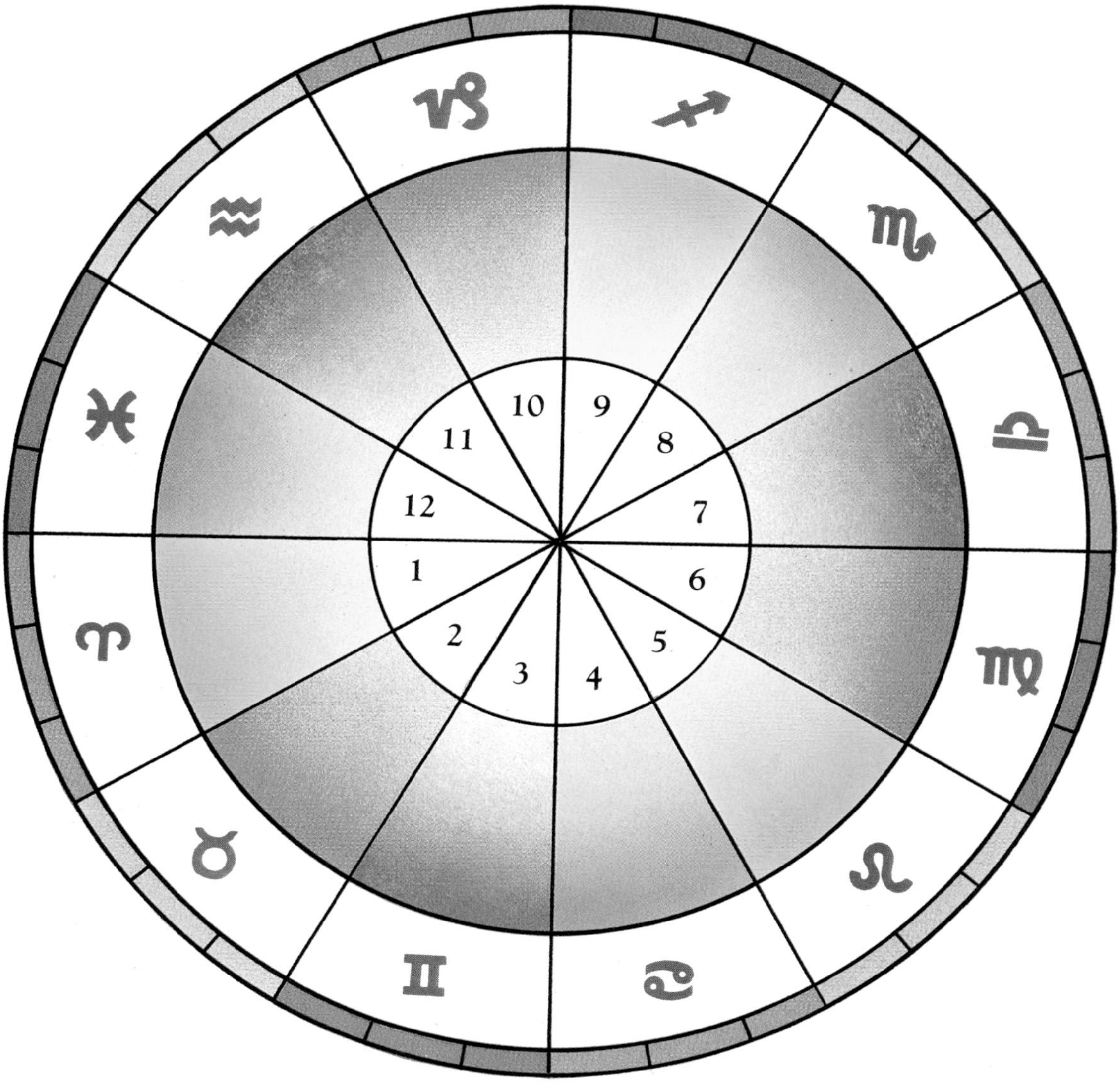

RIGHT *The horoscopic wheel is a graphic framework on which a representation of the heavens at the time of birth (or other event) can be drawn. The narrow outer rim is divided into thirty-six segments of 10° to make the plotting of planetary positions easier. Next comes the twelve 30° segments that contain the zodiac signs; 0° of one sign coincides with 30° of the next at the cusp, the dividing line between signs or houses. The innermost wheel represents the twelve numbered astrological houses. Signs and houses run in anticlockwise order round the chart. The zodiac signs are also subdivided into three qualities – cardinal, fixed and mutable – and four elements – fire, earth, air and water. Both sequences run concurrently anticlockwise from Aries.*

THE MEANING OF THE HOUSES

Astrological houses are divisions of the visible heavens, as seen at any point of time at any place on Earth, with a corresponding division of the invisible heavens hidden beneath the Earth. They are channels through which we enter into relationship with our environment; on a birth chart they are represented by the twelve inner segments. The houses have no names, but are numbered, beginning with the First House, whose cusp is the ascendant, and counted anticlockwise. There are several different systems of house division, that is, dividing up the heavens, and many of them are very complicated. The Equal House System, which divides the circle of the zodiac into twelve equal segments beginning with the ascendant, is the easiest and most used by modern astrologers. For this method, you need an ephemeris that gives the degree of the rising sign and of the midheaven, for the sidereal time of birth.

Each house rules a certain section of life, the first six being rather more concerned with the individual and the last six associated with more public areas of life. Each house is associated with the zodiac sign that bears its number (for example, Leo, the fifth sign of the zodiac is associated with the Fifth House) and with the planet or celestial body that rules the sign (in Leo's case, the Sun).

THE ASSOCIATIONS AND ATTRIBUTES

Some houses are more complicated than others and have wider meanings. Their basic interpretations are as follows. The First House concerns your personality – you, yourself. The Second House concerns business and money, property interests, buying and selling, and material possessions. The Third House governs communications, education, writing, short journeys, close family ties, commerce, trade, and one's intellect. The Fourth House concerns home and private life. The Fifth House involves leisure, love relationships, speculation, sport, children, creativity, and games of chance. The

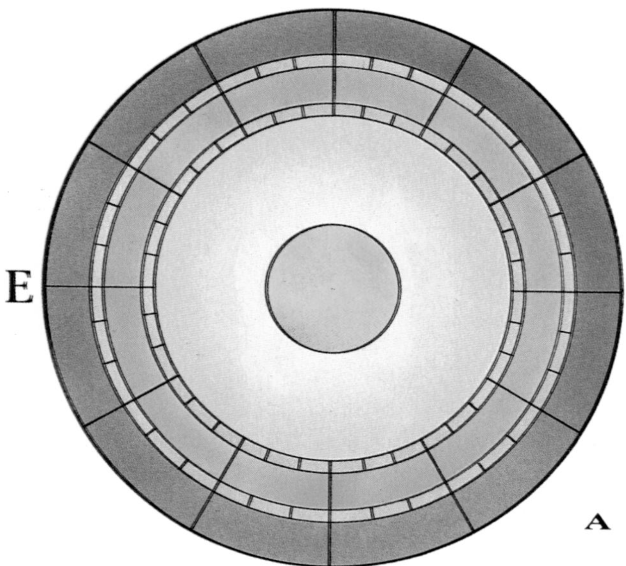

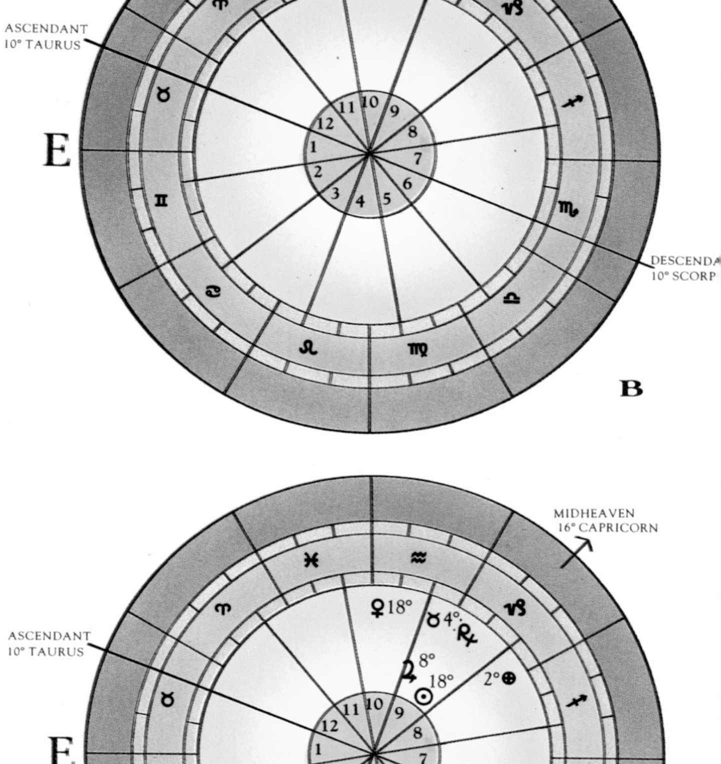

Most modern horoscopes are drawn up on wheel-shaped charts (A). There are three stages to the process. To erect a chart, you need the birth data (time, date and place of birth), an ephemeris for the relevant year and a table of houses for the relevant latitude. To get an accurate view of the heavens, the sidereal time at birth, the time relative to the stars is needed. The ephemeris will give the sidereal time at noon on the birth date, to which must be added (or subtracted if birth was after noon) the difference between noon and birth time, making allowances for summer time. In addition, for every 24 hours of clocktime, there is 24 hours 3 minutes and 56.5 seconds of sidereal time, so an extra 10 seconds for every hour must be added. Finally, time must be added or subtracted depending on the longitude of birth, adding four minutes for each degree or longitude east of Greenwich meridian and subtracting four minutes for each degree west. When the sidereal birth time is established, the ephemeris will give the ascendant, or degree of the rising sign at that time, in this case, 10° Taurus. This forms the horizon of the chart, and the basis for house division. Each house cusp starts at the same degree as the ascendant at 30° intervals round the chart. The houses are numbered anticlockwise. Then the glyphs for the zodiac signs can be filled in, starting with the rising sign (Taurus) and running anticlockwise. Finally, the midheaven, the point overhead at birth, can be obtained from the ephemeris and marked in the chart (B). In the last stage, the positions of the Sun, Moon and planets (from the ephemeris) are filled in, and Fortuna calculated. The complete chart (C) is then ready for astrological interpretation.

Sixth House concerns work and health. The Seventh House is the house of partnerships, personal relationships and marriage. The Eighth House is complex, but it basically concerns longer-term financial matters, stocks, shares and investments; wills, legacies, and shared assets. The Ninth House concerns foreign countries, the Church, the Law, travel, further education, abstract thought, and the future. The Tenth House governs ambition, social status, career, profession and one's place in society. The Eleventh House concerns friendships, intellectual companions, hopes and wishes, ideals, and one's aspirations. The Twelfth House governs the subconscious mind, the inner feelings, escapism and seclusion. It is also concerned with service to others, sorrows, medical matters, drugs, poisons and personal affairs.

QUALITIES AND ELEMENTS

There are other ways of subdividing and interpreting the circle of the zodiac. The qualities or quadruplicities divide the twelve signs into three groups of four signs which are described as cardinal, fixed or mutable.

The cardinal signs are Aries, Cancer, Libra and Capricorn. Cardinal people are leaders, active and energetic people with a goal and purpose in life. The fixed signs are Taurus, Leo, Scorpio and Aquarius. Fixed people are the proprietors of business (those that the cardinal people usually set up) and are usually to be found occupying positions of authority. They are stable, set in their ways, habits and opinions, strong in their likes and dislikes. They seldom change, but if they do, their changes can be drastic. The mutable signs are Gemini, Virgo, Sagittarius and Pisces. Mutable people are the intermediates, having certain qualities of each (cardinal and fixed). They are usually clever, mentally alert, quick and adaptable to circumstance.

Another method of division is by the triplicities, or elements, which divide the circle into four groups containing three signs each, and represent the four elements fire, water, air and earth. The fire signs are Aries, Leo and Sagittarius; the air signs are Gemini, Libra and Aquarius; the earth signs are Taurus, Virgo and Capricorn; and the water signs are Cancer, Scorpio and Pisces.

Fire-sign people are positive, forceful, self-confident, optimistic and sometimes aggressive. Water-sign people are sympathetic, prudent, protective, sensitive, often secretive and possessive. Air-sign people are intellectual, refined, thoughtful, and devoted to the arts and sciences. They work with ideas, and the mind is active and clever. Earth-sign people represent the brain applied to practical and material ends, producing craftsmen, designers, mathematicians, business people, architects, scientists and musicians.

These two patterns mesh so that each sign is unique: there is only one cardinal fire sign (Aries) for example, one mutable air sign and so forth. The power of each element is modified by the quality of the sign, and the quality of the sign is expressed differently through the character of the element.

PLANET PROFILES

The evaluation of the planetary positions in a birth chart depends on the attributes assigned to the planets. Aspects may indicate the relationship the planets have with each other, but can only be fully understood when the nature of the astrological values of the planets are taken into account. Below is a resumé of traditional planetary values.

THE SUN AND MOON

The Sun is the nearest star to Earth and is of vital importance. It is difficult to realize that we are rushing round the Sun at the amazing pace of something like 112 000 km per hour/70 000 miles per hour, and to understand the precarious circumstances under which we exist, because should the solar radiation change even by a tiny fraction, we on Earth might roast or freeze to death. Fortunately, the Sun is a very stable star and such deviations are unlikely. The Sun moves through the zodiac at the rate of about one degree a day, spending approximately one month in each sign.

The Sun is our life force. It provides energy and vitality and represents the positive side of our nature. It is associated with powers of leadership, control and command, and self-expression. It rules the zodiac sign Leo, is exalted (strong and powerful) in Aries, at detriment in Aquarius and at fall in Libra.

Although not a planet, the Moon is our nearest celestial neighbour and has great influence on us. The gravitational pull of the Moon affects the tides on Earth, and this in turn governs our body fluids, which contributes to about 90% of our general make-up. The Moon moves at approximately half a degree an hour, and it glides through all the signs of the zodiac in about one month.

The Moon stands for the receptive and imaginative side of human nature. It governs the emotions, sympathies and affections, and is associated with birth, motherhood and the characteristics inherited from past generations. Astrologically, it can bring changeable and fluctuating conditions. The Moon rules the zodiac sign Cancer, is exalted in Taurus, at detriment in Capricorn and at fall in Scorpio.

MERCURY AND VENUS

Mercury is the planet nearest to the Sun. It rushes round the Sun in just 88 days, and its orbit deviates beyond the ecliptic more than any other planet except Pluto.

Mercury is the planet of communications. It rules thought, speech, writing, short journeys, commerce and trade. It is associated with education, logic, powers of reasoning, sense of perception, and intellectual energy. It is also involved with new technology, radar, and radio communications. In mythology, apart from being the messenger of the gods, Mercury had a mischievous side to his nature, which can sometimes manifest itself in a horoscope. Mercury rules the zodiac signs Gemini and Virgo, is exalted in Virgo, at detriment in Sagittarius and at fall in Pisces.

Venus, second planet from the Sun, can come closer to the Earth than any other planet. It revolves round the Sun in 224.7 days. Venus is the planet of love, harmony, beauty, charm, art, idealism, social interests and fashion, the planet that harmonizes the emotions, and increases understanding. Known as the lesser benefic in astrology, it rules the zodiac signs Taurus and Libra, is exalted in Pisces, at detriment in Aries and at fall in Virgo.

MARS, JUPITER AND SATURN

Mars was named by the ancients after the god of war because of its red colour. It revolves around the Sun in 687 days. In astrology, Mars stands for energy, enthusiasm and initiative. It is quick, decisive and restless. On its positive side it creates courage and endurance, but on its negative side it can cause quarrelsome and reckless behaviour. Mars rules Aries, and traditionally Scorpio, is exalted in Capricorn, at detriment in Libra and at fall in Cancer.

Jupiter is the largest planet in the solar system. It orbits the Sun in 11.9 years, remaining in each sigh for roughly a year. In mythology, Jupiter was king of the gods, the Roman equivalent of Zeus. In astrology, Jupiter is known as the major benefic and the planet of luck, good fortune and opportunity. It is associated with further education, philosophical thinking, foreign countries, languages, the Church, the Law, publishing, travel and the future. On the negative side it can create over-optimism, self-indulgence, gambling instincts and conceit. Jupiter rules Sagittarius, and traditionally ruled Pisces, is exalted in Cancer, at detriment in Gemini, and at fall in Capricorn.

Saturn orbits the Sun in 29.5 years, remaining in a sign for an average of 2.5 years. Astrologically, Saturn is on the one hand the planet of limitation, disappointment and delay, but on the other, it is the planet of wisdom and worth, and stands for stability and security. It is a hard task-master that bestows reward for hard effort. It teaches one to aim for worthwhile success that stands the test of time. Saturn rules Capricorn, and traditionally Aquarius, is exalted in Libra, at detriment in Cancer and at fall in Aries.

URANUS, NEPTUNE AND PLUTO

Uranus orbits the Sun in 84 years. It can remain in a sign for about seven years. In mythology, Uranus was god of the sky. Astrologically, Uranus is the planet of the unpredictable and unexpected. It is associated with change (which can be disruptive or sudden), and with modern science, radio, TV, aeronautics, space travel and science fiction. It bestows originality, versatility and good intellectual ability. Uranus rules Aquarius, is exalted in Scorpio, at detriment in Leo and at fall in Taurus.

Neptune orbits the Sun in a period of 164.8 years. It can remain in a sign for between thirteen and fourteen years. Neptune was known by the ancients as the god of the Sea. In astrology, Neptune is associated with dreams and fantasy, idealism, spiritualism and the imagination. It is also concerned with the arts, poetry, dancing, maritime matters, drugs and poisons. In its negative state it is the planet of deception, pretence and illusion. Its action can be subtle, gradual and sometimes insidious. Neptune rules Pisces, is exalted in Leo, at detriment in Virgo and at fall in Aquarius.

Pluto is at present the last known member of the solar system, and it takes 247.7 years to orbit the Sun. It is named after the god of the underworld. Its orbit is so eccentric that it is thought there is another planet lying out there in the depths of space. In astrology, Pluto marks the beginning and ending of phases and indicates milestones and hurdles in life. It gives one the ability to make a fresh start if conditions are unfavourable. It bestows good powers of analysis and the gift for weighing up people and situations, a wonderful asset if used wisely. Pluto rules Scorpio, and is at detriment in Taurus. Its exaltation and fall is at present being determined.

PLANETARY ASPECTS

Aspects are the relationships within the chart formed by the distribution of the planets. They are calculated by counting the number of degrees between the planets. The number does not have to be precise: each aspect has a tolerance of a few degrees. Reading a chart for aspects is skilled work, as many of the underlying relationships may not be spotted at first glance.

The aspects below are discussed in order of priority. Only the most important are included; there are many weaker ones, but not all astrologers take them into account.

MAJOR ASPECTS

The most powerful aspect is the conjunction, which obviously occurs when two or more bodies occupy almost the same degree in the zodiac. The conjunction can be favourable or otherwise, depending on the nature of the heavenly bodies concerned, the house position in a chart, other aspects involved, and if one planet is the subject's ruling planet.

Next in importance comes the opposition, which is formed when two bodies are 180 degrees, or six signs, apart. Traditionally it is said to be an obstructive or disruptive aspect, but this might not necessarily be so.

The third aspect in line of importance is the square, which is formed when two bodies are 90 degrees, or three signs, apart. This can be a tense, disruptive or challenging aspect, depending mainly on the nature and positions of the planets.

MAJOR ASPECTS

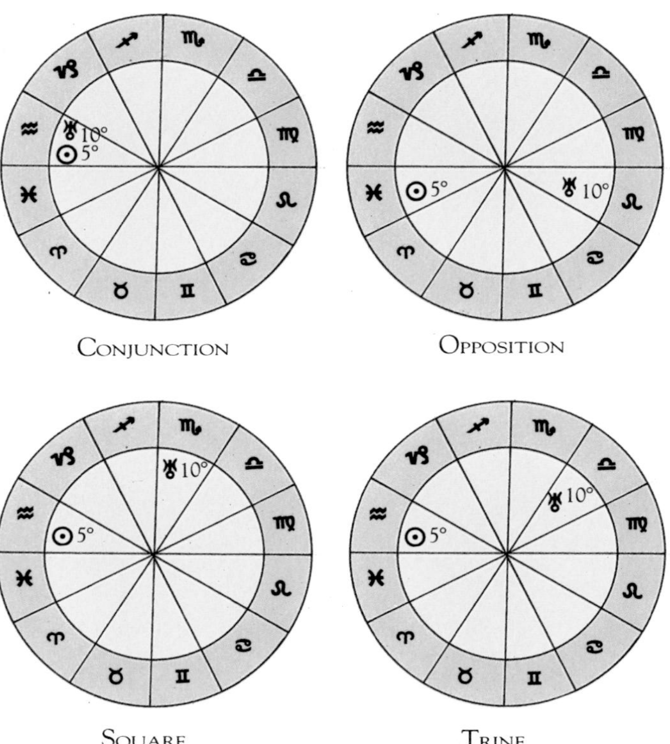

CONJUNCTION OPPOSITION

SQUARE TRINE

Once the positions of the planets in a birth chart have been worked out, the aspects they form must be considered. Aspects are the angles planets make with each other in a chart, measured by counting the number of degrees they are apart. Each aspect has an ideal, exact number of degrees, but a tolerance, called an 'orb' of a few degrees either way is allowed. Aspects vary in strength and influence. The most powerful are the conjunction (exact 0°, orb 8°–9°); the opposition (exact 180°, orb 8°–9°); the square (exact 90°, orb 8°–9°) and the trine (exact 120°, orb 8°–9°). Moderately powerful are the sextile (exact 60°, orb 5°–6°) and the quincunx (exact 150°, orb 2°–3°). Minor aspects include the semi-square (exact 45°, orb 2°) and the semi-sextile (exact 30°, orb 2°). Aspects combine to form patterns or aspects with each other; the most common is the T Square (two planets in opposition and a third in square), grand trine (three planets in trine), grand cross (two oppositions in square with each other) and the yod (two planets in quincunx to a third). The interpretation of aspects depends on the planets involved, and not all negative seeming aspects are as unhelpful as they first appear. When assessing a chart all the aspects must be taken into account together.

MINOR ASPECTS

COMBINED ASPECTS

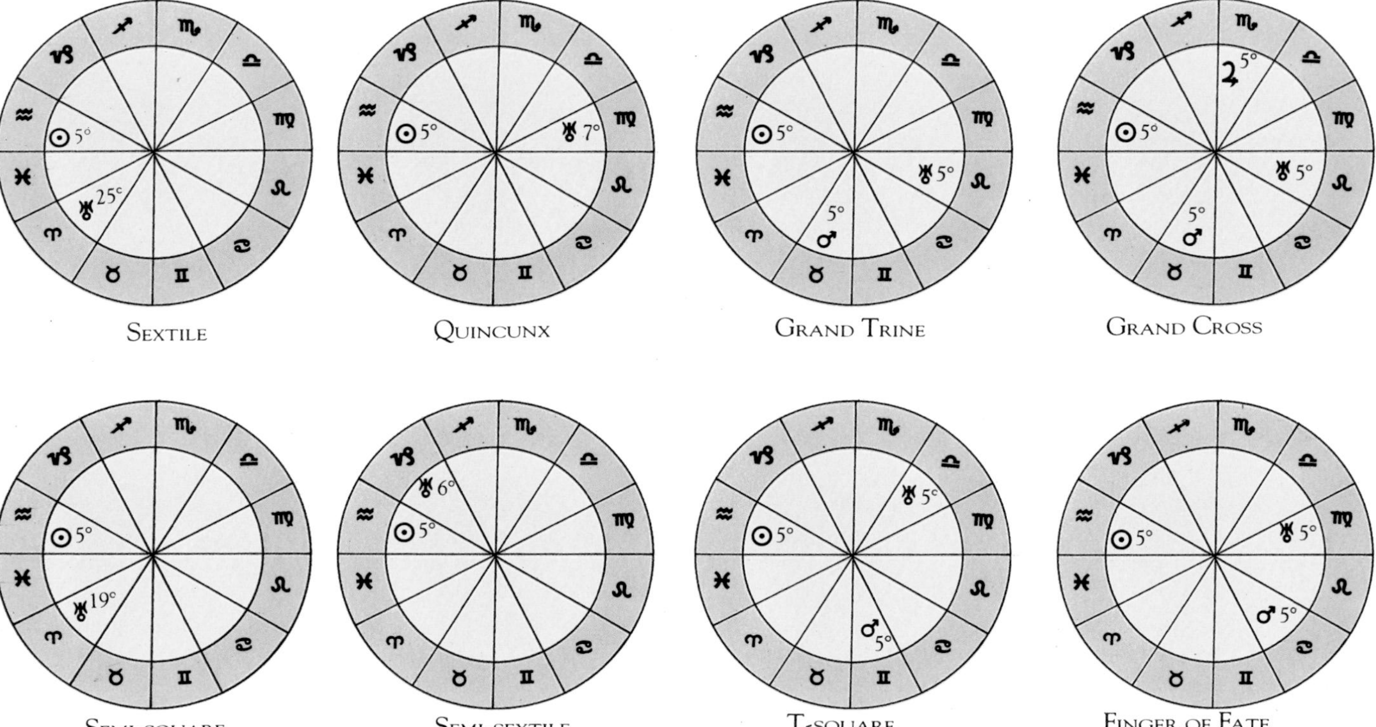

SEXTILE QUINCUNX GRAND TRINE GRAND CROSS

SEMI-SQUARE SEMI-SEXTILE T-SQUARE FINGER OF FATE

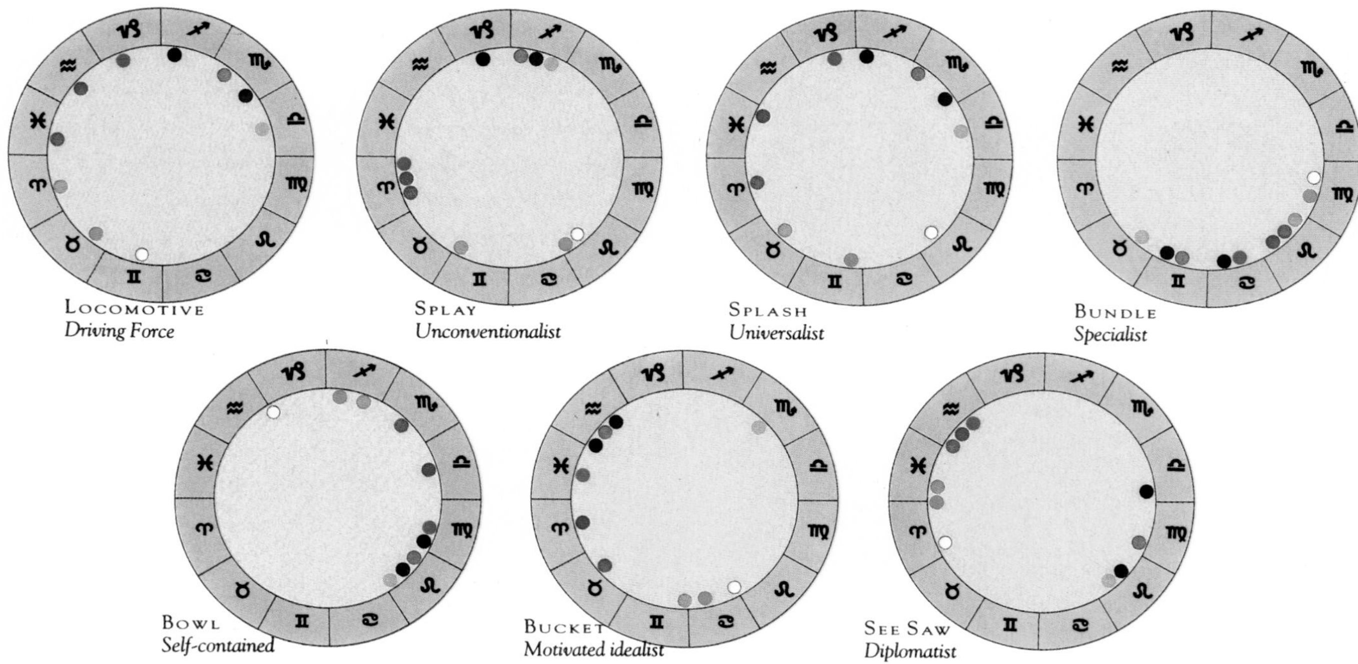

Jones Chart patterns, evolved by the American astrologer Marc Edmund Jones, consider the distribution of planets in a chart to indicate the underlying nature of the chart's subject. There are seven Jones Patterns: Bowl, Bucket, Bundle, Locomotive See-Saw, Splash and Splay.

The fourth aspect is the trine, a favourable aspect formed when planets are 120 degrees, or four signs, apart.

MINOR ASPECTS

The sextile is a favourable aspect but less powerful than the trine. It is half a trine, formed when bodies are 60 degrees, or two signs, apart.

The semi-sextile is a weak but moderately favourable aspect, formed when bodies are 30 degrees, or one sign, apart.

The semi-square is a rather unfavourable aspect formed when bodies are 45 degrees, or 1½ signs apart.

The quincunx is an aspect formed when bodies are 150 degrees apart; it is rather unpredictable and although traditionally regarded as moderate, should not be underestimated.

COMBINED ASPECTS

These occur when two or more aspects combine to form more complex patterns. The commonest is the T-square, formed when two planets in opposition have a third in square to both of them. The Grand Trine occurs when three planets form three trines with each other. The rarest is the Grand Cross, formed by two oppositions in square to each other.

Another important configuration is called the Parallel of Declination, abbreviated as Par. Dec. This occurs when two bodies have the same declination, or distance from the celestial equator. It is immaterial whether both are north or south, or if one is north and the other south. To assess these aspects, attention must be paid to the respective nature of the bodies concerned, the sign occupied or other modifying factors.

The Finger of Fate, or Yod, is a rare configuration; it consists of two quincunxes to a single planet. A quincunx is not regarded as favourable, but the planet at the focal point of the yod will by its nature define the yod.

An interesting focal point in a horoscope is marked by an old Arabic point known as Fortuna or the Point of Fortune. Fortuna, when well placed, indicates success and honour, but the reverse if weak. It can indicate from its house position in a chart and by aspects involved, how one could improve life and find more fulfilment.

THE MOON'S NODES

The Moon's nodes are points on the ecliptic where the Moon moves from north to south latitude or the reverse. The ascending node or north node is called the Dragon's Head (Caput Draconis), and the Dragon's Tail or south node is Cauda Draconis. The north node is thought to be similar in nature to Jupiter and the south node to Saturn. Some astrologers question the value of the nodes.

ASTROLOGY FOR THE AGE OF AQUARIUS?

Where no fixed rules apply, as in the matter of the Moon's nodes, the time has come for matters to be clarified; in fact, a review of astrology generally could be advantageous. It is mostly due to this type of indecision in various different areas of astrology that the subject is sometimes questioned unnecessarily. The dawning of the Age of Aquarius, is surely an opportune time to adjust the vernal point, which is no longer in Aries, and to take advantage of the splendid opportunities now unfolding to discuss scientific questions with astronomers. At this dawning of the New Age of Aquarius, astrology might be established as a science in its own right. It is significant to note that in January 1998, three major planets, Jupiter, Uranus and Neptune, will be in the sign of Aquarius. Perhaps this could be the last milestone marking the beginning of the New Age, when humankind will work for the good of planet Earth, and for all creatures that dwell on it.

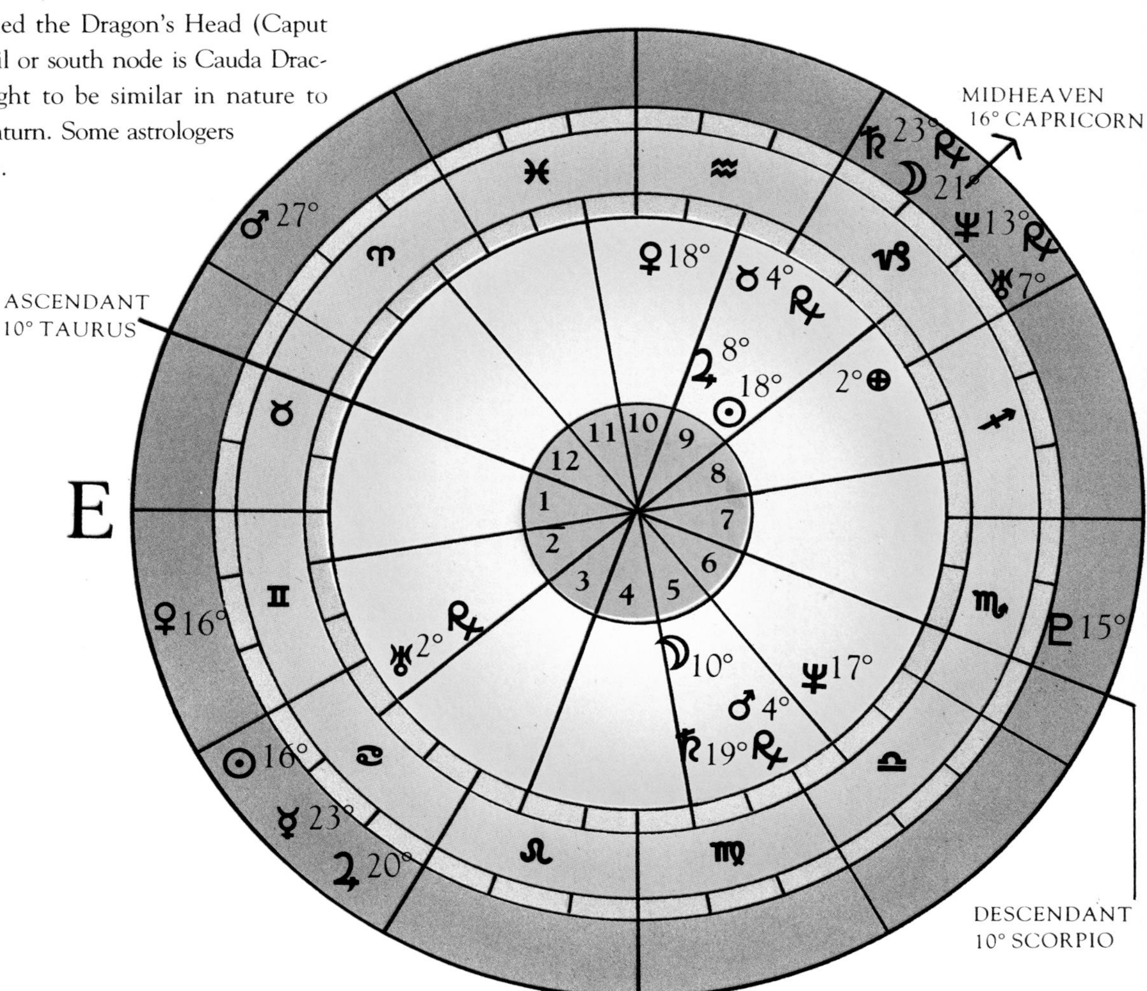

RIGHT *The progressed chart. Astrologers use many methods of progressing a chart, but the idea behind them all is to compare the planetary positions at the subject's birth with their positions at a later date and assess the likely outcome. In this case, the positions for 8 July 1990 are shown. Three planets and the Moon are in Capricorn and the Sun, Jupiter and Mercury oppose them in Cancer. Capricorn occupies the Ninth House (the future) and Cancer occupies the Third House (immediate action). Friction is caused by the intense planetary oppositions, but with the Sun and Jupiter almost in conjunction in Cancer, the outlook is good.*

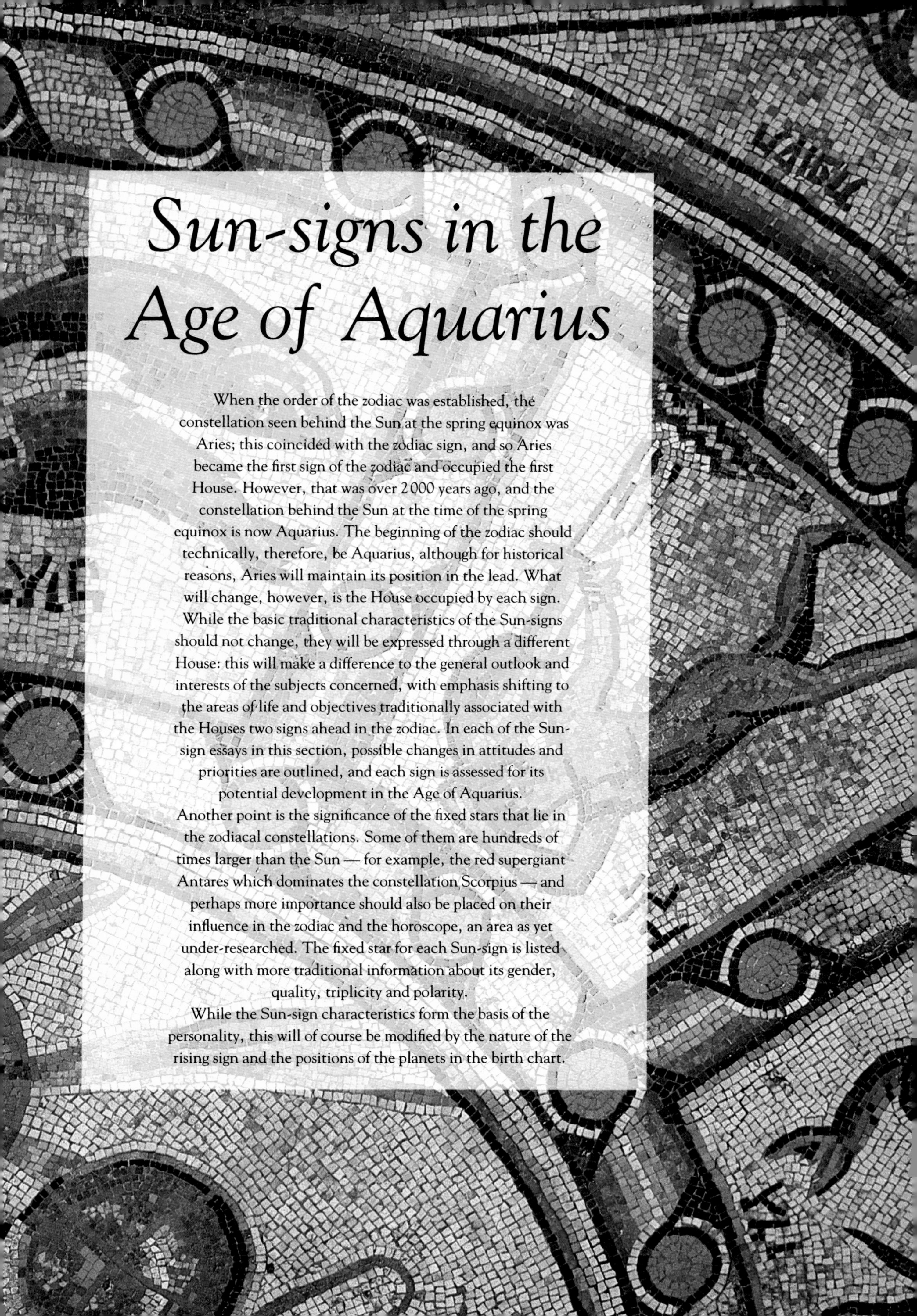

Sun-signs in the Age of Aquarius

When the order of the zodiac was established, the constellation seen behind the Sun at the spring equinox was Aries; this coincided with the zodiac sign, and so Aries became the first sign of the zodiac and occupied the first House. However, that was over 2000 years ago, and the constellation behind the Sun at the time of the spring equinox is now Aquarius. The beginning of the zodiac should technically, therefore, be Aquarius, although for historical reasons, Aries will maintain its position in the lead. What will change, however, is the House occupied by each sign. While the basic traditional characteristics of the Sun-signs should not change, they will be expressed through a different House: this will make a difference to the general outlook and interests of the subjects concerned, with emphasis shifting to the areas of life and objectives traditionally associated with the Houses two signs ahead in the zodiac. In each of the Sun-sign essays in this section, possible changes in attitudes and priorities are outlined, and each sign is assessed for its potential development in the Age of Aquarius.

Another point is the significance of the fixed stars that lie in the zodiacal constellations. Some of them are hundreds of times larger than the Sun — for example, the red supergiant Antares which dominates the constellation Scorpius — and perhaps more importance should also be placed on their influence in the zodiac and the horoscope, an area as yet under-researched. The fixed star for each Sun-sign is listed along with more traditional information about its gender, quality, triplicity and polarity.

While the Sun-sign characteristics form the basis of the personality, this will of course be modified by the nature of the rising sign and the positions of the planets in the birth chart.

Aries the Ram

RULED BY MARS

A Masculine Positive Cardinal Fire Sign

THE SUN IS EXALTED IN ARIES, VENUS AT DETRIMENT AND SATURN AT FALL

POLAR OR OPPOSITE SIGN: LIBRA

FIXED STAR: HAMAL

Aries is the first sign of the zodiac, lasting from approximately 21 March to approximately 20 April.

Aries is ruled by the planet Mars, which gives this sign its individual pioneering and adventurous spirit. Most Arians are daring, independent, active and impulsive, lively, energetic and enthusiastic. It is not unusual to find them among the world's explorers, and leaders of expeditions. They are not afraid to take risks, and rarely abandon things they take on.

Arians with a good birth chart, in which Mars is well placed, will direct their energy, courage, and spirit of enterprise to sensible and useful ends, to further their ambitions. Their outgoing nature can bring a high degree of success in life, if they follow the right type of career. Usually they like to explore untried ground; trade in new areas, and develop fresh ideas and projects. Dull routine work is not for Mars people, who need freedom, and a challenge in life.

At competitive sport and games, Arians generally excel; this gives them an opportunity to burn up some of their high energy reserves. As a rule, their rather restless type of temperament will not allow them to continue with situations they find irritating, whether this concerns work or their personal life. In many instances it pays a partner to take a back seat, to maintain harmony, because Arians find it difficult to compromise. However, if sparks do fly, anger rarely lasts long, and grievances are soon forgotten. But Arians are leaders and they abhor anyone getting in their way. If they are thwarted they can be violent, aggressive, argumentative or foolhardy.

When in love, Arians can be possessive and jealous, yet they are faithful, and rather idealistic. Many have good creative talents, which remain dormant, or sadly neglected, simply because they are too busy with other demanding interests to bother about them.

In the Age of Aquarius, Arians could care more for the local environment, education, writing, communications, and close family ties which are matters concerned with the third zodiac sign.

Aries
Orbis Regens
Mars
Signum Obstans
Libra

Taurus the Bull

RULED BY VENUS

A Feminine Negative Fixed Earth Sign

THE MOON IS EXALTED IN TAURUS, PLUTO AT DETRIMENT, AND URANUS IS AT FALL

POLAR OR OPPOSITE SIGN: SCORPIO

FIXED STAR: ALDEBARAN

Taurus is the second sign of the zodiac, lasting from approximately 21 April to approximately 21 May.

Most Taureans are practical, careful and capable. They like to take life in their stride, and dislike rushing about. Strong, stable, steady and dependable people, with a placid nature that is poised and controlled is typical Taurus; but there is another side to the Taurean character that displays a strong sense of obstinacy if their principles are questioned. The Taurean temper is not easily aroused, but when provoked this sign, symbolized by the Bull, can be fiery, difficult, and stubborn.

Usually, however, Taurus subjects are easy-going, romantic, and strongly attracted to the opposite sex. Usually they are patient, charming, and very affectionate people, but they can be jealous and possessive. As a rule they are kind and considerate people, with a flair for entertaining their friends in a generous manner. They enjoy opportunities to mix business with pleasure, because they are fairly ambitious as a rule, and like to achieve their aims.

As an earth sign, Taurus people are usually happier living in the country, close to Mother Earth, and many find contentment when tending a garden and nurturing plants.

Like the other Venus subjects (Librans), Taureans often show talent in art and design, and many have a liking and aptitude for music, singing, acting and culture.

This sign has a strong sense of self-preservation, and rarely takes risks. Taureans value security, both in personal relationships and in their business life. They make adept business people with the ability to make money – and hold on to it! They like working to a plan, and will not change their ways or opinions.

If a Taurus person fails to realize ambitions early in life, the struggle will continue, until a goal is reached. Taureans will never give up trying, and eventually they are likely to succeed by perseverance and determination.

In the Age of Aquarius, Taureans could become more involved with home and private life, with increased interest in houses, land, real estate and gardens.

Taurus
Orbis Regens
Venus
Signum Obstans
Scorpio

Gemini the Twins

RULED BY MERCURY

A Masculine Positive Mutable Air Sign

MERCURY IS EXALTED IN VIRGO, JUPITER AT DETRIMENT

POLAR OR OPPOSITE SIGN: SAGITTARIUS

FIXED STARS: CASTOR AND POLLO

Gemini is the third sign of the zodiac, lasting from approximately 22 May to approximately 23 June.

Most Gemini people are adaptable, versatile, lively, clever and intelligent. This basically is an intellectual sign that is closely concerned with facts, figures, reason and logic.

Although as a rule good at detailed work, Geminians tend to lack concentration, and are inconsistent and indecisive. They are bright, vivacious, physically active, yet changeable in their moods, whims or fancies. They seem never to be the same from one moment to the next – hence they are often called the 'butterflies of the zodiac'.

Gemini is a dual sign, and like twins they blend and separate, two natures in one. Possibly for this reason they can take on more than one thing at a time, usually becoming quite clever at a number of things, yet rarely specializing in one subject, mostly because they lack staying power, and flit from one thing to another.

The restless, active and agile Geminian mind needs variety, and these Mercury subjects are renowned for starting things and leaving them unfinished. They quickly become bored, and have little patience with mundane matters. As a rule they are talented people, with a keen sense of humour, and a charm of their own, but they have a highly strung nervous system, and often find it difficult to settle to a routine job. Yet Geminis excel at all types of communication; they make good journalists, writers, lecturers, commentators, sales executives, radio or TV presenters and telephone operators.

Physically, Geminians usually retain their youth longer than people born under the other zodiac signs. With their lively imagination and wide selection of interests they have not much time to grow old!

Given the right partner, Geminis can love deeply, but frequently they tend to be fickle, and may be constantly looking for new interests, or seeking the unknown. Many marry more than once or have two meaningful relationships in life.

In the Age of Aquarius, Geminian's interests could shift more to the lighter side of life, to pleasure, creative activities, social life and love relationships; also to new enterprises and speculation in various fields.

Gemini
Orbis Regens
Mercurius
Signum Obstans
Sagittarius

Cancer the Crab

RULED BY THE MOON

A Feminine Negative Cardinal Water Sign

SATURN IS AT DETRIMENT IN CANCER, MARS AT FALL AND JUPITER IS EXALTED

POLAR OR OPPOSITE SIGN: CAPRICORN

FIXED STAR: PRAESEPE

Cancer is the fourth sign of the zodiac, lasting from approximately 23 June to approximately 23 July.

Most Cancerians have a sympathetic, emotional and sensitive nature, that is kind, warm-hearted and affectionate, but they tend to be affected by the phases of the Moon more than the other signs of the zodiac, which makes them quiet, moody and temperamental or changeable at times, and quite difficult to understand. However, their moods are not long-lasting and can vary like the wind. As a rule they are very caring people who will go out of their way to be helpful to others.

Usually, the Cancer personality is gentle, sentimental, very intuitive and imaginative. Moon subjects have a sympathetic heart that is very vulnerable, and easily hurt. If they are upset they will retreat into their shells, to nurse or hide their grievances. They are great worriers, and often worry about things that could never happen, yet they are too shy or reserved to discuss their worries with others.

Cancerians have an emotional link with the past; they will never sever ties with home or loved ones, unless this is absolutely essential. Many are inclined to be hoarders, and store away food, clothes, and anything that might come in useful for a rainy day. Others like collecting works of art, pictures, old books, stamps or trinkets, and will not discard anything of sentimental value.

Cancer people are not usually wildly ambitious; once they become established, they hold on grimly to material assets, and refuse to let go. On the whole, they make good business people, because they are thrifty, shrewd, and careful. There is more tenacity in Cancer than in any of the other signs. A business project in hand will surely be brought to a satisfactory conclusion. But in personal matters, a Cancerian will cling on to a failing relationship when all other signs would call it a day.

Moon subjects tend to be wary of strangers, and are careful and selective when forming new friendships. Most Cancerians have strong feelings towards children, home and loved ones. They like plants, flowers and gardens, and are usually gifted artistically.

In the Age of Aquarius, Cancerians could become more health-conscious, and keen to experiment with new diets. They would be more ambitious and keen to change their daily routine or find the type of work that is more appealing to them.

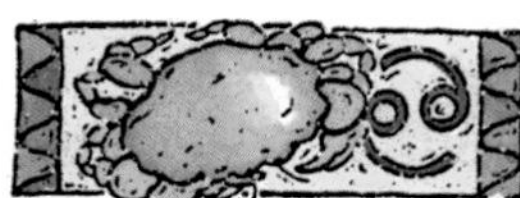
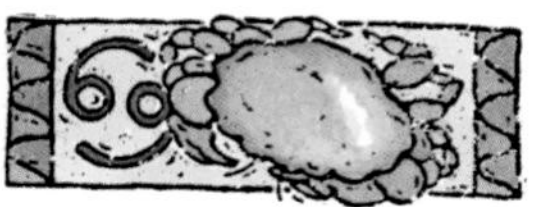

Cancer
Orbis Regens
Luna
Signum Obstans
Capricornus

Leo the Lion

RULED BY THE SUN

A Masculine Positive Fixed Fire Sign

NEPTUNE IS EXALTED IN LEO AND URANUS AT DETRIMENT

POLAR OR OPPOSITE SIGN: AQUARIUS

FIXED STAR: REGULUS

Leo is the fifth sign of the zodiac, and lasts from approximately 24 July to approximately 23 August.

Leo is the sign of strength, pride, confidence and courage. Leo people possess regal dignity; they are leaders, and are usually to be found occupying positions of authority. They have good mental and emotional strength, ambition, a strong will and a good deal of persistence. They love flattery and attention, and revel in compliments. They have a natural charm, and are very generous and affectionate. Leos like the good things in life, nice clothes, furs, jewellery, and luxuries of all kinds – and they will work extremely hard to obtain these things.

They are clever artistically and creatively; many succeed in the entertainment world, and flourish under the glare of the spotlights. They make good organisers, actors, dancers, entertainers, sportsmen, company directors, publicity managers, film, tv and show-business presenters and personnel.

At their best Leos are cheerful, enthusiastic, optimistic and good-natured. They are adept at organizing things – not merely events, shows, and the like – but other people's lives. They are far better at helping others to run their lives than they are at organizing their own.

Personal relationships and marriage are often unlucky for Leos. Strangely they are very sensitive, quite vulnerable and easily hurt. Although very seldom depressed, a Leo can occasionally crumble and hit rock bottom if depression envelops him. Yet as a rule, such glooms will not last long, in fact if things are not going too well, the strength of the Leo character comes to the fore, and Leo is never more determined or persistent than when his back is to the wall. Negative Leos might be pompous, dogmatic, snobbish and patronizing, but most Leos are positive and charming.

Underneath his extrovert personality lies a good and loyal heart, and a generous nature. Although they are free-spenders, Leos are rarely without money. Usually, somehow or somewhere, they manage to find their pot of gold.

In the Age of Aquarius, Leo people could take a high interest in developing new partnerships, both business or personal. As Leo is the sign in polarity with Aquarius, there could be the right blend between the signs that prevents Aquarius from rushing ahead with scientific projects before they are ready. Here, the strength of the Lion and the leadership qualities of Leo could be put to good use.

Leo
Orbis Regens
Sol
Signum Obstans
Aquarius

Virgo the Virgin

RULED BY MERCURY

A Feminine Negative Mutable Earth Sign

MERCURY IS EXALTED IN VIRGO, VENUS AT FALL AND NEPTUNE AT DETRIMENT

POLAR OR OPPOSITE SIGN: PISCES

FIXED STAR: SPICA

Virgo is the sixth sign of the zodiac, lasting from approximately 24 August to approximately 23 September.

Virgo people are dependable, sincere, neat, methodical and precise. They have an enquiring mind and a critical eye for detail. They are hard workers, and very practical. They thrive on constant activity and have lots of nervous energy to burn – hence they find it difficult to relax so are constantly making or mending things, or working on new projects to keep their mercurial minds fully occupied. They see life as a never-ending series of tasks and duties, some pleasant, some difficult – but all of them very necessary.

Precision and neatness comes naturally to a Virgoan; their mental sharpness inclines them to compartmentalize life into self-contained segments. Usually, they aim for perfection, and cannot rest until every tiny detail has been executed to their satisfaction. A Virgo person's flair for detail can dominate the whole personality at times, resulting in criticism, discrimination and a tendency to find fault with others.

Often they show considerable interest in health and hygiene. Many become vegetarians, or take a special interest in diets. At times they worry about health unnecessarily, bordering on hypochondria, and become prey to stomach or digestive disorders.

As a rule, Virgos are quiet, undemonstrative people, quite happy to work by themselves in the background, tending to avoid the limelight and publicity. They are reserved, cautious towards strangers, and can be slow at forming new friendships, but are truthful and loyal to those they trust. They are usually quite happy working in a job that calls for precision, shrewdness and logic. They make good researchers, analysts, teachers, secretaries, literary critics, reporters, dietitians and nurses.

In the Age of Aquarius, Virgoans could become more money-orientated, turning their attention to the manipulation of financial affairs, and dabbling with stocks, shares and longer-term property assets.

Virgo
Orbis Regens
Mercurius
Signum Obstans
Pisces

Libra the Scales

RULED BY VENUS

A Masculine Positive Cardinal Air Sign

SATURN IS EXALTED IN LIBRA, MARS AT DETRIMENT AND THE SUN IS AT FALL

POLAR OR OPPOSITE SIGN: ARIES

FIXED STAR: ZUBENELGENUBI

Libra is the seventh sign of the zodiac, lasting from approximately 24 September to approximately 23 October.

Librans are lovers of harmony and justice. They are sociable, charming people, usually good-natured, easy-going, cheerful, romantic and idealistic, but easily influenced by others. They dislike living alone, and need a happy and lasting relationship.

Indecision is a problem for Librans, who find it difficult to make up their minds, mostly due to their strong sense of justice and the fact that they can clearly see another person's point of view, hence they hesitate to take sides. Their motto seems to be 'Let's wait and see what happens'.

As Venus subjects, Librans have a highly developed sense of beauty. Many are artistically creative, and talented in design or décor. They like home to be comfortable, pleasant and nicely furnished. They have a natural gift for entertaining, and excel at putting people at their ease. Libran people will never willingly hurt another person's feelings because they have a gentleness of manner that is courteous and considerate.

At heart, Librans are sentimental and affectionate. They are inclined to be extravagant with their money – and their feelings! Yet they value a placid lifestyle and pleasant working conditions, well away from discord and arguments. Unpleasantness and a quarrelsome atmosphere can hurt them deeply, and they can then become irritable or moody. Usually Librans have a very even temperament, and never bear malice. They are inclined to compromise so they make good arbitrators and peacemakers. They are not as a rule wildly ambitious, yet they value security.

Librans may be attracted to careers in the luxury trades, including fashion, beauty culture, designing, and art-dealing. Many could do well in the Diplomatic Service, or in the world of entertainment, where they come in contact with the public and can use their Libran charm to advantage.

In the Age of Aquarius, Librans might find an urge to travel, to visit foreign countries and learn a new language, or otherwise to broaden the mind by further education.

Libra
Orbis Regens
Venus
Signum Obstans
Aries

Scorpio the Scorpion

NOW RULED BY PLUTO
TRADITIONALLY RULED BY MARS

A Feminine Negative Fixed Water Sign

URANUS IS EXALTED IN SCORPIO AND THE MOON AT FALL

POLAR OR OPPOSITE SIGN: TAURUS

FIXED STAR: ANTARES

Scorpio is the eighth sign of the zodiac, lasting from approximately 24 October to approximately 22 November.

Most Scorpios have an intense emotional nature. No other sign of the zodiac has more profound and enduring feelings than Scorpio. Pluto people possess a strong sense of purpose, and treat life in a very serious way, with great determination – never doing things by halves. Usually, they work and play hard, and live life to the full. They concentrate fiercely on their objectives; they are highly imaginative, subtle, discerning and persistent.

Scorpio's powerful feelings can be directed into various different areas in life. For many, this will concern their personal life, for others, career or business takes high priority, with an obsession to reach a certain goal. With an analytical mind, capable of penetrating to the very depths of problems, their reasoning is usually right. They have a natural talent for disguising their feelings and it is difficult to penetrate their outer shell.

Scorpio will not compromise, nor accept defeat. Pluto subjects can be very jealous, and often spiteful towards those who stand in their way. They can also be secretive, devious and suspicious. These qualities can apply not only to career, but to close relationships and worldly ambitions.

At the same time, people born under this sign have a great ability to adapt to life's changes, and can accept milestones, turning points or crossroads, willingly leaving one path for another should circumstances demand this. They have the strength and determination to pick up the pieces and start all over again when it is necessary.

There is a strange mysticism and magnetism in the Scorpio personality, often to be seen in their eyes, which seem to delve into one's very soul. Scorpios can burn with anger and resentment if their principles are put to the test. Make a friend of a Pluto person and you have a friend for life; on the other hand – as an enemy, they can be most formidable.

Once they form an opinion – whether it concerns a person or an ideal – the fixity of Scorpio is paramount, and they will rarely, if ever, change their minds.

In the Age of Aquarius, Scorpio could become highly involved with big business, with scientific research projects of importance, especially those that call for the deep analytical skill of the Scorpio mind.

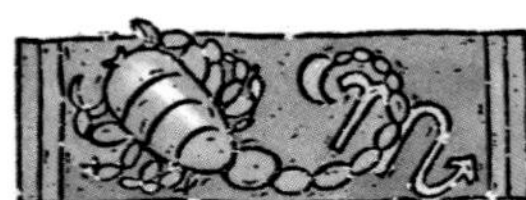

PLUTO
Scorpio
Orbis Regens
Pluto
Signum Obstans
Taurus

Sagittarius the Archer

RULED BY JUPITER

A Masculine Positive Mutable Fire Sign

MERCURY IS AT DETRIMENT IN SAGITTARIUS

POLAR OR OPPOSITE SIGN: GEMINI

FIXED STAR: RUKBAT

Saggitarius is the ninth sign of the zodiac, lasting from approximately 23 November to approximately 22 December.

Typical Sagittarians are optimistic, kind, generous, freedom-loving, versatile and dependable. They have above average mental abilities, possess good judgement and like to enjoy life: many are interested in outdoor sport and games. They have a frank open nature, and are usually popular with friends.

Sagittarians don't like to be tied down; they tend to be restless people, who love freedom, travelling and wandering. They do not care for discipline, or confined spaces, and cannot stand the slightest feeling of claustrophobia, either physical or emotional: for instance working or living in a small room with no open outlook or being tied down to an emotional relationship that is not entirely compatible will really upset them. If physical travel is not possible, then a Sagittarian will travel mentally, studying new subjects, or learning a language, which could keep him in touch with foreign countries and people, either for business or pleasure.

In personal relationships jealousy or possessiveness in a partner will quickly shrivel a Sagittarian's affections; yet Jupiter people as a rule are honest, open-minded and easy to get on with. One failing with this sign is a general lack of tact, and a tendency to speak bluntly without thinking – although such remarks may sound harsh, they are never intended to be harmful or hurtful.

Sagittarians have an adventurous spirit, and in youth or middle age they could often be looking round the corner or over the hill, to see what lies ahead. Similar to their opposite sign Gemini in many ways, they can cope with several projects or interests at the same time. Their inquisitiveness is insatiable, therefore they start to accumulate knowledge from an early age. Yet they tend to lack concentration, and could easily lose interest in a line of study or a hobby, and casually drop the subject as their enthusiasm wanes. Sagittarians need a challenge in life, or they will quickly become bored.

Ruled by Jupiter, the planet of luck, opportunity, and good fortune, Sagittarians are usually fairly lucky people. Their carefree, friendly personality often takes them far in life, and although they can be extravagant and careless over detail, they are one of the most fortunate and likeable of all the signs of the zodiac: they are seldom anyone's enemy but their own!

In the Age of Aquarius, Sagittarians, ruled by Jupiter, should find more success in life without having to struggle so hard to find it. They should have more time to enjoy life and follow their favourite pastime, travel, to their heart's delight.

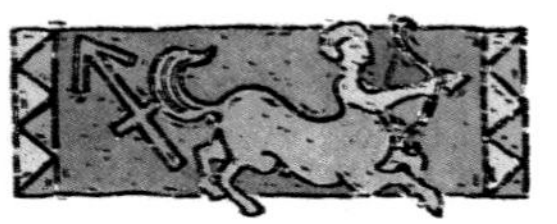

Sagittarius
Orbis Regens
Jupiter
Signum Obstans
Gemini

Capricorn the Goat

RULED BY SATURN

A Feminine Negative Cardinal Earth Sign

MARS IS EXALTED IN CAPRICORN, THE MOON AT DETRIMENT AND JUPITER AT FALL

POLAR OR OPPOSITE SIGN: CANCER

FIXED STAR: ALGIEDI

Capricorn is the tenth sign of the zodiac, lasting from approximately 23 December to approximately 19 January.

Most Capricorn people are reliable, careful, prudent, patient and persevering. They have an orderly mind that can be cool and calculating. They are usually determined and ambitious, with a strong sense of discipline and a good head for business, usually directing their energies towards career interests, status and prestige. The Capricorn way to success is steady upward progress, not the meteoric rise; they value their security too much to chance losing it by overreaching themselves.

As a rule, they are generally rather conventional, or serious. Often personal relationships are difficult, because Saturn subjects will rarely unbend and show their innermost feelings. It takes infinite patience and deft understanding to penetrate their strong wall of defence. Yet those who have the gift to 'get through' to a Capricornian could find no finer nor more enduring love.

Capricorn people tend to be perfectionists. They have the strength of character to bear considerable hardships, disappointments and setbacks in life.

Although many Saturn subjects tend to be loners, or people of few words, often they have a surprising and rather dour sense of humour, and their dry comments on life can be most amusing.

Usually, they are fond of good music, opera, drama and the arts. They are clever with facts, finance, and mathematics, and can devote much time to study to further their career.

Some Capricorn people can be very good company and outwardly quite charming, but beneath this outward cloak they are still Saturn subjects, sensible, determined, clever and superior, with a respect for wisdom, authority and age.

In the Age of Aquarius, Capricorns, often successful in scientific work that calls for mathematical skill, could find much demand for their talents. Good at taking responsibility, Capricorns should flourish.

Capricornus
Orbis Regens
Saturnus
Signum Obstans
Cancer

Aquarius the Water Carrier

NOW RULED BY URANUS
TRADITIONALLY RULED BY SATURN

A Masculine Positive Fixed Air Sign

THE SUN IS AT DETRIMENT IN AQUARIUS AND NEPTUNE AT FALL

POLAR OR OPPOSITE SIGN: LEO

FIXED STAR: SADALMELIK

Aquarius is the eleventh sign of the zodiac, lasting from approximately 20 January to approximately 19 February.

The Aquarian character is kind, friendly but rather distant, and frequently unpredictable. Often difficult to understand, Aquarian people tend to be fairly aloof, but usually this is because others do not follow their reasoning nor understand the working of the Aquarian mind. Their own thinking is often well ahead of its time, and is clear-cut, rational, intelligent and intuitive. Problems in any area of life are approached analytically.

Personal independence is important to those born under this sign, and they will make every effort to maintain it. The Aquarian personality has an aloof glamour that is often fascinating and dynamic, yet is sometimes not all that warm or endearing. In emotional relationships and marriage, an Aquarian likes to retain a certain degree of independence, and this calls for understanding and tolerance from a partner, but when happily married they will be faithful and loyal.

Aquarians are strong believers in the truth, and will not willingly tell a lie. Always a humanitarian with sympathy for the underdog, they are in favour of reform and change, especially the advancement of conditions surrounding human living and working environments. They are very concerned about the well-being of society. Many people think that Aquarius is a water sign, but the liquid that Aquarius is pouring from his urn is from the well of knowledge; he is concerned with pooling the human resource so that all might benefit. Those ruled by Uranus, as are Aquarians, are original, inventive and usually interested in science, modern technology, radio, computers and television. Many are keen on astrology, astronomy, space travel and flying.

In the Age of Aquarius, Aquarians come into their own. Aquarius is the sign of the future, ruled by unpredictable Uranus. The children of the Aquarian age will lead humanity into a glorious future of progress and freedom, but as Aquarian children will be born in all places throughout the world with different backgrounds, culture and religions, the establishment of world-wide harmony may take some time.

Aquarius
Orbis Regens
Uranus
Signum Obstans
Leo

Pisces the Fishes

RULED BY NEPTUNE

A Feminine Negative Mutable Water Sign

VENUS IS EXALTED IN PISCES AND MERCURY AT FALL

POLAR OR OPPOSITE SIGN: VIRGO

FIXED STAR: AL RISCHA

Pisces is the twelfth sign of the zodiac, lasting from approximately 20 February to approximately 20 March.

Endeavouring to evaluate the soft, sensitive and unworldly character of a Piscean is like delving into the mysterious world of dreams and the unknown.

This is a water sign that flows hither and thither, symbolized by two fishes swimming in different directions yet held together by a gossamer thread. These gentle, compassionate people are so very susceptible to outside influences they rarely possess a strong individual character of their own. Usually they are involved with other people's thoughts and feelings, and seem to blend with those close to them.

Most Pisceans tend to live halfway between their secret personal dream world and reality. They are very kind, sensitive people, sympathetic, receptive, unworldly, adaptable and intuitive. They have an extremely active and creative imagination, which gives them a flair for writing, acting, dancing, poetry and music. A true Piscean is unlikely to be highly ambitious or keen on competitive games, yet they will enjoy swimming, sailing and all forms of water sports.

As a rule, routine and an orderly household is foreign to the average Piscean, who can be quite oblivious to chaos or muddle. Many of their ideas are quite impracticable, yet when these concern anything artistic or creative, Pisces can be brilliant! Mostly, they are highly intuitive, and often can be attracted to mysticism, the occult, and spiritual sciences. Basically, however, Pisceans need to identify or belong to someone with a strong character, who can act as a source of inspiration and guidance, and bring out the best in them. Theirs is a rather vague and dreamy personality with a charm of its own. They are romantic and vulnerable, and have an almost overwhelming need for security in personal relationships; they usually seek a kindly, considerate, yet strong-minded partner who is capable of making the decisions.

Pisceans are easily hurt and need plenty of encouragement, as they tend to lack self-confidence. They dislike criticism, arguments or discord, which could make them moody or depressed and upset.

Neptune people are usually very caring, with a strong and genuine desire to help others. Often this attracts them to the sick and needy, to nursing, social work, or to a career in the medical profession.

In the Age of Aquarius, Pisceans could become more involved with second sign interests, such as material resources, business, finance and property.

Pisces
Orbis Regens
Neptunus
Signum Obstans
Virgo

[illegible]

蜜 蜜 蜜 蜜 蜜 蜜 蜜 蜜

[illegible]

吉

章

五鬼

吉

大歲

六害

年驛馬

推年得病日法

甲乙病者鬼起天寶東南來呼名青斛解送即差

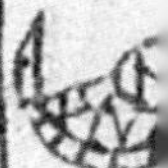

甲乙鬼[illegible]

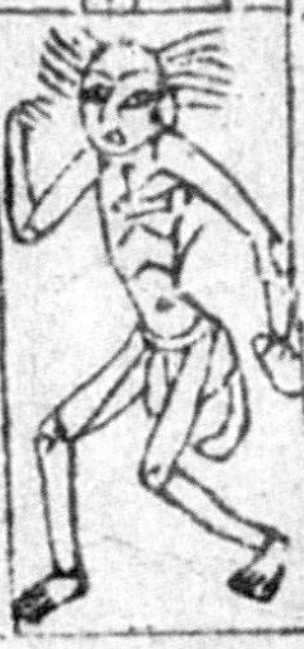

丙丁日病名丑得良呼名赤絕錢財解送立差

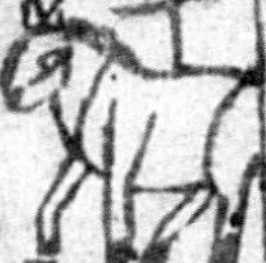

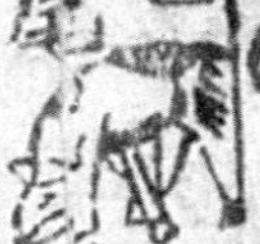

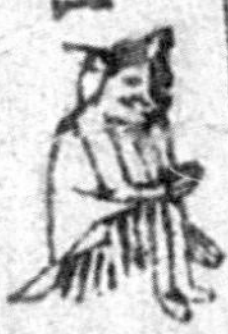

丙丁鬼[illegible]

生人同[illegible]夫

妻危[illegible]十月

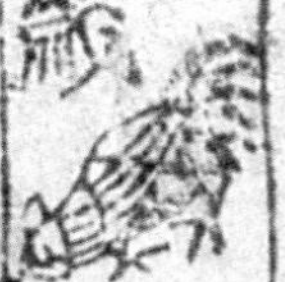

[illegible]生人[illegible]

妻危[illegible]十二月

[illegible]

妻危正月七月

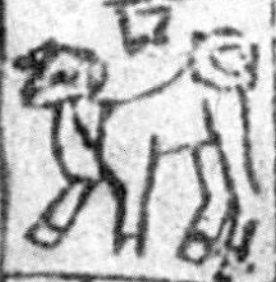

酉生人[illegible]

妻危二月八月

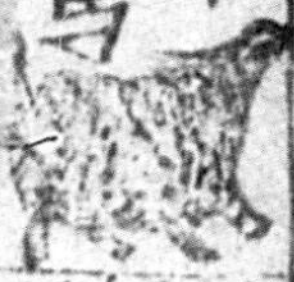

[illegible]

[illegible]

五鬼東北 絕命

太宮西南 生氣

天醫東南 福德

絕體正西 遊魂

五鬼正東 絕命

天醫[illegible]

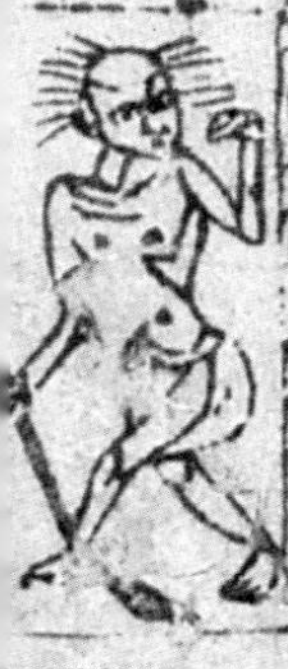

太[illegible]

天醫正南 [illegible]

絕體東北 遊魂

五鬼正北 絕命

太宮西北 生氣

天醫正東 福德

絕體西南 遊魂

五鬼東南 絕命

太宮正北 生氣

天醫東北 福德

絕體正南 遊魂

五鬼正西 絕命

太宮東北 生氣

天醫正北 福德

絕體正西 遊魂

五鬼正南 絕命

太宮[illegible] 生氣

天醫西北 福德

絕體東南 遊魂

五鬼西南 絕命

太宮東南 生氣

天醫西南 福德

絕體正北 遊魂

Dictionary for Astrologers

An A to Z of astrological, astronomical, mythological and historical definitions.

Bold upper-case type indicates a cross-reference.

ABACUS A non-mechanical calculator composed of movable counters mounted on rods or wires or sunk in grooves in a frame.

ABBEN-RAGEL (fl. tenth century AD) Also known as Alcabitius. Arabian astrologer, author of a treatise which was translated into Latin after his death and printed in 1473.

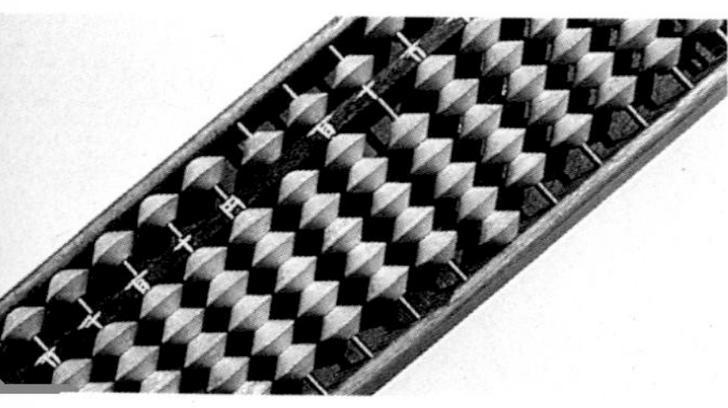

Oriental abacus

ABENEZRA See **ABRAHAM IBN EZRA**

ABERRATION Apparent displacement of a star from its usual position in the sky; a result of the orbital speed of the viewing platform (Earth). All objects seen from Earth appear to shift to and fro up to 20 **ARC** seconds annually.

ABRAHAM The father of the tribes of Israel; as a young man he was known as Abraham the Chaldean (he was living in Ur, the city of the **CHALDEANS**), and studied the stars to determine the best time to sow crops. He also possessed an astrological breastplate, from which he forecast future events.

ABRAHAM IBN EZRA (fl. c AD 1092–1167) Also known as Abenezra. Jewish scholar and mathematician, official astrologer to the Court of Barcelona when it was under Muslim rule. Author of astrological treatises entitled *The Book of the World* and *Sentences of the Constellations*.

ABSCISSION Also called Frustration. If a planet is forming an **ASPECT** to two other planets, the first one to reach **CULMINATION** may produce an abscission, or cutting off, of light that will frustrate, or prevent, the effect of the second aspect.

ABSOLUTE LONGITUDE Position of a planet within the entire circle of the zodiac; essential information for drawing up a **HARMONIC** chart. Conventional birth charts use the position of the planet in a zodiac sign, which is only 30° of the circle. Absolute longitude is calculated by taking 0° **ARIES** as the start of the circle and moving eastwards (anticlockwise). For example, Cancer begins at 90° on the circle; if a planet is at 5° Cancer at the time of birth, its absolute longitude will be 95°.

ABSOLUTE MAGNITUDE The brightness a star would have at a standard distance of ten **PARSECS** (one parsec is 3.26 light years). See also **MAGNITUDE**.

ABU MAASCHAR See **ALBUMASUR**.

Associated with Achernar, Phaeton plunged with his chariot into the River Po

ACAMAR Theta Eridani, a second **MAGNITUDE** double star in the constellation **ERIDANUS**.

ACCELERATION ON THE INTERVAL Adjustment which has to be made between **SIDEREAL** time (the time Earth takes to revolve once relative to a fixed star) and clock or mean time, when calculating a birth chart. To every 24 hours of clock or mean time there are 24 hours 3 minutes 56·5 seconds of sidereal time.

ACCIDENTAL ASCENDANT Position of the **ASCENDANT** at the moment a question is asked of an astrologer setting up a **HORARY** chart.

ACCIDENTAL RULERSHIP Each astrological **HOUSE** is said to be 'ruled' by the planet which rules the sign on its **CUSP**; if a sign is **INTERCEPTED**, its ruler is 'part-ruler' of the house.

ACHERNAR Alpha Eridani, a first-**MAGNITUDE** star in the constellation **ERIDANUS** The River, of which it is currently the brightest member (it is 200 times more luminous than our Sun). See also **ACAMAR**.

ACHILLES **ASTEROID 588.** The first of the **TROJAN ASTEROIDS** discovered (22 February 1906) by Maximilian **WOLF**. In Greek mythology, Achilles was one of the heroes of the Trojan War, the son of **THETIS** the sea goddess by the mortal Peleus. Thetis dipped her son into the River Styx to make him immortal, but forgot to immerse the heel by which she was holding him. He met his death through this vulnerable part, wounded by **PARIS** during one of the battles in the interminable Trojan wars.

ACRONYCHAL RISING The rising after sunset (or setting before sunrise) of a planet that is in **OPPOSITION** to the Sun.

ACRUX Alpha Crucis, the brightest star in the constellation **CRUX AUSTRALIS**.

ACUBENS Alpha Cancri in the zodiac constellation **CANCER**; comes from the Arabian word meaning 'claws'.

ADAMS, Evangeline (1865–1932) American astrologer who brought astrology to the millions in New York with her hugely popular radio programme.

ADAMS, John Couch (1819–1892) English astronomer whose analysis of the orbits of **URANUS** led him in 1845 to predict the existence of the planet **NEPTUNE**. Other astronomers (**LEVERRIER** and **GALLE**) made the same prediction independently, and Neptune was duly observed in 1846.

ADDEY, John (1920–1982) Co-founder and former President of the Astrological Association of Great Britain and editor of its mouthpiece *The Astrological Journal*. Addey spent thirty years investigating and establishing the theory of

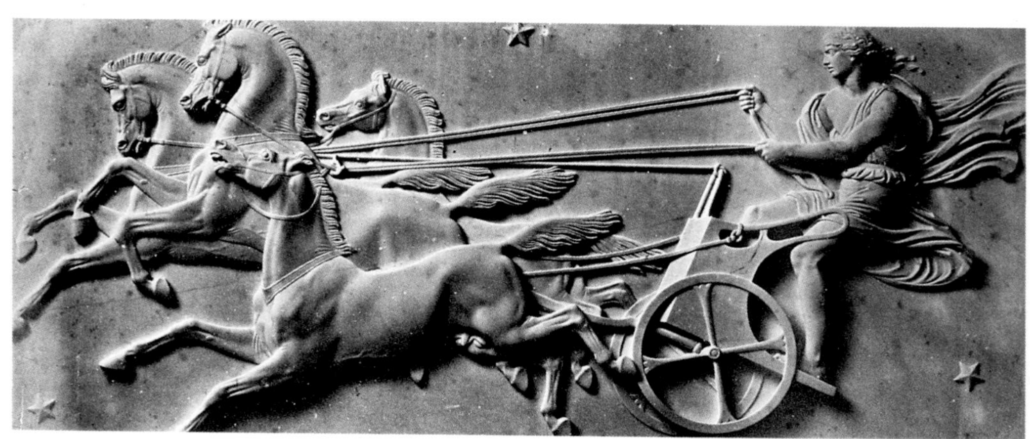

John Adams, Neptune-hunter

HARMONICS, publishing his conclusions in *Harmonies in Astrology* in 1976.

ADHAFERA Zeta Leonis, in the zodiacal constellation **LEO.**

ADJUSTED CALCULATION DATE Also known as the perpetual noon date, used by some astrologers to make **SECONDARY PROGRESSIONS** of a birth chart. Derived from the time of birth, it is calculated by converting the time between birth and noon (for morning births) or noon and birth (in afternoon births) into days. It is a complicated calculation for which special tables are needed and it is based on the **DAY FOR A YEAR** theory (24 hours = 1 day = 1 year, and therefore any part of one day equals the proportional part of a year). The number of days gives the day of the year that will be the adjusted calculation date (for example, forty days would give a date of 9 February, the fortieth day of the year).

ADONIS **ASTEROID** 2101. The second **APOLLO** asteroid; in 1936 it had a near miss with Earth, passing by a mere 2 500 000 km/ 1 553 000 miles away, and was last seen in 1977. In Greek mythology, Adonis was the beautiful youth, one of the many lovers of **APHRODITE**.

AEËTES King of Colchis and son of the Sun god **HELIOS**, and guardian of the Golden Fleece of the sacred ram **ARIES**.

AENEAS **ASTEROID** in the **TROJAN** group; in Greek legend the son of Anchises and **APHRODITE**.

AEROLITES Old name for stony **METEORITES**.

AESCULEPIOS See **ASKLEPIOS**

AETHER In Greek mythology, father of **URANUS**; the god of light and air.

AFFINITY In astrology, a binding by mutual attraction between certain planets.

AFFLICTION Old-fashioned term for an unfavourable or negative **ASPECT**, usually involving a so-called **MALEFIC** planet; also used to describe a planet **BESEIGED** by the two malefic planets. **MARS** and **SATURN** are traditionally called the lesser and greater malefics, but modern astrology does not altogether favour the term.

AGAMEMNON Trojan **ASTEROID** 911, discovered in 1919. In Greek mythology, brother of Menelaus, husband to Clytemnestra and leader of the Greek forces against Troy.

AGE OF AQUARIUS See **AQUARIUS; GREAT YEAR**

AGENA Beta Centauri, second brightest star in the brilliant southern constellation **CENTAURUS**; actually a multiple system (three members discovered so far). Together with **ALPHA CENTAURI** it forms the Southern Pointers which indicate the direction of **CRUX AUSTRALIS.**

AIR See **ELEMENTS**

AIR PUMP Name for the constellation **ANTLIA**.

AIR SIGNS Three signs of the **ZODIAC** associated with the **ELEMENT** of air: **AQUARIUS (FIXED)**, **GEMINI (MUTABLE)** and **LIBRA (CARDINAL)**.

AIRY, Sir George Biddell (1801–92) Astronomer Royal from 1835 to 1881. Determined the mass of Earth by taking readings from a pendulum at the top and bottom of a deep mine shaft; reorganized and re-equipped **GREENWICH OBSERVATORY**, designing much innovative observing equipment himself.

ALBEDO Measure of how much light a body reflects: a perfectly white body reflects all the light that hits it, and has an albedo of 1; a completely black body, which reflects no light, has an albedo of 0.

ALBIREO Beta Cygni, in the constellation **CYGNUS**.

AL-BIRUNI (973–1051) Arabian astrologer, who learned Sanskrit, and visited India. It was partly due to his knowledge and influence that certain Indian ideas were adopted into modern astrology.

ALBUMASUR (Abu Maaschar) (805–885) Astrologer from Bakh (now in Afghanistan) who studied at the famous astronomy school in **BAGHDAD**. His influential treatise *Introductorium in Astronomiam* was one of the first books to be translated and distributed via Spain and into Europe in the early Middle Ages.

ALCHEMY Medieval forerunner of chemistry, inextricably bound up with magic and speculative philosophy. The aim of alchemy was to find the 'philosopher's stone', which would transmute base metals into gold.

ALCOR 80 Ursae Majoris, in the constellation **URSA MAJOR**.

ALCYONE Eta Tauri, third brightest star in the zodiac constellation **TAURUS** and the brightest star in the famous open cluster, the **PLEIADES**. In Greek mythology, Alcyone was the daughter of **ATLAS** and Pleione.

ALDEBARAN Alpha Tauri the brightest star in the zodiac constellation **TAURUS**.

ALEXANDER THE GREAT (356–323 BC) King of Macedonia and conqueror of the Persian Empire who became the shaping spirit and most influential person in the ancient world. Alexander had been taught by **ARISTOTLE** and had some interest in astronomy and astrology.

ALGENIB Gamma Pegasi in the constellation **PEGASUS**.

ALGIEBA Gamma Leonis in the zodiacal constellation **LEO**.

ALGIEDI Alpha Capricornii in the zodiacal constellation **CAPRICORNUS**.

ALGOL Beta Persei in the constellation **PERSEUS**, also known as the Demon Star; Arabian astrologers called it Ras-al-Ghul, the Head of the Demon.

ALHEKA Zeta Tauri, fourth brightest star in the zodiac constellation **TAURUS**.

ALHENA Gamma Geminorum, third brightest star in the zodiac constellation **GEMINI**.

AN

ALMANACK

OR

PROGNOSTICATION for the year of our LORD 1658, Being the ſecond after Biſſextile or Leap year. Calculated for the Meridian of London, and may indifferently ſerve for England, Scotland, and Ireland.

By SARAH JINNER Student in Aſtrology.

London, Printed by J. Streater for the Company of Stationers.

Almanac from 1658

ALIOTH Epsilon Ursae Majoris, the brightest of the seven stars that make up the Plough in **URSA MAJOR**.

ALKAID Eta Ursae Majoris, part of the **PLOUGH**.

ALLEN, William F. See **LEO, ALAN**.

ALMAAK Gamma Andromedae, a splendid **DOUBLE** star in the constellation **ANDROMEDA**.

ALMAGEST A compendium of thirteen astronomical books written sometime during AD 200 by the great Alexandrian astronomer **PTOLEMY**.

Algol, the Head of the Demon

ALMANAC Probably from the Arabic, al-Manakh; a book of tables, containing a calendar of days, weeks and months, giving astronomical and other data.

AL-MANSUR (754–775) Son of Haroun al Raschid and Caliph of **BAGHDAD**, which he founded in 764; he established an observatory, library and school of astronomy which became famous with scholars throughout the world.

ALMUTEN Arabic term for the most influential planet in a birth chart or horoscope.

ALNAIR Alpha Gruis in the constellation **GRUS**.

ALNATH Beta Tauri, second brightest star in the zodiac constellation of **TAURUS**.

ALNILAM Epsilon Orionis, one of the three stars in the 'belt' of the **ORION**.

ALNITAK Zeta Orionis in the constellation **ORION**.

ALPHA First letter of the **GREEK ALPHABET**; used to denote the brightest star in a constellation, although in some cases the alpha is no longer the brightest. See also **CLASSIFICATION OF STARS**.

ALPHA ANDROMEDAE The star **ALPHERATZ**.

ALPHA AQUARII The star SADALMELIK.

ALPHA ARIETIS The star HAMAL.

ALPHA AURIGAE The star CAPELLA.

ALPHA BOÖTIS The star ARCTURUS.

ALPHA CANCRI The star ACUBENS.

ALPHA CANIS MINORIS The star PROCYON.

ALPHA CAPRICORNII The star DENEB AL GIEDI.

ALPHA CASSIOPIAE The star SHEDIR.

ALPHA CENTAURI Brightest of the stars in the constellation CENTAURUS. Together with Beta Centauri (AGENA) forms the Pointers, which indicate the direction of CRUX AUSTRALIS. See also PROXIMA CENTAURI.

ALPHA CETI The star MENKAR.

ALPHA CORONAE BOREALIS The star ALPHEKKA.

ALPHA CRUCIS The star ACRUX.

ALPHA CYGNI The star DENEB.

ALPHA DELPHINI The star SUALOCIN.

ALPHA GRUIS The star ALNAIR.

ALPHA HYDRAE The star ALPHARD.

ALPHA LEONIS The star REGULUS.

ALPHA LIBRAE The star ZUBENELGENUBI.

ALPHA LYRAE The star VEGA.

ALPHA ORIONIS The star BETELGEUX.

ALPHA PEGASI The star MARKAB.

ALPHA PISCIUM The star ALRISCHA.

ALPHA SCORPII The star ANTARES.

ALPHA TAURI The star ALDEBARAN.

ALPHA URSAE MAJORIS The star POLARIS.

ALPHA VIRGINIS The star SPICA.

ALPHARD Alpha Hydrae, the brightest star in the enormous constellation HYDRA.

ALPHEKKA Alpha Coronae Borealis, the only bright star in the constellation CORONA BOREALIS.

ALPHERATZ Alpha Andromedae, one of the leading stars in the constellation ANDROMEDA, which joins on to the Square of PEGASUS.

ALRISCHA Alpha of the zodiacal constellation PISCES.

ALTAIR Alpha Aquilae, in the constellation AQUILA.

ALTAR Name for the constellation ARA.

ALTITUDE The vertical angle between the horizon and a CELESTIAL BODY; in astrology it is expressed in degrees, minutes and seconds.

ALYA Theta Serpentis in the constellation SERPENS.

AMALTHEA Largest of the four inner moons of JUPITER, discovered in 1892 by Edward BARNARD; it is dark red, pocked with craters and a very irregular ellipsoid shape, rather like a tangerine. In Greek mythology, Amalthea was the goat that nursed the infant ZEUS while he was in hiding from his father CRONOS.

AMEN-RA See AMON-RA

AMERICAN FEDERATION OF ASTROLOGERS Organization in Tempe, Arizona, formed by professional astrologers in an effort to formalize astrological training.

AMON-RA Also known as Amen-Ra; king of the gods in ancient Egyptian times, based on the patron of Thebes, Amon; associated with ZEUS by the Greeks; see also JUPITER AMMON.

AMOR ASTEROIDS Group of asteroids (forty so far known) which closely approach the orbit of MARS.

AMPHITRITE ASTEROID 29, discovered in 1854. In Greek mythology, Amphitrite was goddess of the sea, wife to POSEIDON.

ANALEMMA A figure-of-eight shaped scale on a sundial indicating the position of the Sun for the same time every day of the year, thus plotting the path of the Sun's DECLINATION; it shows the difference between true SOLAR TIME and clock or mean time.

ANANKE One of the four outermost moons of JUPITER which have eccentric RETROGRADE orbits.

ANARETA Astrological term of Greek origin, meaning the destroyer, or taker away of life; applies to a planet that unfavourably ASPECTS the HYLEG.

ANATOMY AND THE ZODIAC Each sign of the zodiac is associated with certain parts of the human body, starting at the top with the first sign: ARIES rules the head; TAURUS the neck and throat; GEMINI the arms, shoulders and nerves; CANCER the breasts, stomach and alimentary canal; LEO the spine, back, and heart; VIRGO the bowels and fingers; LIBRA the kidneys, lumbar region and skin; SCORPIO the urinary system and genitals;

A medieval anatomy of the zodiac

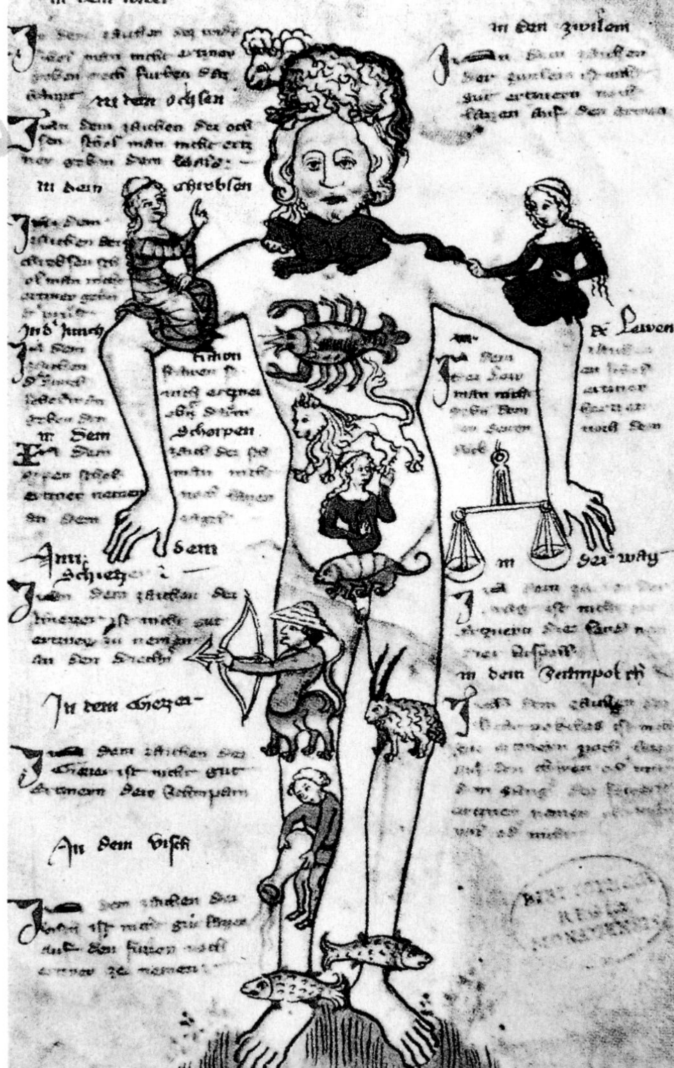

SAGITTARIUS the hips, thighs and buttocks; **CAPRICORN** the bones and knees; **AQUARIUS** the ankles and circulation; and **PISCES** the feet.

ANDROMEDA Large and important northern constellation, containing the stars **ALMAAK** and **ALPHARETZ**. Also contains the Great Spiral M 31, the **Andromeda Galaxy**. In Greek mythology **Andromeda** was the beautiful daughter of the king and queen of Ethiopia, **CEPHEUS** and **CASSIOPEIA**.

ANGELIC ASTROLOGERS Name given to the nineteenth-century revivalist astrologers who took the names of angels and archangels as their *noms de plume*: examples are Raphael (R.C. Smith the **ALMANAC** maker), Seraphial (Walter Richard Old) and **ZADKIEL**.

ANGLES OR PERSONAL POINTS Important angles formed at the points where three **GREAT CIRCLES** (meridian, horizon, and **PRIME VERTICAL**) intersect the **ECLIPTIC**; the **MIDHEAVEN** is where the ecliptic meets the meridian above the place of birth; the **ASCENDANT** is where the ecliptic meets the horizon in the east; and the **VERTEX** is where the ecliptic meets the prime vertical in the west. The North Angle or **IMMUM COELI** (IC) lies opposite the midheaven, at the bottom of a map or chart.

ÅNGSTROM, Anders Jonas (1814–1874) Swedish physicist, the first person to examine the spectra of **AURORAE**, using a **DIFFRACTION GRATING**.

ANGULAR DISTANCE The number of degrees a planet is from 0° **ARIES**: this is the planet's **CELESTIAL LONGITUDE**, the measurement used by astrologers to plot the positions of the **CELESTIAL BODIES** in a **BIRTH CHART**.

ANGULAR HOUSES The first, fourth, seventh and tenth **HOUSES** of a horoscope, which correspond to the **CARDINAL SIGNS**; called angular because they occur at the **ANGLES**.

ANGULAR SIGNS The four **CARDINAL SIGNS** – **ARIES, CANCER, LIBRA** and **CAPRICORN**, because they occur at the **ANGLES**.

ANGULARITY A planet is said to be angular when placed within 8° of the **ASCENDANT, DESCENDANT, MIDHEAVEN** or **IMMUM COELI**.

ANIMALS AND ASTROLOGY The effect of the stars on animal life was discussed by **ARISTOTLE** in his book *History of Animals*.

ANOMALY The **ANGULAR DISTANCE** of a planet or satellite from its **PERIHELION** or **APHELION**.

ANTAPEX The point diametrically opposite the solar **APEX**.

ANTARES Alpha Scorpii, a deep red supergiant that dominates the splendid zodiacal constellation **SCORPIUS**.

ANTINOUS One of Tycho **BRAHE**'s constellations, now included in the constellation **AQUILA**.

ANTIVERTEX Point where the **PRIME VERTICAL** meets the **ECLIPTIC** in the east; the opposite point to the **VERTEX**.

ANTLIA, the Air Pump Small southern constellation just above **VELA**; formerly known as Antlia Pneumatica.

ANTLIA PNEUMATICA Old name for **ANTLIA**.

Ariadne and Bacchus

ANU The Chief God of the Sumerians and Babylonians.

ANUBIS Egyptian god of the underworld, portrayed with the head of a jackal.

ANUNITUM Babylonian fish goddess who, together with **SIMMAH**, represented the zodiac sign **PISCES**.

AORNIS One of the rivers of **HADES**; the name means 'without birds'.

APEX The point on the **CELESTIAL SPHERE** towards which a **CELESTIAL BODY**, such as the Sun or the Earth, is moving.

APHELION The point in its orbit at which a planet, satellite or comet is at the greatest distance from its sun.

APHETA Astrological term meaning the 'giver of life'. See also **ANARETA**.

APHOREL Professional name adopted by the British astrologer F.W. Lacey, co-publisher with Alan **LEO** of *The Astrologer's Magazine*.

APHRODITE Goddess of love and beauty born from the foam produced when SATURN threw the castrated genitalia of his father URANUS into the sea. Aphrodite is associated with the Roman Goddess VENUS, and was worshipped at Corinth as ASHTORETH.

APIAN, Peter Bienewitz (1495–1552) Mathematician whose study of COMETS was the first to note that comet tails always point away from the Sun.

APOGEE The point at which an orbiting body on an elliptical path is at its farthest from Earth.

APOLLO ASTEROID 1862, discovered in 1932; the first of the Apollo Asteroids (there are about thirty in all) which follow Earth-crossing orbits: there is a chance that any one of them may hit Earth. In Greek mythology, Apollo was the son of ZEUS and Leto (sister to ARTEMIS), and often identified with HELIOS the sun god.

APOLLONIUS OF PERGA (c250–200 BC) Greek mathematician credited with the introduction of EPICYCLES and ECCENTRIC orbits to

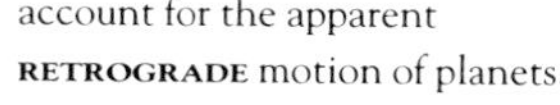

account for the apparent RETROGRADE motion of planets.

APPARATUS SCULPTORIS Old name for constellation SCULPTOR.

APPARENT MOTION The zodiac and planets appear to move from east to west once in every 24 hours, this apparent movement being the result of Earth's rotation on its axis. In reality, the Sun, Moon and planets, owing to their PROPER MOTION, gradually move from west to east through the signs of the zodiac.

APPLICATION Astrological term that refers to a CELESTIAL BODY moving to a point where it will ASPECT another body.

APRIL Fourth month of the GREGORIAN CALENDAR, from the latin *Aprilis*; perhaps named from Etruscan *Apru* or Greek APHRODITE.

APSIDES The points on the orbit of a planet or satellite when it is nearest to or furthest from the body around which it moves.

APUS, the Bee Constellation in the extreme south, was once known as Avis Indica, the Bird of Paradise.

Aphrodite chastises love

The great galaxy Andromeda

AQUARIUS, the Water Carrier Zodiac constellation, one of the originals listed by PTOLEMY. Contains three bright stars above the fourth MAGNITUDE: Beta Aquarii (SADALSUUD), Alpha Aquarii (SADALMELIK) and Delta Aquarii (Scheat), two planetary NEBULAE (Saturn and Helix) and several SPIRAL GALAXIES. **Aquarius the zodiac sign** is the eleventh sign of the zodiac, a MASCULINE POSITIVE FIXED AIR sign ruled by the planet URANUS. The Sun is in DETRIMENT in Aquarius, NEPTUNE is in FALL. Aquarius has no special **myths** or legends, but may be associated with the beautiful youth GANYMEDE, kidnapped by Zeus, who made him cupbearer to the Olympian gods. Although known as the Water Bearer, the liquid Aquarius pours from his urn is not water, but comes from the well of knowledge. The **Age of Aquarius** is a period of 2160 years or so, which we are just entering. Astronomically, it means that the VERNAL POINT has been shunted westwards along the ECLIPTIC by the PRECESSION OF EQUINOXES and the constellation now behind the Sun at that point is Aquarius; astrologically it is extremely important, as it means we are crossing from one great month in the GREAT YEAR to the next.

AQUILA, the Eagle Constellation, one of Ptolemy's original forty-eight, that lies mostly in the north, but is crossed by the CELESTIAL EQUATOR. The chief star is ALTAIR and it contains a substantial flow of the MILKY WAY.

AQUINAS, St Thomas (c1224–1274) Probably the greatest medieval Christian theologian; his work endeavoured to reconcile Christian faith with all that was currently understood about the natural world.

ARA, the Altar Southern constellation lying beneath the sting of SCORPIUS.

ARABIC PARTS Sometimes known as Arabic points. Points are calculated by taking difference between the CELESTIAL LONGITUDES of two planets and referring it to the celestial longitude of the ASCENDANT. One of the better known and most important is the Part of Fortune, or FORTUNA.

ARC Part of the circumference of a circle or ellipse. In astrology it is the orbital distance between two CELESTIAL BODIES or points.

ARC OF VISION In astrology, the shortest distance, measured from the Sun, from which a planet is visible when the Sun is below the horizon.

ARCHER Name for zodiacal constellation SAGITTARIUS.

ARCETRI OBSERVATORY Built by DONATI in 1872 for the University of FLORENCE; major site of SOLAR study.

ARCTURUS Alpha Boötis, a red giant in the constellation BOÖTES; the brightest star north of the CELESTIAL EQUATOR.

ARES In Greek mythology, the son of ZEUS and Hera; the god of war. The Roman MARS.

ARETHUSA ASTEROID 95; in mythology, a sea nymph changed into a fountain by ARTEMIS.

ARGO NAVIS, the Ship *Argo* Huge, ancient and unwieldy southern constellation (last of Ptolemy's original forty-eight) now broken up by modern astronomy into three smaller ones: CARINA, PUPPIS and VELA.

ARIEL One of the five largest of the fifteen moons of URANUS, discovered in 1851 by William LASSELL.

ARIES, the Ram Zodiac constellation lying to the south of ANDROMEDA. Its orange-coloured ALPHA, Hamal, is visible to the naked eye. It is still classed as the first constellaton of the zodiac, although the PRECESSION OF THE EQUINOXES should make it the third. **Aries the zodiac sign** is the first sign of the zodiac and signals the beginning of the circle. Aries is a CARDINAL FIRE sign, ruled by MARS. The Sun is EXALTED in Aries. SATURN is at FALL and VENUS in DETRIMENT. The Aries **myth** is that of the Sacred Ram with the Golden Fleece; JASON and Medea stole the Golden Fleece from its guardian, King AEËTES.

Argo Navis, from a 1742 map

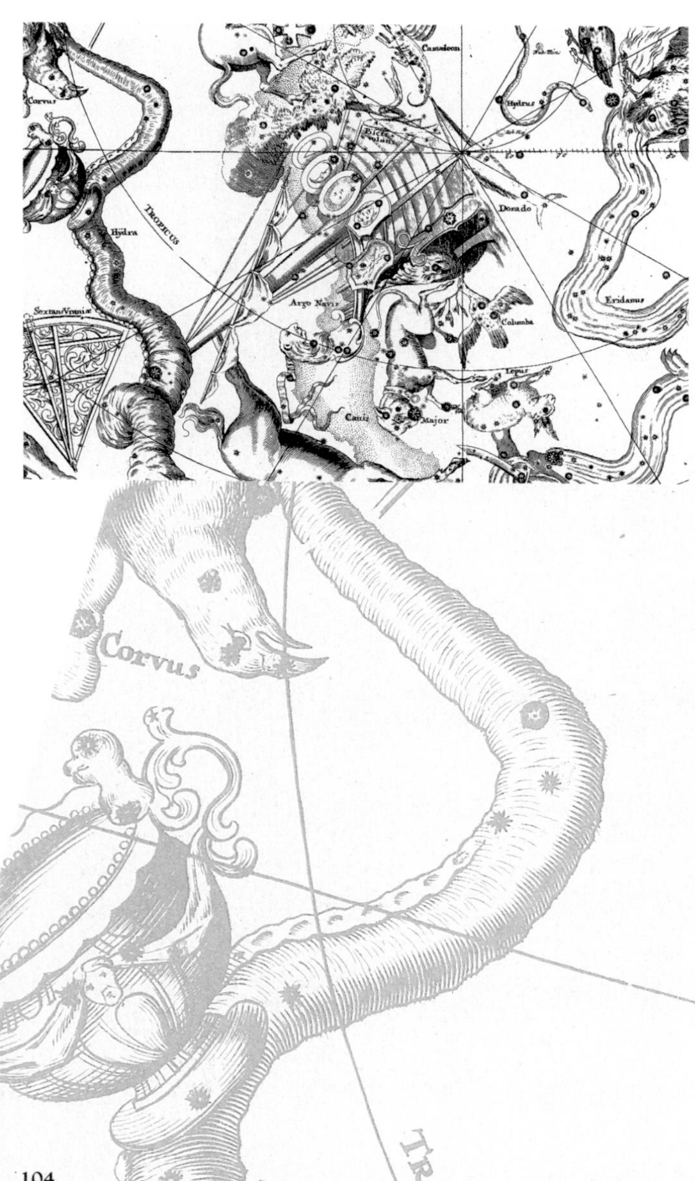

ARISTARCHUS OF SAMOS (310–264 BC) Greek astronomer, who was the first to suggest the HELIOCENTRIC (Sun-centred) view of the solar system.

ARISTOTLE (384–322 BC) Celebrated Greek philosopher and astronomer, pupil of PLATO, tutor to ALEXANDER THE GREAT.

ARKAB Beta Sagittarii in the southernmost zodiac constellation SAGITTARIUS.

ARMILLARY SPHERE Ingenious device used by early astrologers and astronomers to determine the positions of the stars; the instrument comprised of a series of metal rings, mounted on a pedestal. The rings represented the principal circles of the CELESTIAL SPHERE.

ARROW Name for the constellation SAGITTA.

ARTEMIS In Greek mythology the daughter of ZEUS and Leto and twin sister of APOLLO. She was the Virgin Huntress, goddess of the chase, protector of young children and women in childbirth. She was much worshipped in various forms throughout the ancient world and is associated with the Roman goddess DIANA (sometimes identified with the Moon) and SELENE.

ASARU One of the Chaldean names for the planet JUPITER.

ASCENDANT The CUSP of the first HOUSE of a birth chart; marks the rising degree or the ecliptic at the point where it intersects the eastern horizon.

ASCENDING NODE The point at which the Moon's orbit crosses the ECLIPTIC from south to north. See NODES.

ASCENDING OR RISING SIGN The zodiac sign rising in the east at the moment of birth. It is very important in astrological interpretation of birth charts; your ascendant sign can do much to modify the powerful influence of the Sun sign; the ascending sign of people born early in the morning is often the same as their Sun sign, making them ultra 'pure' examples of their sign.

ASHTAROTH OR ASHTORETH The power of the female principle expressed as a goddess: she was known as the goddess of fertility and reproduction among the Canaanites and Phoenicians; the Babylonians called her ISHTAR, goddess of love and war; the Syrians called her Astarte. The Greeks took all these ideas and bound them up into the figure of APHRODITE, later associated with the Roman VENUS.

ASKLEPIOS OR ASLEPIOS Son of APOLLO the Sun god, raised by the centaur CHIRON and taught the arts of healing and medicine.

ASPECT CHART Usually a box-type grid included on printed birth chart forms, and used to calculate ASPECTS for each planet in turn, beginning with the Sun and Moon, and moving outwards from MERCURY to PLUTO.

ASPECT PATTERNS Patterns formed when a line is drawn to connect planets on a birth chart; there are three basic ones: the T SQUARE, the GRAND CROSS and the GRAND TRINE.

ASPECTS Relationships, expressed as angles, between planets at various set points along the ecliptic or between the planets and significant points on the zodiac,

Armillary sphere, 1554

MIDHEAVEN, ASCENDANT, IMMUM COELI, etc. Aspects may be favourable or unfavourable: unfavourable aspects are derived by dividing the 360° of the zodiac by 2, 4, and 8: at 180° planets are in **OPPOSITION**; planets at 90° are in **SQUARE**; and planets at 45° in **SEMI-SQUARE**. (There are other unfavourable aspects, but these are the most important ones.) Dividing the 360° of the zodiac by 3, 6, and 12 produces the beneficial or harmonious aspects: the powerful **TRINE**, 120°; the **SEXTILE**, 60°; and the weaker **SEMI-SEXTILE**, 30°. The **CONJUNCTION** (when two bodies are close together) is the most powerful of all aspects: whether it is good or bad depends on the planets involved. Next is **OPPOSITION**, then **SQUARE**, then **TRINE**. Aspects are described as applying (or separating) when the swifter of the two bodies involved is approaching (or leaving) **EXACTITUDE**.

ASSURBANIPAL (fl. 668–624 BC) King of Assyria, founded a great library of about 25,000 **CUNEIFORM** tablets, concerning astrology, mythology and natural sciences at Nineveh.

ASTARTE Syrian name for **ASHTORETH**.

ASTERISM A group or cluster of stars.

ASTEROIDS Irregular rocky bodies orbiting the Sun, between the paths of **MARS** and **JUPITER**. At least 3 500 have been numbered and named, the largest being **CERES** and the smallest **HATHOR**, about half a kilometre across.

ASTRAEA **ASTEROID**, Discovered in December 1945 by Karl **HENCKE**. In Greek mythology, goddess of justice and innocence, who is supposed to have dwelt on Earth, but when sin became dominant she departed and was metamorphosed into the constellation **VIRGO**.

ASTRAEUS One of the **TITANS**, husband to **EOS**, father to **BOREAS**, **NOTUS** and **ZEPHYRUS**; sometimes claimed to be father of the stars.

ASTROLABE Two-dimensional disc-shaped model of the heavens invented by the Greeks, developed by Muslims, and in widespread use all over Europe from the tenth century.

ASTROLATRY Star worship; prevalent among the **CHALDEANS**.

ASTROLOGICAL ASSOCIATION OF GREAT BRITAIN Founded by John **ADDEY** with Brigadier Roy Firebrace and Joan Rodgers in 1958; Addey became its President in 1961 and edited its magazine *Astrological Journal*.

ASTROLOGICAL HOUSES See **HOUSES**

ASTROLOGICAL STAR Also called the Star in the Ascendant; the celestial body rising on the eastern horizon in the **ASCENDING SIGN**.

Assurbanipal, royal librarian

Augustus Caesar crowned as a god

ASTROLOGICAL SIGNS See **ZODIAC SIGNS**

ASTROLOGICAL YEAR Begins at the **VERNAL POINT** (when Sun crosses the **CELESTIAL EQUATOR**, around 21 March). This used to be at 0° **ARIES**, and this is still the agreed point for the beginning of the zodiac.

ASTROLOGY Literally, 'discourse with the stars'; the study of the positions of the celestial bodies and the interpretation of their effect on the events on Earth and its inhabitants; there are many branches of astrology: see **ELECTIONAL ASTROLOGY; HORARY ASTROLOGY; INCEPTIONAL ASTROLOGY; JUDICIAL ASTROLOGY; MUNDANE ASTROLOGY; NATAL ASTROLOGY.**

ASTRONOMICAL UNIT Mean distance between Earth and Sun (149 987 870 km/ 92 955 630 miles) used as a measurement for stellar distance; abbreviated to AU.

ASTRONOMY The science and study of the planets, stars, the constellations, galaxies and the Universe. The first astronomers were also astrologers and mathematicians.

ASVINS In Hindu mythology a pair of divine twins who were rain-makers and givers of fertility.

ATEN Early expression of the Egyptian Sun God, manifested as the noonday Sun.

ATHENE OR PALLAS ATHENE Daughter of **ZEUS**, goddess of wisdom and the arts, and patron of Athens; equated with the Roman **MINERVA**.

ATLAS Innermost satellite of Saturn, the **SHEPHERD SATELLITE** of Saturn's A ring; also the name given to 27 Tauri, a star in the Hyades cluster in **TAURUS**. In Greek mythology, a mighty giant, the leader of the **TITANS**, condemned by Zeus to carry the world on his shoulders for eternity. Father of the **PLEIADES**.

ATMOSPHERE Gaseous layer enveloping a planet.

ATRIA Alpha Trianguli Australis in the constellation **TRIANGULUM AUSTRALE**.

ATROPOS One of the three Moirai or **FATES**.

ATUM A form of the Egyptian Sun god Ra.

AU See **ASTRONOMICAL UNIT**

AUBREY HOLES Series of fifty-six holes surrounding the ancient monument **STONEHENGE**. Named after the antiquarian John Aubrey (1627–1697), who rediscovered them.

AUGUST Eighth month of the **GREGORIAN CALENDAR** named for the Roman emperor **AUGUSTUS**.

AUGUSTINE of Hippo (AD 354–430) Saint, bishop and one of the greatest Christian thinkers. Formidable opponent of many things he regarded as heretical, including astrology, which he had accepted in his youth.

AUGUSTUS, GAIUS JULIUS OCTAVIANUS (63BC–AD14) The first Roman Emperor, a great believer in astrology.

AURIGA, the Charioteer Brilliant northern constellation (one of **PTOLEMY'S** original forty-eight), with an outstanding alpha, **CAPELLA**.

AURORA OR POLAR LIGHTS Pleasing haloes of lights at either end of the Earth's axis, the result of high speed particles from the Sun colliding with particles in the Earth's upper atmosphere.

AUTUMNAL EQUINOX In northern hemisphere, occurs about the 22 September each year when the Sun is crossing the **CELESTIAL EQUATOR** in a southerly direction, and day and night are equal.

AVENTINE One of the seven hills of Rome; a temple to **MERCURY** was built here.

AVICENNA (980–1037) Also known as Ibn Senna; Arabian mathematician, philosopher, astronomer and physician.

AXIS The imaginary line which joins the north and south pole through the middle of the Earth, and about which the Earth spins, making one revolution in 23 hours 56 minutes and 4 seconds.

AYANAMSA Sanskrit for precession: the difference in degrees between the **SIDEREAL** and **TROPICAL** zodiacs at any given point in time is called the ayanamsa.

AZIMUTH Arc of celestial **GREAT CIRCLE** from **ZENITH** to **HORIZON**; arc of horizon between north or south point, and point where the great circle – passing through a heavenly body and the zenith, cuts the horizon.

AZOTH Alchemists' name for mercury.

AZTECS The Aztecs (fl. third–first century BC) of ancient Mexico were very dedicated astrologers: they foretold events from planetary positions; calculated the horoscopes of children from birth; drew up their own zodiac, comprising twenty signs, and compiled **CALENDARS** that marked favourable or malefic phenomena.

Stonehenge, megalithic indicator of equinoxes and solstices

BA Early Egyptian name for the Soul, which roamed burial places;

BAADE, Walter (1893–1960) German astronomer, discovered **ASTEROID** 944 **HIDALGO** in 1920; resolved and classified large number of stars in **ANDROMEDA** galaxy.

BABYLON (fl. 700 to 100 BC) Capital of Babylonia, on the River Euphrates, the centre of Mesopotamian learning and culture, especially astronomy and astrology; site of the Tower of Babel, a huge **ZIGGURAT**.

BABYLONIAN ASTROLOGY Indivisible from astronomy in Babylonian culture; charting the position of the stars and planets to establish the seasons was essential in an agrarian society for crop planting and flood prediction; astrologers also believed that unusual events in the heavens (**ECLIPSES, COMETS**) presaged human catastrophies such as war. The Babylonians are credited with the origination of the **ZODIAC** as known in the west.

BABYLONIAN DEITIES Babylonian astronomer-priests associated the Sun with the god **SHAMASH**, the Moon with **SIN**, **JUPITER** with **MARDUK**, **VENUS** with **ISHTAR** and **MARS** with **NERGAL**.

BACCHUS Roman god of wine, identified with the Greek **DIONYSUS**.

BACON, Francis (1561–1626) Statesman, scientist, philosopher and astrologer; Chancellor of England in 1618. His *Astrologia Sana* reflected his belief that **CELESTIAL BODIES** had influences apart from light and heat.

BAGHDAD (fl. seventh to tenth centuries) Capital of the Muslim Abassid Kingdom centred on the River Tigris. Site of major observatory, school of astronomy and library set up by Caliph **AL-MANSUR** in AD 829 with the help of Jewish astrologers. Ancient Greek and Babylonian knowledge was passed on to Europe via Islamic expansionism.

BAILY'S BEADS Brilliant points seen along the edge of the **MOON** just before or after a solar **ECLIPSE**, thought to be the result of sun-light shining through the valleys at the Moon's edge; named for retired stockbroker and amateur astronomer Francis Baily (1774–1844), who first observed them in May 1836.

BAKHA Sacred Bull of Hermonthis, Egypt, an incarnation of Menthu, and the personification of the heat of the Sun; he changed colour every hour of the day.

BALANCE Astrological symbol for **LIBRA** the sign the Sun enters about 22 September each year, at the time of the **AUTUMN EQUINOX**, when days and nights are equal length; also the season of grain weighing after harvest, so scales would seem to be an appropriate symbol in an agricultural society.

BARNARD, Edward Emerson (1857–1923) Self-taught astronomer from Nashville, Tennessee; working at **LICK** and **YERKES** observatories, discovered **AMALTHEA** (fifth moon of **JUPITER**) in 1892; in 1916, found the fastest-moving star in the sky, Velox Barnardi, also known as Munich 15040, and Barnard's Star.

BARRED SPIRALS Distinctive, Catherine wheel-shaped galaxies in which the spiral arms extend from a 'bar' through the main nucleus of the system.

BARYCENTRE Common centre of gravity in a multiple star or planet system about which the members of the system orbit; in the Earth-Moon system the barycentre lies well within the

Babylon's Tower of Babel

Earth's sphere, as Earth is eighty-one times as massive as the Moon.

BAYER, Johann (1572–1625) German astronomer who introduced the **CLASSIFICATION OF STARS**.

BAYEUX TAPESTRY Astronomically interesting as it contains the first known illustration of **HALLEY'S COMET**.

BEAKER PEOPLE Early Bronze Age inhabitants of Western Europe known to have drawn up an accurate type of calendar, which marked the **SOLSTICES** and predicted **ECLIPSES**.

BEDFORD BOOK OF HOURS See Book of **HOURS**

BEE Name for the constellation **APUS**.

BEEHIVE Star cluster better known as **PRAESEPE**.

BEER, Wilhelm (1797–1850) German astronomer, brother of the composer **MEYERBEER**; worked with J.H. Mädler on the map of the **MOON**, published in 1837–8.

BEHAVIOUR PATTERNS Biological study of life's rhythms and cycles has produced much evidence to confirm the influence of the planets upon many forms of life. This agrees closely with the claims of astrologers that behaviour patterns may be triggered by a type of cosmic clock. Examples include the yearly swarming of the Pacific Worm.

BELEPHANTES Babylonian astrologer who is reputed to have correctly predicted that **ALEXANDER THE GREAT** would die in **BABYLON**.

BELLATRIX Gamma Orionis, a fixed star in the constellation **ORION**.

BELLONA Roman goddess of war; wife or sister of **MARS**.

BELOMANCY Divination by arrows.

BELTS OF JUPITER System of cloud belts in a constant state of turmoil, with the belts nearest the equator moving slightly faster than those near the poles.

BENEFIC PLANETS **VENUS** and **JUPITER** are traditionally known as the lesser and greater benefics. Venus depicts love, harmony and wealth. Jupiter is the planet of luck and good fortune.

BENEFICIAL ASPECTS See **ASPECTS**

BENETNASCH Alternative name for **ALKAID**.

BERENICE'S HAIR Name for the constellation **COMA BERENICES**.

BEROSSUS (fl. third century BC) Babylonian astrologer and Priest of Bel **MARDUK**, who made a great impact on the classical world with his astrological and historical writings.

BESIEGED In a **BIRTH CHART** or horoscope, a planet situated between two **MALEFICS** (or **BENEFICS**) within the **ORBS** of each is said to be besieged: for example, a planet placed between **VENUS** and **JUPITER** is favourably besieged, but if placed between **MARS** and **SATURN** could be in an extremely unfavourable position.

BESSEL, Friedrich Wilhelm (1784–1846) Founder of modern precision astronomy; in 1838 made first measurement of Earth to a star (61 Cygni) using the **PARALLAX**.

BETA ANDROMEDAE The star **MIRACH**.

BETA AQUARII The star **SADALSUUD**.

BETA ARIETIS The star **SHERATAN**.

BETA BOÖTIS The star **NEKKAR**.

BETA CANIS MAJORIS The star **MIRZAM**.

BETA CENTAURI The star **AGENA**

BETA CYGNI The star **ALBIREO**.

BETA DELPHINI The star **ROTANEV**.

BETA LIBRAE The star **ZUBENALCHEMALE**.

BETA LYRAE The star **SHELIAK**.

BETA ORIONIS The star **RIGEL**.

BETA PEGASI The star **SCHEAT**.

BETA PERSEI The star **ALGOL**.

BETA SAGITTARII The star **ARKAB**.

BETA TAURI The star **ALNATH**.

BETA URSAE MAJORIS The star **MERAK**.

BETA VIRGINIS The star **ZAVIJAVA**.

BETELGEUX Alpha Orionis, bright red supergiant **VARIABLE** in the constellation **ORION**.

BICORPOREAL Double-bodied zodiac signs: **GEMINI**, **SAGITTARIUS**, **PISCES**; **PTOLEMY** classified **VIRGO** as bicorporeal.

BIG BANG THEORY Currently accepted theory explaining the origin of the Universe: it is thought that the original material of the Universe was a ball of extremely hot, dense gas, which 'exploded' between ten and twenty thousand million years ago and has been expanding at a uniform rate ever since, cooling and coalescing into stars and planets on the way.

BIG DIPPER Nickname for **URSA MAJOR**, also known as the Great Bear or the Plough. (Dipper means ladle or scoop.)

BINARY STAR Two stars which form one system, orbiting each other around a common centre of gravity; the larger star is called the primary, the smaller is the companion. First defined by William **HERSCHEL** in 1902. Visual binaries (those which can be seen via a telescope) are commonest (50,000 are known); prototype is Zeta Ursa Majoris, discovered in 1650 by **RICCIOLI**. Eclipsing binaries are close enough to regularly occlude each other, and so their brightness appears to vary; 4 000 examples are known, of which **ALGOL** is the most famous. Spectroscopic binaries are so close together they are indistinguishable through a telescope, even when eclipsing each other. See also **DOUBLE STAR**.

BIORHYTHMS Three rhythmic cycles in human life that run concurrently: the Intellectual (thirty-three days); the emotional (twenty-eight days) and the physical (twenty-three days).

BIOSPHERE Region of Earth's surface (land or water) and the atmosphere above it, which can sustain life. Also called ecosphere; other planets may have biospheres.

Jupiter and Earth compared

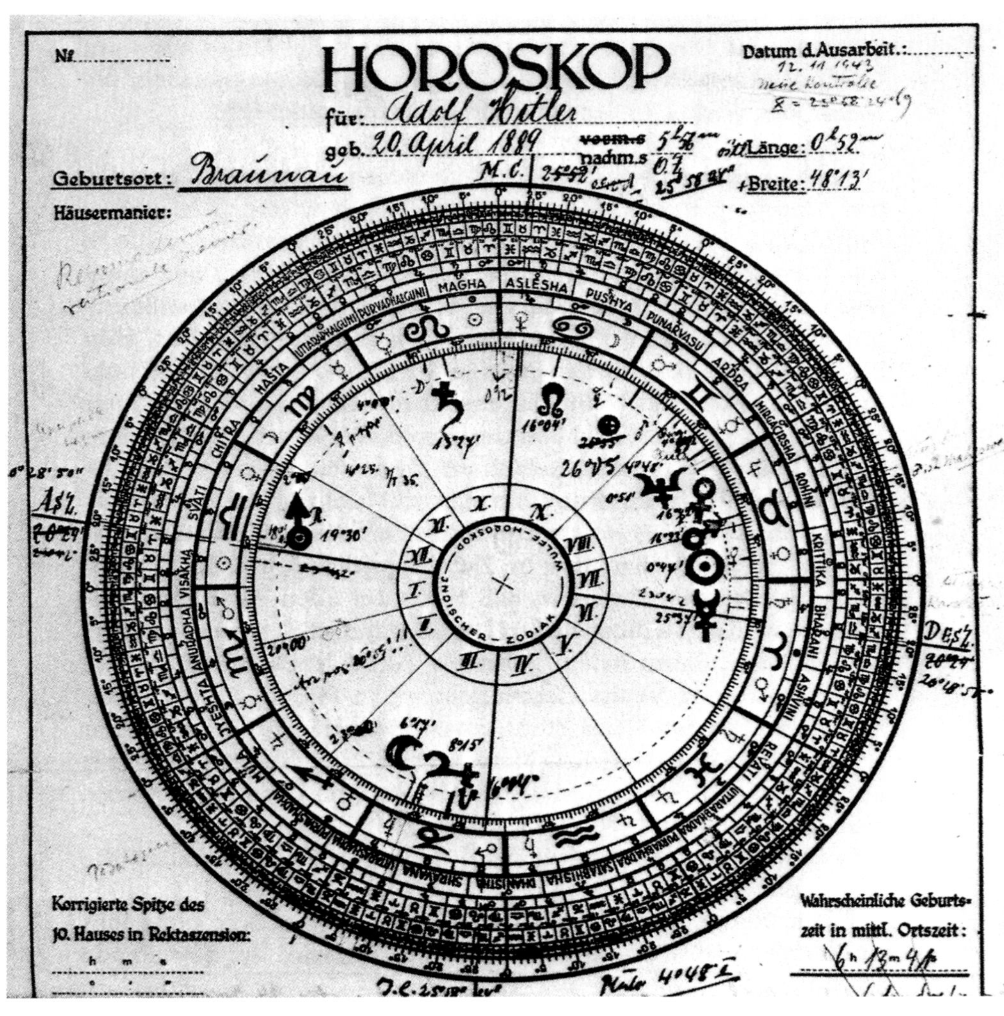

Adolf Hitler's birth chart

BI-QUINTILE Very weak astrological minor **ASPECT** of 144; seldom used by modern astrologers.

BIRR CASTLE Site in Central Ireland of the observatory built by the aristocratic astronomer, the Earl of **ROSSE**.

BIRTH CHART Drawn up from **BIRTH DATA** to show the state of the heavens at the time of birth; also known as a natal CHART; See also **HOROSCOPE**.

BIRTH DATA Date, time and place of birth, from which astrologers can work out the co-ordinates necessary for compiling a **BIRTH CHART**.

BIRTH MOMENT Generally accepted as the first inspiration of breath after the umbilical cord is cut.

BIRTH STONES Astrology has always associated certain gems and precious stones with each sign of the zodiac, but this allocation varies greatly with different cultures and customs. Most selections appear to be roughly colour based, but there are many variations given. A provisional list would assign diamond to **ARIES**, turquoise to **TAURUS**, agate to **GEMINI**, moonstone to **CANCER**, ruby to **LEO**, sardonyx to **VIRGO**, opal to **LIBRA** (the only sign that should wear it), topaz to **SCORPIO**, amethyst to **SAGITTARIUS**, sapphire to **CAPRICORN**, aquamarine to **AQUARIUS** and emerald to **PISCES**; however, other authorities have other ideas, and the list has never been established with authority.

BI-SEPTILE Astrological **ASPECT** of 102° 8", which is a multiple of the **SEPTILE** aspect by 2; **HARMONIC** 7.

BLACK HOLE Area of space in which the pull of gravity is so strong that nothing can escape, not even light.

BLAVATSKY, Helena (1831–1891) Russian mystic and founder of the **THEOSOPHICAL SOCIETY**. Her books include *Isis Unveiled* (1877) and *The Secret Doctrine* (1888).

BLUESTONES Stones from the Prescelly Mountains in Wales, somehow transported between BC 1700 and 1600 to **STONEHENGE**, some 400 km/250 miles away.

BODE, Johann Elert (1747–1826) German astronomer, director of Berlin Observatory from 1772, popularizer of **BODE'S LAW**.

BODE'S LAW Purely numerical relationship between planetary distances; they appear to double until **NEPTUNE** and **PLUTO** are reached, where the sequence is broken.

Madame Blavatsky, mystical theosophist

Background: Tycho Brahe

The Duc de Berry's Book of Hours

BODY Planet, star, asteroid or other celestial object.

BODY AREAS AND THE ZODIAC See **ANATOMY AND THE ZODIAC**

BOLIDE Brilliant exploding **METEOR.**

BOLINGBROKE, Roger (fl. fifteenth century) English wizard reputed to be highly involved with astrology and the Black Arts; hanged for witchcraft.

BOLOGNA Records indicate that a Chair of Astrology was established at the University of Bologna in 1125. First Professor was Cecco **D'ASCOLI.**

BONATTI, Guido (fl.thirteenth century) Italian astrologer, first to make use of midpoints.

BOND, William (1789–1859) First Director of Harvard College Observatory, the first major observatory in the United States; discovered **HYPERION**, eighth satellite of **SATURN**.

BOOK OF HOURS Name for medieval illustrated manuscript showing the months defined by their zodiac signs and the appropriate agricultural activity. Many beautiful books of hours were made during the fourteenth and fifteenth centuries, including the *Bedford Book of Hours* (now in the British Museum) and *Les Tres Riches Heures du Duc de Berri*, probably the most famous example of the genre.

BOOK OF THE DEAD Collection of ancient Egyptian texts, both religious and magical, concerned with guidance for the conduct of the soul through Amenti (Egyptian **HADES**).

BOÖTES, the Herdsman Brilliant northern constellation well known to the ancients, dominated by **ARCTURUS**. In mythology, Boötes was the inventor of the ox-drawn plough.

BOWL One of the seven types of astrological **CHART** patterns devised by American astrologer Marc Edmund Jones.

BOW SHOCK Name given to the 'bow wave' shape made as the **SOLAR WIND** flows against a planetary **MAGNETIC FIELD**.

BRADLEY, James (1693–1762) Third Astronomer Royal; discovered the **ABERRATION** of starlight in 1728, and the **NUTATION** or nodding of the Earth's axis in 1732.

BRAHE, Tycho (1546–1601) Danish astronomer patronized by Frederik II of Denmark; built and equipped a large observatory, Uranienborg, on the island of Hven, where he devised highly accurate maps of the stars, and motions of the planets. Opposed the **HELIOCENTRIC** (Sun-centred) theory of **COPERNICUS**; and put forward the theory that the planets revolved round the Sun and the Sun and Moon revolved round a fixed Earth. His observations formed the basis of the work of his assistant Johannes **KEPLER**.

BRANCHES OF ASTROLOGY See **ELECTIONAL ASTROLOGY; INCEPTIONAL ASTROLOGY; HORARY ASTROLOGY; MUNDANE ASTROLOGY; NATAL ASTROLOGY.**

BROUGHTON, Luke (1824–1899) American physician and astrologer, publisher of the astrological journal *Broughton's Monthly Planet Reader*.

BRUHESEN, Peter van (fl. sixteenth century) Dutch astrologer and physician, author of an astrological almanac.

BRUNO, Giordano (1548–1600) Italian supporter of **COPERNICUS** arrested by the Inquisition in 1593 and burned at the stake for his beliefs.

BUCKET One of the seven types of astrological **CHART** patterns devised by American astrologer Marc Edmund Jones.

BULL Astrological symbol for **TAURUS.**

BUNDLE One of the seven types of astrological chart patterns devised by American astrologer Marc Edmund Jones.

BUTLER, Joseph (1692–1752) English theologian who bitterly attacked astrology; to support his views, he studied astrological treatises in detail, only to discover he himself was becoming a strong supporter of the subject.

CADENT Falling; astrological term for the **HOUSES** which 'fall away' from the **ANGLES**, that is the third, sixth, ninth and twelfth houses, corresponding to the **MUTABLE** signs.

CADUCEUS Staff or wand carved associated with **MERCURY**; carved to represent two snakes twisted round a rod.

CAELA SCULPTORIS See **CAELUM**

CAELUM, the Graving Tool or Chisel Southern constellation introduced by **LACAILLE** in 1752; once known as Caela Sculptoris, the Sculptors Tools.

CAESAR, GAIUS JULIUS, (100 or 102 to 44 BC) Roman emperor interested in astrology and astronomy; wrote a treatise on the stars, *De Astris*; established the **JULIAN CALENDAR** in 46 BC with the help of Egyptian astrologers.

CALENDAR A system to measure time; times, dates and cycles have been vital to survival since the beginning of settled agriculture-based communities which depended on the regular sowing of crops; the first indication of civilization is the attempt to make a calendar, and all established cultures have their own examples. See also **CALENDAR, CHINESE; CALENDAR, EGYPTIAN; CALENDAR, GREGORIAN; CALENDAR, HINDU; CALENDAR, JEWISH; CALENDAR, JULIAN; CALENDAR, MUSLIM; CALENDAR, SOVIET**.

CALENDAR, Chinese Lunar calendar which begins at the first New Moon after the Sun enters **AQUARIUS**. It consists of twelve months with an intercalary month every thirty months.

CALENDAR, Egyptian The Egyptian year began when the star **SOTHIS** (our **SIRIUS**) rose with the Sun, as this coincided with the annual Nile flood; it had twelve months of thirty days each with five extra days, called 'epagomenal', at the end of the year; this gave a slippage of a day every four years and one year over fourteen and a half centuries, when the cycle synchronized again.

CALENDAR, Gregorian Introduced in 1582 by Pope Gregory XIII (1502–1585) in an attempt to improve the **JULIAN CALENDAR**, which slipped by almost ten days; Gregory introduced 1 January as the start of the New Year and decreed that leap years should occur only in years divisible by four. It was not accepted in England until 1752, by which time the slippage was eleven days.

CALENDAR, Hebrew See **JEWISH CALENDAR**.

CALENDAR, Hindu One of the early lunisolar (mixed) calendars with twelve months and an extra month every three years.

CALENDAR, Jewish Combines lunar and solar data; twelve months to a year, alternately twenty-nine and thirty days in a length to keep in step with the Moon; an extra month is added (in the spring) once every three years or so. The Jewish year starts with the New Moon nearest the **AUTUMNAL EQUINOX** in the autumn (between 6 September and 5 October on the **GREGORIAN CALENDAR**).

CALENDAR, Julian The original Roman calendar had only ten months; in 46 BC, with the help of the Egyptian astronomer Sosigenes of Alexandria, Julius **CAESAR** introduced a solar calendar (365.25 days), with a 366-day leap year every four years; New Year's day was 25 March. As the solar year is slightly shorter than that, a discrepancy of nearly eight days accumulated over 1 000 years. The Julian Calendar was finally replaced (1582) in Christian Europe by the **GREGORIAN CALENDAR**, although it took two centuries to fall out of favour completely.

CALENDAR, Mohammedan See **MUSLIM CALENDAR**

CALENDAR, Muslim The most widely used lunar calendar in the twentieth century. It consists of twelve lunar months, the odd months having thirty days and the even ones having twenty-nine; it was established ten years after the flight of Mohammed from Mecca to Medina.

CALENDAR, Soviet First established on 6 October 1923 (Revolution Day) and known as the 'Eternal Calendar'. After further changes it went into effect on 1 January 1930.

CALENDS First day of the month in the Roman calendar; also spelled Kalends. See also **IDES**; **NONES**.

CALLISTO Outermost of the four largest moons of **JUPITER**, a large icy satellite almost the size of **MERCURY**. In Greek mythology, Callisto was one of **ARTEMIS'S** huntresses, who was, inevitably, seduced by **ZEUS**; to deceive **HERA**, Zeus turned her into a bear and put her into the sky as **URSA MAJOR**.

CALYPSO Small moon of **SATURN**; in Greek mythology, the nymph who tempted **ODYSSEUS** to dally on the island of Ogygia.

CAMELOPARDALIS, the Giraffe Northern constellation introduced by **HEVELIUS** in 1690; also known as Camelopardus.

Welsh medieval astrological calendar

CAMELOPARDUS See **CAMELOPARDALIS**

CAMPANELLA, Tommaso (1568–1639) Italian philosopher and Dominican Astrologer-Priest, author of *Astrologia* (1629)

CAMPANUS Thirteenth-century system of **HOUSE DIVISION**.

Ceres, patron of Sicily

CANCER, the Crab Faint zodiac constellation rather like **ORION** in outline; best known for **PRAESEPE** the Cradle (also known as the Beehive), a fine open cluster, visible to the naked eye as a misty patch. **Cancer the zodiac sign** is a FEMININE/NEGATIVE **CARDINAL WATER** sign ruled by the Moon; its symbol is the Crab.

CANES VENATICI, the Hunting Dogs Constellation resolved by **HEVELIUS** in 1690; contains **COR CAROLI**, the prototype **MAGNETIC VARIABLE** and the Whirlpool Gallery, the first recognized **SPIRAL** galaxy discovered by Lord **ROSSE** in 1845.

CANIS MAJOR, the Great Dog One of **PTOLEMY'S** forty-eight constellations, representing one of **ORION'S** hunting dogs; contains **SIRIUS**.

CANIS MINOR, the Little Dog One of **PTOLEMY'S** forty-eight constellations, representing **ORION'S** junior hunting dog.

CANNON, Annie J. (1863–1941) Outstanding astronomer who worked at the Harvard College Observatory; best remembered for her work on the classification of star spectra.

CANOPUS Alpha Carinae in the constellation **CARINA**.

CAPELLA Alpha Aurigae in the constellation **AURIGA**.

CAPRICORN Tenth sign of the zodiac; a feminine negative **CARDINAL EARTH** sign, ruled by **SATURN**; its symbol is the goat. MARS is EXALTED and JUPITER at FULL in CAPRICORN. See **CAPRICORNUS**.

CAPRICORNUS, the Sea Goat Zodiacal constellation in the southern sky: in mythology, Capricornus was the she-goat **AMALTHEA**, placed in the sky by **ZEUS** in gratitude for her care of him when he was an infant in hiding from his father **CRONOS**.

CAPUT DRACONIS The Dragon's Head or Moon's North **NODE**.

CARACOL OBSERVATORY Ancient observatory in the Mayan city of Chichen Itza, Mexico, which shows the extent of pre-Columbian astrological and astronomical skills.

CARDINAL POINTS Points in the zodiac which coincide with the **EQUINOXES** and **SOLSTICES** on the **ECLIPTIC**. The First Point of **ARIES** is where the ecliptic intersects the **CELESTIAL EQUATOR** at the **VERNAL EQUINOX**; the First Point of **LIBRA**, where the ecliptic and equator intersect at the **AUTUMNAL EQUINOX**; the First Point of **CANCER**, when the Sun appears to reach the highest point in its orbit, the **SUMMER SOLSTICE**; and the First Point of **CAPRICORN** when it reaches its lowest, the **WINTER SOLSTICE**. The zodiac signs which occur at the cardinal points are called the **CARDINAL SIGNS**.

CARDINAL SIGNS Four signs of the zodiac that occur on the zodiacal band at the points of the **EQUINOXES** and **SOLSTICES**. The most powerful expression of the elemental energy they represent; the Cardinal **EARTH** sign is **CAPRICORN**; the Cardinal **WATER** sign is **CANCER**; the Cardinal **AIR** sign is **LIBRA**; and the Cardinal **FIRE** sign is **ARIES**. People born under a Cardinal sign are the doers of the world, the initiators, the pioneers.

CARINA, the Keel Southern constellation in the southern sky which was once part of **ARGO NAVIS**.

CARME Eleventh satellite of **JUPITER**; one of the four outer moons with a **RETROGRADE** motion.

CARNAC, Site of a series of alignments of about 2 750 menhirs, or great stones at Brittany, France. Probably used to predict the movements of the sun.

CARTER, Charles (1887–1968) Possibly the most distinguished British astrologer of the first half of this century; learned the first principles of astrology from the works of Alan **LEO** and carried on with this study within the **THEOSOPHICAL SOCIETY**, becoming its President in 1922; author of *The Principles of Astrology* (1925), founder of the magazine *Astrology*; became the first Principal of the Faculty of Astrological Studies.

CASSINI, Giovanni Domenico (1625–1712) Professor of Astronomy at **BOLOGNA** (1650–1669) and later the first Director of the Paris Observatory. Discovered the rotation of **JUPITER** and **MARS** and compiled new tables of Jupiter's satellites; also discovered and gave his name to the Cassini Division, the area between the two brightest rings of **SATURN**.

Annie Cannon

CASSIOPEIA Conspicuous W-shaped constellation in the northern sky, one of **PTOLEMY'S** forty-eight; **CIRCUMPOLAR** from northern latitudes; traversed by the **MILKY WAY**; visible through binoculars. In Greek mythology, Cassiopeia was the queen to King **CEPHEUS** of Ethiopia and mother to **ANDROMEDA**.

CASTOR Alpha Geminorum, a **BINARY** star in the zodiacal constellation **GEMINI**. In Greek mythology, Castor was the mortal son of Leda and **ZEUS**, twin to Polydeuces (Pollux in Latin) and brother to Helen of Troy.

CAUDA DRACONIS The Dragon's Tail or Moon's South **NODE**.

CELESTIAL Relating to the sky.

CELESTIAL EQUATOR The Earth's equator projected into space on to the **CELESTIAL SPHERE**; the zero line of **CELESTIAL LATITUDE**.

CELESTIAL HARMONICS See **HARMONICS**

CELESTIAL HORIZON Plane parallel to the visible horizon, centred on the Earth's centre and extending to the **CELESTIAL SPHERE**.

CELESTIAL LATITUDE The distance of a celestial body north or south of the **ECLIPTIC**.

CELESTIAL LONGITUDE Measurement used by astrologers to plot the celestial bodies in a **CHART**; the distance of a celestial body from 0° **ARIES**, the beginning of the zodiac, stated in degrees (°) and minutes (′) of the zodiac signs: one sign is thirty degrees, one minute is one-sixtieth of a degree. For example, a body is in the first degree of **GEMINI** if it is two signs or 60° from 0° Aries.

CELESTIAL NORTH AND SOUTH POLES Projection of the Earth's North and South Poles on to the **CELESTIAL SPHERE**: the north celestial pole is marked approximately by the **POLE STAR** (currently Polaris); the south celestial pole is not marked by a bright star.

CELESTIAL POLICE Amusing name for group of astronomers who, in 1800, undertook a search for a hypothetical planet supposed to orbit between **MARS** and **JUPITER**; they found asteroids instead.

CELESTIAL SPHERE Imaginary sphere surrounding the Earth, and around which the stars and their celestial bodies appear to move; used by astrologers and astronomers as framework for systems of measurement.

CENTAUR Name for the constellation **CENTAURUS**.

CENTAURUS, the Centaur Striking southern constellation, one of **PTOLEMY'S** original forty-eight. **ALPHA CENTAURI** and **BETA CENTAURI** are known as the Pointers because they appear to indicate the direction of **CRUX AUSTRALIS**, the Southern Cross. Omega Centauri, in the centre of the constellation, is the finest **GLOBULAR CLUSTER** in the sky, and can be seen with the naked eye. Also contains **PROXIMA CENTAURI** nearest star to the sun.

CEPHEID VARIABLES Pulsating stars which expand and contract in size (up to as much as 30 per cent) in a regular rhythmic pattern, changing in brightness as they do. Cepheids are named after their prototype **DELTA CEPHEI** (discovered 1784) in the constellation **CEPHEUS**.

CEPHEUS Northern sky constellation, one of **PTOLEMY'S** original forty-eight; contains Delta Cephei, the prototype of **CEPHEID VARIABLE** and the bright red irregular **VARIABLE**, Mu Cephei, known as the Garnet Star. In Greek mythology, Cepheus was King of Ethiopia, consort to **CASSIOPEIA**, father of **ANDROMEDA**.

CERBERUS In Greek mythology, monster three-headed dog that guarded the doors of **HADES**.

CERES Largest of the **ASTEROIDS**; first of the asteroid belt to be discovered. Seen on 1 January 1801 by Sicilian astronomer Giuseppe **PIAZZI**; named after the patron goddess and protector of Sicily, at Piazzi's request. In Roman mythology, Ceres is the equivalent of Greek **DEMETER**.

CETUS, the Whale Large constellation (one of **PTOLEMY'S** forty-eight that sprawls across the **CELESTIAL EQUATOR**; sometimes identified with the monster sent by **NEPTUNE** to devour **ANDROMEDA**; contains the prototype long-period variable **MIRA** (Omicron Ceti). Cetus obtrudes into the zodiac, and some astrologers believe that this ought to be recognized. See also **OPHIUCHUS**.

Castor and Pollux, the Dioscuri

CHALDEANS General name for the people who colonized Mesopotamia about 3000 BC. Originally referred to Sumerians, later applied to the Babylonians, and came to be equated specifically with astronomers or astrologers.

CHALLIS, James (1803–1862) Director of Cambridge Observatory, England; notorious for failing to recognize the planet **NEPTUNE** in its predicted position in the summer of 1846, although he saw it three times.

CHAMAELEON, the Chameleon Small constellation near the North Pole.

CHAMPOLLION, Jean François (1790–1832) French Egyptologist who deciphered the heiroglyphics on the **ROSETTA STONE**.

CHARIOTEER Name for the constellation **AURIGA**.

CHARLES' WAIN Old name for the **PLOUGH** or Big Dipper in **URSA MAJOR**.

CHARON Pluto's huge icy moon, with an orbit lasting 6.4 days; discovered June 1978 by Dr James Christy at the United States Naval Observatory. In Greek mythology, Charon was the surly ferryman, who carried the souls of the dead across the underground River Styx.

CHART Astrologically, a 'map of the heavens' drawn up for study in the form of a **BIRTH CHART** or **HOROSCOPE**; other charts can be erected (drawn up) for all manner of things: events; the launching of new projects; political matters, and the weather.

CHEIROMANCY See **PALMISTRY**.

CHEIRON See **CHIRON**.

CHELAE Original name for **LIBRA**; means the Scorpion's Claws.

CHEMICAL FURNACE Old name for the constellation **FORNAX**.

CHEOPS The Great Pyramid of Cheops was built with one main passageway aligned towards the star Thuban in the constellation **DRACO**, which was the pole star some 4500 years ago. Cheops or Khefren was second king of the Fourth Dynasty, which flourished before 2500 BC.

CHINESE CALENDAR See **CALENDAR**.

CHINESE ZODIAC Chinese astronomy and astrology is based on the Pole Star and different constellations to the West. The Chinese Solar Year is marked by the **EQUINOXES** and **SOLSTICES**, and the periods between divided into six segments of fifteen or sixteen days, each given a name to do with seasonal weather conditions and crop growing; this makes twenty-four divisions along the **ECLIPTIC**, and is the equivalent of our zodiac: each solar term (Ch'i) equals fifteen of the ecliptic, or half a zodiac sign. The twelve-year cycle with which westerners are more familiar equates with the twelve-year **JUPITER** cycle; each year is named after an animal: Rat, Ox, Tiger, Rabbit (or Cat), Dragon, Snake, Horse, Sheep (or Goat), Monkey, Rooster, Dog and Pig (or Boar), and each animal has its own attributes. Each animal year is also associated with one of the five Elements of Chinese Cosmology, in either its positive or negative quality. The elements, fire, earth, metal, water and wood, run in ten-yearly cycles, one positive element for the first year, then one negative element for the next year, and so on.

Charon meets Psyche, the human soul

CHIRON ASTEROID 2060, a 'mini-planet' discovered in 1977 by Charles Kowal at **PALOMAR**. Large (diameter between 100 and 320 km/72 and 200 miles); possibly a lost moon of **NEPTUNE**, or an **ASTEROID** flung out of the normal belt, or the leader of an undiscovered belt. Some astrologers (notably Barbara Hand Clow) in America assign great weight to it; they claim it is the lost planet that rules **VIRGO**, and **EPHEMERIDES** have been drawn up so that birth charts can be revised to account for this. Not all astrologers agree about its significance. In Greek mythology, Chiron or Cheiron was the wisest and best of the Centaurs, a healer, sage and teacher, also an excellent hunter and sportsman.

CHISEL Alternative name for the constellation **CAELUM**.

CHRISTIE, William Henry (1845–1922) Astronomer Royal from 1881 to 1910 who modernized **GREENWICH OBSERVATORY** and introduced the daily observation of Sun spots.

CHROMATIC ABERRATION False colour effects, or blurred images with coloured fringes around them, as seen through early refractor **TELESCOPES**. Occurs because simple lenses cannot accurately refocus light that has been split into bands of colour by a prism.

CHROMOSPHERE Layer of hot gas that lies in an area surrounding the Sun's **PHOTOSPHERE**, the visible surface of the Sun.

CHRONOCRATORS **JUPITER** and **SATURN**. Known by the ancients as 'Markers of Time'. To them the longest orbits within the solar system were those of **JUPITER** and **SATURN**, Jupiter twelve years and Saturn thirty years. When the conjunctions of Jupiter and Saturn brought periods of global upheaval, these two planets were regarded as the chronocrators.

CIRCINUS, the Compasses Tiny southern constellation near **TRIANGULUM**.

CIRCUMPOLAR STARS Stars that never set.

CLASSIFICATION OF STARS Bright stars which would have been visible to the keen but unaided eyes of the ancient astronomers have individual names, mostly Arabic; these have been kept, but are used in conjunction with the method of classification introduced in 1603 by Johann **BAYER**, who assigned the letters of the Greek alphabet to constellation stars, starting with **ALPHA** for the brightest.

CLAVIUS, Christopher (1537–1612) German Jesuit teacher of mathematics, who masterminded the **CALENDAR** reform of 1582 for Pope Gregory.

CLOCK Name for the constellation **HOROLOGIUM**.

CLOTHO One of the three **FATES** or Moirae.

COAL SACK Dark obscuring cloud in **CRUX AUSTRALIS**; appears silhouetted against the background of the **MILKY WAY**.

COCOON NEBULA Nebula in the constellation **CYGNUS**.

COCYTUS River of **HADES**; its name means 'wailing'.

COLT Name for the constellation **EQUULEUS**.

COLUMBA, the Dove Southern constellation adjoining **CANIS MAJOR** and **CARINA**.

COLURES The **GREAT CIRCLES** projected on to the **CELESTIAL SPHERE** which pass through the **CELESTIAL NORTH** and **SOUTH POLES**.

Chiron instructing Achilles

COMA BERENICES, Berenice's Hair Northern constellation adjoining **BOÖTES**; contains many galaxies. In mythology, the Egyptian queen Berenice, wife of King Ptolemy, vowed to sacrifice her beautiful hair to the gods if her husband returned home safely after vanquishing the Assyrians; when he did so, **ZEUS** placed her hair in the sky.

COMBUST Astrological term referring to a planet whose **LONGITUDE** is within 8.5° of the Sun.

COMETS From the Greek *kometes*, meaning 'hairy star': composed of ice, gases and dust they patrol the Solar System in elliptical orbits; long-term comets take millions of years to circuit the Sun; short-term comets (orbits less than 200 years), of which **HALLEY'S** is the brightest, are believed to be derived from them, pulled away by the gravitational attraction of the planets, especially **JUPITER**.

COMPASSES Name for the constellation **CIRCINUS**.

COMPATIBILITY OF THE ZODIAC SIGNS See **SYNASTRY**

COMPOSITE DEGREE Astrological point which has significance in terms of destiny; to find it, add the **LONGITUDES** of the Sun, Moon and planets as they appear in a **CHART** and divide the result by ten.

CONJUNCTION Astrologically the most powerful **ASPECT**, when two celestial bodies are apparently close together in a **CHART**, that is in the same sign or degree; especially significant if one body is the ruler of the sign. Astronomically, the alignment of two or more planets or a planet and the Sun; inferior conjunction occurs when either **MERCURY** or **VENUS** is in line with the Earth and the Sun; superior conjunction occurs when any of the planets beyond Earth align.

CONSTELLATIONS Groups of stars that appear to observers on Earth to form patterns in the sky; they are not true groups, as some members may be light years away from others. Each civilization has seen different pictures in the sky: the Chinese and the Egyptians for example call Western constellations different names or have entirely different pattern groupings; in Western astronomy, they have kept the names conferred on them by the ancients – mostly mythical beasts or gods. The first attempt at written codification was made by **PTOLEMY**, who listed forty-eight in the **ALMAGEST**, including the twelve zodiacal constellations; Ptolemy's list omitted the southern constellations, which did not appear over Alexandria. (The only place to see all the constellations is on the **EQUATOR**.) With the advent of telescopes and access to the southern skies, the constellation list grew, becoming unmanageably cumbersome; in 1933 the International Astronomical Union went briskly to work and systematized the list, reducing it to the eighty-eight now in use.

COPERNICUS, Nicolaus (1473–1543) Polish astronomer who deduced mathematically that the Sun must be at the centre of the Solar System and the Earth and planets revolve round it; this revolutionary theory negated the long-established **PTOLEMAIC** system and changed the face of astronomy; Copernicus' book *De Revolutionibus Orbium Coelestium* was published as he was on his death bed.

COR CAROLI Alpha Canes Venaticorum in the constellation **CANES VENATICI**; prototype magnetic **VARIABLE**; named by Edmund **HALLEY** in honour of Charles I.

CORONA Literally crown; the part of the solar atmosphere only visible to the naked eye during a solar **ECLIPSE**; composed of ionized gases, with a mean temperature of 1 000 000 K, it extends beyond the **PHOTOSPHERE**.

CORONA AUSTRALIS, the Southern Crown One of **PTOLEMY'S** original forty-eight constellations; easily recognized by its little line of curved stars.

CORONA BOREALIS, the Northern Crown One of **PTOLEMY'S** original forty-eight constellations; adjoins **BOÖTES**; its **ALPHA** is **ALPHEKKA**.

CORRECTION Conversion made between clock time to **SIDEREAL** time in order to calculate the **ASCENDANT** and **MIDHEAVEN** on a **BIRTH CHART**; there are 24 hours 3 minutes 56.5 seconds of sidereal time to 24 hours of clock time.

CORVUS, the Crow Southern constellation, one of **PTOLEMY'S** forty-eight, adjoining **HYDRA**; mythologically, said to represent the crow sent by **APOLLO** to watch the behaviour of his lover Coronis.

COSMIC CLOCKS Discoveries made in the biological study of rhythms and cycles indicate that behaviour patterns are triggered and controlled by some type of timing device or cosmic clock. Behaviour patterns in oysters, for example, which were once associated with the pull of the tides, are now known to coincide with the changing positions of the Moon, when it is New or Full, above or below the horizon. The presence of these unseen influences relative to biological science is an exciting breakthrough for astrology,

Comet West, seen in 1975

Cuneiform dedication to goddess Innin

since it agrees with the astrological ideas concerning the influences of the Sun, Moon and planets on terrestrial life. See also **COSMOBIOLOGY**.

COSMIC CROSS Occasional name for **GRAND CROSS**, an astrological **ASPECT**.

COSMIC RAYS Not really 'rays' but streams of highly charged **PARTICLES** (mainly **PROTONS**) pouring into the top layer of the Earth's atmosphere from deep space; first discovered by Austrian physicist Victor Hess (1883–1964).

COSMIC YEAR Time taken by the Sun (and its attendant Solar System) to make one complete revolution round the centre of the home **GALAXY**; about 225 million years.

COSMOBIOLOGY Study of the effect of cosmic phenomena on human biology and pathology.

COSMOGONY Study of the origins of the Universe.

COSMOLOGY Study of the structure of the Universe.

COURT INTELLIGENCER Title given to the astrologer attached to the Royal Court of England in the seventeenth and eighteenth centuries.

CRAB Name for the constellation **CANCER**.

CRACOW University; Chair of Astrology established in 1460; **COPERNICUS** studied astronomy and astrology here.

CRANE Name for the constellation **GRUS**.

CRATER, the Cup Small constellation (one of **PTOLEMY'S** original forty-eight) adjoining **HYDRA** and **CORVUS**; associated with the wine goblet of **BACCHUS**.

CRESCENT MOON Phase of the Moon during which it appears less than half full to observers on Earth; occurs between New Moon and first quarter and last quarter to New Moon.

CRONUS or CHRONOS One of the **TITANS**, son of **URANUS** and Ghea (Heaven and Earth); castrated his father Uranus with a sickle given to him by his mother; father of the Olympian gods **ZEUS, POSEIDON, HADES, DEMETER, HERA** and **HESTIA**; devoured his own children (to avoid them usurping his power) except for Zeus, who was saved and hidden by his mother **RHEA**; finally toppled from power after the War of the Titans. His Roman equivalent is **SATURN**.

CROW Name for the constellation **CORVUS**.

CRUX AUSTRALIS, the Southern Cross Situated near the Earth's South Pole, the smallest constellation in the sky, almost surrounded by **CENTAURUS**; the Jewel Box cluster (Kappa Crucis) and the dramatic **COAL SACK** nebula.

CULMINATION Astrologically, when a planet reaches the **MIDHEAVEN**; the maximum altitude of a celestial body above the horizon.

CUNEIFORM WRITING Wedge-shaped writing made with a wedge-shaped tool (from Latin *cuneus*) on soft clay tablets; in use from c3800 BC until the Christian era, but not deciphered until 1802 by Georg Friedrich Grotefend (1775–1853).

CUP Name for the constellation **CRATER**.

CUSP Starting point of a **ZODIAC** sign, 0 degrees of that sign; the cusp of an astrological **HOUSE** is its beginning, marked by the dividing line between it and the preceding house; the cusp of the first house on the eastern horizon is called the **ASCENDANT**.

CYCLE OF THE MOON See **METONIC CYCLE**

CYCLE OF THE SUN Twenty-eight-year repeating pattern, when the days of the month fall on the same days of the week again.

CYGNUS, the Swan Very rich, bright and beautiful constellation, often known as the Northern Cross, one of **PTOLEMY'S** original forty-eight; its **ALPHA** is **DENEB**.

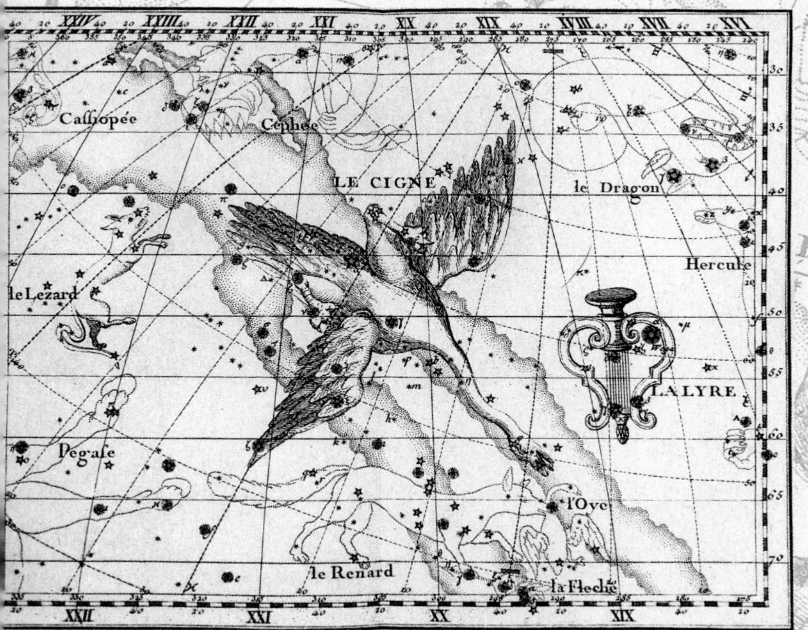

Cygnus, from Flamsteed's star map of 1776

DABIN Fixed star, Beta Capricornii of the zodiacal constellation **CAPRICORNUS**.

DAMASCUS Capital of Syria; in the eighth century, a centre of astrological and astronomical learning rivalling **BAGHDAD**.

DANIEL Old Testament prophet, known in Babylon (and the Bible) as Belteshazzar, master of the magicians, and chief of 'magicians and astrologers'.

DANTE, Alighieri (1265–1321) Italian poet, soldier and politician; studied at the University of **BOLOGNA**; in *The Divine Comedy* (c1300) he condemned astrologers Guido **BONATTI** and Michael **SCOT** for involving astrology with necromancy, but did not condemn astrology itself.

D'ARREST, Heinrich Ludwig (1822–1875) Assistant astronomer at Berlin Observatory; joined **GALLE** in the search for **NEPTUNE**.

D'ASCOLI, Cecco (d. 1327) Professor of Astrology at **BOLOGNA**, burnt at the stake by the Inquisition because of his heretical beliefs, not his astrology.

DATE LINE See **INTERNATIONAL DATE LINE**.

DAY, Sidereal The time the Earth takes to rotate once relative to a fixed star: 23 hours 56 minutes 4.09 seconds of mean Solar Time.

DAY, Solar The time taken by Earth to make one rotation relative to the Sun; varies according to the time of year, but the mean is twenty-four hours.

DAY FOR A YEAR Also known as Secondary **PROGRESSIONS**. Method for progressing a **BIRTH CHART** or **HOROSCOPE** according to the **PROPER** motions of the planets; the positions of the planets the day after birth, are interpreted as relating to the conditions for the first year of life; each day of life represents a year of life, each hour approximately a fortnight; cannot be calculated without the **ADJUSTED CALCULATION DATE** derived from the **BIRTH DATA**. To progress a birth chart by this method for ten years, for example, the astrologer would first work out the Adjusted Calculation Date; then count on ten days from the date of birth in the **EPHEMERIS** for the year of birth, getting to the **PROGRESSED DATE**; the positions of the planets at noon on this day are taken to be the positions of the planets on the Adjusted Calculation Date for the year of the progression (that is ten years after birth year); then the astrologer can evaluate and assess the planetary data and outline trends for the year. Prenatal Secondary Progressions or Regressions are calculated in the same manner but backwards instead of forwards, so that the twenty-four hours immediately before birth correspond to the period up to the first year of life. See also **DIRECTIONS**.

DAYLIGHT SAVING TIME Advance of clocks to provide an extra hour of daylight. Creates many problems for astrologers, who need to know the dates, times and duration of any such saving schemes, all of which affect **BIRTH DATA** and therefore the **BIRTH CHART**. Books which log the complicated time shifts include *The Revised Waite's Compendium of Natal Astrology* and the works of Doris Chase **DOANE**.

DEAN, Dr Geoffrey English astrologer, analytical chemist, and science writer; contributor to *Correlation: a Journal of Research into Astrology*, the twice-yearly publication of the **ASTROLOGICAL ASSOCIATION**. With Arthur Mather compiled *Recent Advances in Natal Astrology* (published 1977 and revised in mid-1980s), a stringent scientific assessment of astrological fact and myth.

DEBILITY Astrological term applied when a celestial body is in **OPPOSITION** to its own sign, or **EXALTATION**; its power and influence are then debilitated or enfeebled.

DECANS OR DECANATES The division of the zodiac signs into thirds, each third comprising 10°; a method of interpretation described by Alan **LEO** in *Practical Astrology* (1911); Leo theorized that the Decans are the 'Faces' of each of the zodiac signs, and supplies tables to simplify this.

DECANS, Egyptian In Egyptian astrology, the division of the year into thirty-six ten-day intervals which corresponded to the thirty-six different constellations which rose in sequence behind the Sun.

DECILE Slightly beneficial astrological **ASPECT** formed when planets are 36° apart.

Dante Alighieri and The Divine Comedy

DECLINATION Celestial equivalent of terrestrial latitude measured from the **CELESTIAL EQUATOR**; a star or planet's position, north or south, is measured in degrees, between 0° at the equator and 90° at the **CELESTIAL POLES** (+ = north; − = south).

DECRESCENT MOON Waning Moon.

DECUMBITURE Meaning 'laying down'. Astrological term for the time or onset of illness; a **HOROSCOPE** erected showing the position of the planets at this point helps astrological assessment of possible nature, prognosis and duration of the illness.

DEE, Dr John (1527–1608) Mathematician, geographer and astrologer, equally interested in the occult arts.

DEFERENT Term used by **PTOLEMY** to account for the motions of the planets; each planet was assumed to revolve about a small circle, the **EPICYCLE**, which in turn revolves about a larger circle, the deferent, centred approximately on the Earth.

DEGREE Measure of the longitudinal division of a circle, used to plot planets' positions in the segments of the zodiac band and to measure the distance between planets to determine the astrological **ASPECTS**. One degree (written °) consists of sixty minutes (written ′); each minute is divided into sixty seconds (written ″).

DEIMOS Smaller of the two moons of **MARS**; tiny (about 12 km/7.5 miles across) and heavily cratered; orbits in 1.262 days.

DE LA RUE, Warren (1815–1889) Born in Guernsey, Channel Islands; pioneer of astronomical photography; took the first good photographs of the Moon in 1852, and much work on the Sun (**SOLAR FLARES** and **SOLAR PROMINENCES**); photographed the total solar **ECLIPSE** of 1860.

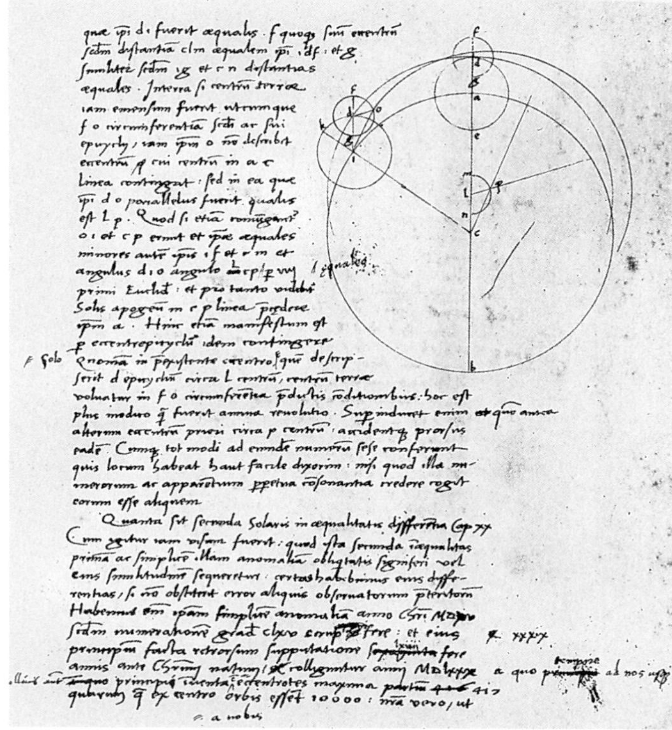

Page from Copernicus' **De Revolutionibus**

DELAUNAY, Charles (1816–1872) Director of Paris Observatory who specialized in the motions of the Moon.

DELINEATION Interpretation of a **MAP** or **BIRTH CHART**, the analysis of the planetary positions in the signs or **HOUSES**, and the **ASPECTS** formed.

DELPHINUS, the Dolphin Small but bright constellation (one of **PTOLEMY'S** original forty-eight) near **AQUILA**.

DELTA CEPHEI Prototype **CEPHEID VARIABLE** discovered by John Goodericke in 1784.

DELTA ORIONIS The star **MINTAKA**.

DELTA SCORPII The star **DSCHUBBA**.

DELTA URSAE MAJORIS The star **MEGREZ**.

DEMON STAR **ALGOL**, the 'Winking Star'.

DEMONIAC ASTROLOGY Form of astrology practised in ancient times; events were predicted by observing the stars, but also invoking evil demoniac forces.

DENDERAH ZODIACS Two representations of the zodiac found on the ceilings of the Egyptian Temple of Hathor at Denderah.

DENEB Alpha Cygni, highly luminous supergiant and brightest star in the constellation **CYGNUS**; one star in the **SUMMER TRIANGLE**.

DENEB AL GIEDI Delta Capricornii, the brightest star in the zodiacal constellation **CAPRICORNUS**.

DENEBOLA Fixed star, Beta Leonis' third brightest star in the zodiacal constellation **LEO**.

DE REVOLUTIONIBUS ORBIUM COELESTIUM **COPERNICUS'S** book expounding his revolutionary **HELIOCENTRIC** theory of the Solar System; published in 1543 and instantly banned by the Church.

DESCENDANT Point where the **ECLIPTIC** meets the horizon in the west; opposite point to the **ASCENDANT**; the western **ANGLE** or **CUSP** of the seventh **HOUSE** in a **BIRTH CHART**.

DESCENDING NODE Point at which an orbit of a celestial body crosses the **ECLIPTIC** from north to south.

DETERMINISM Philosophical theory opposed by the doctrine of free will; theological determinism perceives a purpose (God's) behind events; fatalistic determinism emphasizes humanity's powerlessness at the hands of fate. Astrology was once thought to be fatalistically determinist: what is written in the stars, is or will be; this is no longer the case, as genuine astrology is now considered to be concerned with interpreting future trends in a person's life.

DETRIMENT Astrological term for a planet placed in the sign opposite to the sign it rules; it is in sub-detriment if it sub-rules the sign; traditionally a planet in detriment is thought to be ill-placed, and to lose some of its power.

DEUCALION Greek equivalent of the biblical Noah; son of **PROMETHEUS**, survived the great flood sent by **ZEUS** and guided his ark to rest on Mount **PARNASSUS**; husband of **PYRRHA**, father of **HELLEN**, ancestor to all the Greeks.

DEWEY, E.R. President of the American Foundation for the Study of Cycles, which studies the cyclical nature of almost all activity on Earth from statistical data gathered on every kind of fluctuation, from stock exchange prices to the animal population of the Arctic. In the Foundation's bulletin *Cycles* (August 1970 issue) Dewey publicly concluded that all life on Earth is demonstrably subject to huge, as yet not understood forces, possibly cosmic in origin.

DEXTER ASPECT Early astrological term describing two celestial bodies moving towards an **OPPOSITION**. See also **SINISTER ASPECT**.

DHENEB Zeta Aquilae, third brightest star in the constellation **AQUILA**.

DIALOGUE ON THE TWO CHIEF WORLD SYSTEMS **GALILEO'S** book, written between 1623 and 1633, defending the **HELIOCENTRIC** world view put forward by **COPERNICUS**.

DIANA Roman counterpart of Greek **ARTEMIS**; composite and powerful mythological embodiment of the female principal; goddess of the hunt, of chastity and childbirth; associated with the Moon.

DICHOTOMY Exact half-phase of the Moon, **MERCURY** or **VENUS**.

DIFFRACTION GRATING Form of prism; grooved metal or glass plate which splits light into its separate wavelengths to produce a colour spectrum; used by **ÅNGSTROM** to study the Solar spectrum.

DIGNIFIED Astrological term used of a planet well placed in its own sign or the sign of its **EXALTATION**.

DIONE One of the seven more sizeable moons of **SATURN**

Late Egyptian zodiac from Denderah

(there are 23 moons altogether); discovered in 1684 by **CASSINI**, and notable for the variation in its surface brightness. According to Homer, Dione was one of **ZEUS'S** queens and mother of **APHRODITE**.

DIPHDA Beta Ceti, brightest star in the constellation **CETUS**.

DIRECT OR DIRECT MOTION Astrological term applied to a planet moving forward in the zodiac, or appearing to move in the direction of the signs, for example from **ARIES** to **TAURUS**.

DIRECTIONS Astrologically, future trends.

DIRECTIONS, Primary A method of **PROGRESSION** based on the rotation of Earth and the apparent rising and setting of the planets in the **HOUSES**, taking no account of their **PROPER** motion; the passage of one **DEGREE** of **RIGHT ASCENSION** over the **MIDHEAVEN** of the **BIRTH CHART** is taken to equal one year of life. To make a reading, planets are therefore progressed through the birth chart by one degree for every year desired, and then their **ASPECTS** with their position at the actual birth are drawn up. Also known as One Degree System.

DIRECTIONS, Symbolic or Fixed Increment Method of **PROGRESSING** a chart; directions are not based on any astronomical motion of the planets or **HOUSES**; a fixed annual increment or **PROGRESS** is added to all factors, including the **ANGLES**.

DISPOSITOR Extremely complex astrological rule; the 'Dispositor' of a planet is the ruler of the sign in which it is placed; celestial bodies in **ARIES**, for example, are 'disposed' of by **MARS**. Simplified, the theory is that the ruling planet of the sign on the **CUSP** of the **HOUSE** is the dispositor of a planet actually positioned within that house; the influence of the 'disposed' planet is not removed entirely but merged with the influences of its dispositor.

DISSOCIATE ASPECTS Commonly formed between signs which are themselves in aspect; a body at the beginning of **CANCER** is in **SQUARE** to one at the beginning of **LIBRA**, yet in **TRINE** to one at the beginning of **SCORPIO**; but it is also in trine to one at the end of Libra, although Libra is in square with Cancer; these important **ASPECTS** are often overlooked by astrology students.

DIURNAL Pertaining to, or describing, the day.

DIURNAL ARC The portion of the Sun or planet's travel during which it is above the observer's horizon; the journey from **ASCENDANT** to **DESCENDANT**.

DIURNAL CIRCLE Circle described by the Earth as it rotates on its axis each day.

DIURNAL HOROSCOPE **CHART** erected for a specific day using the **SIDEREAL** time of that day and the birth time of the client. With each additional day after the birthday, the **ANGLES** will **PROGRESS**, according to the increment in the sidereal time at noon on each successive day. Such a chart or map is said to be useful for determining the day when a **DIRECTION** will operate; the arrival of a planet on an angle in the diurnal map is said to produce marked results.

DIURNAL MOTION Apparent daily movement of celestial bodies from east to west.

DOANE, Doris Chase Author of *Time Changes in the World, Time Changes in Canada and Mexico* and *Time Changes in the USA*, all published by the **AMERICAN FEDERATION OF ASTROLOGERS**; list the time shifts and boundary changes that affect the computation of the **SIDEREAL** time of birth from the standard local time.

DOBYNS, Zipporah American astrologer, author of *Expanding*

Diana in repose, by Lucius Cranach

Giovanni Donati

Astrology's Universe (1983), which looks at astrology in an anthropological and psychological context.

DOG STAR Common name for SIRIUS.

DOLPHIN Name for the constellation DELPHINUS.

DOMAL DIGNITY Astrological term describing a planet occupying the sign which it rules (for example, JUPITER in SAGITTARIUS); also applied to a planet in its own HOUSE.

DOMIFICATION Pertaining to the division of the zodiacal HOUSES.

DONATI, Giovanni Battista (1826–1873) Director of Florence Observatory; largely responsible for the transfer of the observatory south to nearby Arcetri; first to make spectroscopic observations of COMETS, and to ascertain that their tails are made of gases; discovered the Great Comet of 1858, which is named after him.

DONATI'S COMET See DONATI.

DOPPLER EFFECT Alteration in pitch (of sound) or wavelength (of light) caused by the speed of a body producing the sound or light. As a body approaches the observer, the lightwaves it emits grow shorter and it appears blue or bluish; as it recedes, the wavelengths grow longer and the light appears red (REDSHIFT); fairly simple way to judge which way a celestial body is moving. First observed and described by Austrian physicist Christiaan Doppler (1803–1853).

DORADO, the Swordfish Southern constellation containing part of the Large MAGELLANIC CLOUD and the splendid Tarantula NEBULA.

DORYPHORY Any planet which acts as a herald or bodyguard to the Sun and rises shortly before it; any planet which rises shortly after the Moon.

DOUBLE SIGNS Traditionally, GEMINI, SAGITTARIUS and PISCES; in life and character, people born under these signs show a curious doubleness, often having two separate vocations, either at the same time or consecutively; frequently there are two marriages and a tendency to bear twins.

DOUBLE STARS Two stars which appear close together; BINARY stars are connected by gravitational attraction; optical doubles only appear to be connected and may actually be light years apart.

DOUBLE SUMMER TIME See DAYLIGHT SAVING TIME.

DOVE Name for the constellation COLUMBA.

DRACO, the Dragon Long, sprawling northern constellation (one of PTOLEMY'S original forty-eight) that twists around URSA MINOR; its alpha, Thuban, seventh brightest member, was the Pole Star in ancient times.

DRAGON Name for the constellation DRACO.

DRAGON'S HEAD See CAPUT DRACONIS.

DRAGON'S TAIL See CAUDA DRACONIS.

DRYDEN, John (1631–1700) English poet and dramatist keenly interested in astrology; compiled BIRTH CHARTS for his sons.

DSCHUBBA Delta Scorpii, fifth brightest star in the zodiacal constellation SCORPIUS.

DUBHE Alpha Ursae Majoris, second brightest star in URSA MAJOR, brighter of the Pointers to the POLE STAR.

DUMB SIGNS CANCER, SCORPIO and PISCES; if MERCURY is afflicted or aspected by a MALEFIC in one of these signs, it is said to indicate a speech impediment.

DUMB-BELL NEBULA M 27, a splendid PLANETARY NEBULA in the constellation VULPECULA; given its name because of its spectacular shape.

DWAD Hindu astrological system which divides each zodiac sign by twelve, giving an ARC of 2.5°; astrological rules governing the significance, attributes and ruler of each dwad are similar to those for DECANS; used to help interpret DIRECTIONS (future trends). See also NAVAMSA.

DWADESHAMSA Term meaning 'one-twelfth'; applies both to division of zodiac circle and division of each sign into DWADS.

DYSIS Greek term marking the western ANGLE or point of setting in a horoscope, at the CUSP of the Seventh HOUSE; same as DESCENDANT.

DYSON, Frank Watson (1868–1939) Astronomer Royal from 1910 to 1933, recognized for his work on solar ECLIPSES.

EA Ancient Babylonian God known as the Antelope of the subterranean ocean, associated with the zodiac signs **CAPRICORN** and **AQUARIUS**.

EAGLE Name for the constellation **AQUILA**.

EARTH Third planet from the Sun; almost 150 million km/93 million miles distant, with an equitorial diameter of 12 756 km/7926 miles; Earth spins anticlockwise once on its axis every 23 hours 56 minutes 4 seconds and orbits the Sun in 365.26 days; the axis inclines 23.5° to the perpendicular.

EARTH See **ELEMENTS**.

EARTH SIGNS **TAURUS**, **VIRGO** and **CAPRICORN** share the **ELEMENT** Earth; people with these signs prominent in their **BIRTH CHART** tend to be practical and cautious.

EARTHSHINE Faint luminosity of the night side of the **CRESCENT MOON**, a result of light from Earth reflecting on to the Moon.

Earthrise, from Apollo 11

EAST **CARDINAL** point of the compass; the point where the Sun rises, highly significant in every culture.

EAST POINT Point where the horizon and **PRIME VERTICAL** intersect in the east.

EASTERN ANGLE Occasionally used as a name for the **ASCENDANT** or the **CUSP** of the **FIRST HOUSE**.

EBERTIN, Reinhold (b. 1901) Cosmobiologist and astrologer; proposes that activities in the cosmos have a direct effect on human biology.

ECCENTRICITY Measure of how far a planet's orbit deviates from the perfectly circular.

ECLIPSE The obscuring of one celestial body by another from an observer's point of view; a total eclipse blots out the whole of the body; partial eclipses (more common) obscure only part of the body.

ECLIPSE OF THALES Historic eclipse accurately predicted by **THALES OF MILETUS** on 28 May 585 BC, which called a halt to the last battle in war of attrition between the Medes and the Lydians, which had been going on for fifteen years.

ECLIPSING BINARY See **BINARY STAR**

ECLIPTIC The apparent annual path of the Sun round the Earth, passing through the twelve zodiacal constellations, so called because **ECLIPSES** occur along it; actually, the projection of the path of the Earth's orbit round the Sun on to the **CELESTIAL SPHERE**; the ecliptic forms an angle of 23.5° to the **CELESTIAL EQUATOR** because the Earth's axis tilts from the perpendicular to that degree. Astrologically, the ecliptic is imaginary centre line that runs down the middle of the zodiac pathway along which the planets travel.

ECLIPTIC LONGITUDE AND LATITUDE Treating the **ECLIPTIC** as the equator of the **CELESTIAL SPHERE**, 0° ecliptic longitude is the meridian between the poles of the ecliptic which passes through the point 0° **ARIES**. Measurements are made in degrees eastwards from this point. Ecliptic longitude is the form generally used by astrologers. Ecliptic latitude, also known as **CELESTIAL LATITUDE**, records positions in terms of degrees north or south of the ecliptic.

EDDINGTON, Sir Arthur (1882–1944) Theoretical astronomer, Director of Cambridge Observatory; his observations of the total **ECLIPSE** of 1919 confirmed **EINSTEIN'S** theory that light bends when caught in a gravitational field (in this case the Sun).

EDWARD VI (1537–1553) King of England from 1547: first patron of Dr John **DEE**, Astrologer Royal and alchemist.

Einstein at Mount Wilson

EGYPTIAN CALENDAR See **CALENDAR**

EIGHTH HOUSE Astrological **HOUSE** associated with eighth zodiac sign **SCORPIO** and ruled by **PLUTO**, now considered to be Scorpio's ruler; it governs long-term finance, shared assets, money from wills, legacies, stocks, shares and investments; also associated with big business and insurance; concerned with the life-force – birth, copulation and death, and attitudes to death and the afterlife; sometimes referred to as the 'House of Crime'!

EIGHTH SIGN OF THE ZODIAC See **SCORPIO**

80 URSAE MAJORIS The star **ALCOR**.

EINSTEIN, Albert (1879–1955) Greatest theoretical physicist of the century, and responsible for many fundamental advances in a wide variety of fields. His monument is the Theory of Relativity, a description of the universe in mathematical terms which would be constant no matter where the observer was positioned.

ELARA Seventh moon of **JUPITER**, discovered in 1905 by Charles **PERRINE**.

ELECTIONAL ASTROLOGY Astrological principles used to find the optimum time to initiate life-changing activities or events, such as starting a business or getting married.

ELECTRIC ASCENDANT Name given to the **ANTIVERTEX** (eastern end of the east-west axis through the birth place) by **JOHNDRO**.

ELECTROMAGNETIC RADIATION Energy released from charged **PARTICLES**, usually when they are accelerated; light, radio waves and X-rays are common examples of electromagnetic radiation; streams of particles called **PHOTONS** oscillate in waves perpendicularly to each other while travelling at the speed of light; just as sea waves rise and fall while making their way forward, so do electromagnetic waves; the distances between the 'wave peaks' indicates the wavelength, which can vary from the barely measurable (gamma rays) to several kilometres (longest radio waves); frequency is the number of waves that can pass a fixed point in one second; so short waves have a much higher frequency than long waves; the shorter the wavelength, the higher the energy of the photons that make it up.

ELECTRON Negatively charged **PARTICLE**.

ELEMENTS Air, Earth, Fire and Water are the four elements considered by **ARISTOTLE** and other ancient Greek philosophers such as **EMPEDOCLES** and **THALES** to be the building blocks of the Universe, each substance using the bricks in a different way or a different proportion. Astrologically, the four elements are shared out among the zodiac signs in a pattern fire–earth–air–water, starting with the first sign **ARIES**. The nature of each element is subtly altered by the **QUALITY** of the sign it governs.

ELEVATION The planet nearest to the **MIDHEAVEN** in a **BIRTH CHART** is elevated above the others and is therefore important.

Sir Arthur Evans

ELEVENTH HOUSE Astrological **HOUSE** associated with the eleventh sign of the zodiac, **AQUARIUS**, and ruled by **URANUS**, the ruler of Aquarius; the house of friendships, society and social life, clubs and societies, intellectual pleasures, and ideals.

ELEVENTH SIGN OF THE ZODIAC See **AQUARIUS**

ELLIPSE Elongated circle.

ELLIPTICAL ORBITS Non-circular orbits defined by Johannes **KEPLER** in the *Laws of Planetary Motion*; according to the first Law of Planetary Motion, planets move round the Sun in elliptical orbits.

ELONGATION Furthest **ANGULAR** distance of a planet from the Sun.

EMPEDOCLES (fl. fifth century BC) Greek philosopher living in Sicily who theorized that the four **ELEMENTS**; fire, water, earth and air; were 'continually in motion, sometimes becoming One through Love (that is, gravitational or magnetic attraction), but at others being torn asunder through Disharmony'; he considered the Universe to be spherical.

ENCELADUS Second reasonable-sized moon (500 km/ 310.5 miles across) among **SATURN**'s extensive satellites.

ENCKE'S COMET Discovered in 1818 by French astronomer Jean Louis **PONS**; has the shortest period of return (3.3 years) of any **COMET** and was named for Johann Franz Encke (1791–1865), who calculated its orbit.

ENIF Epsilon Pegasi, currently the brightest star in **PEGASUS**.

ENTRAIL DIVINATION Predicting future events by studying the entrails of freshly slaughtered animals; the state of the heart, liver and so on are examined. Popular with **ETRUSCANS** and Romans: may have had a zodiacal basis, but further than that it is difficult to establish exactly how it worked.

ENUMA ELISH Akkadian creation myth (the Akkads were a Semitic people from South Arabia who took over Sumerian civilization in Mesopotamia in about 3000 BC).

EOS In Greek mythology, goddess of the dawn; wife to **ASTRAEUS** and mother of the winds **BOREAS**, **NOTUS** and **ZEPHYRUS**. Identified with Roman Aurora.

EPHEMERAL MAP **CHART** erected for the time of an event; judged by **HORARY ASTROLOGY**.

EPHEMERIDES Plural of **EPHEMERIS**.

EPHEMERIS Printed details of the astronomical positions of the planets in the past and the future and other astrological and astronomical data essential for the correct construction of **CHARTS**; also used by astronomers and nautical navigators.

EPICYCLES Small circles used by **PTOLEMY** in an endeavour to explain planetary motion in a **GEOCENTRIC** universe; planets were thought to describe a succession of small circles centred on the path of a large circle (the **DEFERENT**) surrounding the Earth.

EPIMETHEUS One of the moons of **SATURN**; in Greek mythology the brother of Prometheus.

EPOCH Reference date chosen for comparing astronomical reference points; star positions logged in 'epoch 2000' will change slightly over the next few centuries.

EPSILON ORIONIS The star **ALNILAM**.

EPSILON URSAE MAJORIS The star **ALIOTH**.

EQUAL HOUSE SYSTEM See **HOUSE DIVISION**.

EQUATION OF TIME Difference between true **SOLAR TIME** and mean solar time; represented by **GREENWICH MEAN TIME** or Universal Time.

Entrail divination in the fourth century BC

EQUATOR Imaginary line girdling the Earth at 0° latitude and equidistant from North and South Poles; the **CELESTIAL EQUATOR** is a further imaginary projection of this line onto the **CELESTIAL SPHERE**.

EQUINOCTIAL YEAR Interval between successive passages of the Sun through the **VERNAL POINT** 0° **ARIES** (0° **LIBRA** in the southern hemisphere), a period of 365 days 5 hours 48 minutes and 46 seconds. Also called the Tropical Year.

EQUINOX The two occasions every year when the **ECLIPTIC**cuts the **CELESTIAL EQUATOR**; the Sun appears directly overhead at the **EQUATOR** and has no **DECLINATION**; days and nights are equally long. See also **AUTUMNAL EQUINOX**; **SPRING EQUINOX**

EQUINOX SIGNS **ARIES** and **LIBRA**.

EQUINOXES, Precession of The slow movement of the **VERNAL POINT** or **EQUINOX** clockwise along the **ECLIPTIC**. Every seventy-two years, the point slips 1°; when the vernal point was set by astronomers over 2 500 years ago, it was at 0° **ARIES**; although it is still referred to as the First Point of Aries it is in fact about to enter Aquarius.

EQUULEUS the Foal (or Colt) Small northern constellation; in mythology, represents the colt given to **CASTOR** by **MERCURY**.

ERATOSTHENES OF CYRENE (c276–c194 BC) Greek astronomer, mathematician, geographer and Chief Librarian at the Library and Museum of Alexandria; attempted to measure the circumference of the Earth (40 225 km/25 000 miles); he overestimated by roughly 6 000 km/4 000 miles.

ERDA Nordic goddess of the earth, also name given to the eldest of the Norns, the equivalent of the Greek **FATES**.

ERIDANUS, the River Huge constellation (one of **PTOLEMY'S** original forty-eight) that starts in the southern sky; contains **ACHERNAR** and **ACAMAR**; in mythology, Eridanus was a river god, associated with the River Po; **PHAETON** was supposed to have plunged to his death in here after losing control of the Sun's chariot.

ERIDU The world's oldest known city, founded by the Sumerians c5000 to 3000 BC on the Euphrates in Mesopotamia.

EROS **ASTEROID 433**, discovered in 1898. First known **MARS** approach asteroid. In Greek mythology, the god of love.

ESCAPE VELOCITY Speed needed to escape from the pull of a body's gravitational field.

ESSENTIAL RULERSHIP Astrological **HOUSES** are said to be ruled by the planet which rules the sign on its **CUSP**, but the planet ruling the sign corresponding to a house is called the essential or natural ruler of that house. **VENUS**, therefore, is the essential ruler of the Second and Seventh Houses because it rules the second and seventh signs, **TAURUS** and **LIBRA**.

ETA CARINAE Bright star in the constellation **CARINA**, partly obscured by the **HOMONCULUS NEBULA**.

ETA TAURI The star **ALCYONE**.

ETA URSAE MAJORIS The star **MIZAR**.

ETA VIRGINIS The star **ZANIAH**.

ETRUSCANS Ancient people of what is now northern Italy, whose sophisticated cities in Etruria (modern Tuscany) reached the height of their power c500 BC.

EUPHROSYNE **ASTEROID 31**: fifth largest of the known asteroids, diameter 370 km/230 miles; Euphrosyne was one of the three Graces.

EUROPA Smallest of the four main moons of **JUPITER**, slightly smaller than our own Moon; mysteriously smooth surface; orbits Jupiter in three and a half days. In mythology, Europa was the daughter of the king of Phoenicia whom **ZEUS** carried off, disguising himself as a white bull; she became the mother of Minos.

EVANS, Sir Arthur (1851–1941) British archaeologist whose excavation of Knossos, Crete, resulted in the discovery of the **MINOAN CIVILIZATION**.

EVECTION Inequality of the Moon's motion caused by slight changes in the shape of its orbit.

EVENING STAR **VENUS** at the greatest **ELONGATION** in the westerly direction.

EXALTATION Astrological term; each planet has a sign in which it is exalted, and when it is placed in that sign it is in exaltation.

EXCITATION, Law of One of the most exact and useful laws in astrology, dealing with the actual onset of a future event or trend, called a **DIRECTION**: 'If at the time that a progressed body is in **ASPECT** to another by direction, and either of these bodies forms an aspect by **TRANSIT**, with either of the two directional bodies, then this transit will excite the direction into immediate operation.' For example, if the progressed Sun in 0° **CANCER** is in **TRINE** to **JUPITER** in 0° **SCORPIO**, then any transit of the Sun or Jupiter, over any point in aspect with 0° Cancer, or 0° Scorpio will cause the direction to act.

EXOSPHERE Outermost part of the Earth's **ATMOSPHERE**.

EYSENCK, Hans Jurgen (b. 1916) Controversial psychologist who emphasizes the role of heredity rather than environment in intelligence. Worked with Michel **GAUQUELIN** on the statistical correlation between astrological data and personality types: results published in 1981 in *Personality and Individual Differences* indicated a strong connection between introverts and the prominence of **SATURN'S** influence in the **BIRTH CHART**, and extroverts and the prominence of **JUPITER** and **MARS**.

An ephemeris for 1701

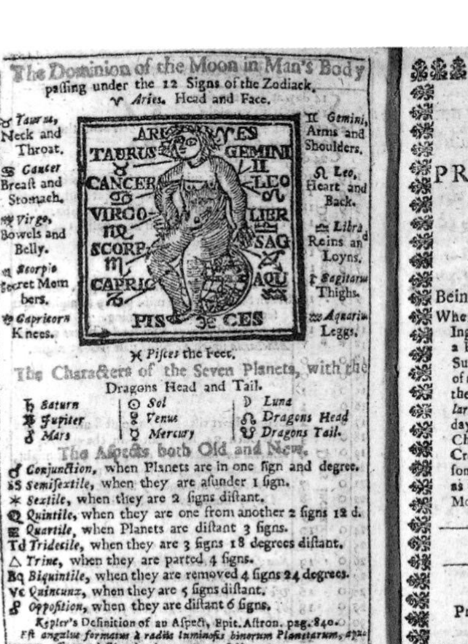

The Dominion of the Moon in Man's Body passing under the 12 Signs of the Zodiack.

♈ *Aries*. Head and Face.

♉ *Taurus*, Neck and Throat.
♊ *Gemini*, Arms and Shoulders.
♋ *Cancer* Breast and Stomach.
♌ *Leo*, Heart and Back.
♍ *Virgo*, Bowels and Belly.
♎ *Libra* Reins and Loyns.
♏ *Scorpio* Secret Members.
♐ *Sagitarius* Thighs.
♑ *Capricorn* Knees.
♒ *Aquarius* Leggs.

ARIES TAURUS GEMINI CANCER LEO VIRGO LIBER SCORP SAG CAPRIC AQU PISCES

♓ *Pisces* the Feet.

The Characters of the Seven Planets, with the Dragons Head and Tail.

♄ *Saturn*	☉ *Sol*	☽ *Luna*
♃ *Jupiter*	♀ *Venus*	☊ *Dragons Head*
♂ *Mars*	☿ *Mercury*	☋ *Dragons Tail.*

The Aspects both Old and New.

☌ *Conjunction*, when Planets are in one sign and degree.
SS *Semisextile*, when they are asunder 1 sign.
✶ *Sextile*, when they are 2 signs distant.
Q *Quintile*, when they are one from another 2 signs 12 d.
□ *Quartile*, when Planets are distant 3 signs.
Td *Tridecile*, when they are 3 signs 18 degrees distant.
△ *Trine*, when they are parted 4 signs.
Bq *Biquintile*, when they are removed 4 signs 24 degrees.
Vc *Quincunx*, when they are 5 signs distant.
☍ *Opposition*, when they are distant 6 signs.

Kepler's Definition of an Aspect, Epit. Astron. pag. 840.
Est angulus formatus à radiis luminosis binorum Planetarum, apud terram, efficax ad stimulandam naturam sublunarem.

WING

WING.
A
PROGNOSTICATION,
for the Year of our
LORD GOD
1701.
Being the 1st after Bissextile or Leap-year:
Wherein is contained the time of the Sun's Ingress into the Four Cardinal Signs, with a Figure of the Heavens at the time of the Sun's Ingress into *Aries*, with the Calculation of a visible *Lunar* Eclipse, all Calculated from the Tables lately published in my *Scientia Stellarum*. A Table shewing the hour of the day by a Rod, or hand stick, also a pleasant Chronology of memorable things since the Creation of the World, to all which is added some useful things for the Information of such as understand not the motions of the Sun and Moon.

By *John Wing*, Math.

CAMBRIDGE,
Printed by *John Hayes*, Printer to the University, 1701.

FACE Defined by Alan **LEO** as the sixth part (5°) of a zodiac sign, or half a **DECAN**; just as the decans represent different aspects of a sign and have different rulers, so do the faces; interpretation of the faces is important when a very detailed **CHART** is requested. The use of faces has fallen out of favour somewhat, but is still of interest to astrological students.

FACULAE Bright patches on the Sun associated with **SUNSPOTS**; appear just before a spot breaks out, and generally persist for a time after the spot has vanished.

FACULTY OF ASTROLOGICAL STUDIES, Sussex, England; founded in 1948, under the presidency of Charles **CARTER**: has trained students in most countries of the world.

Alan Leo's explanation of faces

FALL Astrological term describing a planet placed in the sign opposite its sign of **EXALTATION**; a planet so placed is said to be weak in its effects.

FALLOWS, Fearon (1789–1831) Born in Cumberland, England; in 1821 established the Royal Observatory at the Cape of Good Hope, South Africa (now the South African Astronomical Observatory).

FALSE CROSS Large symmetrical pattern formed in the southern sky by the stars Iota and Epsilon Carinae (of the constellation **CARINA**) and Kappa and Delta Velorum (of the constellation **VELA**).

FAMILIARITY Term used by **PTOLEMY** to indicate an **ASPECT** or parallel between two bodies, or their mutual disposition, as when each is in the other's zodiac sign or **HOUSE**.

FATALISM See **DETERMINISM**

FATES Greek (and later Roman) myth to explain the individual patterns of birth, life and death; the Three Fates (also known as the Moirae to the Greeks and the Parcae to the Romans) were **CLOTHO** (spinner of life's thread); **LACHESIS** (who measured it) and **ATROPOS** (who cut it); possibly originally symbolic of the phases of the Moon. Fate herself was Moira, the oldest power in the Universe.

The Fates, by Michelangelo

FAUNUS Roman equivalent of Greek **PAN**; half man, half goat, god of woods, fields, flocks and shepherds.

F-CORONA Outer part of the Solar **CORONA**; extends for several million kilometres, eventually merges with interplanetary dust and particles, producing the **ZODIACAL LIGHT**.

FEBRUARY Second month of **GREGORIAN CALENDAR**; perhaps named from the latin *februa*, a feast of purification.

FEMININE SIGNS Traditionally, **TAURUS, CANCER, VIRGO, SCORPIO, CAPRICORN** and **PISCES**, the 'even' zodiac signs representing **EARTH** and **WATER**; said to be in principle reserved and receptive.

FIDDLER CRAB Prime example of the effect of events in the Solar System on the biology of life forms on Earth; the fiddler crab changes colour in accordance with the position of the Moon.

FIDUCIAL Prescribed reference point, often associated with a **FIXED STAR**, used as a marker to make comparative measurements; used in **SIDEREAL** astrology.

FIFTH HOUSE Astrological **HOUSE** associated with fifth zodiac sign **LEO** and ruled by the Sun; traditionally known as a fortunate house, as it is in **TRINE** (120° favourable **ASPECT**) with the **FIRST HOUSE**; represents pleasure, holidays, social life, affairs of the heart, children, new enterprises, speculation, and games of chance; source of strength, energy, and enthusiasm to enjoy the opportunities and happiness available in life.

FIFTH SIGN OF THE ZODIAC See **LEO**

FIGURE Alternative name for astrological **CHART**.

FINGER OF FATE Also called the Finger of God; its astrological name is a **YOD**. A complex **ASPECT** consisting of two **QUINCUNXES** to a single planet. A quincunx is a fairly weak 150° aspect; its effect in a **CHART** could cause indecision in matters concerning the planet at the focal point.

FIRE See **ELEMENTS**

FIREBRACE, Brigadier Roy See **ASTROLOGICAL ASSOCIATION**.

FIRE SIGNS **ARIES, LEO** and **SAGITTARIUS**; also known as the Fire **TRIPLICITIES**.

FIRE TRIANGLE The three **FIRE** signs: **ARIES, LEO** and **SAGITTARIUS**.

FIRMAMENT Ancient astronomical term for the heavenly **SPHERE** of the **FIXED STARS**.

FIRST HOUSE Astrological **HOUSE** associated with the first zodiac sign **ARIES** and ruled by **MARS**; contributes, with other factors, to the personality, disposition, temperament, physical body, health and appearance of the subject.

An Etruscan version of Pan

FIRST POINT OF ARIES Agreed 'beginning' of the **TROPICAL ZODIAC** and **ECLIPTIC**; 0° **ARIES**; once coincided with the northern hemisphere's **VERNAL EQUINOX**, but this has now slipped backwards (see **PRECESSION OF THE EQUINOXES**); used by astronomers and astrologers alike as a reference point, but known to astrology as **ABSOLUTE LONGITUDE**.

FIRST POINT OF LIBRA 0° **LIBRA**; point opposite the **FIRST POINT OF ARIES** which once coincided with the northern hemisphere's **AUTUMNAL EQUINOX** when the Sun passes into the southern hemisphere.

FIRST SIGN OF THE ZODIAC See **ARIES**

FISHES Symbol for **PISCES**.

FIXED CROSS Rare and powerful **ASPECT**; a **GRAND CROSS** formed by four planets making two **OPPOSITIONS** in the **FIXED SIGNS** on a **BIRTH CHART**; interpretation depends on the planets concerned.

FIXED INCREMENT DIRECTIONS Symbolic method of progressing a chart not based on any astronomical motion of the planets or **HOUSES**; a fixed annual increment is added to all factors including the **ANGLES**; this is a very ancient method of **PROGRESSION** and appears to be as satisfactory as more difficult systems.

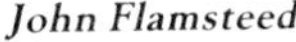

John Flamsteed

FIXED SIGNS **TAURUS, LEO, SCORPIO** and **AQUARIUS**. Fixed sign subjects show tenacity of purpose, fixed opinions, and resistance to change.

FIXED STARS Stars of the constellations, so far from Earth that they appear to be stationary; the brightest of the fixed stars, visible to the naked eye, were considered by ancient astrologers to be important in a **HOROSCOPE**.

FLAMSTEED, John (1646–1719) First Astronomer Royal, appointed by Charles II in 1675; his observatory, Flamsteed House (designed by Sir Christopher Wren), is now part of the National Maritime Museum at **GREENWICH**.

FLARES, Solar See **SOLAR FLARES**.

FLARE STARS Faint **RED DWARFS** which show sudden short-lived increases in brilliance lasting

Flora receiving tribute
Background: flowers for Aquarius

any time from a minute to an hour, possibly due to intense flares above their surfaces.

FLORA ASTEROID 8 discovered in 1847; in Roman mythology, the goddess of flowers, youth and spring.

FLORENCE In medieval times, Florence boasted an official city astrologer, appointed to study the city's progress .

FLOWERS AND ZODIAC SIGNS Relationships between flowers, plants and zodiac signs tend to be arbitrary, but the following selection seems appropriate: ARIES – Red Geranium, Nasturtium, Honeysuckle, Gorse, Thistle; TAURUS – Red Rose, Coltsfoot or Bull's foot, Cypress, Cherry; GEMINI – Iris, Fleur-de-Lys, Ferns and Nut trees; CANCER – Honesty or Moonwort, Lily of the Valley, Silver Birch; LEO – Marigold, Sunflower, Heliotrope, Bay tree; VIRGO – Rosemary, Cornflowers and the Elder tree; LIBRA – The White Rose, Love in the Mist, Chinese Cherry; SCORPIO – Red Peony, Red Poppy, Holly and Firethorn; SAGITTARIUS – Pinks, Sage, Chestnut and Mulberry trees; CAPRICORN – Snowdrop, Hemlock, Pine and Blackthorn; AQUARIUS – Orchids, Blue Gentian, Lime and Lemon trees; PISCES – Opium Poppy, Water-Lily, Willow tree.

FLY Name for the constellation MUSCA.

FLYING FISH Name for the constellation VOLANS.

FLYING HORSE Alternative name for the constellation PEGASUS.

FOAL Name for the constellation EQUULEUS.

FOMALHOUT Alpha Piscis Austrini in the southern constellation PISCIS AUSTRINUS; known to astronomers as one of the FOUR WATCHERS OF THE HEAVENS.

FORNAX, the Furnace Southern constellation once known as Fornax Chemica, the Chemical Furnace; contains several galaxies.

FORTIFIED Astrological term applied to a planet when it is strongly placed, that is in EXALTATION in a congenial zodiac sign or well aspected (see ASPECTS).

FORTUNA Most familiar of the ARABIC POINTS, also known as Pars Fortuna or Part of Fortune, or Fortuna; calculated in a CHART by adding together the ABSOLUTE LONGITUDES of the ASCENDANT and the Moon and subtracting that of the Sun (360° can be added or subtracted if this is necessary, to bring the result into the range of 0–360). Fortuna is said to indicate, by its sign and HOUSE position, how best to adapt to circumstances and find the right way to adjust inner hopes to outer needs.

FORTUNE TELLING Attempts to predict actual events; reputable astrologers dissociate themselves from fortune telling, preferring to forecast trends rather than specific happenings.

FOUNDATION FOR THE STUDY OF CYCLES American institution which collects and correlates statistical information on the cyclical nature of almost all activities on Earth; results published in the journal *Cycles*. See also E.R. DEWEY.

FOUR-FOOTED SIGNS Traditionally, ARIES, TAURUS, LEO, SAGITTARIUS and CAPRICORN.

FOURTH HOUSE Astrological HOUSE associated with the fourth zodiac sign CANCER and ruled by the Moon; concerns home and private life, and is associated with houses and land; is also involved with the beginning and end of life, birth and death.

FOURTH ZODIAC SIGN See CANCER

FOUR WATCHERS OF THE HEAVENS Ancient name for the four very bright FIXED STARS ALDEBARAN, ANTARES, FOMALHOUT and REGULUS: they form a square in the sky, with Antares at the west point, Aldebaran at the east, Fomalhout at the south and Regulus at the north; when they were first named, they were positioned at the EQUINOCTIAL and SOLSTICIAL points, but the PRECESSION OF THE EQUINOXES and the slow movement of the fixed stars means that this is no longer the case; also known as the Guardians of the Heavens and the Royal Stars.

FOWLER, Alfred (1868–1940) English astronomer, specialized in spectroscopic work.

FOX Name for the constellation VULPECULA.

FREYJA Another name for FRIGG or FRIGGA.

FRANKLIN-ADAMS, John (1843–1912) English amateur astronomer who made the first photographic star map of the entire sky, which became the standard astronomical chart for more than fifty years following its publication in 1913–14.

FRAUNHOFER LINES Dark lines in the Sun's spectrum caused by absorption of some of the wavelengths in the cooler parts of the solar atmosphere; named for their first observer, Joseph von Fraunhofer (1787–1826).

FRIDAY Sixth day of the week; named for FREYJA in germanic languages and VENUS in latin languages.

FRIGGA ASTEROID discovered 12 November 1862; named for the Scandinavian goddess Frigg, equated with VENUS and wife of ODIN.

FULL MOON Phase of the Moon when it is opposite the Sun, and therefore its whole disc is illuminated; in astronomy, alternative beginning point of a LUNATION; astrologically less important than a NEW MOON, unless it falls in a sensitive place in a CHART.

FURNACE Name for the constellation FORNAX.

GAEA OR GE Greek goddess of Earth, who evolved spontaneously from formless chaos, gave birth to **URANUS** (the Heavens) and Pontus (the Sea); coupled with Uranus to produce the Giants, the one-eyed Cylopes and the **TITANS**.

GALACTIC CENTRE Gravitational centre of the **MILKY WAY** and source of intense radio emission; located in the direction of **SAGITTARIUS**, some 30000 **LIGHT YEARS** from Earth; very densely packed and difficult to study. See also **SAGITTARIUS A**.

GALACTIC HALO Spherical-shaped collection of old stars and globular clusters surrounding the nucleus and main part of the **GALAXY**; it is the 'ghost' of the original gas cloud from which the galaxy coalesced.

GALACTIC NEBULAE Birth place of the stars; clouds of dust and gas out of which new stars condense; also known as Gaseous Nebulae; a good example is the Great Nebula (M42) in the 'Sword' of **ORION**.

GALACTIC POINT Point where the plane of the Solar System cuts the plane of our **GALAXY**.

GALATEA **ASTEROID** in the first group of 100 to be discovered; first observed in August 1862 by German astronomer Ernst Tempel. In Greek mythology, Galatea was a sea-nymph, in love with the beautiful Acis and beloved by the jealous cyclops Polyphemus.

GALAXY Complete star system containing billions of stars; our home galaxy is the **MILKY WAY**; over three million are visible, but few of these have yet been classified. There are five main types of galaxies: **BARRED SPIRALS**, **ELLIPTICAL**, **IRREGULAR**, **LENTICULAR**, and **SPIRAL**.

GALEN (Claudius Galenus) (fl. AD 130–201) Greek physician and philosopher; founded experimental physiology, and was interested in the use of astrology in the treatment of diseases.

GALILEAN SATELLITES OF JUPITER Four largest satellites of **JUPITER: CALLISTO, EUROPA, GANYMEDE** and **IO**; first seen by **GALILEO** through his **TELESCOPE** in 1609; they are the middle group of the sixteen known Jupiter moons or satellites which orbit almost level with the planet's equatorial plant.

The Galactic Centre, Sagittarius A

GALILEO (Galileo Galilei) (1564–1642) Italian mathematician, astronomer and physicist, born at Pisa; Professor of Mathematics at the University of Pisa until 1591, when he took up the same post in Padua; great critic of **ARISTOTLE'S** theories; first to realize the astronomical potential of the newly invented **TELESCOPE**, built his own (1609) and made great improvements on the original; made observations of the Sun and **SUNSPOTS**, the craters and mountains of the Moon, the phases of **VENUS** and the larger satellites of **JUPITER** among other things, all of which led him to conclude that Aristotle had been wrong and that the Sun, not the Earth, was the centre of the Solar System; this confirmed the mathematical theories of **COPERNICUS**, but went against theological teaching based on ancient and venerable authority (**PTOLEMY**).

GALLE, Johann Gottfried (1812–1910) German astronomer; together with **D'ARREST** located **NEPTUNE** in September 1846; first (1873) to use an **ASTEROID** (**FLORA**) to determine solar **PARALLAX**.

GALTON, Sir Francis (1822–1921) Cousin of Charles Darwin, trained as a medical doctor; made great study of heredity and theorized on the relationship between lines and patterns on the palms of the hands and congenital disorders.

GAMMA ANDROMEDAE The star **ALMAAK**.

GAMMA AQUILAE The star **TARAZED**.

GAMMA AURIGAE Former designation for **ALNATH**, now classified as Beta Tauri.

GAMMA BOÖTIS The star **SEGINUS**.

GAMMA GEMINORUM The star **ALHENA**.

Zeus abducting Ganymede

GAMMA LEONIS The star **ALGIEBA**.

GAMMA LYRAE The star **SULAPHAT**.

GAMMA PEGASI The star **ALGENIB**.

GAMMA RAYS High frequency intense called **X-RAYS**; **ELECTRO-MAGNETIC RADIATION** of extremely short wavelength and high frequency.

GAMMA URSAE MAJORIS The star **PHAD**.

GANYMED **ASTEROID 1036**, one of the **AMOR** group, discovered by **BAADE** in 1924; 35 km/22 miles across, probably the largest of the close approach asteroids.

GANYMEDE One of the **GALILEAN SATELLITES OF JUPITER**, largest known satellite in the Solar

System (diameter 5 276 km/3 280 miles), larger than MERCURY or PLUTO; orbits JUPITER once every 7.15 days. In Greek mythology Ganymede was handsome youth abducted by a besotted ZEUS to be cup-bearer to the gods on Olympus.

GARNET STAR Mu Cephei, a bright red VARIABLE star in the constellation CEPHEUS.

GASEOUS NEBULAE See GALACTIC NEBULAE.

GASSENDI, Pierre (1592–1655) French astronomer, friend of GALILEO and KEPLER; biographer of Tycho BRAHE, COPERNICUS and REGIOMONTANUS; made the first recorded observations (in 1631) of a TRANSIT of MERCURY across the face of the Sun.

GAUQUELIN, Professor Michel (b. 1928) French psychologist and statistician who has researched into the statistical correlation of birth data and character as interpreted astrologically.

GAUSS, Karl Friedrich (1777–1855) German mathematician and physicist; calculated the orbit of the first ASTEROID discovered, CERES, in 1801; did much work on magnetism and magnetic fields and gave his name to a measurement of magnetism.

GAUSS UNIT Measurement of a magnetic field; Earth has a weak magnetic field varying from 0.3 to 0.6 gauss. Named for Karl Friedrich GAUSS.

GEB Egyptian god of the Earth, the twin and lover of sky goddess NUT; depicted as impregnating NUT with the stars.

GEGENSCHEIN See ZODIACAL LIGHT.

GEMINI, the Twins Brilliant zodiacal constellation in the northern sky, one of PTOLEMY'S original list; its ALPHA, CASTOR is now secondary in brightness to the beta (POLLUX); there are eleven other stars above fourth MAGNITUDE and the MILKY WAY crosses it. **Gemini the zodiac sign** is

Ptolemy's geocentric Solar System

the third sign of the zodiac, a MUTABLE AIR sign ruled by MERCURY. JUPITER is in DETRIMENT in Gemini. The **Gemini myth** centres on the twin sons of LEDA and ZEUS, Castor (Castor the mortal) and Pollux (the immortal); when Castor was slain in battle, Pollux was grief-stricken; Zeus immortalized both brothers and placed them in the heavens.

GEM STONES AND THE ZODIAC See BIRTH STONES

GENETHLIALOGY Branch of astrology that deals with the interpretation of the BIRTH CHART.

GENITURE Alternative name for BIRTH CHART or NATIVITY

GEOARC Term applied to one of the HOUSE DIVISIONS of a CHART erected for a given moment to consider the effect on an individual relative to the daily orbit of a given point on the Earth's periphery.

GEOCENTRIC Earth-centred; until COPERNICUS, it was believed that the bodies in the Solar System orbited in a complex manner about the still Earth in the centre, a theory first fully formulated by ARISTOTLE and handed on by PTOLEMY via HIPPARCHUS. Astrology is based on a geocentric world view as it deals with the influence of the celestial bodies on the inhabitants of Earth, therefore the fact that the Earth goes round the Sun, and not vice versa.

GEOCENTRIC EPHEMERIS EPHEMERIS that gives positions of the planets and other astronomical information from an Earth-centred viewpoint.

GEOGRAPHICAL LATITUDE See LATITUDE

GEOGRAPHICAL LONGITUDE See LONGITUDE

GEOMANCY Divination of the underlying geometric forces of the Earth.

GEORGIAN PLANET Obsolete name for URANUS; given to the planet by its discoverer HERSCHEL in 1782, in honour of his patron George III.

GEOSTATIONARY Describes an orbit in which a satellite appears to hang stationary over a point on its PRIMARY'S equator; also called synchronous, because to appear stationary a satellite would have to be orbiting at the same rate as its primary.

GIBBOUS Describes the phase of the Moon or an INFERIOR PLANET half way through its cycle.

GIENAH Epsilon Cygni, third brightest star in the northern constellation CYGNUS.

GIRAFFE Name for the constellation CAMELOPARDALIS.

GIRTAB Kappa Scorpii, sixth brightest star in the constellation SCORPIUS and part of the Scorpion's distinctive 'sting' (the other two stars are SHAULA and LESATH).

Background: Geomantic centre of the Islamic world

GIVER OF LIFE See HYLEG

GLOBULAR CLUSTERS Symmetrical star systems containing up to a million stars; unlike constellations, stars in a globular cluster are all at the same distance from an observer and all evolved at the same time; they are the oldest inhabitants of any GALAXY.

GLYPHS Astrological symbols identifying the zodiac signs, celestial bodies and ASPECTS; also known as a sigil; possibly originated from the ideograms of the Egyptians or the symbols used on clay tablets by early Mesopotamian astrologers. Glyphs are used as convenient shorthand.

GNOMON Ancient instrument (usually a perpendicular column) for determining the altitude of the Sun, the principle of which was passed from the Babylonians to the Greeks; also the pointer which casts the Sun's shadow onto a SUNDIAL: it always points to the CELESTIAL POLE.

GNOSTICS Breakaway heretical Christian sects of the second century; the name derives from the Greek *gnosis* meaning knowledge, interpreted as meaning special knowledge revealed in a mystical revelation to the gnostics alone; gnostics considered all physical matter inherently evil.

GOAT Symbol for the zodiac sign CAPRICORN.

GRAFFIAS Beta Scorpii, currently the seventh brightest star in the zodiacal constellation SCORPIUS.

GRAND CROSS Rare astrological configuration which occurs when there are two sets of OPPOSITIONS in SQUARE to each other in a CHART; oppositions can be considered as either opposing or challenging, but interpretation depends on the planets and signs involved.

GRAND TRINE Powerful ASPECT pattern in a CHART occurring when three planets form

three **TRINES**, one with the other; a trine is considered a good aspect, but interpretation depends on the planets and signs involved.

GRAPHOLOGY Study of character from the shape and flow of handwriting.

GRAVING TOOL Name for the constellation **CAELUM**.

GRAVITY Mutual attraction between masses; defined by Sir Isaac **NEWTON** in 1697 as a force between any two masses proportional to the product of the masses and inversely proportional to the square of the distance between them. All masses are positively charged and therefore constantly attract all other masses, which is why the planets do not fly out of their orbits round the Sun and why they can affect each other.

GREAT BEAR See **URSA MAJOR**

GREAT CIRCLES Imaginary circles projected on to the **CELESTIAL SPHERE**, used by astrologers and astronomers to plot positions of the stars and planets.

The brass bar marking the Greenwich meridian

GREAT DOG See **CANIS MAJOR**

GREAT RED SPOT Most outstanding and famous feature of the planet **JUPITER**: first observed by Robert Hooke (1635–1703) in 1664, it is a huge swirling weather system – at its largest, 40 000 km/25 000 miles long and 11,200 km/7 000 miles wide, almost the same surface area as Earth.

GREAT YEAR Period of approximately 26 000 years, the time it takes for the **CELESTIAL NORTH POLE** to describe a complete circle in the heavens, and for **VERNAL POINT** to pass westwards through each of the twelve zodiac signs (see **PRECESSION OF THE EQUINOXES**); the period spent in each sign (approximately 2 160 years) is known as a 'Great Month'. See also **PLATONIC YEAR**.

GREATER BENEFIC Astrologically, the planet **JUPITER**. See also **BENEFIC**.

GREATEST ELONGATION See **ELONGATION**

GREEK ALPHABET Used by Joseph **BAYER** in 1603 to classify the stars of a constellation in terms of their **MAGNITUDE**; as there are only twenty-four letters in the Greek alphabet, other systems had to be devised to name stars in very rich constellations, or the 'new' discoveries that sprang into vision through the **TELESCOPE**. See also **ALPHA**; **CLASSIFICATION OF STARS**.

GREEN, Charles (1735–1771) English astronomer who accompanied the explorer Captain Cook on his journeys, in order to study the 1769 **TRANSIT** of **VENUS**.

GREEN FLASH Brief but vivid flash of green seen on clear summer days just before the Sun disappears below the horizon, occasionally just before it rises; the flash lasts longer in polar regions; produced by a side effect of local variations in the Earth's atmosphere.

GREENWICH MEAN TIME (GMT) Standard time in Britain and Western Europe; the mean solar time on the **PRIME MERIDIAN** (longitude 0°) chosen by the members of the International Meridian Conference in 1884 as the line running through the centre of the observatory at Greenwich, in London; time zones are measured in whole hours east and west of the prime meridian: eastern times are ahead, western times are behind. Also known as Universal Time. See also **LONGITUDE**.

GREENWICH ROYAL OBSERVATORY Established in 1675 under the patronage of Charles II, principally to improve navigational systems by finding a reliable way to fix **LONGITUDE** from a ship in motion; first forty-three years under the directorship of the first Astronomer Royal, John **FLAMSTEED**, but there was not enough data to produce an efficient nautical almanac until 1766, under Nevil Maskelyne, the fifth Astronomer Royal. After that, Greenwich devoted itself to tracking the motion and position of heavenly bodies until late into the nineteenth century, when Sir William **CHRISTIE** introduced modern instruments enabling researchers to study the nature as well as the movements of stars and planets; in 1948, the instrumentation was moved to Herstmonceux Castle in Sussex, England; this has proved unsatisfactory and in 1990 the observatory was re-established in Cambridge, England; the original Wren buildings at Greenwich are now a museum. See also **LA PALMA OBSERVATORY**.

GREGORIAN CALENDAR See **CALENDAR, GREGORIAN**

GRIMALDI, Francesco Maria (1618–1663) Italian physicist, Professor of Mathematics at **BOLOGNA**; discovered the refraction of light and formulated a wave theory to explain the movement of light.

GRUS, the Crane Distinctive constellation, one of the **SOUTHERN BIRDS**; its bright, white **ALPHA**, Alnair, is 230 times as luminous as the Sun and the beta, Al Dhanab appears orange coloured.

GUARDIANS OF THE HEAVENS See **FOUR WATCHERS OF THE HEAVENS**

HADES In Greek mythology, lord of the Underworld, brother of ZEUS; called DIS by the Romans; also known as PLUTO, which means wealth, as he owned all the gold and precious metals in the Earth.

HAEDI Eta, Zeta, and Epsilon Aurigae, a triangular pattern of stars in the constellation AURIGA, near the ALPHA, CAPELLA; the name means 'kids'.

HALE, George Ellery (1868–1938) American astronomer, inventor of the spectroheliograph (1892), who discovered the magnetic fields of SUNSPOTS; organized the finance for the establishment of several large TELESCOPES, notably at YERKES, MOUNT WILSON and MOUNT PALOMAR, of which he was the first Director in 1934.

HALE OBSERVATORIES Discontinued name for the observatories at MOUNT WILSON and MOUNT PALOMAR.

HALL, Asaph (1829–1907) American astronomer who discovered the two moons of MARS, DEIMOS and PHOBOS, in 1877.

HALLEY, Edmond (1656–1743) Astronomer Royal in 1720; best remembered for his COMET; also studied the motion of stars, the gaseous nature of NEBULAE, METEORS, planetary orbits and ECLIPSES; determined the distance of the Sun from the TRANSITS of VENUS.

HALLEY'S COMET Comet visible to the naked eye; has been observed all over the world for 3 000 years or more; named for Edmond HALLEY, who plotted its elliptical orbit round the Sun, and correctly predicted its return every seventy-six years.

HAMAL Alpha Arietis, in the zodiacal constellation ARIES.

HARDING, Karl Ludwig (1765–1834) German astronomer, Professor of Astronomy at the University of Göttingen, compiler of a star atlas and discoverer of ASTEROID JUNO.

HARE Name for the constellation LEPUS.

HARMONIA ASTEROID 40, discovered 31 March 1856 by Hermann Goldschmidt (1802–1866).

HARMONIC ASTROLOGICAL CHART BIRTH CHART drawn up according to the HARMONICS theories of John ADDEY; the natal positions of the planets have to be converted to ABSOLUTE LONGITUDE before the chart can be drawn up.

Will Hay, entertaining amateur astronomer

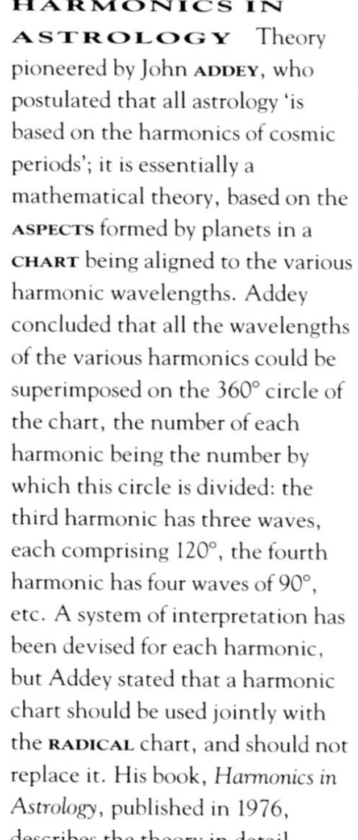

HARMONICS IN ASTROLOGY Theory pioneered by John ADDEY, who postulated that all astrology 'is based on the harmonics of cosmic periods'; it is essentially a mathematical theory, based on the ASPECTS formed by planets in a CHART being aligned to the various harmonic wavelengths. Addey concluded that all the wavelengths of the various harmonics could be superimposed on the 360° circle of the chart, the number of each harmonic being the number by which this circle is divided: the third harmonic has three waves, each comprising 120°, the fourth harmonic has four waves of 90°, etc. A system of interpretation has been devised for each harmonic, but Addey stated that a harmonic chart should be used jointly with the RADICAL chart, and should not replace it. His book, *Harmonics in Astrology*, published in 1976, describes the theory in detail.

HARMONY OF THE SPHERES See MUSIC OF THE SPHERES

HARRIOT, Thomas (1560–1621) English astronomer and mathematician, tutor to Sir Walter Raleigh; began making observations by TELESCOPE at the same time as GALILEO, studied the moons of JUPITER and made the first map of the Moon.

HARVEST MOON In the northern hemisphere, the FULL MOON nearest to the AUTUMNAL EQUINOX.

HATHOR ASTEROID 2340, tiny celestial object only a few kilometres across, discovered in 1976 at MOUNT PALOMAR: in Egyptian mythology, a goddess of love and fertility.

HAWKEYE SCIENTIFIC SATELLITE Launched on 3 June 1974 into a highly elliptical polar orbit around the Earth, to collect data concerning the interaction of the SOLAR WIND and the Earth's MAGNETOSPHERE.

HAY, Will (1888–1949) Popular professional stage and film comedian, and a keen amateur astronomer; in 1933 discovered the white spot, named after him, on SATURN.

HEBE ASTEROID 6, discovered in July 1847 by Karl Ludwig HENCKE; in Greek mythology, the daughter of ZEUS and HERA, cup-bearer to the gods until replaced by GANYMEDE.

HECABA OR HECUBA ASTEROID 108 of the TROJAN group; in Trojan legend, second wife to King Priam and mother of nineteen of his fifty children, including HECTOR, Paris, Helenus and Cassandra; mother of TROILUS by APOLLO.

HECATE ASTEROID 100, discovered in July 1868; in Greek mythology, companion to Persephone, honoured by ZEUS and the Olympian gods as a dreaded divinity who consorted with dead souls.

HECTOR ASTEROID 624 in the TROJAN group, twice the size of the others and shaped like a dumb-bell; in Trojan legend, son of King Priam, a great hero, murdered by ACHILLES.

HEIS, Eduard (1806–1877) German astronomer, expert on VARIABLE STARS and authority on ZODIACAL LIGHT.

HELEN In Trojan legend, daughter of ZEUS and LEDA, sister of CASTOR and POLLUX, reputed to be the most beautiful woman in the world; although married to Menelaus, King of Sparta, eloped with Paris, Prince of Troy, and sparked off the interminable Trojan Wars.

HELENE Small satellite of SATURN, discovered in 1980; co-orbital with DIONE, which is almost four times its size.

HELIACAL RISING Rising of a celestial body at the same time as the Sun; also used to denote the time when a body is first visible in the dawn sky.

HELICON In Greek mythology, the home of APOLLO and the MUSES; one peak of MOUNT

Helen abducted by Paris

PARNASSUS, containing the sacred springs Aganippe and Hippocrene.

HELIOCENTRIC Sun-centred.

HELIOCENTRIC ASTROLOGY Interpretation of a BIRTH CHART drawn up to show the true positions of the planets, relative to the Sun as centre; in practice this usually only affects the smaller, fast-moving planets and the Moon. These positions give a true picture of the pure Ego, the Real Self, before it becomes modified by the character-forming patterns of the GEOCENTRIC positions, that guide, bend or distort the original energies emanating from the Sun when they reach the point on Earth where the subject is born. Very helpful in MUNDANE ASTROLOGY, which involves mass psychology; especially interesting when working with TRANSITS, in the case of the slower-moving, outer planets, and will often explain the prolonged effects of these transits, as a planet moves between the heliocentric and geocentric positions. Heliocentric EPHEMERIDES giving the positions of the planets from 1800 to the year 2000 are available for astrological study.

HELIOCENTRIC BIRTH CHART Drawn up from HELIOCENTRIC EPHEMERIDES and shows the true position and movements of the planets; there is no RETROGRADE MOTION in a heliocentric chart.

HELIOCENTRIC EPHEMERIS EPHEMERIS which gives positions of the planets and other astronomical information from a Sun-centred viewpoint.

HELIOCENTRIC THEORY Theory that the planets revolve around the Sun, and not the Earth, first put forward by Greek philosopher ARISTARCHUS in the third century BC, and promptly dismissed; next advanced almost 1600 years later by Nicholas COPERNICUS in *De Revolutionbus Orbium Coelestium* (1543); his theory was purely mathematical, but was supported by the empirical observations of GALILEO. The theory was not universally accepted until KEPLER formulated his laws of motion (1609–1618).

HELIOPOLIS The City of the Sun, a Greek form of Baalbek in Syria; also a site of Sun worship in ancient Egypt.

HELIOS or HELIUS Greek Sun god who rode across the heavens every day on a chariot drawn by snow white horses, descending into the ocean at night; son of HYPERION and Theia, brother of SELENE.

HELIOSPHERE Area of space in which the interplanetary MAGNETIC FIELD and the SOLAR WIND dominate the interstellar medium.

HELIOTROPE In classical mythology, associated with the sea nymph Clytie who loved APOLLO; deserted by him she was changed into a sunflower, or heliotrope, which turns its 'face' to the Sun.

HELIUM Second lightest chemical element, and lightest of the inert gases; first identified in 1868 by James LOCKYER in the Solar Spectrum, and named for HELIOS. Helium composes about 27 per cent of the Universe and is currently believed to be synthesized in stars.

HELLE In Greek mythology, daughter of Athanas and Nephele, who fled with her brother Phrixus

Sun-god Helios in his chariot

on the back of a flying **RAM** with a golden fleece; fell to her death into the straits of the Dardanelles, an area later called Hellespont.

HELLENES What the Greeks called themselves, after Hellen, son of Deucalion and Pyrrha, the legendary ancestor of their race.

HELLENIZATION The huge spread of Greek civilization, culture and language that enveloped the whole of the Mediterranean and Middle East after the imperial expansion of **ALEXANDER THE GREAT** in the fourth century BC.

HELLESPONT See **HELLE**.

HEMISPHERE Half a sphere; the Earth's sphere is divided laterally by the Equator and longitudinally by a **MERIDIAN** going through both Poles.

HENCKE, Karl Ludwig (1793–1866) German amateur astronomer; discovered two **ASTEROIDS**: **ASTRAEA** in 1845 and **HEBE** in 1847.

HENDERSON, Thomas (1798–1844) First Astronomer Royal for Scotland (1834); Director of the Royal Observatory at the Cape of Good Hope; made the first **PARALLAX** measurement of Alpha Centauri in 1832.

HERA Sister and wife to **ZEUS**; goddess of marriage and childbirth and renewed her virginity every year by bathing in a sacred spring at Argos; identified as **JUNO** by the Romans.

HERACLES Greek name for **HERCULES**.

HERCULES Large but undistinguished constellation, one of **PTOLEMY'S** original forty-eight; its **ALPHA**, Rasalgethi, is a red supergiant but now third brightest star in the group; also contains two **GLOBULAR CLUSTERS**, one (M 13) visible to the naked eye. In Greek mythology, Hercules was the most famous hero; son of Alcmene by **ZEUS** (in disguise as her husband Amphitrion); **HERA** persecuted him, driving him mad so that he killed his own children; as penance he had to complete twelve seemingly impossible labours, after which he was made immortal.

HERDSMAN Name for constellation **BOÖTES**.

Hermes, the Greek Mercury

HERMES **ASTEROID 1937UB**; a tiny member of the **APOLLO** group, discovered 28 October 1938: came within 800 000 km/500 000 miles of Earth (the nearest so far), but disappeared soon afterwards. In Greek mythology, the messenger of the gods, son of **ZEUS** and the nymph Maia; one of the busiest deities on Olympus: fertility god, patron of travellers and commerce, god of gambling and luck, inventor of the lyre, gymnastics, olive culture, boxing, the alphabet and musical notation, and enjoyed power over animals. Some of his attributes later passed on to **APOLLO**; the Romans called him **MERCURY**.

HERMES, Rule of Astrological hypothesis that the Moon influences the moment of impregnation, or conception, as well as that of birth; according to the Rule, the **ASCENDANT** or **DESCENDANT** at birth is the place of the Moon at conception, and the place of the Moon at birth is the ascendant or descendant at conception. Before a **CHART** for the time of conception can be calculated, it must be ascertained whether the Moon at birth is above or below the horizon, and in either case, whether it is waxing or waning. A conception or epoch chart is useful for correcting the time of birth.

HERMES TRISMEGISTUS Thrice Greatest Hermes, a god hero, and a manifestation of the Egyptian god **THOTH** in the guise of the Greek god **HERMES**; a favourite with the inhabitants of Alexandria.

HERMETIC ART Art or science of **ALCHEMY**, named for **HERMES TRISMEGISTUS**, who was supposed to have invented it.

HERMETIC BOOKS Forty-two books of impenetrable mystery, fabled to have been written at the dictation of **HERMES TRISMEGISTUS**, dealing with the life and thought of ancient Egyptians; known collectively as the Hermetica; regarded by Giordano **BRUNO** as more important than the Bible (one of the reasons why he was burnt at the stake).

HERMETICA See **HERMETIC BOOKS**

HERSCHEL, Caroline Lucretia (1750–1848) Member of the astronomical Herschel family; born in Hanover, went to England in 1772 to assist her brother Friedrich Wilhelm; discovered eight comets and several star clusters and nebulae; published a revised edition of **FLAMSTEED'S** star catalogue in 1798; awarded the Gold Medal of the Royal Astronomical Society in 1828.

Hermes Trismegistus

HERSCHEL, Friedrich Wilhelm ('William') (1738–1822) Hanover born musician who moved to Bath, England, in 1766; took up astronomy as a hobby when he was thirty-five, built several highly efficient **TELESCOPES** and became probably 'the best observer of all time'. Observed and listed almost 850 **DOUBLE STARS**, confirming the **BINARY** nature of many, and did much work on the nature of nebulae; he made his greatest discovery 13 March 1781, when he observed **URANUS**.

HERSCHEL, John Frederick William (1782–1871) Son of Friedrich Wilhelm **HERSCHEL**; continued his father's work, discovering a further 525 nebulae and star clusters; made detailed survey of southern skies from Royal Observatory at the Cape of Good Hope, South Africa, publishing his results in 1847.

HERSTMONCEUX See **GREENWICH**.

HERTZPRUNG, Ejnar (1873–1967) Danish astronomer who developed the **HERTZPRUNG-RUSSELL DIAGRAM** independently from **RUSSELL**.

HERTZSPRUNG-RUSSELL DIAGRAM Graph which plots star temperature against star brightness; a star's position on the graph shows whether it is a normal star, a supergiant, a **RED GIANT** or a **WHITE DWARF**. See also **HERTZPRUNG**; **RUSSELL**.

HESPERIA **ASTEROID 69**, discovered by **SCHIAPARELLI** 29 April 1861.

HESPERIDES Three mythical sisters who guarded the apple tree given by **GE** to **HERA** as a wedding present and which produced the famous 'golden apples'.

HESPERUS Name given to **VENUS** when it is the evening star, in the western sky.

HESTIA **ASTEROID 46**, discovered 16 August 1857; in Greek mythology, daughter of **CRONOS**, older sister of **ZEUS** and goddess of the sacred hearth; known as Vesta by the Romans.

HEVELIUS, Johannes (1611–1687) Polish astronomer, designed and built the best observatory of its time at Gdansk, but it burnt down in 1679; discovered four comets, made an improved map of the Moon, which he published as *Selenographia* in 1647, catalogued 1500 stars and listed several constellations.

HIDALGO **ASTEROID 944**, discovered in 1920 by W.H. **BAADE**; has an unusual comet-like orbit.

HIEROGLYPHS Sacred writing; the picture characters of ancient Egyptian writing. Undeciphered by western scholars until 1882, when French Egyptologist J.F. **CHAMPOLLION** decoded the **ROSETTA STONE**.

HIMALIA Sixth moon of **JUPITER**, largest of the non-**GALILEAN SATELLITES OF JUPITER**; discovered in 1904 by American astronomer Charles Dillon Perrine (1878–1951).

HIPPARCHUS OF NICAEA (c190–c120 BC) Sometimes known as Hipparchus of Rhodes because he is said to have spent much of his later life there; one of the greatest of the Greek astronomers and mathematicians. Among his many achievements were the invention of trigonometry, a catalogue of star positions; the discovery of the **PRECESSION OF THE EQUINOXES** and the measurement of the size of the Moon by **PARALLAX**.

HIPPOCAMPUS Mythical sea-beast with the head and shoulders of a horse and tail of a fish or dolphin; the steed of **NEPTUNE**.

HIPPOCRENE Sacred fountain of the **MUSES** on Mount **HELICON**.

HOMUNCULUS NEBULA Patchy white cloud of dust and gas surrounding **ETA CARINAE** in the constellation **CARINA**; first observed in the late 1830s.

HONE, Margaret (1892–1969) One of the best-known teachers of modern astrology. Helped to found the **FACULTY OF ASTROLOGICAL STUDIES**, of which she eventually became President; author of two standard textbooks, *The Modern Textbook of Astrology* and *Applied Astrology*.

Herschel's home-made telescope

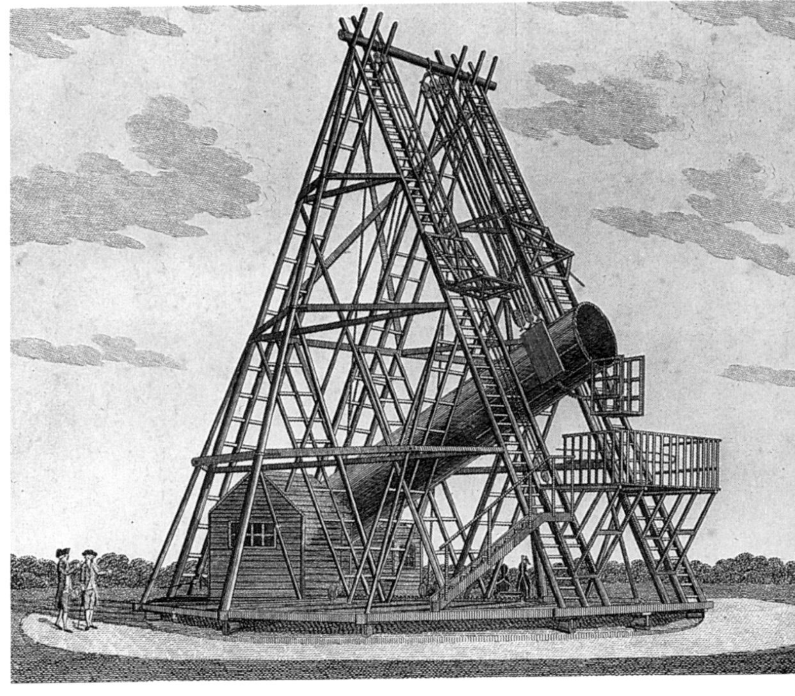

Preparing a horoscope, 1617-19

HORARY ASTROLOGY From the Greek *hora*, an hour; a branch of astrology in which a chart is set up for the moment the inquirer asks a question, and then studied for an answer.

HORIZON A GREAT CIRCLE on the CELESTIAL SPHERE which is everywhere 90° away from the observer's ZENITH; also known as the Celestial Horizon or the Rational Horizon; the visible or apparent horizon is confined to the limit of an observer's vision.

HOROLOGIUM, the Clock Dim constellation bordering on ERIDANUS.

HOROSCOPE From the Greek *hora*, an hour, and *skopein*, to observe; defined by Charles CARTER as 'a diagram of the heavens erected for any time and place, for the purpose of astrological study.'

Zeus at Amalthea's breast (see Horn of Plenty)

HORN OF PLENTY Also known as the Cornucopia; in Greek mythology the horn from the she-goat that suckled the infant ZEUS; supposed to provide endless good fortune.

HORROCKS, Jeremiah (1619–1641) English clergyman, mathematician and keen amateur astronomer; accurately predicted and observed the TRANSIT of VENUS.

HORSE According to Greek mythology, the creation of POSEIDON, identified by the Romans with NEPTUNE.

HORSE'S HEAD NEBULA Immense dark cloud, three LIGHT YEARS across, that obscures the eastern part of the constellation ORION.

HORUS Major sky god in the pantheon of ancient Egypt; the falcon-headed son of ISIS and OSIRIS, often represented as a winged sun-disc.

HOUR ANGLE Angle made by the HOUR CIRCLE of a celestial body and the MERIDIAN; the time which has elapsed since the body crossed the meridian.

HOUR CIRCLE A GREAT CIRCLE on the CELESTIAL SPHERE that passes through the CELESTIAL EQUATOR, one or both CELESTIAL POLES and a celestial body; it measures DECLINATION. The zero hour circle coincides with the observer's MERIDIAN.

HOURS, Book of See BOOK OF HOURS

HOUSE CUSPS The CUSP of an astrological HOUSE is its beginning, the dividing line between it and its predecessor; in a BIRTH CHART the cusp of the FIRST HOUSE on the eastern HORIZON marks the degree of the ASCENDANT or rising sign. See also HOUSE DIVISION.

HOUSE DIVISION Methods of dividing up the sky into HOUSES; there are many and various methods of doing this, and more controversy has been generated in astrological circles on this subject than almost anything else. The problem is finding a method of division which will not fail in polar regions. Attributed to PTOLEMY, the **Equal House System** is the simplest to calculate and understand, does not fail at the polar regions, and is the preferred method of many modern astrologers. It is based on the equal division of the ECLIPTIC into twelve 30° segments beginning at the eastern HORIZON (as calculated on the BIRTH CHART for the SIDEREAL time of birth) and counting back anticlockwise. The **Porphyry System** (introduced in the second century) is a modification which makes three equal divisions along the ARC of the Ecliptic between the MERIDIAN and the HORIZON. **Space Systems**, notably those developed by thirteenth-century mathematician **Campanus** and later by REGIOMONTANUS, were based on equal division of the PRIME VERTICAL; circles linking these divisions passed through the Ecliptic, marking the HOUSE CUSPS; Regiomontanus used the CELESTIAL EQUATOR rather than the Prime

Horus, the dominant Egyptian god

Vertical. The **Morinus House System** developed by **MORIN** in the seventeenth century is similar to the Regiomontanus Method. The **Time-Based Systems** are mathematically complex. By far the best one, although unjustly neglected, is that developed by the Arabic astrologer **Alcibitius**; it is based on the division by three of the **QUADRANTS**, the resultant points being projected on to the **CELESTIAL SPHERE**, and is the only time-based system that does not fail in the polar regions. Alcibitius' method was taken up and developed by **PLACIDUS** but made unnecessarily complex. It is based on the time taken by any degree on the zodiac circle to move from the Ascendant to the Midheaven, that is one half of its **DIURNAL ARC**; this time is divided by three and the result determines at what point the degree will mark the cusp of a house. Each cusp has to be separately calculated, the process repeated for the **NOCTURNAL ARC** (using the **DESCENDANT** and the **IMUM COELI**) and the system does not account for distortion in polar regions. Similar to the Alcibitius system is the Koch House System, devised in the 1970s by Dr Walter Koch; also known as the Birthplace House system, as it uses the **OBLIQUE ASCENSION** of the birthplace to calculate the intermediate **HOUSE CUSPS**. However, it fails in the polar regions above latitudes of 67°. Birth charts drawn up under the various house systems differ slightly (especially if the Placidus system is used) as the planets are sometimes positioned in different houses; in this case, the interpretations should be used together.

HOUSES Astrological Also known as Mundane Houses; the houses are an intellectual concept, divisions of the visible heavens, as seen at any point of time at any place on Earth, with a corresponding division of the invisible heavens, hidden beneath the Earth. They have no names and no physical correlation in the real world, but represent every department of human life; they are channels through which man enters into relationship with his environment. There are twelve houses, corresponding to the twelve zodiac signs (but not coterminous with them in a **BIRTH CHART**), and ruled by the planets that rule the signs; they are also classified according to their **TRIPLICITIES**: houses which correspond to **EARTH** signs are associated in general with material and worldly circumstance; houses corresponding to **AIR** signs correspond with mental activities and social interaction; houses that correspond with **WATER** signs are associated with emotional life; and houses associated with **FIRE** signs are associated with character, personality and individual expression. (For further details see **FIRST HOUSE, SECOND HOUSE, THIRD HOUSE**, etc.) The fixed houses are constant, regardless of which zodiac sign or planet is passing through at the time of a **HOROSCOPE** or **BIRTH CHART**; for example, the First House, corresponding to the **CARDINAL FIRE** sign **ARIES** and ruled by **MARS** is associated with the basic material of the self, and is the home of the **ASCENDANT**; therefore, whichever zodiac sign is rising, and to what degree it has risen, and the position of any planets are very important in the forming of the basic personality and may extensively modify the broad characteristics of the **SUN SIGN**. The methods of **HOUSE DIVISION** are many, various and sometimes extremely complicated. See also **HOUSE CUSPS**.

HOYLE, Sir Fred (b. 1915) British astronomer, best known for his support of the **STEADY STATE THEORY** of **COSMOLOGY** developed at Cambridge University.

HUBBLE, Edwin Powell (1889–1953) American astronomer; worked most of his career at **MOUNT WILSON**; made the definitive classification of galaxies, measured the **RED SHIFT** of the spectra of galaxies and established the fact that things move away faster the more distant they are, that is, recessional velocity increases with distance ('Hubble's Law'); this lends support to the **BIG BANG** theory of the origin of the Universe. The Hubble Space Telescope, recently launched into orbit above Earth and the most scientific satellite so far constructed, is named in his honour.

HUMOURS Medieval doctrine based on the theories of Hippocrates (fifth century BC), which attempted to explain the nature of humanity; he proposed the division of the four humours: blood, phlegm, black bile and yellow bile; these gave rise to four temperaments: sanguine, phlegmatic, melancholic and choleric. Healthy personalities were a mixture of these temperaments and illnesses were thought to occur when one predominated.

HUNTER Name for the constellation **ORION**.

The Four Humours inspect a painting

HUNTER'S MOON The **FULL MOON** following the **HARVEST MOON**; around the time of the **AUTUMNAL EQUINOX** in the northern hemisphere.

HUNTING DOGS Name for the constellation **CANES VENATICI**.

HUNTING THE MOON Sometimes kown as 'Chasing the Moon'; concerns a difficult square **ASPECT** between the Moon and **SATURN**; in a **BIRTH CHART**, this is a depressing aspect, that by **TRANSIT** and **PROGRESSION** recurs throughout an individual's life, according to the cycles of the Moon and Saturn, which roughly coincide; the Moon takes about twenty-eight years, and Saturn about thirty to return to its original position in the birth chart; during these progressed cycles the **SQUARE**, **OPPOSITION** and **CONJUNCTION** will be formed at intervals of about seven years, which will activate the original difficult square aspect in the birth chart.

HYADES Sparkling star cluster in the zodiacal constellation **TAURUS**; second nearest cluster to Earth; rise at dusk in the autumn and are considered to signify rains; in Greek mythology, the Hyades were daughters of **ATLAS** and Aethra.

HYDRA, the Watersnake Largest constellation in the sky, one of **PTOLEMY'S** original forty-eight; its **ALPHA**, **ALPHARD**, is often called the 'Solitary One' because no other star appears near it. In Greek mythology, the many headed monster that infested the Lernean Marshes; it was the Second Labour of **HERCULES** to kill this beast, who grew two heads every time one was cut off; he solved the problem by ordering his charioteer to burn the neck stumps as soon as the heads were off.

Hercules slaying the Hydra

HYDRUS, the Little Snake Constellation in the far south.

HYGEIA **ASTEROID 10**, discovered in 1849; in Greek mythology, the goddess of health.

HYLEG Ancient Greek astrological term meaning giver or sustainer of life; also known as Apheta. The doctrine of the hyleg held that a certain point or body in a **BIRTH CHART**, usually the Sun, Moon, **ASCENDANT** or **FORTUNA**, decided by its strength or weakness the length of life. Such complex rules were given to determine exactly the hylegiacal element of each chart that it is doubtful if the doctrine has any real meaning. See also **ANARETA**.

HYPERION Eighth moon of **SATURN**, discovered in 1848. In Greek mythology, a **TITAN**, the father of **HELIOS**, **SELENE** and Eos.

HYPOGEON 'Under the Earth'; astrologically, it concerns the lower heavens, including such terms as **NADIR**, **IMUM COELI** and the **FOURTH HOUSE**.

IAPETUS Third largest satellite of **SATURN**, with a diameter of 1460 km/900 miles; orbits every seventy-nine days. First observed by **CASSINI** in 1671. In Greek mythology, Iapetus was one of the **TITANS**, father to **ATLAS**, Prometheus and Epimetheus.

IASION Alternative mythological name for Alpha Geminorum or **CASTOR**.

IAU See International Astronomical Union.

IBIS Sacred bird of the ancient Egyptians, revered as an incarnation of **THOTH**.

IBN SENNA See **AVICENNA**

IBN SHAPRUT (915–990) Jewish physician and astrologer at the court of the Caliph of **BAGHDAD**; also taught at the Academy of Cordova in Spain.

IC See **IMUM COELI**

ICARIUS Mythological character represented by the constellation **BOÖTES**. An Athenian who was taught viniculture by **DIONYSUS**, killed by shepherds made drunk by his wine; led to his grave by his dog Moera, his daughter Erigone hanged herself from grief; she is supposed to have become the constellation **VIRGO** and his dog became **PROCYON**, the **ALPHA** of **CANIS MINOR**.

ICARUS **ASTEROID 1566**, one of the **APOLLO** group discovered by **BAADE** in 1949; so far the only asteroid found to approach the Sun within the orbit of **MERCURY**. In mythology, the son of the labyrinth-builder Daedalus, who escaped from Crete by flying on wings designed by his father; he flew too close to the Sun, which melted the wax securing the wings, and he plunged to his death in the Aegean Sea.

I CHING The Book of Changes; ancient Chinese oracular treatise possibly dating from 3000 BC.

ICHTHUS Greek name for the zodiac sign **PISCES**.

IDES Fifteenth day of March, May, July and October and the thirteenth day of every other month in the ancient Roman **CALENDAR**; Julius **CAESAR** was assassinated on the Ides of March; see also **CALENDS**; **NONES**.

IKEYA-SEKI Extremely bright **COMET** observed in 1965.

IMUM COELI Often written **IC**; opposite point on a **CHART** to the **MIDHEAVEN**; the point in the sky that lies directly beneath the subject's feet at the moment of birth.

INCEPTIONAL ASTROLOGY Branch of astrology concerned with 'beginnings'; indicates the prevailing astrological conditions at the start of an enterprise and indicates possible outcome; connected with **ELECTIONAL ASTROLOGY**, but not manipulative.

INCLINATION Angle between the plane of an orbit and a reference plane.

INCONJUNCT Astrological term for a planet which neither forms **ASPECTS** in a **CHART** nor is in parallel, **DECLINATION** or mutual disposition to another planet; also refers to any two signs or **HOUSES** which have no **FAMILIARITY** with each other.

INDIAN Name for the constellation **INDUS**.

INDIAN ASTROLOGY Astrology is important in India, and still used to assess the success of marriages, business ventures, important decisions in life; its origins are lost in time, but it is very complicated, inextricably linked with Hindu religion and the philosophy of **KARMA**, and therefore unlike astrology in the West. One of the most noticeable differences is the importance accorded to the Moon over the Sun; the **ECLIPTIC** is divided into twenty-eight **LUNAR MANSIONS** or nakshatras, according to the constellations seen behind the Moon; and the Moon's **NODES** are considered extremely influential. Apart from the Moon and the Sun, only the visible planets (**MERCURY**, **VENUS**, **MARS**, **JUPITER** and **SATURN**) are taken into account as there is no ancient authority for viability of the non-visible planets (**URANUS**, **NEPTUNE**, **PLUTO**) discovered later.

INDUS, the Indian Small, dim southern constellation near **GRUS**.

INFERIOR CONJUNCTION Astronomical occurrence when an **INFERIOR PLANET** (**MERCURY** or **VENUS**) comes between Earth and the Sun, and has the same **RIGHT ASCENSION**.

INFERIOR PLANETS **MERCURY** and **VENUS**, the two planets between Earth and the Sun; also known as Inner Planets.

Icarus plunging to his doom
Background: North Indian horoscope

Part of the Ishtar Gate from Babylon; now in Berlin

Isis and the child-god Horus

INFORTUNES Astrological term sometimes applied to **MARS** and **SATURN**; otherwise known as **MALEFIC**.

INFRARED ASTRONOMY The study of the infrared radiation produced by the Sun, planets, stars and other celestial bodies; the infrared ('below red') part of the electromagnetic spectrum lies between the red end of the visible spectrum (see **LIGHT**) and shortwave radio wavelengths, the range between one to 1 000 micrometres. The Earth's atmosphere will not allow the majority of these wavelengths to penetrate, and so astronomical observations have to be made from above the atmosphere or, less satisfactorily, from high altitudes on Earth's surface; infrared observations allow the penetration of the stellar dust that blots out many of the visible stars and allows comprehensive study of the **GALACTIC CENTRE**; it can also be used to study other galaxies and the chemical composition of the planets of the Solar System.

INFRARED RADIATION See **INFRARED ASTRONOMY**

INGRESS Astrological term for the entry of the Sun, Moon or any planet into a sign or quadrant of the zodiac; the Sun makes an ingress into the **CARDINAL** signs at the **EQUINOXES** and **SOLSTICES**.

INNER PLANETS See **INFERIOR PLANETS**.

INNES, Robert (1861–1933) Scottish astronomer who in 1915 discovered the star **PROXIMA CENTAURI**, the nearest known star to the Sun.

INNES' STAR **PROXIMA CENTAURI**; see also Robert **INNES**.

INTERCALARY Term describing an extra day (or month) inserted into the regular **CALENDAR**; for example, every four years an extra day is inserted into February; the Latin verb 'calare' which forms the root of the word means to proclaim: the Romans considered alterations to the calendar a subject for solemn proclamation.

INTERCEPTED HOUSES Astrological **HOUSES** produced by **HOUSE DIVISION** systems other than an Equal House system will produce intercepted houses, that is houses not coterminous with a zodiac sign. See also **INTERCEPTED SIGNS**.

INTERCEPTED SIGNS Term for signs contained within a **HOUSE** but not occupying the **CUSP**.

INTERNATIONAL ASTRONOMICAL UNION The governing body of the world's astronomical interests.

INTERNATIONAL DATE LINE The **MERIDIAN** 180° east and west of the **PRIME MERIDIAN**, that is, exactly opposite it; marks the difference in time between east and west. Westbound travellers crossing this meridian put the date forward one day; eastbound travellers lose a day. The meridian deviates when it crosses land to avoid date confusion in adjacent land areas.

INTERNATIONAL TIME ZONES Twenty-four equal longitudinal divisions of the globe, starting from the **PRIME MERIDIAN** and moving westward; each zone represents 15° of **LONGITUDE** and one hour in time; the time is the same throughout the zones, but changes by one hour when crossing from one zone to the next; **LOCAL TIME** therefore changes by four minutes for every degree of longitude.

INTERPOLATION Astrological term used when computing the position of a planet for a certain moment, between two known positions, which are usually provided by an **EPHEMERIS**; also refers to the method of determining the **CUSPS** of **HOUSES** for an intermediate **LATITUDE** that lies on either side of the one required.

INTERPRETATION An astrologer's individual judgement or reading of a **HOROSCOPE** or **BIRTH CHART**; also applies to the analysis and translation of planetary **TRANSITS** and **PROGRESSIONS**.

INTERPRETERS Babylonian term for the five known planets, each associated with one of the Babylonian gods; thought to predict the fate of individuals and nations; also known as the Wanderers.

INTRUDERS IN THE ZODIAC Portions of non-zodiacal constellations which obtrude into the **ZODIAC** ; part of **OPHIUCHUS** (between **SCORPIUS** and **SAGITTARIUS**) **ORION, SEXTANS** and **CETUS**.

IO Innermost of the **GALILEAN SATELLITES OF JUPITER**; slightly larger than the Earth's Moon (3 640 km/2 75 miles diameter); in Greek mythology, the daughter of Inachus, one of **ZEUS's** many mistresses.

ION **PARTICLE** which changes according to the number of electrons it carries: more electrons make it negative, less make it positive.

IONOSPHERE Layer of the Earth's atmosphere that extends from about 64 to 480 km/40 to 300 miles above the surface of the Earth; important for communications as it reflects certain radio waves.

IOTA AQUARIDES Minor **METEOR** shower, seen in August.

IRIS **ASTEROID 7**, discovered in 1847; fourth brightest of the asteroids; in Greek mythology, the goddess of the rainbow.

ISHTAR Babylonian goddess of love and war; known as **INNANA** in Sumeria, in Syria as **ASTARTE**, in Phoenicia as **ASHTORETH**; powerful female deity whose attributes were later shared out between **APHRODITE** (Roman **VENUS**) and **ARTEMIS** (Roman **DIANA**).

ISIDORUS OF SEVILLE (c570–636) Bishop of Seville, a Spanish scholar and encyclopaedist; one of the first, at that time, to separate astrology from astronomy.

ISIS Principal goddess of ancient Egypt, wife of **OSIRIS**, the mother of **HORUS**, and called the 'Queen of Heaven'.

ISLAMIC ASTRONOMY The spread of Islam from the seventh to the tenth centuries played a major part in the development of mathematics, astronomy and astrology in Europe, as Islamic expansionism in Spain brought the ancient Greek texts to Europe. In the heart of the Islamic empire, Caliph **AL-MANSUR** of Baghdad established a major observatory and library in the city, making it the astronomical capital of the world; the Arabic names of many of the **FIXED STARS** date from this time.

IVAR **ASTEROID 1627**, a tiny member of the close approach **AMOR** group.

Islamic lion

JACOB BEN TARIK Established a school of astrology in **BAGHDAD** in the eighth century AD.

JAIPUR ASTRONOMICAL OBSERVATORY Indian observatory established by Maharaja Sawai Jai Singh II (1688–1744), a learned ruler, deeply interested in astronomy and mathematics. In 1727 he founded the city of Jaipur, where he built an open-air observatory (one of five constructed at his orders) containing eighteen large instruments.

JANSKY, Karl (1905–1950) American radio engineer of Czech descent. In 1931, while conducting research for Bell Telephone Laboratories, he detected radio waves from the **MILKY WAY**.

JANSSEN, Pierre Jules César (1824–1907) French astronomer specializing in solar phenomena. He founded the **MEUDON** and Mont Blanc observatories.

JANTAR MANTAR OBSERVATORY An ancient and well-equipped observatory near Delhi, India. Its name derives from local pronunciation of the Sanskrit words *Jantra*, instrument, and *Mantra*, calculations.

JANUARY First month of the **GREGORIAN CALENDAR**; dedicated by the Romans to **JANUS**.

JANUS One of the smaller satellites of **SATURN**, discovered in 1978. It is co-orbital with **EPIMETHEUS**. In Roman mythology, Roman deity, patron of endings and beginnings and guardian of the *Patulicus*, the Opener, and *Clusivius*, the Closer.

JAPAN There is great interest in astrology in modern Japan, where the Association of Professional Astrologers has some 200 000 members.

JASON Hero of the myth of Jason and the Argonauts. His father, Aeson, King of Iolcus, was deposed and imprisoned by his half-brothers, Pelias and Neleus. Pelias seized the kingdom, but the child Jason was secretly entrusted to **CHEIRON** the Centaur. As a young man, Jason demanded the return of his kingdom; Pelias asked for the Golden Fleece in return. With a band of heroes, Jason sailed to Colchis in the ship *Argo* and with the help of Medea the sorceress, whom he married, seized the Fleece.

JEANS, Sir James (1877–1946) English astronomer, astrophysicist, writer and broadcaster. His theory of the origin of the solar system was that material extracted from the Sun by a passing star condensed to form the planets.

JET STREAMS Powerful winds, ranging between about 160–320 km/h/100–200 miles per hour, which blow at a level near the **TROPOPAUSE** in the Earth's atmosphere.

JEWEL BOX Popular name for **KAPPA CRUCIS**.

JEWISH CALENDAR See **CALENDAR, JEWISH**

JODRELL BANK The radio and astronomical observatory, also a research and teaching centre, of the University of Manchester, sited near Macclesfield, Cheshire, England. Sir Bernard **LOVELL** was its director (1951–1981).

JOHANNES HISPALENSIS (fl. mid-twelfth century) Renowned astrologer who wrote a popular treatise, *Epitome Totius Astrologiae*.

Gnomon at Jai Singh Observatory, Jaipur

Jason and the Golden Fleece

prominence in the 1970s; he maintained that women were fertile when the Sun and Moon returned to the exact angular relationship that they occupied in the individual's **BIRTH CHART**.

JONES, Marc Edmund American astrologer, deviser of the **JONES CHART PATTERNS**.

JONES' CHART PATTERNS Seven astrological **CHART** patterns – the **BOWL, BUCKET, BUNDLE, LOCOMOTIVE, SEE-SAW, SPLASH** and **SPLAY**, each created by the grouping of the planets in a birth chart – devised by the American astrologer Marc Edmund Jones. He claims that these shapes indicate an individual's characteristics and facilitate the interpretation of a **HOROSCOPE**, see **BOWL, BUNDLE, BUCKET, LOCOMOTIVE, SEE-SAW, SPLASH** and **SPLAY**.

Part of Jantar Mantar Observatory

JOHNDRO, Edward American astrologer who is said to have pioneered work on the **VERTEX** and **ANTIVERTEX**.

JOINT RULERSHIP Before all the planets known today were discovered, each of the five known planets ruled two zodiac signs. **MERCURY** ruled **GEMINI** and **VIRGO**; **VENUS** ruled **TAURUS** and **LIBRA**; **MARS** ruled **ARIES** and **SCORPIO**; **JUPITER** ruled **SAGITTARIUS** and **PISCES**; and **SATURN** ruled **CAPRICORN** and **AQUARIUS**. (The Sun and Moon ruled the signs **LEO** and **CANCER** respectively). Following the discovery of **URANUS, NEPTUNE** and **PLUTO**, Uranus became the ruler of Aquarius (sub-ruler Saturn); Neptune ruled Pisces (sub-ruler Jupiter); and Pluto ruled Scorpio (sub-ruler Mars).

JONAS, Dr Eugen Czech psychiatrist whose work came to

C.G. Jung

JONES, Sir Harold Spencer (1890–1960) Tenth British Astronomer Royal, who arranged the transfer of the Royal Observatory from **GREENWICH** to **HERSTMONCEUX**.

JOVE Alternative name for **JUPITER**.

JOYS An old and rather ill-defined astrological term. Planets are said to be in their 'Joys' when they reside in their own sign, in the house of which they are the sub-ruler, or in the sign in which they are in **EXALTATION**. For example, the **MOON** is in its 'Joys' when in **CANCER**, the sign it rules; in the fourth **HOUSE**, its own house; or in **TAURUS**, where it is exalted.

JULIAN CALENDAR See **CALENDAR**

JULIAN DAY Used by astronomers, this contains no divisions. Its starting point was set by the French mathematician Joseph Scaliger (who named the calendar for his father, Julius) at 1 January 4713 BC, spanning 6 661 years up to and including AD 1948. Each day has a number: 1 January 1948 is designated J.D. (Julian Day) 2 432 552.

JULIAN YEAR The year of 365 and one-quarter days, based on solar rotation, established by the **JULIAN CALENDAR**.

JULIUM SIDUS The great **COMET** seen at the death of Julius **CAESAR**, said by the Romans to be his soul.

JULIUS II (1443–1513) Pope 1503–1513, reflected the great popularity of astrology in Europe at the time when he consulted an astrologer regarding the most favourable day for his papal coronation.

JULY Seventh month of the **GREGORIAN CALENDAR**; named in honour of **JULIUS CAESAR**.

JUNE Sixth month of the **GREGORIAN CALENDAR**; perhaps associated with **JUNO**.

JUNG, Carl Gustav (1875–1961) Swiss psychiatrist. He showed great interest in astrology and in such paranormal faculties as clairvoyance and telepathy. His research into some 500 of his patients' marriages, involving the casting and study of more than 1 000 **HOROSCOPES** and **BIRTH CHARTS**, revealed many similarities in the placing of the woman's Moon and the man's Sun, indicating compatibility.

JUNO **ASTEROID 3**
Discovered in 1804 by **HARDING**, it has a diameter of 288 km/179 miles. In Roman mythology, the wife and sister of **JUPITER (JOVE)**, Queen of Heaven and protectress of women and marriages; identified with the Greek deity **HERA**.

JUPITER AMMON
Name given to **JUPITER** by his Libyan worshippers.

JUPITER Largest planet in the Solar System and fifth in line from the Sun. Its equatorial diameter is 142 700 km/88 680 miles and its mean distance from the Sun is 775 880 000 km/484 300 000 miles. It rotates on its axis in 9 hours 51 minutes and orbits the Sun in 11.9 years. A system of swirling, multi-coloured cloud belts is visible on its surface, but its outstanding feature is the **GREAT RED SPOT**, very prominent since 1878. Jupiter has sixteen known moons or satellites: the four largest – **IO, EUROPA, CALLISTO** and **GANYMEDE**, known as the **GALILEAN SATELLITES** – may easily be seen with a small **TELESCOPE**. In Roman mythology, Jupiter was the King of Gods, known also as **JOVE**; identified with the Greek **ZEUS**. The son of **SATURN (CRONOS)**, whose throne he took, he controlled lightning and thunderbolts. Revered as the supreme guardian of Rome, his temple dominated the Capitoline Hill.

JUPITER RETURN
Once every twelve years, **JUPITER**, having travelled round the zodiac, returns to its original position in an individual's **BIRTH CHART**. Astrologers believe that this return exerts a favourable effect. See also **PLANETARY RETURNS**.

JUVENTAS Roman name for the Greek goddess **HEBE**, daughter of **ZEUS** and **HERA** and cup-bearer to the Olympian deities until replaced by Ganymede.

Jupiter and Cetus, by Ingres

KABALAH A Hebrew word meaning 'tradition'. The Kabalah is a mystical discipline of Jewish origin, embodying occult interpretations of the Bible and a complex astrological system.

KAKATYCHE OR KATOTYCHE Greek term for ill fortune, sometimes applied astrologically to the **SIXTH HOUSE**.

KANT, Immanuel (1724–1804) German philosopher and cosmologist who theorized that the Moon's tide-raising powers explained why it always presented the same face to the Earth. He also suggested that the **MILKY WAY** was simply a nebula, and predicted the existence of **URANUS** before **HERSCHEL**.

KAPPA CRUCIS The **JEWEL BOX CLUSTER**.

KAPPA SCORPII The star **GIRTAB**.

KAPPA VELORUM The star **MARKEB**.

KAPTEYN, Jacobus (1851–1922) Dutch astronomer noted for work in photographic astrometry, for measurement of the **PROPER MOTION** of stars and for the discovery of **STAR STREAMS**.

KAPTEYN TELESCOPE A 39 in. (99 cm) Anglo-Dutch telescope at **ROQUE DE LOS MUCHACHOS** observatory, La Palma. Taking wide-angle photographs with minimum distortion, it is used for the accurate establishment of star patterns.

KARMA Eastern philosophical term referring to the way in which one's actions in one stage of existence profoundly affect one's destiny in the next stage, or to the transmigration of the soul through successive reincarnations.

K-CORONA Term for the inner part of the solar **CORONA**; consists of highly active free electrons and supplies a major part of the solar corona's brilliance.

KEEL Name for the constellation **CARINA**.

KELVIN, William Thompson, First Baron (1824–1907) Scottish mathematician and physicist; Professor of Natural Philosophy, Glasgow University, 1846–1899. Lord Kelvin helped to establish the Second Law of Thermodynamics, indicating how an absolute temperature scale could be derived from it. See also **K SYMBOL**

The heirarchy of the Kabalah

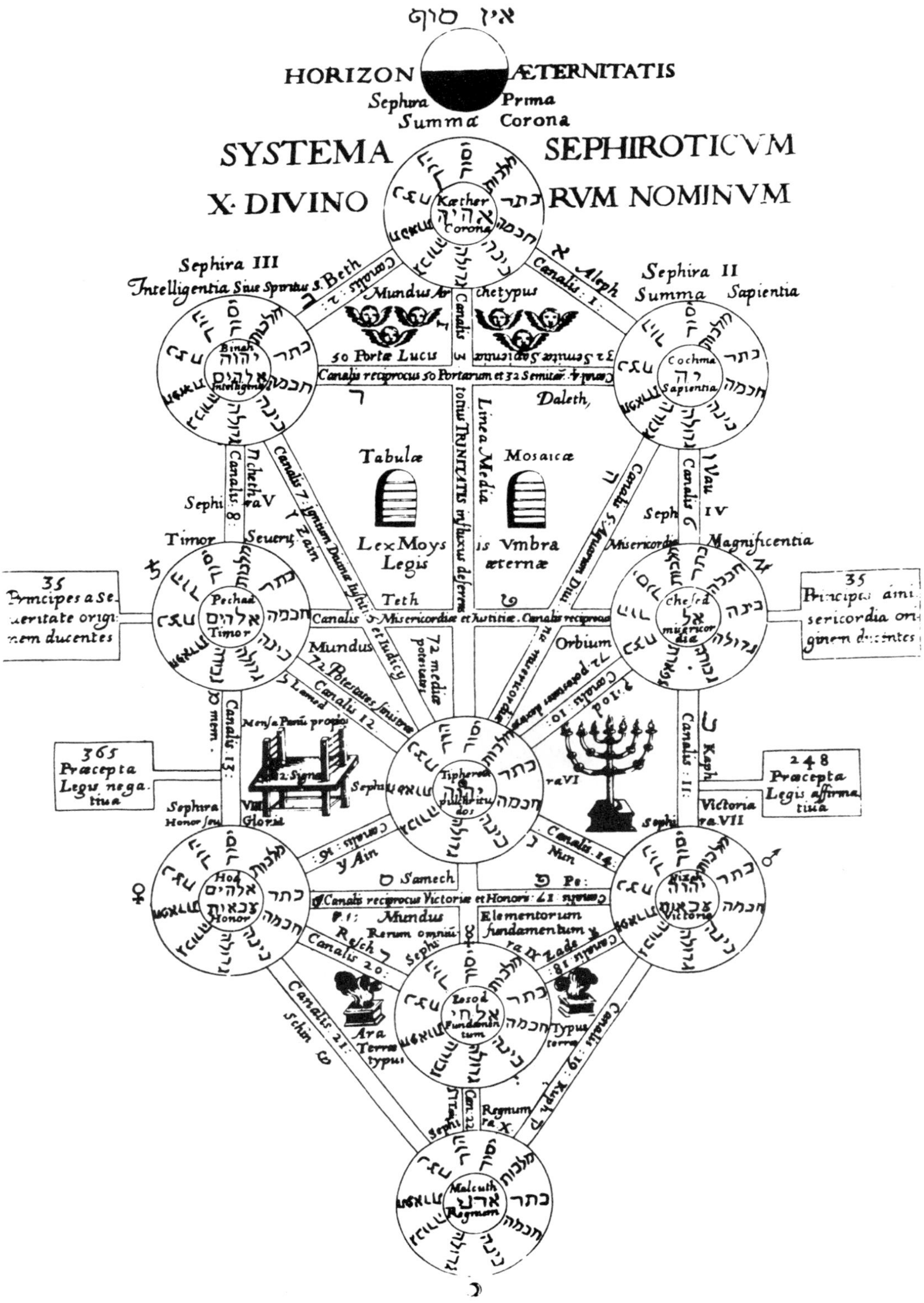

KENNEDY SPACE CENTER Experimental space flight establishment near Cape Canaveral, Florida; NASA's launch and control centre for the first manned **MOON** flight.

KEPLER, Johann (1571–1630) German astronomer and mathematician; assistant and then successor to Tycho **BRAHE**, and one of the founders of modern astronomy. Kepler studied planetary motion and concluded that the Sun must be at the centre of the solar system, with the planets moving around it in **ELLIPTICAL ORBITS**. Having verified Copernicus' **HELIOCENTRIC THEORY**, he drew up his three Laws of Planetary Motion (1609–18).

KEPLER'S LAWS OF PLANETARY MOTION Three laws established by Johannes **KEPLER**: The planets move in **ELLIPTICAL ORBITS** around the Sun, which stands at one focus of the **ELLIPSE**. (2) The imaginary line (radius vector) joining the centres of a planet and the Sun describes equal areas of space in equal times; thus, a planet moves fastest when nearest to the Sun, and slowest when furthest away. (3) The square of the time taken to complete an **ORBIT** is proportional to the cube of the planet's mean distance from the Sun.

KEPLER'S STAR A **SUPERNOVA** that appeared in **OPHIUCHUS** in 1604.

KEW ROYAL OBSERVATORY Near Kingston, Surrey; established by King George III (reigned 1760–1820).

KEYHOLE NEBULA A dark dust cloud nebula, outlined by the brilliant **CARINA** nebula, named by Sir John **HERSCHEL**. Its changing appearance is thought to be due to illumination by the **VARIABLE STAR** Eta Carinae.

KEYWORDS A series of words, based on a system introduced by Margaret **HONE**, devised for teaching purposes.

Kennedy Space Center

Keywords indicate the astrological values, **QUALITIES**, principles and motivation of the Sun, Moon, planets, zodiac signs and **HOUSES**.

KHAYYAM, Omar (c1050–c1153) Persian poet, famous in the west through Edward FitzGerald's translation of his (attributed) *Rubáiyát*; also a mathematician and astronomer, interested in astrology, science and medicine. He prepared improved astronomical tables and wrote a book on algebra.

KIBLAH The point to which Muslims turn when they pray: the direction of the Kaaba (part of the Great Mosque) at Mecca. The word is also used for the *mihrab*, the mark on a mosque wall indicating the required direction.

KILOPARSEC Term for 1 000 **PARSECS** or 3 260 **LIGHT YEARS**.

KIRKWOOD GAPS Areas of the **ASTEROID** belt where there are very few asteroids; noted in 1857 by the American mathematician Daniel Kirkwood (1814–1895).

KITT PEAK NATIONAL OBSERVATORY Research centre for ground-based optical astronomy in the Quinlan Mountains, Arizona. Its several remarkable **TELESCOPES** include the 401 cm/158 in. Mayall Telescope and the McMath Solar Telescope, the largest in the world.

KOCAB Beta Ursae Minoris of the North Polar constellation **URSA MINOR** (one of **PTOLEMY'S** original forty-eight).

KOCH HOUSE SYSTEM See **HOUSE DIVISION**

KOHOUTEK'S COMET Discovered near **JUPITER'S** orbit in 1973 by L. Kohoutek.

KONKOLY OBSERVATORY Hungary's major astronomical observatory.

KON-TIKI Legendary Sun King of the territory of the Incas in medieval Peru.

KOPFF'S COMET Discovered by the Heidelberg astronomer Kopff in 1906; last observed in 1983.

KOPPERNICK, Nicolaus Name sometimes used for **COPERNICUS**.

KORAN Holy book of the Muslims, containing 114 *Suras* (chapters) of religious teachings said to have been dictated to the prophet Mohammed at Mecca by an angel.

KOSMOBIOLOGIE German astrological magazine founded in 1928 by Reinhold **EBERTIN**.

KRAFFT, Karl Ernst (1900–1945) Swiss astrologer who worked for German intelligence services during World War II. His successful prediction of the attempted assassination of Adolf Hitler in Munich in November 1939 provoked his arrest as being involved in the plot; he was released to work on translations of **NOSTRADAMUS**, commissioned by Goebbels. In 1941, he was arrested again, and died on the way to Buchenwald concentration camp.

KRONOS See **CRONOS**.

K SYMBOL Sometimes used for the **KELVIN** unit of temperature.

KUFIC Ancient Arabic characters in which the **KORAN** is said to have been first written.

KUIPER, Gerrit Pieter (1905–1973) Dutch astronomer especially noted for the discovery of **MIRANDA** and **NEREID**, satellites of **URANUS** and **NEPTUNE** respectively. He contributed to NASA's space research.

KUMBHA The water pot or urn of ancient Indian Zodiacs; the **SANSKRIT** equivalent to **AQUARIUS**.

KUN the Tails; name associated by **BABYLONIAN ASTROLOGERS** with the zodiacal constellation of **PISCES**, the Fishes.

KUSARIKKU Mythical name associated with the Fish-Goat symbol of the constellation and zodiac sign **CAPRICORN**.

LACAILLE, Nicholas Louis de (1713–1762) French astronomer, 'father of southern astronomy'; who made observations at the Cape of Good Hope, South Africa; named fourteen southern constellations.

LACERTA, the Lizard Small and rather obscure constellation near **CEPHEUS**.

LACEY, F.W. Associate of Alan **LEO**, with whom he co-founded *The Astrologer's Magazine*.

LACHESIS In Greek mythology, one of the three **FATES**.

LADON In Greek mythology, the dragon that guarded the Garden of the **HESPERIDES**.

LALANDE, Joseph Jerome Le Français (1732–1807) French mathematician and astrologer, who became Director of the **PARIS OBSERVATORY** in 1795.

LAMBDA SCORPII The star **SHAULA**.

LAMBDA TAURI Currently the fifth brightest star in the zodiacal constellation **TAURUS**; an eclipsing **BINARY**.

LANGRENUS, Michael Florentius (1600–1675) Belgian mapmaker who eventually became Mathematician and Cosmographer to Philip IV of Spain; drew up and published the first significant map of the Moon in 1645.

LA PALMA OBSERVATORY See **ROQUE DE LOS MUCHACHOS OBSERVATORY.**

LAPLACE, Pierre Simon de (1749–1827) French astronomer and mathematician who formulated the Nebular Hypothesis regarding the origin of the Solar System, suggesting that the Sun was formed from a gas cloud which, as it contracted and grew hotter, began to rotate rapidly and bulge at its equator, throwing off rings of material which condensed to form planets.

LAS CAMPANUS OBSERVATORY Major observatory near La Serena, Chile, operated by the Carnegie Institute of the USA.

LASER Acronym for Light Amplification by Simulated Emission of Radiation; device producing a beam made up of rays of identical wavelengths (coherent light) and phases.

Mirror reflecting laser beams

LA SILLA OBSERVATORY European Southern Observatory (ESO), one of the three important observatories in Chile (the others are Cerro Tololo and **LAS CAMPANAS**).

LASSELL, William (1799–1880) British astronomer; built his own reflecting **TELESCOPES**, and observed several faint planetary satellites and some 600 nebulae.

LATITUDE, Celestial See **CELESTIAL LATITUDE**.

LATITUDE, Ecliptic See **ECLIPTIC LATITUDE**.

LATITUDE, Terrestrial angular distance of any location from the Earth's Equator, which is 0° latitude; measured north and south of the equator, with the North Pole at 90°N and the South Pole at 90°S; used with the other geographical co-ordinate, **LONGITUDE**, to pinpoint exactly a place on the globe. Not to be confused with **CELESTIAL LATITUDE**.

LEAVITT, Henrietta Swan (1868–1921) American astronomer who specialized in the study of **CEPHEID VARIABLES**; worked for some time at the Harvard College Observatory.

LEDA One of the small outer satellites of **JUPITER**, discovered in 1974 by C. Kowal. In Greek mythology, the mother of **CASTOR** by her husband Tyndarus, and **POLLUX** and **HELEN** by **ZEUS**.

LEMAITRE, Georges Edouard (1894–1966) Belgian astrophysicist, Professor of Astronomy at University of Louvain from 1927; known for his work on the expanding Universe.

LEMNOS Volcanic island in the north Aegean; in Greek mythology, the resting place of the blacksmith god Hephaestos (**VULCAN** to the Romans).

LEMURES Roman name for malevolent night-walking spirits or spectres of the dead.

Alan Leo, aka William F. Allen

LENORMAND, Marie Anne (1772–1843) French cartomantic fortune teller and astrologer known as the 'Sybil of the Faubourg St Germain'; frequently consulted by Napoleon.

LENTICULAR GALAXY Lens-shaped galaxy, flattened like a **SPIRAL** but with no 'arms'; rather rare.

LEO, the Lion Impressive zodiacal constellation, one of **PTOLEMY'S** original forty-eight; its **ALPHA, REGULUS,** was known to the ancients as one of the **FOUR WATCHERS OF THE HEAVENS**. **Leo the zodiac sign** is the fifth sign of the zodiac, a **MASCULINE POSITIVE FIXED FIRE** sign ruled by the Sun; **URANUS** is in **DETRIMENT** in Leo, **NEPTUNE** in **EXALTATION**. The Leo **myth** is associated with the Nemean Lion, a huge beast with an impenetrable hide, strangled by **HERCULES** in the fulfilment of the first of his Twelve Labours.

LEO, Alan (W.F. Allen) (1860–1917) Most noted professional astrologer of his time (he took his astrological name from his **ASCENDING SIGN**); led the twentieth-century revival of astrology, writing many books on the subject aimed specifically at students, including *Practical Astrology*; together with fellow astrologer F.W. Lacey, founded *The Astrologer's Magazine*, later *Modern Astrology*.

LEO MINOR, the Little Lion Small, faint constellation which butts on to **URSA MAJOR**.

LEONID METEORS Noted **METEOR** shower in the zodiacal constellation **LEO**; appears around 17 November every year, but the finest displays tend to occur every thirty-three years.

LEONOV, Alexei (b. 1934) Soviet Cosmonaut, made the first walk in space from the Soviet Spacecraft Voskhod II on 18 March 1965.

LEPUS, the Hare Small distinctive constellation, one of **PTOLEMY'S** original forty-eight, south of **ORION**.

LERNAEAN HYDRA See **HYDRA**

LESATH Upsilon Scorpii, eighth brightest star in the zodiacal constellation **SCORPIUS** and one of the stars in the 'sting' of the Scorpion.

LESSER BENEFIC Astrological term for **VENUS**, considered to create love and harmony when well placed in a **CHART**; see also **BENEFIC**.

LETHE In Greek mythology, the river of forgetfulness which ran through **HADES**, whose waters obliterated the remembrance of earthly existence from the minds of dead souls.

LETO Roman version of the Greek Latona; mother, by **ZEUS**, of **APOLLO** and **ARTEMIS**.

LE VERRIER, Urbain Jean Joseph (1811–1877) French astronomer and chemist; correctly predicted the existence of **NEPTUNE** following close observation of the irregularities in **URANUS'** motion; also postulated the existence of the hypothetical planet **VULCAN** near **MERCURY**.

LEXELL'S COMET First recognized short-period **COMET**, observed in 1770 by Charles **MESSIER** and named for Finnish astronomer Anders Lexell (1740–1784), who plotted its orbit.

LIBER ASTRONOMICUS Popular medieval treatise on astrology and astronomy by Guido **BONATTI**.

LIBRA, the Scales Rather dim, unremarkable zodiacal constellation, one of **PTOLEMY'S** originals, once known as Chelae Scorpionis, the Scorpion's Claws. **Libra the zodiac sign** is the seventh sign of the zodiac, a **MASCULINE POSITIVE CARDINAL AIR** sign, ruled by **VENUS**; the Sun is in **FALL** in Libra; **MARS** is in **DETRIMENT**; **SATURN** is in **EXALTATION**. There is no specific **myth** associated with Libra: Greek legends associate it with Mochis, inventor of weights and measures; it also covers the time of weighing the harvest.

Lick Observatory
Background: James Lick

LICK OBSERVATORY Astronomical Observatory of the University of California sited 1 238 m/4 200 ft above sea level on top of Mount Hamilton, northern California; completed in 1888, it was financed by eccentric gold rush millionaire James Lick, who is buried beneath one of its large **TELESCOPES**.

LIGHT **ELECTRO-MAGNETIC RADIATION** in the narrow visible range from about 700 **NANOMETRES** (red range) to 400 (violet range); the fundamental 'building block' or quantum of light is the **PHOTON**. Light travels in waves (which are in turn made up of oscillating particles) at a speed of 299 793 km/186 300 miles per second.

LIGHT PLANETS Term sometimes applied to the Moon, **MERCURY** and **VENUS**, referring to their low gravities and consequent swiftness of motion.

LIGHT SPEED See **LIGHT**

LIGHT YEAR Measurement of stellar distance; the distance travelled by a beam of light in one year (through the vacuum of space): $9{\cdot}46 \times 10^{12}$ km/$5{\cdot}87 \times 10^{12}$ miles.

LIGHTS Astrological term for the Sun and Moon; also known as luminaries.

LILLY, William (1602–168) English astrologer who predicted the Great Fire of London (1666); wrote several books on astrology (including *Christian Astrology* in 1647) and an autobiography which describes other, less upright, astrologers working in his time.

LIMB Edge of the detectable disc of a planet or moon.

LION Astrological symbol for **LEO**; traditionally associated with the Nemean Lion, a monstrous animal with a pelt so impenetrable that **HERCULES** had to strangle it.

LIPPERSHEY, Hans (c1570–c1619) Dutch optician; inventor of the refracting **TELESCOPE**.

LITHOPANSPERMIA The theory that germs of life or possibly even complex living organisms were brought to Earth by **METEORITES** or cosmic dust.

LITHOSPHERE The Earth's crust.

LITTLE BEAR Name for the constellation **URSA MINOR**.

LITTLE DOG STAR Procyon, or Alpha Canis Minoris, the brightest star in **CANIS MINOR**.

LITTLE SNAKE Alternative name for constellation **HYDRUS**.

LIZARD Name for constellation **LACERTA**.

LOCKYER, Joseph (1836–1920) English astronomer and founder of Sidmouth Observatory, Devon; detected **HELIUM** in the Sun.

LOCOMOTIVE One of the seven **BIRTH CHART** patterns devised by Marc Edmund Jones.

LODESTAR Pole Star, currently **POLARIS**.

LOMONOSOV, Mikhail (1711–1765) First great Russian astronomer; supporter of the theories of **COPERNICUS**; observed a **TRANSIT** of **VENUS** in 1761, and deduced that the planet had a dense atmosphere with an unbroken cloud layer.

LONGITUDE, Absolute See **ABSOLUTE LONGITUDE**.

LONGITUDE, Celestial See **CELESTIAL LONGITUDE**.

LONGITUDE, Ecliptic See **ECLIPTIC LONGITUDE**.

LONGITUDE, Terrestrial imaginary vertical lines which provide east/west co-ordinates that will pinpoint a point on the globe when taken with **LATITUDE**; measured 180° east and west from the **PRIME MERIDIAN** (0° longitude) at **GREENWICH** in London. There are twenty-four lines of longitude, each covering 15° of a circle and each representing a different time zone an hour ahead (west) or an hour behind (east) its neighbour. Not to be confused with **ABSOLUTE LONGITUDE** or **CELESTIAL LONGITUDE**.

LORD Astrologically, the most powerful planet or body in a **CHART**.

LORD OF A HOUSE Planetary ruler of the zodiac sign that occupies the **CUSP** of a **HOUSE**.

LORD OF THE HOROSCOPE Astrological term referring to the most powerful or influential planet or body in a **CHART**; determined by the nature of the planet, its position in the chart and how it is aspected (see **ASPECTS**). Often known under its old Arabic name, Almutoen.

LOVELL, Sir Bernard (b. 1913) British astronomer, Professor of **RADIO ASTRONOMY** at the University of Manchester, and Director of **JODRELL BANK** (1951–1981).

LOWELL OBSERVATORY Founded in 1894 in Flagstaff, Arizona, by Percival **LOWELL**; operates eight **TELESCOPES**, four of which are based in the Anderson Mesa dark-sky site, southeast of Flagstaff.

LOWELL, Percival (1855–1916) American astronomer, founder of the **LOWELL OBSERVATORY**; predicted the existence of **PLUTO** and observed the canal patterns on **MARS**, which led him to the conclusion that the planet was inhabited.

LUCIFER From the Latin meaning 'light bringer'; often applied to **VENUS** when it is in the **MORNING STAR** position; also the name of Satan, the angel of the morning, before his fall from grace. See also **HESPERUS**.

LUMINARIES See **LIGHTS**

LUNA Latin for Moon; the Romans credited the Moon with powers over the human mind and believed that lunatics were adversely affected by the waxing of the moon.

LUNAR Pertaining to the Moon.

LUNAR CYCLES See **MONTHS**

LUNAR ECLIPSE Occurs when the Moon passes through the shadow of the Earth. Total eclipses when the Sun, Earth and Moon are in **OPPOSITION** (that is, their centres align) and the Moon is at one of its **NODES** (the two points where its orbit crosses the **ECLIPTIC**): then the Moon is immersed in the Earth's shadow for up to two hours. Lunar eclipses can be predicted; up to three can occur in any one year. Astrologically, a lunar eclipse can have a powerful effect if it falls on a sensitive part of a **PROGRESSED BIRTH CHART**.

LUNAR MANSIONS Also known as Lunar Stations. System of dividing the **ECLIPTIC** into twenty-eight equal segments to match the constellations seen behind the Moon rather than the Sun; supposed to transmit influences, not unlike the **HOUSES**; important in **INDIAN ASTROLOGY** (where they are called *nakshatras*) and **CHINESE ASTROLOGY**.

LUNAR RETURN CHART Compiled for the time at which the Moon returns to its position in the subject's **BIRTH CHART**.

LUNAR STATIONS See **LUNAR MANSIONS**

LUNAR YEAR Twelve **SYNODIC MONTHS**, about 354 days. See also **SOLAR YEAR**.

Luna or Selene, Moon-goddess

LUNATION The time taken for the Moon to proceed through its phases; measured from one **NEW MOON** to the next or one **FULL MOON** to the next; same as a **SYNODIC MONTH** (the mean of which is 29 days 12 hours 44 minutes 2.9 seconds).

LUND OBSERVATORY Founded in 1672 at Lund, Sweden; present building dates from 1867. Its western wing houses a **MERIDIAN CIRCLE** circle and a small planetarium.

LUPUS, the Wolf Undistinguished southern constellation, one of **PTOLEMY'S** original forty-eight, bordering on **SCORPIUS** and **CENTAURUS**.

LYCAON In Greek mythology, a king of Arcadia, who angered **ZEUS** by serving him human flesh; he and all save one of his sons were transformed into wolves.

LYNX, the Lynx· Large, rather dull northern constellation adjoining **URSA MAJOR**, named by **HEVELIUS** in his star map of 1690.

LYOT, Bernard Ferdinand (1897–1952) French astrophysicist, inventor of the coronograph used to observe the Solar **CORONA** in the absence of an **ECLIPSE**.

LYRA, the Lyre Small but interesting northern constellation, one of **PTOLEMY'S** original forty-eight; contains the spectacular Ring Nebula, visible through a small telescope and the double **DOUBLE** star Epsilon Lyrae. Mythologically, the lyre, oldest of stringed instruments, is associated with **APOLLO, HERMES** and **ORPHEUS**.

LYRE Name for the constellation **LYRA**.

LYSITHEA Tenth satellite of **JUPITER**, one of the small outer group, discovered in 1938 by American astronomer Seth Barnes Nicholson (1891–1963).

MACH, Ernst (1838–1916) Austrian physicist and philosopher who gave his name to the 'Mach Number', expressing the ratio of the speed of a body to the speed of sound in the surrounding atmosphere. Also proposer of the Mach Principle, which states that the mass of a body is generated by forces originating in all the matter of the Universe, exerting pressure on that body.

MACROCOSM From Latin *macro* and Greek *kosmos*: the 'great world'. Mediaeval philosophers saw man, the 'Microcosm', as a miniature model of the Macroscosm, the Universe.

MAFFEI GALAXIES Two INFRARED sources close to the plane of the MILKY WAY, possibly GALAXIES belonging to our own group, discovered by the Italian astronomer Paolo Maffei in 1968.

MAGELLANIC CLOUDS Two small GALAXIES near the MILKY WAY. The larger, Nubecula Major, is some 8° in diameter; Nubecula Minor is about half that size. They cannot be observed north of latitude 15°N. Named for the Portuguese navigator Ferdinand Magellan (1480–1521), who first recorded them in 1519.

MAGI Plural of magus; the 'three wise men' who followed the star to Bethlehem are referred to as astrologers in ancient texts.

MAGNETIC FIELDS Areas of moving charged particles around a planet generated by the planet's own magnetism; one of the fundamental forces of nature.

MAGNETIC STORMS Outbursts of magnetic activity which disturb the Earth's MAGNETIC FIELD; usually caused by SOLAR FLARES or other changes in the Sun.

MAGNETIC VARIATION Angle between the direction of Magnetic North and True North at any particular location on the surface of the Earth. Its value can change with time.

MAGNETOBIOLOGY Study of the effect of natural or artificial magnetic fields on biological organisms.

MAGNETOSPHERE Huge region around the Earth, defined by the SOLAR WIND flowing past the Earth's MAGNETIC FIELD; twenty or thirty times larger than the Earth, it is pear-shaped, being flattened where it faces the Sun and tailing off behind. The flow of the Solar Wind and the orbital path of the Earth means that the magnetosphere is constantly changing shape; trapped inside are the belts of charged PARTICLES called VAN ALLEN BELTS.

MAGNITUDE Measure of the brightness of a star. VISUAL MAGNITUDE indicates how bright a star looks to an observer on Earth. ABSOLUTE MAGNITUDE indicates how bright a star would be observed from a distance of 10 PARSECS. Stars are classified within their constellations by their magnitudes (both visual and absolute are usually given). The lower the number, the brighter the star; the faintest objects so far recorded have a magnitude of 26. Magnitudes higher than zero are expressed as minus figures: SIRIUS, the brightest star in the sky, has a magnitude of −1.4 and the Sun is −26.8.

MAIA One of the seven bright stars in the brilliant PLEIADES open cluster; in Greek mythology, eldest daughter of ATLAS and PLEIONE, leader of the PLEIADES and mother of HERMES by ZEUS.

MAJOR ASPECTS See ASPECTS

MAKARA Indian name for the zodiac sign CAPRICORN.

MALEFIC ASPECT See ASPECTS

MALEFIC PLANETS Traditionally MARS and SATURN are called the lesser and greater malefics respectively; many modern astrologers deprecate such terms.

MANSIONS See LUNAR MANSIONS

MANZILS See LUNAR MANSIONS

MAP Chart of the heavens drawn up for astrological or astronomical study; often referred to as a BIRTH CHART, nativity, natus or geniture.

MARCAB Alpha Pegasi, in the constellation PEGASUS.

MARCH Third month of the GREGORIAN CALENDAR, named for MARS.

MARDUK Supreme god of Babylonian myth, the son of EA

Mars, Roman god of War

and Damkina; identified by the Romans with **JUPITER**.

MARIA MITCHELL OBSERVATORY On Nantucket Island, Mass.; founded in 1902 to honour America's first female astronomer, **MARIA MITCHELL**. (1818–1899).

MARINER'S COMPASS Name for the constellation **PYXIS**.

MARIUS, Simon (1570–1624) German astronomer, the first to view the **ANDROMEDA GALAXY** by **TELESCOPE**, in 1612.

MARKEB Kappa Velorum in the constellation **VELA**.

MARS Fourth planet from the Sun, just over half the size of Earth (diameter 6 750 km/4 219 miles); it orbits the Sun in 687 days and a Martian day lasts 24.7 hours. First observed closely by **GALILEO** through his **TELESCOPE** in 1610; its red colour is due to persistent dust storms. Mars has two moons, **DEIMOS** and **PHOBOS**. Astrologically, Mars rules **ARIES**, is **EXALTED** in **CAPRICORN**, at **DETRIMENT** in **LIBRA** and at **FALL** in **CANCER**. Mars is associated with the body's muscular system, the blood and the adrenal glands; Mars subjects show positive traits of leadership, bravery, decisiveness and the pioneering spirit; on the negative side, they can be foolhardy, aggressive, brutal and thoughtless. In Roman mythology, Mars is the god of war, equated with the Greek Ares.

MASCULINE ZODIAC SIGNS The ancients divided the signs of the zodiac into masculine and **FEMININE** groups. The masculine signs, related to positive, outgoing or aggressive phenomena, are the **FIRE** signs **ARIES**, **LEO** and **SAGITTARIUS**, and the **AIR** signs **LIBRA** (although Libra, a **VENUS** subject, is the most diplomatic and easy-going sign), **AQUARIUS** and **GEMINI**.

MATUTINE Term for a star or planet that rises with the Sun in the morning, or for planets already above the horizon at sunrise.

Medusa slain by Perseus

MAUNA KEA OBSERVATORY Splendidly sited observatory on the summit of Mauna Kea mountain, Hawaii, at an elevation of 4 267 m (14 000 ft).

MAXWELL, James Clerk (1831–89) Scottish physicist who became first Professor of Experimental Physics at Cambridge in 1871; famous for his theory of **ELECTROMAGNETIC RADIATION**.

MAY Fifth month of the **GREGORIAN CALENDAR**; named for the nymph **MAIA**, mother of **HERMES**.

MAYAN ASTROLOGY The Maya, an Indian people of Central America, devised a series of **CALENDARS**, one of 365 days, one of 360 days, and a third, pertaining to religion and ritual, of 260 days. They studied the positions of the planets, notably **VENUS**, and could predict **ECLIPSES**. Keen astrologers, they drew up **HOROSCOPES** for the newly born.

MC Abbreviation for **MEDIUM COELI**; see **MIDHEAVEN**.

MEAN SUN For the purpose of timekeeping, an imaginary sun moving at a constant rate along the **CELESTIAL EQUATOR**.

MECHAIN, Pierre (1744–1805) French astronomer specializing in **COMETS**; discoverer of **ENCKE'S COMET** and eight others between 1781 and 1799.

MEDICI, Catherine de (1519–1589) Wife, later widow, of King Henry II of France. She brought the astrologer **NOSTRADAMUS** to her court, but terminated the association when alarmed by his necromantic activities.

Mayan ruins of Palenque, Mexico

MEDICINE AND ASTROLOGY Until the eighteenth century, medical training included instruction in astrology as an aid to diagnosis and treatment.

MEDIUM COELI (MC) Latin for **MIDHEAVEN**.

MEDUSA In classical mythology, the most hideous of the three serpent-haired Gorgons.

MEGALITHIC SITES The great stone menhirs and other megalithic markers on sites throughout western Europe are believed to have been erected to mark the positions of the Sun, Moon and planets. See also **CARNAC; STONEHENGE**.

MEGAPARSEC Equivalent to one million **PARSECS**.

MEGREZ Delta Ursae Majoris in the constellation **URSA MAJOR**.

MELPOMENE **ASTEROID 18**, discovered in 1852; has a diameter of about 150 km/93 miles. In Greek mythology, one of the nine **MUSES**; her domain was Tragedy.

MENHIRS See **MEGALITHIC SITES**

MENKAR Alpha Ceti in the constellation **CETUS**

MENKALINA Beta Aurigae in the northern constellation **AURIGA**.

MENSA, the Table Southern constellation identified by **LACAILLE** in 1752 as *Mons Mensae* ('Table Mountain'); a small part of the larger **MAGELLANIC CLOUD** lies within it.

MERAK Beta Ursae Majoris, one of the stars that make up the distinctive **PLOUGH** pattern in **URSA MAJOR**.

MERCURY Nearest planet to the Sun; less than half the size of **EARTH**, with a diameter of 4880 km/3030 miles, it rushes round the Sun in a period of 88 days, but rotates on its own axis in 59 days, so that a Mercurian day lasts almost two-thirds of its year. No moons. Astrologically, Mercury rules **GEMINI** and **VIRGO**, is at **DETRIMENT** in **SAGITTARIUS**, and at **FALL** in **PISCES**. Mercury is associated with the brain, the nervous system and the respiratory system. Mercury subjects may be very intellectual, perceptive, versatile, quick-minded; on the negative side, they may be argumentative, cynical, hypercritical and inconsistent. In Roman mythology, Mercury was the son of **JUPITER** and **MAIA**, the messenger of the gods; equated with the Greek **HERMES**, god of science, commerce and travellers, including thieves and vagabonds. He is represented as a youth with a winged hat and sandals, carrying a staff representing two twisted snakes, called a caduceus.

MERIDIAN Imaginary **GREAT CIRCLE** on the Earth's surface, passing through the North and South Poles and all places with the same **LONGITUDE**; the corresponding celestial meridian passes through both **CELESTIAL POLES**; see also **PRIME MERIDIAN**.

Mercury, from Izmir, Turkey

MERIDIAN CIRCLE A telescope sited on a north/ south **MERIDIAN** so that it can measure the **RIGHT ASCENSION** and **DECLINATION** of a star as it crosses that meridian; these co-ordinates are used to establish the star's **PROPER MOTION**.

MEROPE One of the stars in the **PLEIADES** visible to the naked eye; in Greek mythology, one of the daughters of **ATLAS** and **PLEIONE** and wife of **SISYPHUS**.

MESOPOTAMIA Literally, the area 'between the waters'; the fertile crescent between the rivers Tigris and Euphrates that water the area between the Mediterranean and the Persian Gulf; the cradle of Sumerian and Babylonian civilization.

MESOSPHERE Layer of the earth's atmosphere that lies above the **STRATOSPHERE**. The upper mesosphere merges into the **THERMOSPHERE**.

MESSIER, Charles (1730–1817) French astronomer who made a catalogue of more than 100 stars, **GALAXIES** and the like, assigning each an **M NUMBER**.

METEOR Small particle of interplanetary dust that, moving through Earth's upper **ATMOSPHERE** at immense speed, burns itself out in a radiant streak. Meteors often manifest themselves annually, sometimes in showers or streams.

METEORITE A body that survives its entry from space into the atmosphere and reaches Earth, sometimes as a fireball.

METIS **ASTEROID 9**, discovered in 1848; it has a diameter of 150 km/93 miles.

METONIC CYCLE A nineteen-year cycle of the **MOON**, following which the Moon's **PHASES** repeat themselves on the same days of the year.

METOSCOPY The study of facial lines and of moles or marks on the body, which are said to be indications of character.

MEUDON OBSERVATORY Founded in 1876 by **JANNSEN** at an ancient castle near Paris. It was enlarged in around 1950 and by 1953 its activities included **RADIO ASTRONOMY**.

M51 The **WHIRLPOOL GALAXY**.

MICHEL DE NOTRE DAME See **NOSTRADAMUS**

MICROCOSM See **MACROCOSM**

MICROMETER Instrument for measuring the angular separation of celestial bodies, diameters of planets, etc; invented by the Englishman William Gascoigne in 1636.

MICROSCOPE Name for the constellation **MICROSCOPIUM**.

MICROSCOPIUM, the Microscope Small southern constellation near **GRUS**.

MICROWAVE RADIATION Comprised of **ELECTROMAGNETIC** waves between the **INFRARED** and **RADIO** spectrum, this reaches Earth through the **RADIO WINDOW**.

MIDAS **ASTEROID 1981**, one of the **APOLLO** group, discovered by Charles Kowal.

MIDHEAVEN The point where the **ECLIPTIC** crosses the subject's **MERIDIAN**, or line of longitude at birth. Opposite to the **IMUM COELI**.

MIDNIGHT SUN At certain times of year, in locations inside the Arctic and Antarctic Circles, the Sun may be seen above the horizon at midnight; it is always visible at the North Pole when it is north of the **CELESTIAL EQUATOR**.

MIDPOINT Point midway between two points, bodies or planets; established by adding together the **ABSOLUTE LONGITUDE** of each body and dividing the result by two.

Minerva, Roman goddess of wisdom

MILKY WAY Name given to the GALAXY, containing the Solar System which is of SPIRAL type with the Sun and its family of planets moving along one arm of the spiral.

MIMAS Innermost satellite of SATURN, with a diameter of 390 km/242 miles and locked in synchronous rotation with the planet; discovered by William HERSCHEL in 1789.

MINERVA Roman goddess of wisdom and patron of the arts, also a warlike deity; associated with the Greek ATHENA.

MINOAN CIVILIZATION Bronze Age civilization that flourished on Crete from c2500 BC. Knossos, its centre, was destroyed by fire and earthquake in c1400 BC. It is named from Minos, in Greek mythology the ruler of Crete and son of ZEUS and EUROPA.

MINOR PLANETS See ASTEROIDS

MINOS In Cretan mythology, son of ZEUS and EUROPA, king of Crete, considered to be the father of Minoan civilization.

MINTAKA Delta Orionis in the constellation ORION.

MINUTE OF ARC See ARC

MIRA Omicron Ceti in the constellation CETUS; a RED GIANT that varies greatly in brightness, it is the prototype long-period VARIABLE.

MIRACH Beta Andromedae, in the constellation ANDROMEDA.

MIRANDA Satellite of URANUS, discovered in 1948; named for a Shakespearean character, like its fellow moons.

MIRZAM Beta Canis Majoris in the constellation CANIS MAJOR.

MITCHELL, Maria (1818–1889) American woman astronomer, founder of the observatory that bears her name.

MITHRA OR MITHRAS Persian god of light, the friend and protector of mankind; identified with the Sun.

MIZAR Zeta Ursae Majoris, one of the seven stars constituting the PLOUGH or Big Dipper in URSA MAJOR.

MNEMOSYNE In Greek mythology, the goddess of memory; daughter of URANUS and GAEA and mother, by ZEUS, of the nine MUSES.

M NUMBERS The astronomer MESSIER placed his initial, M, before the numbers he assigned to the celestial objects in his catalogue.

MODUS EQUALIS A term sometimes applied to the equal house system of HOUSE DIVISION.

MOERA See ICARIUS

MOIRA In Greek mythology, the power of fate.

MONDAY Second day of the week; named for the MOON.

M11 The WILD DUCK CLUSTER.

MONOCEROS, the Unicorn Constellation situated near ORION , and crossed by the CELESTIAL EQUATOR and the MILKY WAY.

MONS MENSA See MENSA

Knossos, centre of Minoan culture

The Moon, Earth's influential companion

MONTH The time it takes the Moon to work through its cycle of phases: around 29/30 days. There are various kinds of month, depending on how measurement is taken, but to astrologers the most important are the SIDEREAL MONTH and the SYNODIC MONTH. The synodic month is the interval between New Moons, a period of 29 days 12 hours 44 minutes and 2.7 seconds. The sidereal month is the time taken by the Moon to make two successive passages across a FIXED STAR: it varies by up to seven hours, but the mean is 27.32 days. See also METONIC CYCLE; SAROS.

MOON Earth's only satellite; next to the Sun, the most spectacular celestial object in the sky and subject of much study; its regular changes of shape (phases) have been recorded by every civilization, as have the ECLIPSES. The Moon has a diameter of 3 448 km/2 142 miles, and orbits the Earth in a mean period of 29.53 days. Astrologically, the Moon rules CANCER, is EXALTED in Taurus, at DETRIMENT in CAPRICORN and at FALL in SCORPIO. After the Sun, it is the most important and influential celestial body in a CHART, affecting instinctive behaviour and inherited characteristics. Moon subjects are sensitive and imaginative, maternal, receptive and shrewd; on the negative side, they can be moody, gullible and unreliable. Almost every culture has a mythology about the Moon; it has many names which differ according to various cultures. In Greek mythology, the Moon was said to be HECATE before rising and after setting, and ASTARTE when a crescent Moon. The Romans called her DIANA, to the Greeks she was ARTEMIS and was also associated with SELENE; the Moon has always had a strong connection with the feminine power.

Background: Kepler's notation for the Music of the Spheres

MOONS Satellites that orbit the planets in the Solar System; MERCURY and VENUS have no moons; Earth has one; MARS has two; JUPITER has sixteen known moons, SATURN has at least seventeen, URANUS has fifteen, NEPTUNE has six (so far) and PLUTO one.

MOON MANSIONS See LUNAR MANSIONS

MOON'S NODES The Moon's north NODE, called the Dragon's Head, is the point on the ECLIPTIC where the ascending Moon crosses from south to north latitude. Its south node, when it is called the Dragon's Tail.

MOON'S PHASES In order, these are the New Moon, when it is first seen after conjunction with the Sun; the first crescent; the first quarter; the GIBBOUS, when it is half-full, and the full. The phases then reverse.

MORIN DE VILLEFRANCHE French astrologer at the court of Anne of Austria, queen-regent of France (1641–1643). He developed the Morinus system of astrological HOUSE DIVISION.

MORINUS HOUSE SYSTEM See MORIN DE VILLEFRANCHE; HOUSE DIVISION.

MORNING STAR The planet VENUS.

MOUNT PALOMAR OBSERVATORY Sited east of San Diego, California, Mount Palomar was formerly combined with the MOUNT WILSON OBSERVATORY, when the two were jointly known as the Hale Observatory. It is famous for the HALE reflector, a 508 cm/200 in. TELESCOPE completed in 1946 and at that time the largest in the world.

MOUNT STROMLO OBSERVATORY One of Australia's major observatories, founded in 1924 and sited near Canberra.

MOUNT WILSON OBSERVATORY Solar observatory near Pasadena, California, founded by George HALE.

M27 The DUMB-BELL NEBULA.

MU CEPHEI An irregular VARIABLE called the GARNET STAR; in the northern constellation of CEPHEUS.

MULLARD OBSERVATORY RADIO ASTRONOMY observatory at the University of Cambridge, England.

MUNDANE ASTROLOGY Branch of astrology concerned with nations, political parties and such inanimate objects as buildings, ships or vehicles.

MUSCA AUSTRALIS, the Southern Fly Small but fairly rich constellation.

MUSES The nine daughters of ZEUS and MNEMOSYNE; in Greek mythology the patrons of arts, sciences and of such attributes as memory and meditation. They were Calliope, Clio, Erato, Euterpe, MELPOMENE, Polyhymnia, TERPSICHORE, THALIA and URANIA; they lived on Mount HELICON with APOLLO.

MUSLIM CALENDAR See CALENDAR, MUSLIM

MUSIC OF THE SPHERES In the ancient Greek world view, which persisted long into the fifteenth century, the Earth was the centre of the Solar System, and the Sun, Moon and planets were thought to orbit it. Some authorities considered them to be mounted on crystal spheres nested within each other, and the heavenly sounds made by the spheres as they gracefully revolved was called the Music of the Spheres; other philosophers considered that the planets vibrated at different pitches as they moved at different rates, and that their music corresponded to their rate of motion. Also known as Harmony of the Spheres, as it was considered that all things in Nature were inherently harmonious. PYTHAGORAS claimed that humans could not hear the music because their souls were out of harmony with them.

MUTABLE SIGNS GEMINI, VIRGO, SAGITTARIUS and PISCES; mutable signs emphasize the flexible, adaptable changeable side of life. See also CARDINAL SIGNS, FIXED SIGNS.

MUTUAL RECEPTION Two planets are in mutual reception if, in a CHART each is placed in the sign ruled by the other.

MYCENAEAN CIVILIZATION A culture that flourished in Greece, Crete, Cyprus and the Aegean islands c4000–1000 BC. Excellent architects and craftsmen, the Myceneans used a form of writing in Linear B. They are identified with the Achaeans, a dominant group during the Homeric siege of Troy.

NABURIANNU (c500 BC) Babylonian mathematician and astronomer who computed astronomical tables to establish the **AYANASMA.**

NADIR Point on the **CELESTIAL SPHERE** lying exactly below the observer's feet; the intersection of the **PRIME VERTICAL** and the **MERIDIAN**. Also known as the North Point. See also **ZENITH**.

NAIADS In Greek mythology, nymphs of freshwater lakes, brooks and streams.

NAKSHATRAS Hindu name for the **LUNAR MANSIONS**.

NANJING OBSERVATORY Astronomical research laboratory, founded in 1934, sited on one of the peaks of the Purple Mountain, northeast of Nanjing, China; publishes the *Astronomical Bulletin* of the Chinese Astronomical Society; also known as the Purple Mountain Observatory.

NANOMETRE One thousand-millionth of a metre abbreviated to nm: a microscopic unit of measurement used to measure **LIGHT** wavelengths.

NASHIRA Gamma Capricornii, fourth brightest star in **CAPRICORNUS**.

NATAL ASTROLOGY Branch of astrology concerned with the erection and interpretaton of **BIRTH CHARTS**, compiled for a person's time of birth.

NATAL CHART **BIRTH CHART**

NATIVE The person for whom a **BIRTH CHART** or **HOROSCOPE** is erected.

NATIVITY Another name for **BIRTH CHART**.

NAVAMSA Term in Hindu astrology; subdivision of a zodiac sign by nine, as a **DECAN** is a subdivision by three. Different qualities were ascribed to each navamsa. See also **DWAD**.

NAVAMSA CHART In Hundi astrology the ninth **HARMONIC** chart.

NEAP TIDES Smaller tides which occur at the first or last of the Moon's quarters. See also **TIDES**.

NEBUCHADNEZZAR (fl. 604–561 BC) Famous Babylonian ruler who reestablished the country's power base by recapturing lost provinces, rebuilt much of Babylon itself, and restored most of the temples in the country.

NEBULA Cloud of dust and gas in space; may be light and hazy or dark, and appear in many different shapes and sizes; either produce their own light (by gas fluoresence) or the dust motes reflect starlight; dark nebula only shows up against a bright background (see **COAL SACK NEBULA**).

NECROMANCY Fortune telling or prophesying by contacting the dead; in some cases, mixed up with black magic or witchcraft.

NEGATIVE SIGNS Astrologically, the **EARTH** and **WATER** signs: **TAURUS, CANCER, VIRGO, SCORPIO, CAPRICORN** and **PISCES**, which alternate in the zodiac circle with the **POSITIVE** signs. Negative in this case implies receptiveness, latent potential, veiled power, reserved strength waiting for activation, a gathering in rather than an outpouring; the principle is similar to the Chinese concept of **YIN/YANG**.

NEKKAR Beta Boötis in the constellation **BOÖTES**.

NEMEAN LION See **LION**

NEMESIS Daugher of **OCEANUS**; the goddess of vengeance, and retribution.

NEMESIUS (fl. fourth century) Philosopher who theorized that the return of all the celestial bodies to their original positions at the birth of the cosmos would mean the death of the cosmos and its subsequent rebirth into a new cycle.

NEPTUNE Eighth planet from the Sun, discovered by **GALLE** 23 September 1846, although its existence had been predicted by **ADAMS** and **LEVERRIER**; has a diameter of about 48 000 km/31 000 miles (much the same as **URANUS**) and seventeen times Earth's mass; orbits the Sun at a distance of 4 493 million km/2 793 million miles and takes between 164 and 179 years to complete its orbit; thought to have only two moons, **NEREID** and **TRITON** until Voyager II's flyby in August 1989, which revealed the existence of four more moons, a ring system, a magnetic field and a Great Dark Spot twice the size of Earth. Neptune appears pale blue through binoculars.
Astrologically, Neptune is the ruler of **PISCES** and the **TWELFTH HOUSE**; its positive traits are idealism, spirituality, imagination, sensitivity, creativity; on the negative side, Neptune can promote deceitfulness, carelessness, sentimentality, indecision and impracticality. Neptune is associated the spinal canal, mental and nervous processes. In **mythology**, Neptune

Neptune, from a Tunisian mosaic

was the Roman equivalent of **POSEIDON**, god of the Sea, married to Amphitrite, daughter of **NEREUS**, and father of **TRITON**.

NEREID Smaller of the first two discovered satellites of **NEPTUNE**; takes 365 years to track around in a huge elongated orbit.

NEREIDS Sea nymphs, daughters of **NEREUS**.

NEREUS Greek sea god, sometimes called the 'Old Man of the Sea', father of the **NEREIDS**, one of whom married **NEPTUNE**.

NERGAL Sumerian god, ruler of the Underworld; also associated with **MARS**.

NESTOR ASTEROID 659 In the **TROJAN** group, discovered in 1908: in Trojan legend, the only son of Neleus spared by **HERCULES** in the Trojan War.

NET Name for constellation **RETICULUM**.

Hogarth's view of Newton's laws of gravity

NEUTRAL POINT Point between two celestial bodies, where their gravitational pull is equal.

NEUTRINO Extremely tiny **PARTICLE** with no electrical charge; travels at the speed of light and is capable of penetrating huge distances in matter. Neutrinos are produced in the heart of the Sun and similar stars.

NEUTRON STARS Tiny very dense stars in which all the **PROTONS** have been compressed into neutrons; what is left after the death of a **SUPERNOVA**; in effect, very strong magnets which spin rapidly, pushing out waves of **ELECTROMAGNETIC RADIATION**. Their effect on life in the Universe has yet to be assessed. See also **PULSARS**.

NEW MOON Appearance of the Moon as a thin crescent, after its **CONJUNCTION** with the Sun; in astrological terms, the time of the conjunction itself, very important in **MUNDANE** and **NATAL ASTROLOGY**.

NEWTON, Sir Isaac (1642–1727) Mathematician, physicist and philosopher; invented the reflector **TELESCOPE** (1671) and formulated the theory of **GRAVITY**, which he reluctantly published in his great work *Philosophiae Naturalis Principia Mathematica* ('The Mathematical Principles of Natural Philosophy') (1687).

NIAS, D.K.B. Co-author with Professor **EYSENCK** of *Astrology, Science or Superstition?* (1982).

NICE OBSERVATORY Private concern built in 1881; reputed for work on **ASTEROIDS**, **COMETS** and **DOUBLE STARS**.

NIDABA Sumerian goddess of writing and music.

NILE Egyptian river, the inadvertent cause of the invention of the **EGYPTIAN CALENDAR**; in order to accurately predict the mighty but fruitful Nile flood, Egyptian astronomers studied the dawn sky and found that the rising of the bright star **SOTHIS** (**SIRIUS**) occurred just before the flood. They based their **CALENDAR** on this regular occurrence.

19 TAURI The star **TAYGETE**.

NINEVEH Capital of the Assyrian Empire from the eighth century BC; destroyed by the Medes in 612 BC.

NIOBE Goddess of maternal sorrow.

NINTH HOUSE Astrological **HOUSE** associated with the zodiac sign **SAGITTARIUS** and ruled by **JUPITER**; concerned with travel, exploration, long journeys into the unknown, both mental and physical; rules foreign countries, languages, further education, the Church, law, inspiration, prophecy and dreams.

NINTH SIGN OF THE ZODIAC See **SAGITTARIUS**

NOCTILUCENT CLOUDS Sheets of rippling silvery clouds observed in northern latitudes in high summer; they float 80 km/50 miles above Earth and are lit from beneath by the Sun when it is below the observer's **HORIZON**; possibly composed of a layer of dust thinly coated with water ice.

NOCTURNAL ARC Portion of the Sun's (or planet's) travel during which it journeys below the horizon.

NOCTURNAL DIVINITIES Aztec gods of the night; Aztec astronomers divided the night sky into nine segments, each one representing a deity.

NODAL LINE Line drawn to join the Moon's **NODES**.

NODES Points where the orbits of the planets and the Moon cross the **ECLIPTIC**; the points at which they have no **DECLINATION**; astrologically, the Moons nodes are considered to be significant, especially in **INDIAN ASTROLOGY**.

NONES Ninth day before the **IDES** of a month according to ancient Roman calculation. See also **CALENDS**.

NOON DATE See **ADJUSTED CALCULATION DATE**

The Nile bordering Africa

NORMA, the Rule Small, obscure constellation near **ARA** and **LUPUS**.

NORNS In Norse mythology, the equivalent of the **FATES**; **ERDA** or Urd, Verandi and Skuld.

NORTH NODE See **NODES**

NORTH POINT See **NADIR**

NORTH POLE STAR See **POLE STAR**

NORTHERN CROSS See **CYGNUS**

NORTHERN CROWN See **CORONA BOREALIS**

NORTHERN LIGHTS See **AURORA BOREALIS**

Nostradamus, foreteller of doom

NOSTRADAMUS (Michel de Nostredame) (1503–1566) French physician and astrologer; published an annual **ALMANAC** but is renowned for his books of rhyming predictions, *Les Centuries* (1555–58).

NOTUS The southwest wind; son of **EOS** and **ASTRAEUS**; called Auster by the Romans. See also **WINDS**.

NOVA Star which suddenly flares into brightness, shines very brightly for a short time, then fades back into obscurity; mostly members of **BINARY** systems, thought to be caused by the equivalent of a nuclear explosion in the star.

NOVEMBER Eleventh month of the **GREGORIAN CALENDAR**; named for the Latin for 'nine', *novum*, as it was the ninth month of the **JULIAN CALENDAR**.

NUBECULA MAJOR Larger of the **MAGELLANIC CLOUDS**.

NUBECULA MINOR Smaller of the **MAGELLANIC CLOUDS**.

NUMEROLOGY Study of the symbolic and magical properties of numbers. **PYTHAGORAS** suggested that numbers are the basis of all reality.

NUT Egyptian goddess of the sky, depicted arching over her twin and lover **GEB**, the Earth god, her body forming the Egyptian **FIRMAMENT**; she was supposed to swallow the stars in the morning and give birth to them again at night.

NUTATION Slight nodding or oscillation of the Earth's axis; result of the Moon's orbit being inclined 5° to the Earth orbit, therefore causing variable gravitational effects which alter the Earth's tilt slightly (nine seconds of **ARC**) over a period of 18.6 years; discovered by James **BRADLEY**.

NYSA **ASTEROID 44**, brightest known asteroid. In Greek mythology, the Libyan mountain where **DIONYSUS** hid from the wrath of **HERA** and invented wine.

OANNES Babylonian god with the body of a fish and the head and feet of a human.

OBERON Outermost satellite of **URANUS**; about the size of the Earth's Moon.

OBLIQUE ASCENSION Component of the calculations used in the Koch system of **HOUSE DIVISION**. In northern latitudes, it is the **R A** *minus* the ascensional difference (for north declination) or *plus* the ascensional difference (for south declination); in southern latitudes, the rule is reversed. Ascensional difference is the angle between a rising star or planet and the part of the equator which is simultaneously rising.

OBLIQUITY OF THE ECLIPTIC Angle of the tilt between the **ECLIPTIC** and the **CELESTIAL EQUATOR**; currently (1990) 23° 26′ 26″; it varies over a period of 40 000 years from between 21° 55′ and 28° 18′.

OCCIDENTAL MOON Term describing the Moon relative to the Sun when it is decreasing in light, from **FULL MOON** to **NEW MOON**.

OCCIDENTAL PLANETS Planets placed on the right hand or western or right hand side of a **CHART**.

OCCULTATION Occurs when a distant celestial body is hidden or eclipsed by a nearer one.

OCCURSIONS Astrological term for celestial occurrences such as the formation of **ASPECTS**, **INGRESS**, etc.

OCEANUS One of the **TITANS**, an ancient Greek god of the Sea.

OCTAGON ROOM Room in **GREENWICH OBSERVATORY** cunningly designed by Sir Christopher Wren with high windows to allow the use of long **TELESCOPES**.

OCTANS, the Octant Faint southern constellation containing the current, and unremarkable, South Pole Star, Sigma Octantis.

OCTANT Name for constellation **OCTANS**.

OCTILE Alternative name for the **SEMI SQUARE**.

OCTOBER Tenth month of the **GREGORIAN CALENDAR**; named for the latin for eight, *octo*, because it was the eighth month of the **JULIAN CALENDAR**.

ODIN Greatest of the Norse gods; god of wisdom, poetry, agriculture and the dead; often depicted as one-eyed (his eye representing the Sun). Some association with **MERCURY**.

Oceanus, the Roman god of the sea

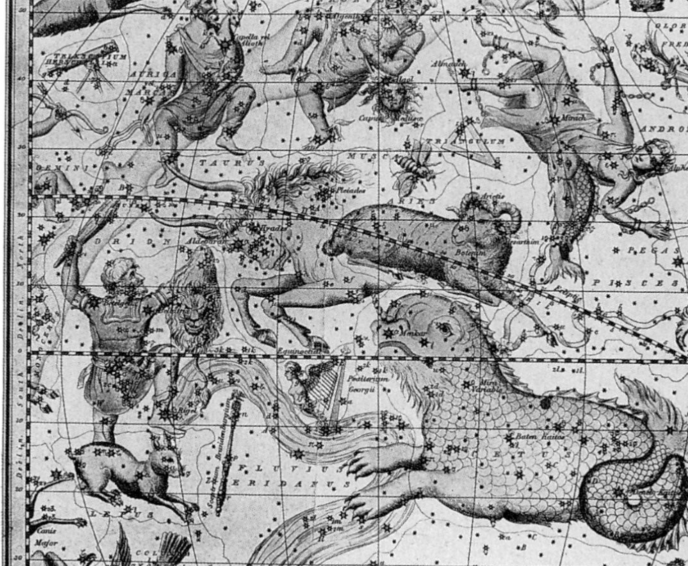

ODYSSEUS See **ULYSSES**

OEBALUS In Greek mythology King of Sparta, father of Tyndareus, Hippocoon and **ICARIUS**.

OLBERS, Heinrich (1758–1840) German medical doctor and amateur astronomer; discovered two of the first **ASTEROIDS** (**PALLAS** and **VESTA**), and sponsored and supported the career of Friedrich Wilhelm **BESSEL**.

OLBERS' COMET Bright, long period **COMET** seen three times (1815, 1887 and 1956) and expected again 2025; its orbit was plotted by Friedrich Wilhelm **BESSEL**, who named the comet for his patron Heinrich **OLBERS**.

OLD, Walter Richard One of the **ANGELIC ASTROLOGERS**, known as **SERAPHIAL**.

OLJATO **ASTEROID 2201**, one of the **APOLLO** group rediscovered in 1979; possibly the burnt-out remains of a **COMET**.

OLYMPIA Valley in Elis, Peloponnesus, centre of **ZEUS** worship and site of the first **OLYMPIC GAMES** held to honour him in 776 BC.

OLYMPIAN ZEUS or **JOVE** Ivory and gold statue of the king of the gods by Phidias (d. 432 BC), the greatest sculptor of ancient Greece; sixty feet high and supported by four lions, the statue dominated the Temple of Zeus at Olympia.

OLYMPIC GAMES Founded by **HERCULES** to honour **ZEUS**; first Olympiad in 776 BC and the last in AD 392; they were revived in 1896 as an international sporting event.

OLYMPUS Mountain home of the Greek Gods in Thessaly.

OMEGA CENTAURI Brightest **GLOBULAR CLUSTER** in the **GALAXY**, visible to the naked eye in the constellation **CENTAURUS**.

OMICRON CETI See **MIRA**

ONE DEGREE METHOD Used to **PROGRESS** a chart using the **FIXED INCREMENT** or symbolic method; uses one degree of **ARC** to equal one year of life. See **DIRECTIONS**.

ONSALA SPACE OBSERVATORY Radio Observatory near Göthenburg, Sweden.

OPEN CLUSTERS Cluster of stars which are close to each other and move in a group through space.

Orion the Hunter

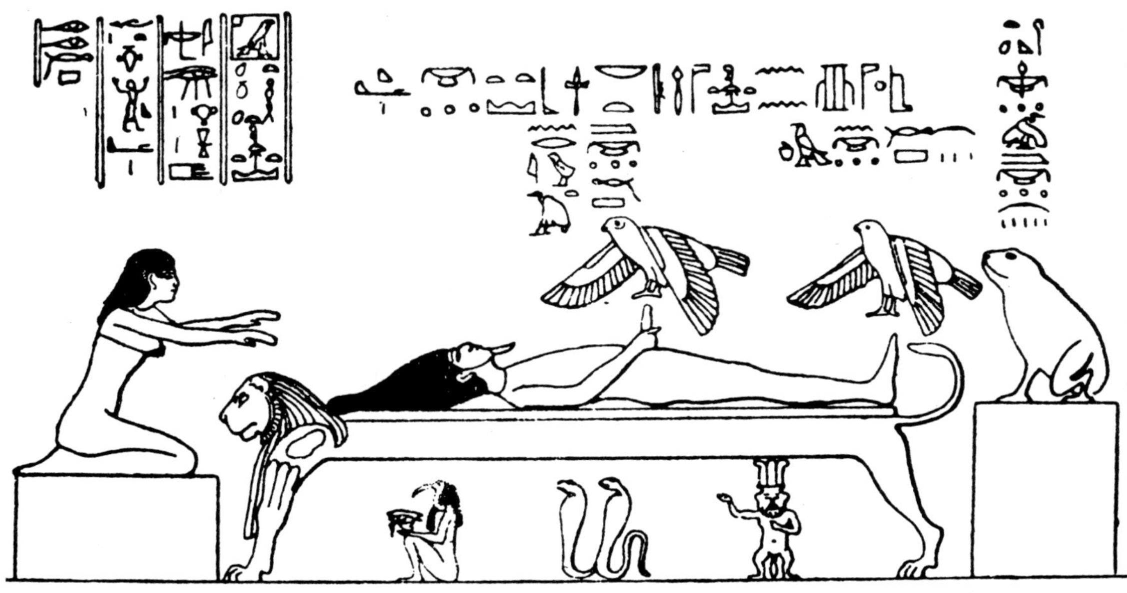

Osiris begetting Horus

OPHIUCHUS, the Serpent-Bearer Huge but ill-defined constellation, one of PTOLEMY'S orginal forty-eight; its ALPHA is Rasalhague.

OPPOLZER, Theodor Egon Ritter von (1841–1886) Austrian astronomer; catalogued every Solar and Lunar ECLIPSE from 1207 BC to AD 2163, published in 1887 as the *Canon of Eclipse*.

OPPOSITION Two celestial bodies 180° apart in a CHART; the second most important astrological ASPECT.

OPS Early Roman Goddess of Plenty, later identified with Rhea, the wife of SATURN.

OPTICAL DOUBLES Stars which appear to be close together to an observer on Earth, but could be in reality light years apart; see also BINARY STARS; DOUBLE STARS.

ORBIT Path a celestial body describes within the gravitational field.

ORBS Astrological term for the number of degrees allowed in a CHART for different ASPECTS when these are forming or separating from EXACTITUDE, and the aspect could still be effective.

ORCUS Roman name for the Underworld, the abode of DIS.

ORIENTAL PLANETS Planets on the eastern side of the chart, moving over the horizon towards the MERIDIAN. See also OCCIDENTAL PLANETS.

ORIENTAL MOON Term describing the Moon relative to the Sun when it is increasing in light, from NEW MOON to FULL MOON.

ORION, the Hunter Spectacular constellation, one of PTOLEMY'S original forty-eight, which straddles the CELESTIAL EQUATOR and is therefore visible from both hemispheres; the brightest star is Beta Orionis, or Rigel, a giant DOUBLE STAR, the seventh brightest in the sky; the ALPHA is BETELGEUX, a red VARIABLE supergiant; the three stars that make up Orion's Belt are Alnilam (Epsilon Orionis), Alnitak (Zeta Orionis) and Mintaka (Delta Orionis); below the belt lies Orion's Sword, which contains the splendid Orion Nebula (M42, also called the Great Nebula), at the heart of which lies Theta Orionis, a multiple star with four components, known as the Trapezium. In Greek mythology Orion was a very dashing hunter, son of POSEIDON; blinded by Oenopion of Chios to revenge the rape of his daughter Merope, he restored his sight by staring into the rising Sun, but was later accidentally killed by ARTEMIS and his image set in the heavens.

ORION NEBULA See ORION

ORION'S BELT Distinctive pattern of three stars (Alnilam, Alnitak and Mintaka) that cross the centre of ORION.

ORPHEUS In Greek mythology, son of Oeagrus and Calliope, considered the greatest poet and musician of his time; given a lyre by APOLLO, with which he charmed HADES while trying to retrieve his wife Eurydice from the Underworld. The lyre was put into heavens as LYRA.

ORRERY Mechanical model of the Solar System used to plot the movements of the celestial bodies; named for Irish peer Charles Boyle, Fourth Earl of Orrery (1676–1731).

OSIRIS Ancient Egyptian god of the Underworld; son of NUT and brother of SET, husband to ISIS.

OUTER PLANETS Planets beyond Earth; also known as the SUPERIOR PLANETS.

OWL Symbol of ATHENE and the sacred bird of Athens; said to be lucky for those born under the sign of LEO.

OWL NEBULA PLANETARY NEBULA M97 in the constellation URSA MAJOR; discovered by Pierre MECHAIN in 1781; it looks like an owl's face.

Rowley's Orrery (bottom)

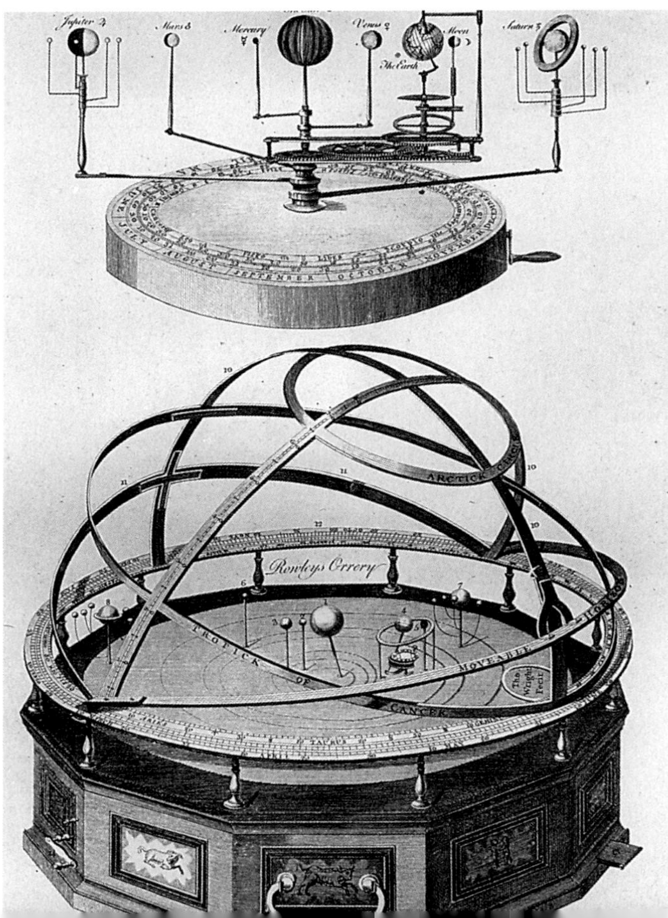

PAINTER Name for the constellation **PICTOR**.

PAINTER'S EASEL Alternative name for the constellation **PICTOR**.

PALAMEDES In Greek mythology, son of Nauplius and Clymene and one of the heroes who fought against the Trojans; reputed inventor of the scales, dice and lighthouses.

PALES Roman god of sheep and shepherds.

PALLAS **ASTEROID 2**, discovered by **OLBERS** in March 1802; third brightest asteroid in the sky; named for **PALLAS ATHENE**.

PALLAS ATHENE See **ATHENE**

PALMISTRY Cheiromancy, the ancient art of telling fortunes from the lines on the subject's hand. Palmists divide palms into five distinct zones (called Mounts) named after the Sun (Apollo in palmist terms), Moon (Luna in palmist terms) and the five planets **MERCURY, VENUS, MARS, JUPITER** and **SATURN**.

PALOMAR See **MOUNT PALOMAR**

PAN In Greek mythology, misshapen god, half man, half goat; lover of many nymphs.

PANDORA Third satellite of Saturn in terms of distance, discovered in 1980 from photographs taken by Voyager I; small and icy, it is a shepherd satellite (along with **PROMETHEUS**) of Saturn's F ring. In Greek mythology, Pandora was the equivalent of Eve; created by the gods as companion to the first mortal Epimetheus (brother of Prometheus), she opened a forbidden box and unleashed the troubles of the world.

Pan and Olympus

PANOPE One of the **NEREIDS**.

PANSPERMIA Theory first put forward in 1906 by Swedish chemist and Nobel Prize winner Svante Arrhenius which suggested that life came to Earth by means of a **METEORITE**.

PARACELSUS, Theophrastus Bombastus Von Hohenheim (1490–1541) Swiss physician, chemist and alchemist; extremely interested in astrology, believing that 'influences from the Sun and planets and stars act invisibly on man'.

PARALLAX Mathematical method of determining a star's distance. Any object viewed from two different positions appears to shift slightly relative to its background; a nearby star observed from the same place on Earth at six-monthly intervals will show apparent movement against background stars (as the Earth itself moves half-way round its orbit in six months, it provides two different viewing positions). The distance the star appears to move is expressed as an angle; parallax is defined as half this angular distance and can be used trigonometrically, to calculate the linear distance.

PARALLEL DECLINATION Abbreviated as Par. Dec. Occurs when two bodies are the same distance or **DECLINATION** from the **CELESTIAL EQUATOR**; whether both are north or both south, or one north and the other south is immaterial.

PARCAE Roman equivalent of the Greek **FATES**.

PARIS In Greek legend, son of King Priam of Troy and abductor of **HELEN**; killed **ACHILLES** at the seige of Troy, but was himself fatally wounded.

PARIS OBSERVATORY Oldest observatory in the world still functioning; built to the order of Louis XIV in 1667 by Charles Perrault.

PARKES OBSERVATORY Australian centre for **RADIO ASTRONOMY**, and national radio observatory; situated in New South Wales.

PARNASSUS Twin peaked mountain near Delphi, Greece; home of **APOLLO** and the **MUSES**; also sacred to **DIONYSUS**. See also **HELICON**.

PARSEC Distance a star would have to be from the observer to show a **PARALLAX** of one second of **ARC**; one parsec equals 3.26 **LIGHT YEARS**.

PARTHENON Great temple at Athens, began c445 BC, dedicated to **ATHENE**.

PARTHENOPE **ASTEROID 11**, discovered in May 1850 by De Gasparis; it is 150 km/93 miles across. In classical mythology, one of the Sirens who lured Odysseus.

PART OF FORTUNE See **FORTUNA**

PART RULER See **ACCIDENTAL RULERSHIP**

PARTICLES Tiny subdivisions of matter; examples are electron, neutron, **PROTON, PHOTON**.

PASIPHAE Eighth satellite of **JUPITER**, discovered in 1908; very small (diameter 150 km/93 miles) with a **RETROGRADE** orbit, indicating that it may be a captured **ASTEROID**. In Greek mythology, the wife of King **MINOS** of Crete, mother of **ARIADNE**, also mother of the Minotaur fathered on her by **ZEUS** in disguise as a white bull. See also **EUROPA**.

PATIENTIA **ASTEROID 451**, discovered December 1899; one of the largest known asteroids, with a diameter of 276 km/172 miles.

PATROCLUS **ASTEROID 617**, one of the brightest of the **TROJANS**; discovered October 1906. In Trojan legend, the beloved cousin of **ACHILLES**, slain by **HERCULES**.

PAVO, the peacock Southern constellation, one of the **SOUTHERN BIRDS**.

PEACOCK Name for the constellation **PAVO**.

PEGASUS, the Flying Horse Distinctive northern constellation, one of PTOLEMY'S original forty-eight; contains the famous Square of Pegasus made up of four stars, ENIF, SCHEAT, MARKAB and ALPHERATZ (now classified in the constellation ANDROMEDA). In Greek mythology, the winged flying horse, offspring of POSEIDON and Medusa.

PEKING OBSERVATORY Also called Beijing Observatory; established in 1958 as the research centre for the Chinese Academy of Sciences; five observation centres (Shahe, Xinglong, Miyun, Huairou and Tianjin) form part of the institute. Ancient Beijing Observatory, built in the reign of the Ming emperor Zhengtong (1436–1449), is situated in the old city of Beijing.

PENTAGRAM Five-pointed star used in magic and occult practice.

PENUMBRA Region of partial shade surrounding the main shadow cast by a nonluminous body; especially the area around the total shadow of the Moon in an ECLIPSE. It also applies to the lighter outer area of SUNSPOTS.

PERIGEE Point in the orbit of the Moon or satellite which is nearest to Earth; the point of any satellite nearest its PRIMARY.

PERIHELION The point on the orbit of a planet or COMET at which it is nearest to the Sun.

PERIODS Planetary According to Charles CARTER, planetary influences tend to be more active at certain periods in life than at others. The Moon rules infancy. Childhood up to puberty, or possibly later, is influenced by MERCURY, which gives way to VENUS; at about the age of 25 the Sun takes over, followed by MARS from about 41 to 56; then JUPITER takes over and rules until 68 or so, followed by SATURN who rules old age. URANUS is thought to rule extreme longevity, and NEPTUNE possibly rules senility. Carter had no period assigned to PLUTO.

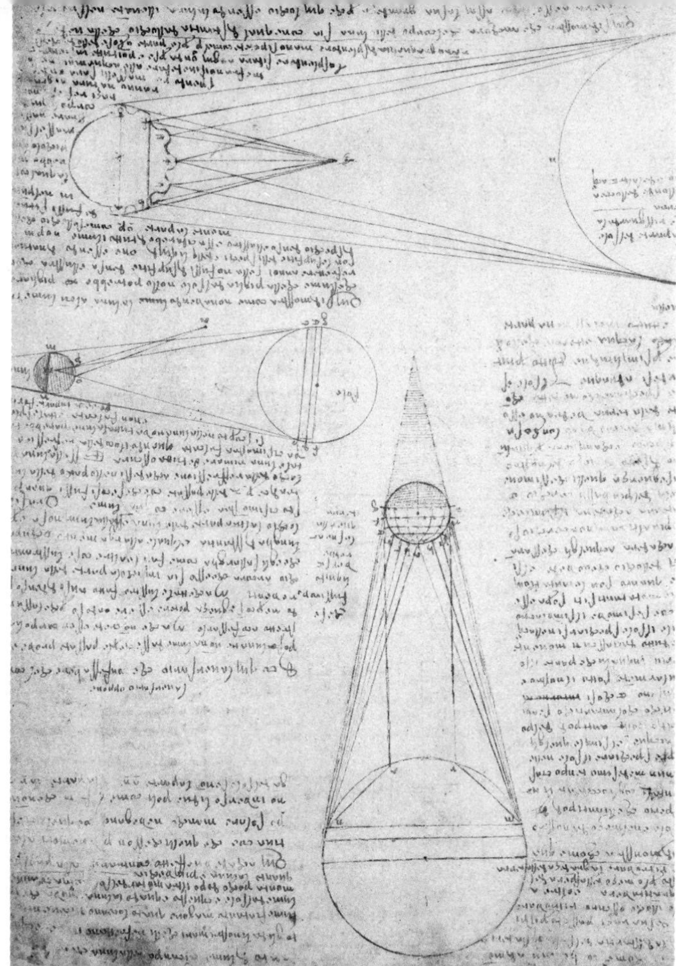

Leonardo's notes on parallax

Ruben's Judgement of Paris

Persephone abducted by Hades

PERPETUAL NOON DATE See **ADJUSTED CALCULATION DATE**

PERRINE, Charles Dillon (1878–1951) American astronomer who discovered **HIMALIA**, one of **JUPITER'S** satellites, and several comets.

PERSEID METEORS Annual **METEOR** shower with its **RADIANT** in the constellation **PERSEUS**. First recorded by Chinese astronomers in July AD 36; very reliable performers, peaking around 11 August every year.

PERSEPHONE In Greek mythology, daughter of **DEMETER** and wife of **HADES**. Identified with the Roman Proserpina.

PERSEUS Prominent northern constellation, one of **PTOLEMY'S** original forty-eight; lies across the **MILKY WAY**, and contains several objects visible to the naked eye, including the prototype **ECLIPSING BINARY, ALGOL**. In Greek mythology, Perseus was the son of **ZEUS** and Danae; it was his task to kill the Gorgon Medusa, who turned all who looked upon her to stone. He succeeded with the help of the gods. Returning triumphant, Perseus rescued and then married **ANDROMEDA**.

PERSEUS ARM Neighbouring spiral arm of the **MILKY WAY** to the Orion Arm, home of our Sun.

PERTURBATION Disturbance or displacement in the orbit of a planet or other celestial body, created by the gravitational effects of other bodies.

PHAD Gamma Ursae Majoris, one of the severn stars that form the **PLOUGH** in the constellation **URSA MAJOR**.

PHAETHON **ASTEROID 3200** of the **APOLLO** group, found in 1983 during an infrared satellite mission. In Greek mythology, son of **HELIOS**, who drove his father's chariot so wildly across the heavens that **ZEUS** had to strike him down with a thunderbolt, and he fell to his death in the River Po. See also **ERIDANUS**.

PHAROS OF ALEXANDRIA Island in the bay of Alexandria famous for its lighthouse, which was listed as one of the **SEVEN WONDERS OF THE WORLD**.

PHASES OF THE MOON See **MOON'S PHASES**

PHEKDA OR PHECDA Alternative name for **PHAD**.

PHILOCTETES Famous archer in the Trojan War, companion to the hero **HERCULES**.

PHILOSOPHER'S STONE Hypothetical supreme object of **ALCHEMY**; a substance supposed to change baser metals into silver or gold.

PHILOSOPHIAE NATURALIS PRINCIPIA MATHEMATICA Published in 1687, written by Sir Isaac **NEWTON**; expounds his theory of **GRAVITY**; often referred to as *Principia* for brevity.

PHLEGETHON River of liquid fire in **HADES**.

PHOBOS Innermost moon of **MARS**.

PHOCIS Area in northern Greece, location of **MOUNT PARNASSUS**.

PHOEBE Outermost satellite of **SATURN**; it has a **RETROGRADE** motion and an orbital period of 550 days. In Greek mythology, name given to **ARTEMIS** as goddess of the Moon.

PHOEBUS Another name for **APOLLO**.

PHOENIX, the Phoenix Southern constellation, lying near **ACHERNAR**; one of the **SOUTHERN BIRDS**. Its **ALPHA** is Ankaa. In Egyptian myth, the Phoenix was a unique bird that lived for more than a thousand years then immolated itself to be reborn from the ashes.

Associated with **SOTHIS**; see **CALENDAR, EGYPTIAN**.

PHOTOSPHERE Visible luminous surface of the Sun; more generally the dividing line between the inside and outside of a star.

PIAZZI, Guiseppe (1746–1826) Italian mathematician and astronomer; Director of the observatory at Palermo, Sicily; compiled several star catalogues and discovered **CERES**, the first **ASTEROID**, in 1801.

PIC DU MIDI OBSERVATORY Observatory of the University of Toulouse, France; one of the highest observatories, with an altitude of 2438 m/8000 ft.

PICTOR, the Painter Unremarkable southern constellation near **CANOPUS**.

PISCES, Age of The period lasting 2 160 years which began roughly at the time of the birth of Jesus Christ and is just drawing to an end; see **GREAT MONTH**; **GREAT YEAR**.

PISCES, the Fishes Zodiac constellation lying to the south of **PEGASUS**: large but rather faint, with Eta as its brightest star and **AL RISCHA** as its **ALPHA**. **Pisces the zodiac sign** is the twelfth and last sign of the zodiac; it is a **FEMININE MUTABLE WATER** sign, ruled by **NEPTUNE**. **VENUS** is **EXALTED**, **MERCURY** is at **FALL** in Pisces. There is no special myth associated with Pisces, but the Babylonians knew the constellation as Kun or the Tails and associated it with the river goddesses **ANUNITUM** and **SIMMAH**. **The Age of Pisces,** the 2160-year-long **GREAT MONTH** from which we have just emerged, saw the foundation and development of Christianity. The fish was the secret symbol of the early Christian sects, and Jesus had twelve disciples whom He called his Fishers of Men.

PISCIS AUSTRALIS The Southern Fish One of **PTOLEMY'S** original fortyeight constellations; its **ALPHA** is **FOMALHOUT**, one of the **FOUR WATCHERS OF THE HEAVENS**. Also known as Piscis Austrinus.

PISCIS AUSTRINUS See **PISCIS AUSTRALIS**

PLACIDUS DE TITO (fl. seventeenth century) Astrologer and mathematician; devised a complicated method of **HOUSE DIVISION**.

PLANET, Angular Planet placed within 8° of the **ASCENDANT, DESCENDANT, MIDHEAVEN** or **IMUM COELI**.

PLANET From the Greek word meaning 'to wander', a celestial body that moves (in comparison to the perceived infinitely slow progress of the fixed stars); specifically the name given to the bodies that orbit the Sun.

PLANETARY CONJUNCTION See **CONJUNCTION**

PLANETARY IMPACTS The effects planets have on business, politics, trade and financial matters; demonstrated by the American astrologer Evangeline **ADAMS**.

PLANETARY INFLUENCES In astrology, influences can be interpreted as effects; it is rather a misleading term, with a fine line of difference in meaning. It is better to say the effect of an **ASPECT**, rather than the influence of one.

Philosopher's 'egg' or stone

PLANETARY MOTION See **KEPLER'S LAWS OF PLANETARY MOTION**

PLANETARY NEBULA Symmetrical or circular **NEBULA** with a star at its centre. There are about 1 000 catalogued in the **GALAXY**.

PLANETARY NODES Two points at which planetary orbits intersect the **ECLIPTIC**.

PLANETARY PERIODS See **PERIODS, PLANETARY**

PLANETARY RETURNS See **RETURNS, PLANETARY**

PLANETARY SATELLITES See **MOONS**

PLANET DISTRIBUTION See **JONES CHART PATTERNS**

PLANET EXALTATION See **EXALTATION**

PLANET FALL See **FALL**

PLANETS, Inferior See **INFERIOR PLANETS**

The Pharos of Alexandria, 280 BC

PLANETS, Superior
See SUPERIOR PLANETS

PLANETS DETRIMENT
See DETRIMENT

PLANETS IN MUTUAL RECEPTION
See MUTUAL RECEPTION

PLATO (c428–348 BC) Greek philosopher, mathematician and astronomer and pupil of Socrates; founded his Academy in Athens c387.

PLATONIC CYCLE The amount of time it would take for all the stars and constellations to return to their former positions, relative to the EQUINOXES.

PLATONIC MONTH Twelfth part of the PLATONIC YEAR; the time taken for the Vernal Point to precess westwards through one sign of the zodiac; about 2 100 years.

PLATONIC YEAR Period of about 26 000 years, the time taken for the CELESTIAL NORTH POLE to describe a huge circle round the pole at the ECLIPTIC and for the VERNAL POINT to precess right round the zodiac and return to the FIRST POINT OF ARIES. Also called GREAT YEAR.

PLEIADES Lovely open star cluster known as the Seven Sisters, in the zodiac constellation TAURUS. The seven bright stars are ALCYONE, ATLAS, ELECTRA, MAIA, MEROPE, PLEIONE and TAYGETE. Can be seen easily with the naked eye, but through a TELESCOPE about 3 000 stars can be seen. Their name stems from the Greek word *plein*, to sail; their rising indicated a safe time for sailing and their setting marked the end of the season. In Greek mythology, they were the seven daughters of Atlas and Pleione and companions of ARTEMIS.

PLEIONE Mother by ATLAS of the PLEIADES.

PLINY THE ELDER (AD 23–79) Gaius Plinius Secundus Roman encyclopedist, author of *Historia Naturalis* (AD 77), in which he discussed the celestial system and the superior planets.

PLOUGH Group of seven bright stars which form the distinctive Plough, in the northern constellation URSA MAJOR: the stars are Alkaid (Eta Ursa Majoris), MIZAR, ALIOTH, Megrez, PHAD, MERAK and DUBHE.

PLUTO Ninth planet from the Sun, smallest in the Solar System; discovered 18 February 1930 by Clyde Tombaugh at the Flagstaff Observatory Arizona, although its existence had been predicted in 1916 by Percival LOWELL. Smaller than MERCURY, with a diameter of approximately 3200 km/2000 miles and a very ECCENTRIC 247.7-year orbit that takes it 17° from the ECLIPTIC on occasion; has one known satellite, CHARON. Astrologically, Pluto rules the zodiac sign SCORPIO and the EIGHTH HOUSE; it is at DETRIMENT in TAURUS; its EXALTATION and FALL have not yet been determined as it takes so long to move through the zodiac signs, spending over twenty years in each one. Associated anatomically with the gonads, Pluto is thought to influence the larger things in human existence; massive upheavals (earthquakes, volcanoes), big business and high finance, beginnings and endings of phases, life and death; can be a force for creation or destruction on the negative side can indicate cruelty. In Greek mythology, Pluto is another name for HADES.

PLUTUS In Greek mythology, the god of earthly riches.

POLAR SIGN Zodiac sign directly opposite another.

POLARIS Alpha Ursae Minoris, brightest star in the constellation URSA MINOR and currently the POLE STAR.

POLARITY In astrology, the relationship between opposite signs of the zodiac.

POLES, Celestial See CELESTIAL NORTH AND SOUTH POLES

POLE STAR The star lying closest to the CELESTIAL NORTH POLE; currently POLARIS. The Pole Star changes as the CELESTIAL NORTH POLE traces its circle through the sky. See PRECESSION OF THE EQUINOXES. There is no star to mark the exact South Pole at the moment.

POLICE, Celestial See CELESTIAL POLICE

POLITICAL ASTROLOGY Branch of astrology related to MUNDANE ASTROLOGY; erecting and interpretation of CHARTS for governments inanimate objects, countries and cities.

POLLUX Beta Geminorum, brightest star in the constellation GEMINI; in classical mythology, the

Roman name for the Greek Polydeuces, son of ZEUS and LEDA, immortal twin to CASTOR.

POLYDEUCES Greek name for POLLUX.

POMONA Roman goddess of fruitfulness, and fruit in general.

PONS, Jean Louis (1761–1831) One of the great COMET trackers, discovering thirty-seven between 1803 and 1827; had an unlikely start in astronomy as a handyman at Marseilles Observatory and rose through the ranks to become Director of Florence Observatory. Comets named after him include Pons- Brook (1812) and Pons-Winnecke (1819).

POOP Name for the constellation PUPPIS.

POSEIDON God of the sea; eldest son of CRONOS (Saturn) and RHEA, brother of ZEUS and HADES; said to have created the horse and taught men how to bridle them; fathered PEGASUS on Medusa. Husband of Amphitrite, daughter of NEREUS, and father of TRITON. Identified with the Roman NEPTUNE.

POSITION ANGLE Position in the sky of one celestial object with reference to another; measured from the north point of the major object, through east, south and west.

POSITIVE SIGNS ARIES, GEMINI, LEO, LIBRA, SAGITTARIUS and AQUARIUS; the FIRE and AIR signs: according to Charles CARTER, related to the creative, outgoing or aggressive side of nature; relates with the NEGATIVE signs as Yang does to Yin in Chinese philosophy (see YIN/YANG).

POSTUMIUS AULUS In Roman mythology, led the Romans to victory at the Battle of Lake Regillus. To celebrate his victory he founded the Temple of CASTOR and POLLUX in the Forum; also reputed to have built the Temple of CERES.

The planets and their days

PRAESEPE Beautiful open cluster (M44) in the zodiac constellation CANCER; first observed by HIPPARCHUS, finally resolved by GALILEO; known as the Crib or Cradle or the Beehive.

PRECESSION Movement backwards; see EQUINOXES, PRECESSION OF.

PRECESSIONAL YEAR Another name for the GREAT YEAR.

PREDICTIVE ASTROLOGY Branch of astrology that deals with DIRECTIONS; various methods are used to predict future influences.

PRIAM In Trojan legend, King of Troy when the city was sacked by the Greeks; husband of HECUBA, father of fifty sons, including HECTOR and PARIS; killed by PYRRHUS, son of ACHILLES.

PRIAMUS ASTEROID 884, discovered by Max WOLF in September 1917; one of the TROJANS, named for King PRIAM of Troy.

PRIMARY Principal star in a BINARY; body around which satellites orbit.

PRIMARY DIRECTIONS See DIRECTIONS, PRIMARY

PRIME MERIDIAN Imaginary GREAT CIRCLE on the Earth's sphere which passes through the North and South Poles and 0° longitude at GREENWICH OBSERVATORY. See also MERIDIAN.

PRIME VERTICAL Depending on the place of birth, a GREAT CIRCLE at right angles to the MERIDIAN, cutting the HORIZON at the east and west and passing through the ZENITH and NADIR.

The Plough, January 1946

PRINCIPIA Short name for PHILOSOPHIAE NATURALIS MATHEMATICA.

PROCYON Alpha Canis Minoris in the constellation CANIS MINOR; eighth brightest star in the sky.

PROGNOSTICATION From prognosticate, to foretell, give advance information, to predict, or to forecast; in astrology, relates to the various forms of PROGRESSING a CHART or HOROSCOPE, to look into the future.

PROGRESS To prepare a CHART for the future, making calculations based on the astrological date in the BIRTH CHART.

PROGRESSING See PROGRESS

Pluto dines with Proserpina

PROGRESSIONS Specialized side of astrology dealing with future trends. Several methods of progression exist: PRIMARY DIRECTIONS, SECONDARY PROGRESSIONS, the DIURNAL HOROSCOPE, Tertiary Progressions and TRANSITS. Astrologers usually have a preference for one method, which they find gives the best results.

PROMETHEUS Second satellite (in terms of distance) of SATURN, discovered by Voyager photographs in 1980; along with PANDORA, SHEPHERD SATELLITE to Saturn's F ring; also named for active volcano on IO, one of JUPITER'S satellites. In Greek mythology, one of the TITANS, sons of IAPETOS and the sea nymph Clymene; stole fire from Olympus to give to humanity, for which he was severely punished by ZEUS.

PROMINENCES, Solar See **SOLAR PROMINENCES**

PROMITTOR Indicates the promise of fulfilment; astrologically, refers to the potential shown by the planets, through **PROGRESSIONS** and **DIRECTIONS.**

PROPER MOTION The planets in a **CHART** are carried round clockwise in the signs as they rise, due to the anticlockwise rotation of Earth on its axis; proper or true motion of the planets is anticlockwise through the degrees of the signs.

PROPUS Eta Geminorum in the constellation **GEMINI**.

PROROGATOR Another name for **APHETA**, or 'Giver of Life'; See also **HYLEG**.

PROSERPINA Roman equivalent of **PERSEPHONE**.

PROTEUS In Greek mythology, the prophetic old man of the sea, shepherd of **POSEIDON'S** flocks of seals.

PROTON Fundamental **PARTICLE**: nucleus of the hydrogen atom; carries a positive electric

PROXIMA CENTAURI Nearest known star to our Sun (1.31 **PARSECS** or just over four **LIGHT YEARS**).

PSYCHE **ASTEROID 16**, discovered March 1951 by De Gasparis; largest metallic iron asteroid so far found. In Greek mythology, Psyche represents the human soul.

PTOLEMAIC SYSTEM **GEOCENTRIC** system to explain the Solar System expounded by **PTOLEMY** and accepted as viable until **COPERNICUS** proved it invalid.

PTOLEMY, Claudius (c AD 100–c170) Greek astronomer and mathematician, lived and worked in Alexandria, centre of the **HELLENISTIC** empire; renowed for his major work the **ALMAGEST**, the greatest astronomical work of the ancient world. Ptolemy described fortyeight constellations, and established the **GEOCENTRIC** theory of the Solar System, a crystallization of ancient Greek theories from **ARISTOTLE**, **HIPPARCHUS** and **PYTHAGORAS**; in the Ptolemaic system the Sun, Moon and five planets known at the time (**MERCURY**, **VENUS**, **MARS**, **JUPITER** and **SATURN**) move around the Earth; the fixed stars were considered to be literally fixed to a huge sphere beyond the planets, the **VAULT OF HEAVEN**.

Illustrations from Ptolemy's star catalogue

PULSARS Very dense **NEUTRON STARS** that emit very strong radio waves in pulses (hence the name); first discovered in 1967 by radio telescope at the Mullard Radio Astronomy Observatory at the University of Cambridge.

PULSATING STARS Stars which expand and contract.

PUPPIS, the Poop Southern constellation, part of the archaic constellation **ARGO**, most of it visible in low northern latitudes; the brightest star is Suhail Hadar (Zeta Puppis) and it contains several bright open clusters.

PURBACH, Georg von (1423–1461) Austrian astronomer and professor at Vienna in 1450, teacher of **REGIOMONTANUS**; compiled a catalogue of lunar **ECLIPSES** (1459).

PURPLE MOUNTAIN OBSERVATORY See **NANJING OBSERVATORY**

PYGMALION In Greek mythology, king of Cyprus who sculpted a statue of a beautiful woman then fell in love with his creation; **APHRODITE** granted the statue life, and Pygmalion married the creature.

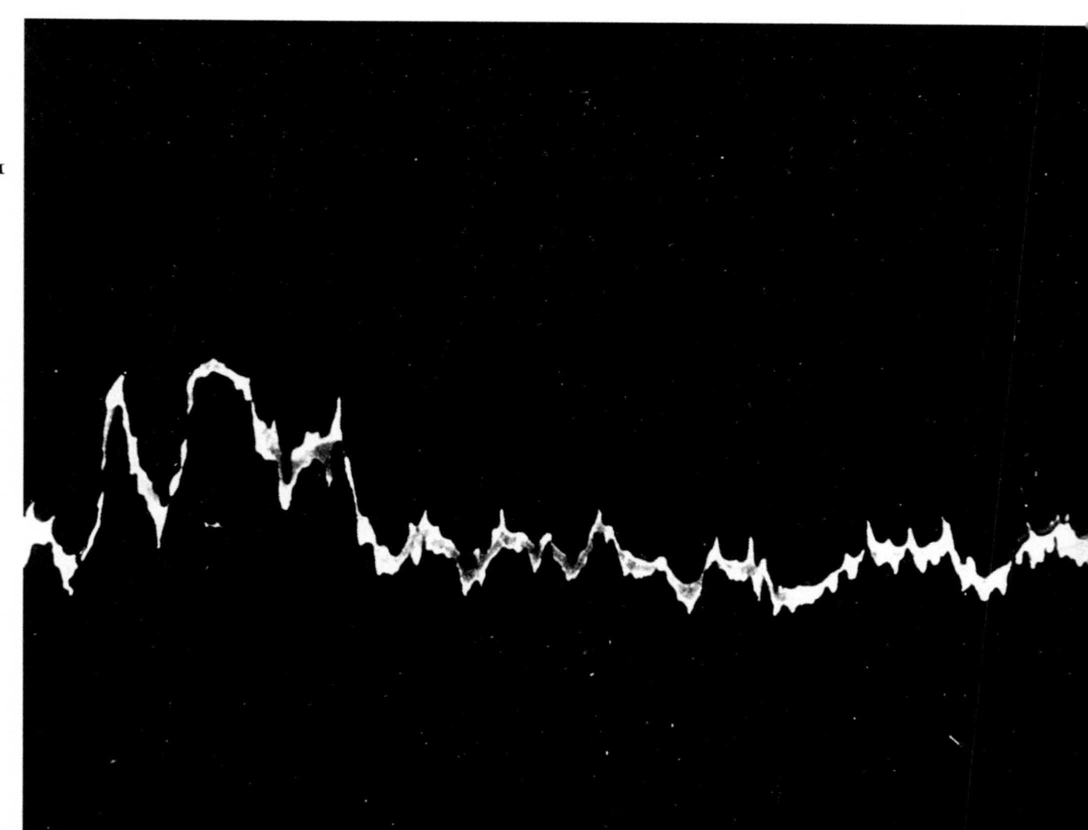

Emissions from a pulsar

PYRAMIDS The Great Pyramids of Egypt were conceived as astronomical instruments as well as tombs; their bases were aligned almost precisely with the four **CARDINAL POINTS**; the **GREAT PYRAMID** of Cheops contained a passageway in alignment with the then **POLE STAR**, **THUBAN**.

PYROMANCY Divination by fire, or from the pictures seen in fires.

PYRRHA Wife of **DEUCALION** mother of **HELLEN**, forefather of all the Greeks.

PYTHAGORAS (c572–500 BC) Greek philosopher, mathematician and religious thinker; one of the first to claim that the Earth was a sphere and that the planets orbit in cycles.

PYTHON In Greek mythology, monster serpent and shedragon, spawned on **MOUNT PARNASSUS** from the mud of the great flood, and guarded the oracle at Delphi; killed by **APOLLO**, who took over the oracle.

PYXIS, the Compass southern constellation, originally part of the archaic **ARGO**.

Claudius Ptolemy

QUADRA EUCLADIS Former name for constellation NORMA.

QUADRANTIDS METEOR shower which occurs annually around 3 or 4 January; first noticed in 1835; so named because they occur in part of the constellation BOÖTES, once known as Quadrans Muralis (the Mural Quadrant); a spectacular display occurred in 1977.

QUADRANTINE LUNATION Astrological term sometimes used with reference to the important ASPECTS (conjunctions, squares and oppositions) of the Sun and Moon.

QUADRANTS The four quarters of a CHART; when applied to the zodiac, the two oriental quadrants run from ARIES to GEMINI inclusive and LIBRA to SAGITTARIUS inclusive; the two occidental quadrants run from CANCER to VIRGO inclusive and from CAPRICORN to PISCES inclusive.

QUADRATURE Position of the Moon or a planet at 90° to the Sun; the Half Moon is at quadrature; astrologically, a celestial body in SQUARE ASPECT to the Sun.

QUADRUPEDAL Refers to the FOUR-FOOTED SIGNS.

QUADRUPLICITIES Four groups into which the twelve signs of the zodiac are divided; each quadruplicity represents a QUALITY (CARDINAL, FIXED or MUTABLE). See also TRIPLICITIES.

QUALITIES Three astrological qualities, CARDINAL, FIXED and MUTABLE, assigned alternately to the twelve signs of the zodiac, beginning with the cardinal ARIES. Also called the QUADRUPLICITIES. See also TRIPLICITIES.

QUASARS Abbreviation for **Quas**i-stell**ar** Radio Sources; discovered in 1963 by RADIO ASTRONOMY. Compact sources of intense radiation, probably BLACK HOLES; not all quasars are radio sources, and some astronomers prefer to call them Quasi-stellar objects.

QUERENT In HORARY ASTROLOGY, the person asking the question of the astrologer. See also QUESITED.

QUESITED In HORARY ASTROLOGY, the person, object or thing that is subject to the enquiry. See also QUERENT.

QUETZALCOATL ASTEROID 1915 in the AMOR group. In Mexican mythology, the Plumed Serpent, a powerful Aztec god.

QUICKSILVER Alchemists' name for MERCURY.

QUINCUNX Astrological ASPECT of 150°, or five signs apart; regarded as a moderate and rather unpredictable aspect; its position and aspects with other planets in a CHART needs careful assessment. Integral part of the FINGER OF FATE or YOD configuration.

QUINTILE Weak minor astrological ASPECT of 72°.

RA Abbreviation for RIGHT ASCENSION.

RA or **RE** Ancient Egyptian Sun god, supposed ancestor of all the Pharaohs; worshipped at HELIOPOLIS; after c1990 BC, assimilated with the Theban deity Amen, the pair were often represented by a RAM.

RADAR Acronym from **RA**dio **D**irection **A**nd **R**anging; system to locate a moving object by broadcasting ultra-high-frequency radio waves and measuring the time and location of their return; developed in World War II to detect shipping and aircraft. See also RADAR ASTRONOMY.

RADAR ASTRONOMY Study of celestial objects by RADAR; the range of radar transmitters and receivers used on Earth limits investigation to the Solar System.

RADIAL MOTION Movement of a body directly away from an observer; see also RADIAL VELOCITY; TRANSVERSE MOTION.

RADIAL VELOCITY Speed of a body directly away from or towards an observer; measured by observing the DOPPLER EFFECT on the radiation emitted by the moving body. See also RADIAL MOTION.

RADIANT Apparent focal point of a METEOR shower, where the showers appear to originate, or the point from which light radiates.

RADIATION BELT Area in the MAGNETOSPHERE of a planet, within which streams of electrically charged PARTICLES are trapped by the planet's magnetic field. On Earth this can cause auroral displays and radio interference. See also RADIATION ZONES; VAN ALLEN BELTS.

RADIATION ZONES Areas surrounding a planet's MAGNETOSPHERE which contain trapped charged PARTICLES; MERCURY, Earth JUPITER, SATURN, URANUS and NEPTUNE have radiation zones.

RADICAL CHART Prime basic chart drawn up for a person's time of birth or a specific event; sometimes referred to as a RADIX chart.

RADIO ASTRONOMY Study of the universe by measuring radio waves received on Earth from space; such waves were first discovered by American physicist Karl JANSKY in 1931, but their significance as a method of interpreting the universe was not realized for many years. Advances in radio astronomy were made possible by the building of huge disc-shaped telescopes to gather in the radio waves. See JODRELL BANK; VERY LARGE ARRAY.

RADIO GALAXIES Distant galaxies that are powerful sources of RADIO WAVES.

RADIO STARS Stars emitting strong RADIO WAVES. See also PULSARS.

RADIO WAVES ELECTROMAGNETIC RADIATION of varying wavelengths from beyond the INFRARED and MICROWAVE band of the spectrum.

RADIO WINDOW Area in the Earth's atmosphere that allows the penetration of radiation of wavelengths varying from about 20 mm to about 30 m.

RADIX RADICAL CHART of a birth time, and the basic roots from which everything concerning the FIGURE is judged.

RADIX MEASURE Used for symbolic or **FIXED INCREMENT DIRECTIONS** and introduced by Dr Gornold, the mean daily motion of the Sun 59′ 8″ a year of direction. Tables are published to give the progress by this ratio for any given number of days or years. Some astrologers prefer the actual solar motion at the rate of 1° = 1 year, applying this to all celestial bodies.

RAHU In **INDIAN ASTROLOGY**, the Sanskrit name for the Moon's North **NODE**, the Dragon's Head; in Hindu legends, the Demon that causes **ECLIPSES**.

RAM Symbol for the zodiac constellation and sign **ARIES**; represents the Ram with the Golden Fleece from whose back **HELLE** fell to her death; in Egyptian mythology associated with **RA**.

RAMADAN Ninth month of the Mohammedan Year and the Muslim Holy Month, in which the Koran was revealed to Mohammed.

RAMC Abbreviation for **RIGHT ASCENSION** of the **MIDHEAVEN**.

RAMESES II (c1300–1236 BC) Pharaoh of Egypt, which he ruled for sixty-seven years, bringing great prosperity to the land; keenly interested in astrology and was responsible for establishing the four **CARDINAL SIGNS**.

RAMMANU-SUMAUSAR (fl. seventh century BC) High-ranking astrologer in the court of the Assyrian king Assurbanipal (reigned 668–625 BC), founder of the library at **NINEVEH**.

RASALGETHI Alpha Herculis, a **VARIABLE RED GIANT** in the constellation **HERCULES**.

RAS-AL-GHUL The star **ALGOL**.

RASALHAGUE Alpha Ophiuchi in the constellation **OPHIUCUS**.

Air traffic Radar dish

Background: Regiomantanus' condensed edition of Ptolemy's Almagest.

RECEPTION, Mutual See **MUTUAL RECEPTION**

RECTIFICATION Astrologically, a method for adjusting a time of birth which is uncertain, by considering the physical appearance, temperament, and events in a person's life.

RED DWARF Faint star, smaller and cooler than the Sun; burns very slowly, and so lives a long time.

RED GIANT Huge ageing star that has consumed all the hydrogen available to it so that its core has contracted and its atmosphere expanded.

REDSHIFT Amount by which the wavelength of **ELECTROMAGNETIC RADIATION** increases as a result of the expansion of the Universe, or the recession of the source of radiation; the **SPECTRUM** of an object approaching shifts towards the blue end; the spectrum of an object moving away shifts to the red end. Also known as the **DOPPLER EFFECT**.

REFLECTING TELESCOPE See **TELESCOPE**

REFRACTING TELESCOPE See **TELESCOPE**

REFRANATION Term used in **HORARY ASTROLOGY** to describe the situation if one of two planets applying to an **ASPECT** turns **RETROGRADE** before the completion of this aspect.

REGIOMONTANUS Name adopted by Johannes Müller (1436–1476) from his birthplace Königsburg. German astrologer, mathematician, and astronomer; published **EPHEMERIDES** 1475–1506 and developed a system of **HOUSE DIVISION**.

REGRESSION OF THE MOON'S NODES Movement of the Moon's **NODES**, or the nodal axis, backwards round the zodiac (due to the gravitational pull of the Sun on the Moon), at a rate of about 3.18 minutes of arc a day, completing the full circle in 18.6 years.

Ram, from Egyptian zodiac

REGRESSIONS Also known as Pre-Natal Secondary **DIRECTIONS**. Calculated in the same way as ordinary Secondary Directions, but reversed and counted backwards, so that twenty-four hours or one day before birth would correspond to the first year of life.

REGULUS Alpha Leonis, sometimes called the Lion Star or Royal Star, in the zodiac constellation **LEO**. One of the **FOUR WATCHERS OF THE HEAVENS**.

REINMUTH, Karl (1892–1979) Astronomer at Königstuhl Observatory, Heidelberg, where he concentrated on the study of **ASTEROIDS**, discovering many and drawing up a catalogue of 6 500, published in 1953.

Tomb of Rameses II, Karnak

REMUS In Roman mythology, twin brother of **ROMULUS**, son of **MARS** and **RHEA SYLVIA**.

RENAISSANCE Period of European history characterized by the rediscovery of classical knowledge and an interest in scientific matters; the renaissance also saw a revival of astrology.

RETARDATION The relative difference between the times of the rising of the Moon on consecutive nights; it can be more than an hour, or a mere fifteen minutes at **HARVEST MOON**. The deviation is caused by the Moon's motion as it passes north or south of the **ECLIPTIC**.

RETICULUM, the Net Far southern constellation, small but distinct, first described by **HEVELIUS**.

RETICULUM RHOMBOIDUS Old name for the constellation **RETICULUM**.

RETROGRADE MOTION The apparent backward motion of a planet as seen from Earth. Occurs when a fast-moving **INFERIOR PLANET** (**MERCURY** or **VENUS**) overtakes the Earth and starts to move behind the Sun, or when **SUPERIOR PLANETS** come into **OPPOSITION** behind the Sun; in both cases, they appear to the Earth-based observer to be moving backwards. Also refers to the clockwise motions of some **PLANETARY SATELLITES**; most planets and moons orbit anticlockwise. Astrologically, retrograde describes a planet moving backwards through the zodiac signs; a retrograde planet is said to have diminished power and influence in a **CHART**.

RETURNS, Planetary A planet 'returns' when it has travelled right round the zodiac and returns to the same position it occupied in the **RADICAL CHART** or **BIRTH CHART**; a return has significance to the **NATIVE**, especially with regard to the **SUPERIOR PLANETS** (excluding **MARS**, which comes round every two and a half years); **JUPITER** returns every twelve years, **SATURN** every twenty-nine and a half years, **URANUS** every eighty-four years (therefore experienced by the fortunate few). Noone (at present) can experience a **NEPTUNE** or **PLUTO** return: Nepturn takes 146 years, and Pluto 248 years to orbit the Sun. Some astrologers believe that half returns (when the planets are at exactly half-way round their course and therefore in **OPPOSITION** to their positions in the Birth Chart) are also significant, especially the half return of Uranus, which occurs in the early forties, well known as a time of upheaval and reassessment in people's lives.

REVOLUTION Time taken by one celestial body to revolve around another.

RHABDOMANCY Dowsing; divination or prophecy by the use of rods or twigs.

RHADAMANTHUS In Greek mythology, son of **ZEUS** and Europa, ruler of part of Crete; became one of the Judges of **HADES**.

RHEA Second largest satellite of **SATURN**; an icy moon 1530 km/950 miles across. In Greek mythology, one of the **TITANS**, daughter of **URANUS** and **GAEA**, sister of and wife of **CRONOS** (Saturn), who fathered her children, **ZEUS**, **DEMETER**, **HADES**, **HERA**, **HESTIA** and **POSEIDON**. Sometimes identified with **CYBELE**.

RHEA SYLVIA Vestal Virgin, mother of **ROMULUS** and **REMUS** by **MARS**; because she had disgraced her calling, her children were abandoned, but were suckled by a shewolf and survived.

RHODE OR RHODOS In Greek mythology, said to be the daughter of **POSEIDON**; wife of the sun god **HELIOS**.

RHOMBOIDAL NET Name for the constellation **RETICULUM RHOMBOIDUS**.

RICCIOLI, Joannes Baptista (1598–1671) Astronomer of **BOLOGNA**; drew up map of the Moon in 1651.

RICHTER, Charles Francis (1900–1985) American seismologist who devised a method of measuring the strength of earthquakes, known as the Richter Scale.

RIGEL Beta Orionis, a beautiful blue-white giant, brightest star in the constellation **ORION** and seventh brightest star in the sky.

RIGHT ASCENSION Abbreviated to **R A**; celestial equivalent of longitude. Zero of right ascension is the **FIRST POINT OF ARIES** or the Vernal Point, and it is measured eastwards from this along the **CELESTIAL EQUATOR** to the point where the **HOUR CIRCLE** of the celestial body in question cuts the celestial equator. Sometimes given in degrees, but more usually in **SIDEREAL TIME**, 15° being equal to one hour, 1°

Romulus and Remus

equalling four minutes. Not to be confused with **CELESTIAL LONGITUDE**, which is measured from the First Point of Aries along the **ECLIPTIC**.

RIGIL KENT Alternative name for **ALPHA CENTAURI**.

RIMMON Babylonian god of storms.

RING GALAXIES Galaxies in which the nucleus is surrounded by a ring of stars.

RING NEBULA Well-known ring doughnut-shaped **PLANETARY NEBULA**, M57 in the constellation **LYRA**; it is over 5000 years old and still expanding.

RISING PLANET A planet rising in the **ASCENDING SIGN**; a rising planet often seems to become part ruler of a **HOROSCOPE** and could have a powerful influence on the subject's life. See also **RULERSHIP**.

RISING SIGN The zodiac sign rising in the east at the **ASCENDANT** in a **CHART**.

RIVER Name for the constellation **ERIDANUS**.

ROCHE, Edouard (1820–1883) French mathematician and astronomer who in 1848 originated the **ROCHE LIMIT** for planetary satellites.

ROCHE LIMIT Minimum distance that a satellite can orbit its mother planet before stress rips it apart; measured as 2.5 times the radius of the planet.

RODGERS, Joan See **ASTROLOGICAL ASSOCIATION**

RØMER, Ole (1644–1710) Danish astronomer who determined the speed of **LIGHT** in 1675.

ROMULUS Founder of Rome; twin brother of **REMUS**, son of **MARS** and **RHEA SYLVIA**; killed his brother and was taken to Olympus by his father where he was worshipped by the Romans as Quirinus.

ROQUE DE LOS MUCHACHOS Internationally funded observatory on the 'Mountain of the Boys' on La Palma, Canary Islands. Started in 1985 as a joint venture between Spain, the United Kingdom, Republic of Ireland, Denmark, Sweden and the Netherlands. Sited 2 400 m/7 870 feet above sea level, it makes an excellent base for the observation of the northern hemisphere.

ROSETTA STONE Discovered in 1799 during excavations near Rosetta at the western mouth of the **NILE** delta; a basalt slab inscribed in three languages. Greek, Egyptian Demotic and hieroglyphic, providing a key at last to Egyptian hieroglyphics, and consequently Egyptian culture. Deciphered by **CHAMPOLLION**.

The Rosetta Stone

The Isaac Newton telescope at Roque de los Muchachos Observatory

ROSSE, William Parsons, Third Earl of (1800–1867) Amateur astronomer and builder of a huge reflecting **TELESCOPE** with a reflector 183 cm/72 in. across at Birr Castle in Ireland. Through it he made the first studies of **SPIRAL GALAXIES** among other things.

ROTA IXIONIS Wheel of Ixion, a name sometimes given to the little crown of stars in the constellation **CORONA AUSTRALIS**. In Greek mythology, Ixion was punished by **ZEUS** for attempting to seduce **HERA** by being lashed for eternity to a wheel of fire rolling through the heavens.

ROTANEV Beta Delphini in the constellation Delphinus, named by Nicolaus **VENATOR**.

ROTATION The revolution of a celestial body on its axis.

ROYAL OBSERVATORY GREENWICH See **GREENWICH**

ROYAL STARS See **FOUR WATCHERS OF THE HEAVENS**

RUDHYAR, Dane (1895–1985) French astrologer, musician, poet-artist and philosopher who published many books expounding his ideas of a holistic Universe, the realization of all our inner potential and the need for a global society; born Chennevière in Paris, he moved to the USA in 1916, changing his name to Rudhyar, derived from a Sanskrit word *rudra*, meaning dynamic action, electrical power, transforming energy. His major work is *The Planetarization of Consciousness*.

RUDOLPHINE TABLES Astronomical calculations and observations made by Tycho **BRAHE**, completed after his death by his assistant Johannes **KEPLER** and published in 1627; named in honour of Rudolph II, the Holy Roman Emperor from 1576 to 1612 (Brahe had been imperial astronomer at the court in Prague).

RULE Name for the constellation **NORMA**.

RULER OF THE HOROSCOPE Otherwise known as Lord of the Horoscope; usually the ruler of the **FIRST HOUSE**, but not if this body is weak, in which case it could be a body well aspected and strong that is rising on the **ASCENDANT**, or a powerful planet on the **MIDHEAVEN**. In Arabian astrology it was called the Almuten.

RULERSHIPS Each zodiac sign has a planetary ruler. As there are twelve signs and only ten celestial bodies (so far), **MERCURY** and **VENUS** rule two signs each (respectively **GEMINI** and **VIRGO** and **TAURUS** and **LIBRA**); **MARS** rules **ARIES**, the Moon rules **CANCER**, the Sun rules **LEO**, **PLUTO** rules **SCORPIO**, **JUPITER** rules **SAGITTARIUS**, **SATURN** rules **CAPRICORN**, **URANUS** rules **AQUARIUS** and **NEPTUNE** rules **PISCES**. Before Uranus, Neptune and Pluto were discovered, Aquarius was ruled by Saturn, Pisces by Jupiter and Scorpio by Mars.

RUNES The twenty-four symbols of an ancient alphabet, devised for carving on hard stone; originated among the Gothic tribes of northern Europe in the third century AD. Although used as a straightforward recording alphabet, runes each had their own magic symbolism and were used to interpret the trends and the relationship of the individual and the environment.

RUSSELL, Henry Norris (1877–1957) American astronomer who developed **HERTZPRUNG-RUSSELL DIAGRAM** independently from **HERTZPRUNG**.

RUTILICUS Zeta Herculi, second brightest star in the constellation **HERCULES**.

RYLE, Sir Martin (1918–1984) Astronomer Royal (1972–1982); a pioneer of **RADIO ASTRONOMY**, he won the 1974 Nobel Prize for work on **PULSARS**.

Runic inscription from Frösön, Sweden

SABIK Eta Ophiuchi, second brightest star in the constellation OPHIUCHUS.

SADALMELIK Alpha Aquarii, second brightest star in the zodiac constellation AQUARIUS.

SADALSUUD Beta Aquarii, the brightest star in the zodiac constellation AQUARIUS.

SAGAN, Dr Carl (b. 1934) American physicist, astronomer, biologist and Pulitzer Prize winner; renowned astronomer and pioneer in the search for life elsewhere in the Universe.

SAGITTA, the Arrow Small but a quite distinctive constellation, one of PTOLEMY'S original forty-eight.

SAGITTARIUS, the Archer Southern zodiacal constellation, one of PTOLEMY'S originals; its brightest star is Kaus Australis (Epsilon Sagittarii) and there are fifteen others above the fourth MAGNITUDE; also contains many VARIABLE STARS, CLUSTERS and NEBULAE, including the Lagoon and Omega Nebulae. The richest part of the MILKY WAY flows through Sagittarius, and the centre of the GALAXY SAGITTARIUS A, lies just beyond the star clouds in this area. **Sagittarius the zodiac sign** is the ninth sign of the zodiac, a MASCULINE, POSITIVE MUTABLE FIRE SIGN ruled by JUPITER; mercury is at DETRIMENT in Sagittarius. Its symbol is a centaur, and the Sagittarius **myth** is associated with CHIRON, the wise Centaur.

SAGITTARIUS A Name used to describe a source of intense radio emission located on the west shoulder of the large star cloud in SAGITTARIUS; the centre of our GALAXY; discovered and explored by RADIO ASTRONOMY. Most of the work on Sagittarius has been done at the VERY LARGE ARRAY in New Mexico.

SAILS Name for the constellation VELA.

SAINT MICHEL OBSERVATORY Observatoire de Haute Provence (OHP), a centre for astrophysics established in Provence, France, in 1946. Important studies on COMETS, GALAXIES and RADIAL VELOCITY have been carried out here.

SAIPH Kappa Orionis, sixth brightest star in the constellation ORION.

S. ANDROMEDAE SUPERNOVA in the ANDROMEDA NEBULA, the first to be discovered (1885) outside the MILKY WAY.

SARGAS Theta Scorpii in the zodiacal constellation SCORPIUS.

SAROS Period of 18 years 11.3 days following which the Sun, Moon and Earth return to almost their same relative positions.

SASSANIAN EMPIRE (fl. AD 224) Founded by Ardashir, descendant of the mighty Persian potentate Xerxes; centred on Ctesiphon.

SATELLITES, Planetary See MOONS

SATELLITES OF JUPITER See JUPITER; MOONS

SATELLITES OF MARS See MARS; MOONS

SATELLITES OF NEPTUNE See MOONS; NEPTUNE

SATELLITES OF SATURN See MOONS; SATURN

SATELLITES OF URANUS See MOONS; URANUS

SATELLITIUM Astrological term for a group of three or more celestial bodies within a few degrees of each other in a CHART.

SATURDAY Seventh day of the week, named for SATURN.

SATURN Second known largest planet in the Solar System. Diameter at its equator 120000 km/74500 miles. Its journey round the Sun takes 29½ years and a Saturn day is 10 hours 39.4 minutes long. It has a beautiful ring system that lies in the plane of its equator. Astrologically, Saturn rules the zodiac sign CAPRICORN, is EXALTED in LIBRA, at DETRIMENT in CANCER, and at FALL in ARIES. It is thought to govern the skin and bones. In Roman mythology, Saturn is identified with the Greek CRONOS, son of URANUS and father of ZEUS. In ancient times, when it was the outermost planet, it was regarded as the planet of limitation. Saturn has two faces, one as the planet of endurance, perseverance, and self-discipline, necessary when dealing with difficult conditions, disappointment and delay, and on its other side, it is the planet of wisdom, worth, and stability, bringing success from hard effort and dedication to duty.

SCALES Symbol for the constellation and zodiac sign LIBRA.

SCHEAT Name of two fixed stars: Beta Pegasi, an orange VARIABLE STAR in the constellation PEGASUS; and Delta Aquarii, third brightest star in the zodiac constellation AQUARIUS.

SCHIAPARELLI, Giovanni Virginio (1835–1910) Italian astronomer, Director of Brera Observatory, Milan (1862);

Saturn

Giovanni Schiaparelli

discovered **HESPERIA** in April 1861, and did pioneer work on the planets **MERCURY**, **VENUS**, **URANUS** and, especially, **MARS**.

SCHWARZSCHILD, Karl (1873–1916) German astronomer and pioneer of theoretical astrophysics; did important work on the gravitational fields of mass, and the theory of **BLACK HOLES**.

SCINTILLATION The twinkling of a star; this is an effect of the Earth's atmosphere, and depends on the prevailing weather conditions.

SCORPIO Eighth sign of the zodiac, a **FEMININE NEGATIVE FIXED WATER** sign, once ruled by **MARS**, but now by **PLUTO**. The Moon is at **FALL** and **URANUS** is **EXALTED** in Scorpio. It represents the Scorpion sent by **HERA** to sting **ORION** in punishment for his vanity – he had boasted that he could kill any animal, large or small. **ZEUS** put the Scorpion into the heavens as the zodiac constellation **SCORPIUS**.

SCORPION Name and symbol for the zodiacal constellation **SCORPIUS**.

SCORPIUS, the Scorpion Magnificent zodiacal constellation which, unlike other asterisms meant to represent an animal, really does form a picture rather like a scorpion in the sky. It has twenty stars above the fourth **MAGNITUDE**, dominated of course by its Alpha, **ANTARES**. Beta Scorpii is the star Graffias. The star Shaula, in the scorpion's 'sting', is only just below first magnitude. Scorpius is associated with the zodiac sign **SCORPIO**.

SCOT, Michael (c1175–1234) British astrologer and occultist who was attached to the court of King Frederick II of Sicily and Naples. He translated many valuable works of Greek and Arab writers and was a talented exponent of **JUDICIAL ASTROLOGY**.

SCULPTOR, the Sculptor Constellation formerly known as Apparatus Sculptoris; not very rich in stars, but contains several faint galaxies, including a dwarf elliptical galaxy discovered in 1976.

SCULPTOR'S TOOLS Name for the constellation **CAELUM**.

SCUTUM, the Shield Small constellation bordering on **AQUILA**; contains the Wild-Duck open cluster M11 and is crossed by the **MILKY WAY**.

SEASONS Times of the year that coincide with the **EQUINOXES** and **SOLSTICES**; differences in day lengths and climate are the result of the Earth's axial tilt of 23.5.

SECOND HOUSE Astrological **HOUSE** associated with the second sign of the zodiac, **TAURUS**, and ruled by **VENUS**; the second house rules possessions of all kinds, material assets, business and money, principles and moral values.

SECOND SIGN OF THE ZODIAC See **TAURUS**

SECONDARY DIRECTIONS See **DIRECTIONS**

SECONDARY PROGRESSIONS See **DIRECTIONS**

SEE-SAW CHART See **JONES CHART PATTERNS**

SEGINUS Gamma Boötis in the constellation **BOÖTES**.

SEISMOLOGY The study of earthquake phenomena.

SELENE In Greek mythology, goddess of the Moon; daughter of **HYPERION** and Theia, identified approximately with the Roman **DIANA**.

SELENOGRAPHY The study of the Moon's surface.

SELEUCIS. Nicator (c358–281 BC) One of **ALEXANDER THE GREAT**'s generals; conquered **BABYLON** in 312BC and set up a rival city, Seleucis.

SEMELE In Greek mythology, daughter of Cadmus and Harmonia; mother, by **ZEUS**, of **DIONYSUS**.

SEMI-ARCS OF THE SUN The Sun's **DIURNAL** (daily) **ARC** is when it is travelling from the **ASCENDANT** to the **DESCENDANT**, and above the **HORIZON**. Its **NOCTURNAL ARC** is when it is moving from the descendant to the ascendant, below the horizon. A line drawn from the **MC** to the **IC**, corresponding to the axis, cuts these arcs into four semi-arcs, called quadrants.

SEMI-QUINTILE Astrological **ASPECT** of 36°; a **QUINTILE** is 72°.

SEMI-SEXTILE Astrological aspect of 30° or one sign; a **SEXTILE** is 60°.

SEMI-SQUARE Astrological **ASPECT** of 45°; a square is 90°.

SEPTEMBER Ninth month of the **GREGORIAN CALENDAR**; named from the Latin word for seven (*septem*) because it was the seventh month of the **JULIAN CALENDAR**.

SEPTILE Obtained by dividing the 360° of the zodiac by seven, resulting in a degree of 51° 4″. This is used mainly for **HARMONICS** and is the Seventh Harmonic.

SERAPHIAL See **ANGELIC ASTROLOGERS**

SERAPIS Egyptian God Apis, Lord of the Underworld. The place identified as **HADES** by the Greeks, and **ORCUS** or Dis by the Romans.

SERPENS, the Serpent A constellation divided into two parts, the head portion Caput, and the body portion Cauda. Possibly representing the serpent that fought with **OPHIUCHUS** and must have been decapitated. The Caput section has six stars above fourth **MAGNITUDE**, but the Cauda has only three above fourth magnitude. Alpha Serpentis (Caput) is the star called Unukalhai, magnitude 2.65.

SERPENT Name for the constellation **SERPENS**.

SERPENT-BEARER Named for the constellation **OPHIUCHUS**.

SERPENTARIUS Ancient name for the constellation **OPHIUCHUS**.

SESQUIQUADRATE An astrological **ASPECT** of 135°.

SESQUIQUINTILE An astrological **ASPECT** of 108°.

SET OR SETH Egyptian equivalent to the Greek **TYPHON**.

SEVEN SISTERS Name sometimes given to the **PLEAIDES**.

SEVEN WONDERS OF THE WORLD The ancient list of the Seven Wonders consists of the Pyramids of Egypt, the Hanging Gardens of Babylon, the Tomb of Mausolus (Mausoleum), the Temple of **DIANA** at Ephesus, the Colossus of Rhodes, the Statue of **ZEUS (JUPITER)** by Phidias, and the **PHAROS** of Alexandria. A later list quotes The Coliseum of Rome, The Catacombs of Alexandria, The Great Wall of China, **STONEHENGE**, The Leaning Tower of Pisa, The Porcelain Tower of Nanking and The Mosque of San Sophia at Constantinople (now Istanbul).

SEVENTH HOUSE Astrological **HOUSE** associated with the seventh sign of the zodiac **LIBRA** and ruled by **VENUS**; rules partnerships and relationships, business or personal; also the house of marriage.

SEVENTH SIGN OF THE ZODIAC See **LIBRA**

SEXTANS, the Sextant Obscure constellation between **LEO** and **HYDRA**; it intrudes slightly into the zodiac.

SEXTANT Name for the constellation **SEXTANS**.

SEXTILE Astrological **ASPECT** of 60°, or two signs apart.

SEYFERT, Carl (1911–1960) American astronomer who specialized in the study of certain types of **GALAXIES** with highly condensed nuclei which are now named after him. See **SEYFERT GALAXIES**.

SEYFERT GALAXIES Named after Carl **SEYFERT**; very bright, compact **SPIRAL** or **BARRED SPIRAL** galaxies, so closely packed that they look like stars, and strong sources of **RADIO WAVES** and **ELECTROMAGNETIC RADIATION** above and below the visible **SPECTRUM**.

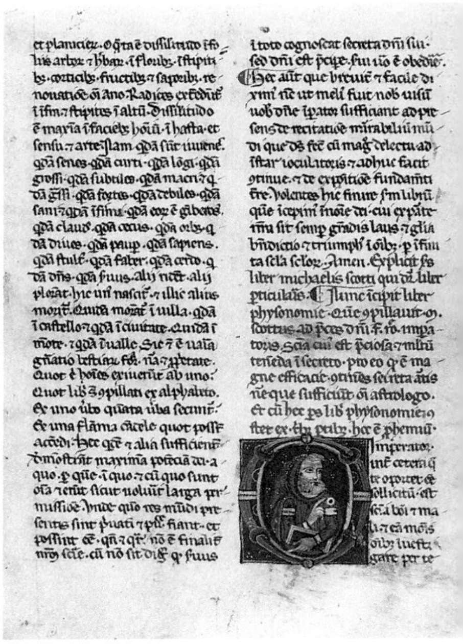

The Colossus of Rhodes

Michael Scot

Babylonian image of the Sun-god Shamash

SHADOW BANDS Slow-moving bands of shadow seen before or after a total **ECLIPSE**.

SHAMASH Akkadian Sun god, son of **SIN** the Moon god, depicted as sailing across the sky in a boat.

SHAPLEY, Harlow (1885–1972) American astronomer; first to draw up an accurate map of the **MILKY WAY** from his observations of **CEPHEID VARIABLES** and **GLOBULAR CLUSTERS**.

SHARATAN Beta Arietis, second brightest star in the zodiac constellation **ARIES**.

SHAULA Lambda Scorpionis, part of the 'sting' in the Scorpius's tail.

SHEDIR Alpha Cassiopiae in the constellation **CASSIOPIA**.

SHELIAK Beta Lyrae in the constellation **LYRA**: the prototype **ECLIPSING BINARY**.

SHEPHERD SATELLITE Moons which orbit with planetary rings; **SATURN** has eight such shepherds, and **URANUS** has two. See **MOONS**.

SHERATAN Beta Arietis in the zodiacal constellation **ARIE**

SHIELD Name for the constellation **SCUTUM**.

SHOOTING STARS Popular name for **METEORS**.

SIBYL In classical mythology, a prophetess inspired by a deity.

SICKLE OF LEO Curved pattern of stars in the zodiac constellation **LEO**, dominated by the star **REGULUS** (Alpha Leonis).

SIDEREAL Pertaining to the stars.

SIDEREAL CLOCKS Clocks that show the time relative to the stars; ordinary clocks show mean time relative to the Sun (**SOLAR TIME**). See also **SIDEREAL DAY**.

SIDEREAL DAY The time the Earth takes to rotate once relative to a **FIXED STAR**; it lasts 23 hours, 56 minutes and 4.09 seconds of **GREENWICH MEAN TIME** or Universal Time.

SIDEREAL MONTH Time taken for the Moon to make two successive passages across a **FIXED STAR**; it varies by up to seven hours, but the mean is 27.32 days. See also **MONTH**.

SIDEREAL TIME Time that is measured relative to the stars.

SIDEREAL YEAR The time taken for the Earth to travel once round the Sun relative to a **FIXED STAR**; also expressed as the interval between successive journeys of the Sun over a star: 365 days 6 hours 9 minutes 9.5 seconds.

SIDEREAL ZODIAC See **ZODIAC, SIDEREAL**.

SIDING SPRING OBSERVATORY Major Australian observatory, built on top of a volcanic peak near Coonabarabran, New South Wales. Contains much of the equipment moved from **MOUNT STROMLO**, whose position near the industrially polluted skies of Canberra makes astronomical observation difficult.

SIGILS Another name for **GLYPHS** or symbols.

SIGMA OCTANTIS Called the South Pole Star, it lies within 7° of the **POLE**, but its position will have increased to 1° by the end of this century. It lies in the constellation **OCTANS**.

SIGNS OF THE ZODIAC See **ZODIAC SIGNS**

SIMMAH One of the Babylonian fish-goddesses that represents **PISCES**.

SIN Akkadian Moon god. See also **SHAMASH**.

SINISTER ASPECT Old astrological term describing celestial bodies moving towards a **CONJUNCTION**.

SINOPE Tiny satellite of **JUPITER**, ninth to be discovered (1914).

SIRIUS, the Dog Star Alpha Canis Majoris in the constellation **CANIS MAJOR**; brightest star in the sky.

SISYPHUS **ASTEROID 1866**, one of the **APOLLO** group. In Greek mythology, son of **AEOLUS** and husband of **MEROPE**; known as the 'Crafty One', he was punished in **HADES** by having to push a huge boulder up a steep hill forever.

SIXTH HOUSE Astrological **HOUSE** associated with **VIRGO**, the sixth sign of the zodiac and ruled by **GEMINI**; it rules work and subordinates and is the house of health, although well-being is not entirely assessed from this house.

SIXTH SIGN OF THE ZODIAC See **VIRGO**

61 CYGNI **BINARY** star in the constellation **CYGNUS**, the first star to be measured by the method of **PARALLAX** in 1838, by **BESSEL**.

SKYLAB First American space station, launched on 14 May 1973.

SLIPHER, Vesto Melvin (1875–1969) American astronomer, Director of **LOWELL** Observatory (1916–1952); initiated the search for **PLUTO**, and was the first to appreciate the importance of **REDSHIFT** in the measurement of **GALAXIES**.

SMITHSONIAN ASTROPHYSICAL OBSERVATORY Merged with the **HARVARD COLLEGE OBSERVATORY** in 1973 to become the Center for Astrophysics; situated in Cambridge, Massachusetts.

SMYTHE, William Henry (1788–1865) English hydrographer, founder of the Royal Geographical Society; he established an observatory at Bedford, and wrote *Cycle of Celestial Objects* and the *Bedford Catalogue*.

SOCRATES (c469–399 BC) Great Athenian philosopher, tutor to **PLATO**; condemned to death for introducing new gods to his pupils.

SOLAR Pertaining to the **SUN**.

SOLAR APEX The point on the **CELESTIAL SPHERE** towards which the Sun (and its attendant Solar System) are moving. It lies in the constellation **HERCULES**.

SOLAR CHROMOSPHERE See **CHROMOSPHERE**

SOLAR CONSTANT The total amount of solar radiation reaching the Earth; the value is 1.95 calories per square centimetre per minute.

SOLAR CORONA 'Crown' round the Sun, lying beyond the **CHROMOSPHERE**, only visible to the naked eye during a total **ECLIPSE** of the Sun.

SOLAR CYCLE Period of about eleven years. Its mean since 1715 is 11.04 years.

SOLAR DAY Time taken by the Earth to make one revolution relative to the Sun. This varies according to the time of year, but its mean is 24 hours.

SOLAR ECLIPSE When the Moon is in line between the Sun and Earth and passes in front of the Sun, it blocks out the Sun's disc, and we have an eclipse of the Sun, but when the Sun is completely obscured by the Moon, there is a total Solar eclipse.

SOLAR FACULAE Often associated with sunspots; bright patches which seem to lie at a higher level above the spots. Sometimes faculae can be seen just before a sunspot breaks out, and can last for a while after the spot has disappeared.

SOLAR FLARES A brilliant burst of light occurring near a sunspot.

SOLAR PROMINENCES Hot bright clouds of gas projected from the Sun like flames, some can attain lengths of thousands of miles.

SOLAR SYSTEM The group of **PLANETS**, moons, planetary satellites, **COMETS**, **ASTEROIDS** and other material or bodies within the gravitational field of the Sun.

SOLAR TIME True solar time is the time given by a sundial. Some sundials have a device called an **ANALEMMA**, which measures the equation of time, which is the difference between true solar time and mean solar time, now called Universal Time or **GREENWICH MEAN TIME**.

SOLAR WIND A continuous stream of charged **PARTICLES** emitted in all directions by the Sun.

SOLSTICE See **SUMMER SOLSTICE**; **WINTER SOLSTICE**

SOLSTITIAL COLURE **GREAT CIRCLE** on the **CELESTIAL SPHERE** that joins the points of the summer and winter **SOLSTICES**.

Solar Eclipse 1979, from Manitoba, Canada

Solar prominences

SOMBRERO HAT GALAXY Spiral galaxy lying forty-one million **LIGHT YEARS** away in **VIRGO**.

SOSIGENES Egyptian astronomer who assisted Julius Caesar to devise the **JULIAN CALENDAR**, which was laid down in 46 BC.

SOTHIS Egyptian name for **SIRIUS**.

SOUTH AFRICAN ASTRONOMICAL OBSERVATORY The headquarters are at the site of the old Royal Observatory at the Cape, but its main telescopes are at Sutherland, about 640 km/200 miles northeast of Cape Town.

SOUTH NODE Point where a planet or body crosses the **ECLIPTIC** and moves from the northern to the southern latitudes.

SOUTHERN BIRDS Constellations in the southern sky, named for birds: **GRUS**, **PAVO**, **PHOENIX** and **TUCANA**.

SOUTHERN CROSS See **CRUX AUSTRALIS**

SOUTHERN CROWN See **CORONA AUSTRALIS**

SOUTHERN FISH See **PISCES AUSTRALIS**

SOUTHERN FLY See **MUSCA AUSTRALIS**

SOUTHERN LIGHTS See **AURORA**

SOUTHERN SIGNS Six zodiac signs from **LIBRA** to **PISCES** inclusive.

SOUTHERN TRIANGLE Star pattern in the constellation **TRIANGULUM AUSTRALE**; consists of Alpha Trianguli Australis, **ATRIA**, and Beta and Gamma Trianguli Australis.

SPACE SHUTTLE Reusable winged manned space transporter.

SPARTA Ancient Greek city-state in the Peloponnese; Spartans were noted for their hard, disciplined life.

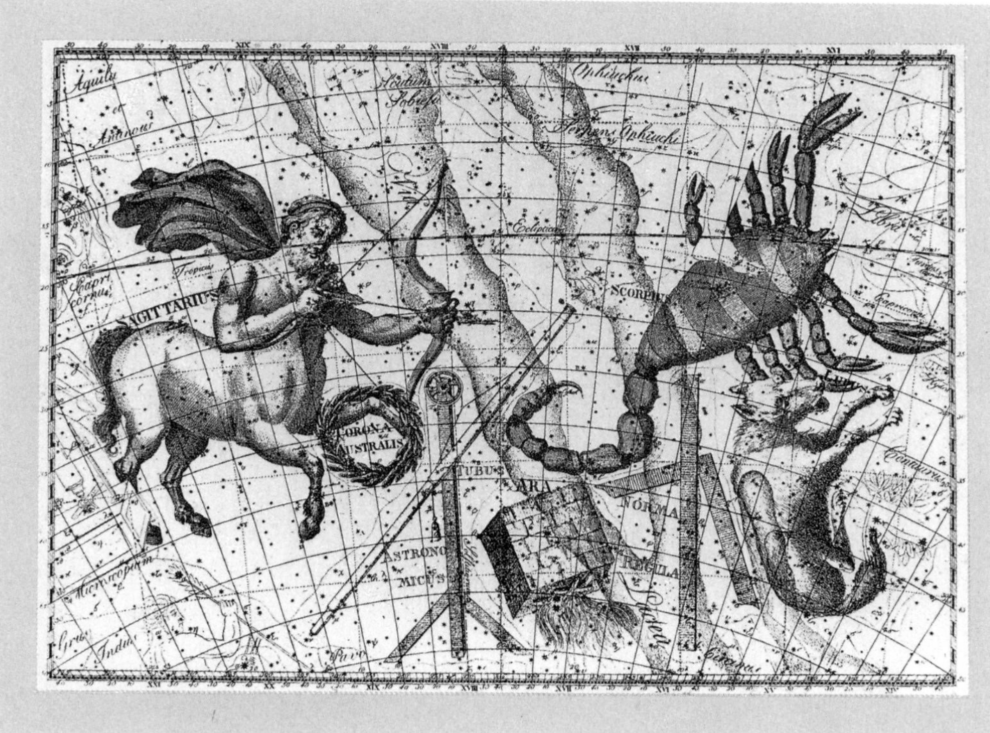

Some southern zodiac signs and constellations

SPECTROSCOPE Instrument used by astronomer to analyse the nature of light from stars in our own galaxy, or even from more distant sources. The device splits white light into a series of wavelengths, and their relative colours of the spectrum.

Spiral galaxy in Ursa Major

SPECTRUM The entire range of wavelengths of electromagnetic radiation.

SPICA Alpha Virginis, a bright blue-white close **BINARY** type star, in the zodiac constellation **VIRGO**.

SPIRAL GALAXY Galaxy shaped like a Catherine Wheel, with cool stars in the centre and hot stars on the outer spiral arms. The **MILKY WAY** is a spiral galaxy.

SPLASH Types of astrological chart based on the grouping of the planets, devised by American astrologer **MARC EDMUND JONES**.

SPLAY One of the **JONES CHART PATTERNS**.

SPRING TIDES Occur when the Sun and Moon are in line with the Earth and their attractive forces are combined; tides are consequently higher.

SQUARE An astrological aspect that measures 90° and is therefore three signs apart in a chart. It is evaluated as a difficult or inharmonious **ASPECT**.

SQUARE Alternative name for the constellation **NORMA**.

STANDARD TIME The official or legal time used by any place in the world. It is calculated from the agreed international point of zero longitude, set at Greenwich England. The world is divided into twenty-four standard time zones, each defined by successive meridians of 15° geographical longitude, representing one hour difference in time from the next meridian. Zones to the east of Greenwich are ahead of Greenwich, and zones to the west are behind Greenwich, and have to be adjusted accordingly to obtain **GREENWICH MEAN TIME** or Universal time. The **INTERNATIONAL DATE LINE** is the meridian 180° east and west from Greenwich, crossing the Pacific Ocean. Very useful books giving information on time changes in the world are available; see **DOANE**.

STANDARD TIME ZONES See **STANDARD TIME**.

STAR CLOUDS Huge groups of old, cool stars towards the centre of the **MILKY WAY**.

STAR CLUSTERS Star clusters are divided into two groups, the **GLOBULAR CLUSTERS** and **OPEN CLUSTERS**. It was from the study of globular clusters that astronomer **SHAPLEY** could determine that the centre of the **MILKY WAY** lies in the direction of **SAGITTARIUS**.

STAR OF BETHLEHEM This famous 'Star' is associated with the 'Planet of Kings', **JUPITER**, according to several reliable sources. One of the first was Johannes **KEPLER** who connected this 'Star' with the **CONJUNCTION** of the planets Jupiter and **SATURN** at the time of Christ's birth. Such a conjunction occurred three times in the year 7 BC in the sign of the Fishes. A triple conjunction only occurs every 139 years, and in **PISCES** once in 900 years.

STAR TYPES Various star types are listed in this dictionary under their alphabetical headings, i.e. **BINARY STARS**, **CEPHEID VARIABLES**, **ECLIPSING BINARIES**, **FLARE STARS**, **RED GIANTS**, **RED DWARFS**, **DOUBLE STARS** and **VARIABLES**.

STATIONARY CELESTIAL BODIES see **RETROGRADE MOTION**.

STEADY STATE THEORY Theory of **COSMOLOGY** which regards the Universe as essentially unchanging throughout time.

STELLAR MAGNITUDE SCALE see **MAGNITUDE**

STELLIUM Astrologically this is indicated by three, four or more planets within a few degrees of each other in a chart.

STEWARD OBSERVATORY The observatory of the University of Arizona, Tucson. Its main telescopes are situated on **KITT PEAK**.

The magi and the Star of Bethlehem

STOCKHOLM OBSERVATORY Originally founded in 1748, it was moved in 1931 to the suburbs of Saltsjobade.

STOICS A school of Greek philosophers founded by Zeno of Citium (335–263 BC). His system stated it was necessary for man to live in harmony with nature. They were attracted to astrology and divination.

Stonehenge

STONEHENGE Situated on Salisbury Plain west of Amesbury, this is the most famous prehistoric monument in Britain. It was originally of late Neolithic construction, and later repaired or rebuilt by the Beaker Folk. It is thought to have been a huge astronomical clock and centre of worship, connected in some way with the Sun. Its outer circle was built from local sarsen stones, and two inner circles of Blue Stones, thought to have come from the Prescelly Mountains. Large stone lintels capped the first and third circles, and the whole was surrounded by a ditch with fifty-six Aubrey holes. The Heel Stone, which marks sunrise on Midsummer's Day, stands alone.

STRATOSPHERE A layer of the Earth's atmosphere which lies above the tropopause – the upper limit of the troposphere – and extends as far as the mesosphere.

STYX The river in the Underworld across which CHARON, the surly boatman, ferried the souls to the realm of HADES.

SUALOCIN Alpha Delphini in the constellation DELPHINUS; named by Nicolaus VENATOR, who reversed the letters of his own forename.

SUB-DETRIMENT A planet placed in a sign opposite to the one it rules, or sub-rules, is said to be in its detriment or sub-detriment. See SUB-RULERSHIP.

SUB-RULERSHIP Before the planets URANUS, NEPTUNE and PLUTO were discovered, the ancients had the signs and their rulers magically worked out. From the positions of the Sun and Moon in LEO and CANCER respectively, the planets ruled the signs in their proper order from the Sun. MERCURY ruled GEMINI and VIRGO, VENUS ruled TAURUS and LIBRA, and MARS ruled ARIES and

Charon crossing the Styx

SCORPIO. **JUPITER** ruled **PISCES** and **SAGITTARIUS** and **SATURN** ruled **AQUARIUS** and **CAPRICORN**, but when the modern planets were discovered it muddled the system. Uranus became ruler of Aquarius, Neptune ruler of Pisces, and Pluto became ruler of Scorpio. The former rulers of these three signs were regarded as having the lesser status of co-rulers.

SUCCEDENT HOUSES The **HOUSES** which correspond to the four fixed signs; the **SECOND**, **FIFTH**, **EIGHTH** and **ELEVENTH HOUSE**.

SULAPHAT Gamma Lyrae in the constellation **LYRA**.

SUMMER SOLSTICE The point at which the Sun is at its highest **DECLINATION** in the sky, and we have the longest day and the shortest night; usually about 21 June in the northern hemisphere and 22 December in the southern; a **CARDINAL POINT**, at 0° **CANCER**. See also **WINTER SOLSTICE**.

SUMMER TRIANGLE **ALTAIR**, a white first **MAGNITUDE** star in the constellation **AQUILA**, together with Deneb in **CYGNUS** and Vega in **LYRA**, form a very fine triangle known as the Summer Triangle.

SUN The nearest star to Earth and of vital importance to all life on our planet. If the amount of Solar radiation changed even by a minute fraction life could become impossible. Fortunately however the Sun is a stable star, and although eventually it will use up all its nuclear fuel and collapse, it will last for at least another five thousand million years. Its mean distance from Earth is 150 million km/9 million miles.
Astrologically, the Sun rules **LEO**, is **EXALTED** in **ARIES**, at **DETRIMENT** in **AQUARIUS** and at **FALL** in **LIBRA**. The Sun is associated with the spine and heart, fatherhood, children, creativity and play. Sun-ruled subjects are characterized by generosity, organizing ability, magnanimity and affection; on the negative side, there may be pomposity, arrogance, condescension and bombast.
In **mythology** the sun was worshipped as a God by primitive peoples; he was known as **SHAMASH** by the Assyrians, Mithras by the Persians, **RA** by the Egyptians. Ra, whose name means Sun, was by some said to be the son of Atum, but it was usually believed that he was self-created. Ra symbolized the Sun at the height of its power and Atum, as an old man, was identified as the setting sun. Known by the Greeks as Helios, who climbed to heaven in a chariot drawn by white horses to give light each day, and in the evening disappeared down into the ocean. He was recognized by the Romans as Sol. Sometimes called **HYPERION**, and in later times identified with **APOLLO**.

SUNDAY First day of the week, named for the **SUN**.

SUNDIAL TIME see **SOLAR TIME**

SUNSPOTS Dark patches on the surface of the Sun. Sunspots have a dark central region called the umbra, which is surrounded by a lighter greyish area known as the penumbra. Sunspots are associated with strong **MAGNETIC FIELDS**. The number of spots varies and conforms to a cycle which extends over a period of about eleven years.

Zodiac sundial, Greenwich

SUPERGIANTS Enormous stars, such as **ANTARES**, and **BETELGEUX** with radii about 1 000 times that of the Sun.

SUPERIOR CONJUNCTION Term describing a planet when it is on the other side of the Sun and cannot be seen from Earth.

SUPERIOR PLANETS These are the planets beyond the Earth's orbit. **MARS**, **JUPITER**, **SATURN**, **URANUS**, **NEPTUNE** and **PLUTO**.

SUPERNOVA A celestial disaster, the complete disintegration of a star in an awesome explosion.

SWAN Name for the constellation **CYGNUS**.

SWIFT'S COMET Also called the Great Comet of 1862, it was discovered in July 1862 by Lewis Swift (1820–1913), American astronomer, who specialized in hunting **COMETS**. In early September 1862 the comet was exceedingly bright, but it rapidly faded.

SWORDFISH Name for the constellation **DORADO**.

SYMBOLIC DIRECTIONS Otherwise known as **FIXED INCREMENT** directions, which are all **DIRECTIONS** that are not based on any astronomical motion of the planets or houses. In all symbolic methods, there is a fixed annual increment, which is added to all factors, including the angles.

SYNASTRY A careful and detailed study involving the comparison of charts, to ascertain compatibility, harmony, discord, etc, between those concerned.

SYNCHRONOUS ORBIT see **GEOSTATIONARY**

SYNODIC MONTH The interval between New Moons, lunations, a period of 29 days 12 hrs 44 mins 2.7 seconds.

SYNODIC PERIOD The interval between the successive oppositions of a superior planet.

SYNTHESIS The art of blending together all the aspects, influences, etc, to be found in a nativity, and making a complete summary of everything. The ability to do this expertly bears the mark of a gifted and experienced astrologer.

SYRINX In Greek mythology, the nymph pursued by **PAN**; she was changed into a reed, from which he made his pipes.

SYZYGY A term of Greek origin which means yoking together. It is loosely applied to a conjunction or opposition, especially of a planet with the Sun, and close to the ecliptic. It also applies to the position of the Moon in its orbit when New or Full.

TABLE Name for the constellation **MENSA**.

TABLES OF HOUSES Astrological tables that show the degrees of the signs that occupy the **CUSPS** of the astrological **HOUSES** and the **ASCENDANT** in different latitudes for every degree of **RIGHT ASCENSION** (that is, every four minutes of **SIDEREAL TIME**).

TACITUS, Publius or Gaius Cornelius (c AD 55–120) Roman historian, author of books on oratory and the history of the Roman Empire among other subjects; he considered the planet **SATURN** to have great power over human affairs. Tacitus is the name given to a lunar crater.

TAILS Translation of the Babylonian word **KUN**; name for the zodiac sign **PISCES**.

TANTALUS In Greek mythology, king of Lydia and son of **ZEUS**; gave away the gods' secrets to mortals and was punished by being confined to water without being able to drink and starved while in the full sight of food.

TANTRAS Sanskrit religious books of the sixth and seventh centuries AD.

TARANTULA NEBULA Faintly visible **NEBULA** on the southeast edge of the large **MAGELLANIC CLOUD**.

TARAZED Gamma Aquilae, second brightest star in the constellation **AQUILA**; lies near the **ALPHA**, **ALTAIR**.

TAROT CARDS Probably devised in northern Italy in the fourteenth century; the Tarot pack consists of seventy-eight cards; the Lesser or Minor Arcana, and twentytwo cards, each representing a symbolic character, forming the Greater or Major Arcana.

TARTARS Asiatic tribes led by Ghenghis Khan who rampaged round thirteenth-century Europe; name possibly derived from **TARTARUS**.

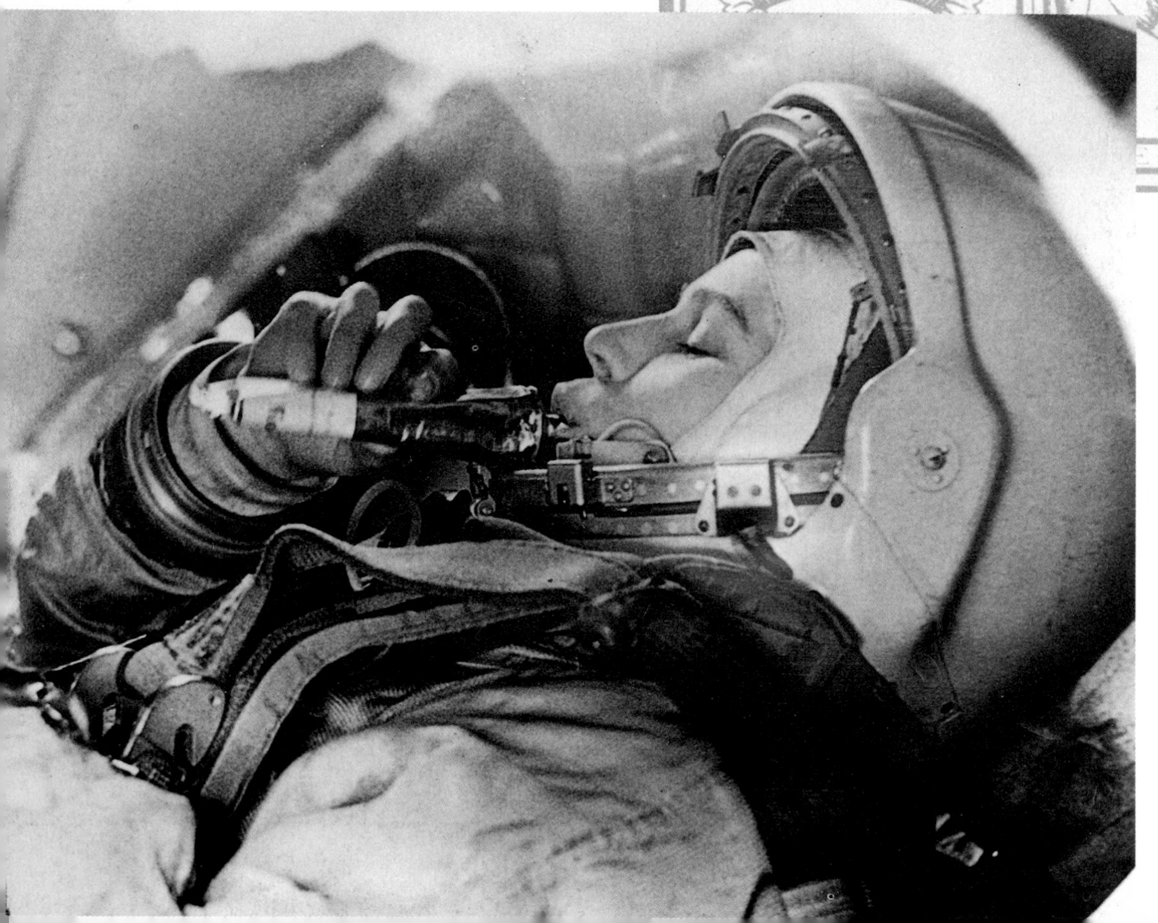

Tereshkova in space, 1963

TARTARUS Nethermost pit of **HADES**.

TAU CETI Fifth brightest star in the constellation **CETUS**; nearest star to Earth that is similar to the Sun.

TAURID METEORS Slow-moving **METEOR** shower with its **RADIANT** in the constellation **TAURUS**; visible every year between 20 October and 30 November, at their brightest between 3 and 10 November.

TAURUS, the Bull One of the brightest, richest zodiac constellations, and one of **PTOLEMY'S** originals; its **ALPHA**, **ALDEBARAN**, makes the 'eye' of the bull and is one of the **FOUR WATCHERS OF THE HEAVENS**; its beta is **AL NATH**; also contains the famous open clusters of the **PLEIADES** and the **HYADES**, the Crab **NEBULA**. **Taurus the zodiac sign** is the second sign of the zodiac, a **FEMININE NEGATIVE fixed EARTH** sign ruled by **VENUS**. The Moon is **EXALTED** in Taurus, **PLUTO** at **DETRIMENT** and **URANUS** at **FALL**. The Taurus **myth** is associated with the white bull – **ZEUS** in one of his many disguises – which abducted **EUROPA**, taking her to Crete, where she gave birth to Minos, **RHADAMANTHUS** and Sarpedon, and fathered the **MINOTAUR** on **PASIPHAË**.

TAYGETE 19 Tauri, one of the stars in the **PLEIADES** cluster in the constellation **TAURUS**.

TEBBUTT'S COMET The Great Comet, discovered by Australian astronomer John Tebbutt, 13 May 1861.

TEKTITES Rounded pieces of a glass-like substance, thought to be of extra-terrestrial origin.

TEE SQUARE Astrological **ASPECT** formed when two planets are in **OPPOSITION** to each other, and a third planet is **SQUARE** to both.

TELESCOPE Optical instrument which allows observation of celestial objects beyond naked eye visibility. Telescopes are either **refracting** or **reflecting**; refracting telescopes, the first design for which was patented by **LIPPERSHEY**, use glass lenses to gather in light from distant objects and focus it onto a plate. Reflecting telescopes, the first of which was designed by Sir Isaac **NEWTON**, use two mirrors, a curved one to collect the light and a second one to direct the image to a plate for observation. The largest refracting telescope is that at **YERKES OBSERVATORY** (the lens is 1.01 m/40 in. across); for very large telescopes, the reflecting type is better, and the **HERSCHEL** reflecting telescope at **ROQUE DE LOS MUCHACHOS** has mirrors 4.2 m/165 in. across. Radio telescopes are groups of large parabolic dishes which collect radio waves. See **VERY LARGE ARRAY**.

TELESCOPE Name for the constellation **TELESCOPIUM**.

TELESCOPIUM, the Telescope Small, rather insignificant constellation, near **ARA**.

TELESTO Small satellite of **SATURN**, discovered in 1980; coorbital with **TETHYS** and **CALYPSO**.

TEMPEL-TUTTLE COMET Short-period **COMET**

Tarot trump cards
Background: Tarot cards

first recorded by **MECHAIN** in 1790 but later independently 'discovered' by German astronomer Ernst Tempel, 19 December 1865, and Horace Tuttle in 1858; its period is about thirty-three years and is next due at **PERIHELION** in 1998.

TENTH HOUSE Astrological **HOUSE** associated with the tenth sign of the zodiac, **CAPRICORN**, and ruled by **SATURN**: governs ambition, prestige, career, and main aims in life.

TENTH SIGN OF THE ZODIAC See **CAPRICORN**

TERESHKOVA, Valentina (b. 1937) Soviet cosmonaut, first woman to journey into space, making fortyeight orbits round the Earth on the Russian spaceship Vostok 6 in June 1963.

TERPSICHORE In Greek mythology one of the **MUSES**: she represents dancing and song, and carries a lyre.

TERRESTRIAL EQUATOR The Earth's equator, the imaginary circle round the centre of the Earth equidistant from the North and South Poles.

TERRESTRIAL PLANETS Alternative name for **MERCURY** and **VENUS**; also called inferior planets or inner planets.

TETHYS Satellite of Saturn discovered by **CASSINI** in 1684; with a diameter of 1050 km/650 miles it dwarfs its two coorbiters, **CALYPSO** and **TELESTO**. In Greek mythology, one of the **TITANS**, a goddess of the sea, daughter of **URANUS** and **GAEA**, wife of **OCEANUS**.

TETRABIBLOS Greek term meaning four books; compiled by **PTOLEMY**, they contain the oldest surviving records of the ancient astrological systems, and are dated from c AD 132–160.

THALES OF MILETUS (c625–547 BC) Greek philosopher active in Ionia (western Turkey) who made many advances in geometry; accurately predicted the **ECLIPSE** of 585 BC.

THALIA One of the **MUSES**, representing comedy and poetry.

THAMMUZ Sumerian, Assyrian and Babylonian god of regeneration.

THEBE One of the four smaller inner satellites of **JUPITER**; small (80 km/50 miles diameter) dark moon discovered in 1980 during Voyager flybys. In Greek mythology, the wife of Zethus, founder of Thebes.

THEMIS **ASTEROID 24**, discovered by De Gasparis in April 1853. In Greek mythology, one of the **TITANS**, and the goddess of order.

THERMOSPHERE Part of the Earth's **ATMOSPHERE** that begins about 80km/50 miles above the surface.

THESEUS In Greek mythology, son of Aegeus of Athens; a great hero, his most famous exploit was the killing of the Minotaur of Crete.

THESPIUS In Greek mythology, father of fifty daughters, which he gave to **HERCULES** after the hero had killed the Lion of Mount Cithaeron that was laying waste Thespius' country.

THETA ORIONIS Multiple star system in the **ORION NEBULA**.

THETA SCORPII The star **SARGAS**.

THETA SERPENTIS The star **ALYA**.

THETIS In Greek mythology, a sea goddess, daughter of **NEREUS**; sought after by **ZEUS** and **POSEIDON**, but eventually married Peleus and became the mother of **ACHILLES**.

THIRD HOUSE Astrological **HOUSE** associated with the third sign of the zodiac, **GEMINI**, and ruled by **MERCURY**; concerns relations, family ties, communication, education, writing, correspondence, books and short journeys.

THIRD SIGN OF THE ZODIAC See **GEMINI**

THOAS In Greek legend, son of Andraemon; took forty ships to fight against the Trojans.

THOR Nordic god armed with a hammer, son of **ODIN**; equated with Roman **VULCAN**.

Earl Rosse's telescope

THOTH Powerful ancient Egyptian moon god, said to have created himself by calling his own name. God of time, astronomy, writing and language; he had magical powers and acted as interpreter for the gods. Identified by the Greeks with **HERMES TRISMEGISTUS**, the Thrice Greatest Hermes.

THUBAN Alpha Draconis in the northern constellation **DRACO**; in 3000 BC it was the **POLE STAR**.

THURSDAY Fifth day of the week; named for Donar or **THOR** in germanic languages and for **JUPITER** in latin languages.

TIDES Regular movement of the Earth's seas due to the gravitational pull of the Moon and, to a lesser extent, the Sun. The attraction of the Moon causes the waters beneath it to bulge, and at the same time there is a lesser bulge on the opposite side of the Earth. These bulges coincide with the high tide. As the Earth turns once daily on its axis, there are two high tides and two low tides, as these bulges sweep by. High spring tides are caused when the Sun and Moon are in line with the Earth, and their forces are pulling in the same direction.

TIME See **DAYLIGHT SAVING TIME; GREENWICH MEAN TIME; SIDEREAL TIME; SOLAR TIME; STANDARD TIME; SUNDIAL TIME**

TIME ZONES See **INTERNATIONAL DATE LINE; STANDARD TIME ZONES**

TITAN Saturn's largest satellite, with a diameter of 5150 km/3200 miles; discovered 25 March 1655 by Christiaan Huygens. In Greek mythology, the Titans were children of **URANUS** and **GAEA**: Cronus, Hyperion, Oceanus, Iapetus, Phoebe, Rhea, Themis, Tethys and Mnemosyne (although other names are also given); they rose against their father and deposed him, and waged a ten-year war with **ZEUS**, son of the Titan **CRONOS**, which they lost.

TITANIA Largest satellite of **URANUS**, with a diameter of 1580 km/982 miles, discovered in 1787 by William **HERSCHEL**; named for the Queen of the Fairies in *Midsummer Night's Dream*.

TIU Norse god of war, son of **ODIN** and brother of **THOR**; equated with **MARS**. Also called **TIW** or **TYR**.

TOKYO ASTRONOMICAL OBSERVATORY Founded in 1888, it is still Japan's National Observatory, associated with the University of Tokyo.

TOPOCENTRIC HOUSE SYSTEMS Time-based systems of **HOUSE DIVISION**.

TORO **ASTEROID 1685**, tiny (5 km/3 miles across) member of the **APOLLO** group, discovered 17 July 1948 by A. Wirtanen at **LICK**.

TOUCAN Name for the constellation **TUCANA**.

TRANSITS Astronomically, the passage of any celestial body across a fixed point; the passage of a small body across a large. **MERCURY** and **VENUS** make regular transits across the Sun, when they can be seen as small black dots moving from east to west. Mercury transits occur around 7 May and 9 November every three to thirteen years: the next are due on 1993 and 1999. Venus transits are rarer, but visible to the naked eye; they occur around 7 June and 8 December, and are next due in 2004 and 2012. Astrologically, transits are the movements of the Sun, Moon and planets. The importance of transits varies relative to their **RADICAL** (or **BIRTH CHART**) strengths, the points involved and the speed of the transiting planet. The slower-moving outer planets are more important than the faster ones.

TRANSVERSE MOTION Motion across the observer's line of sight. See also **RADIAL MOTION**.

TRAPEZIUM See **THETA ORIONIS**.

TREPTOW OBSERVATORY Situated not far from Berlin, a centre for astronomical education now known as the Archenhold Observatory, in honour of its first Director, F.S. Archenhold (in office 1891–1931).

TRIANGLE Name for constellation **TRIANGULUM**.

TRIANGULUM, the Triangle Small constellation, one of **PTOLEMY'S** original forty-eight, lying between **ANDROMEDA** and **ARIES**.

Titans and Olympians in battle

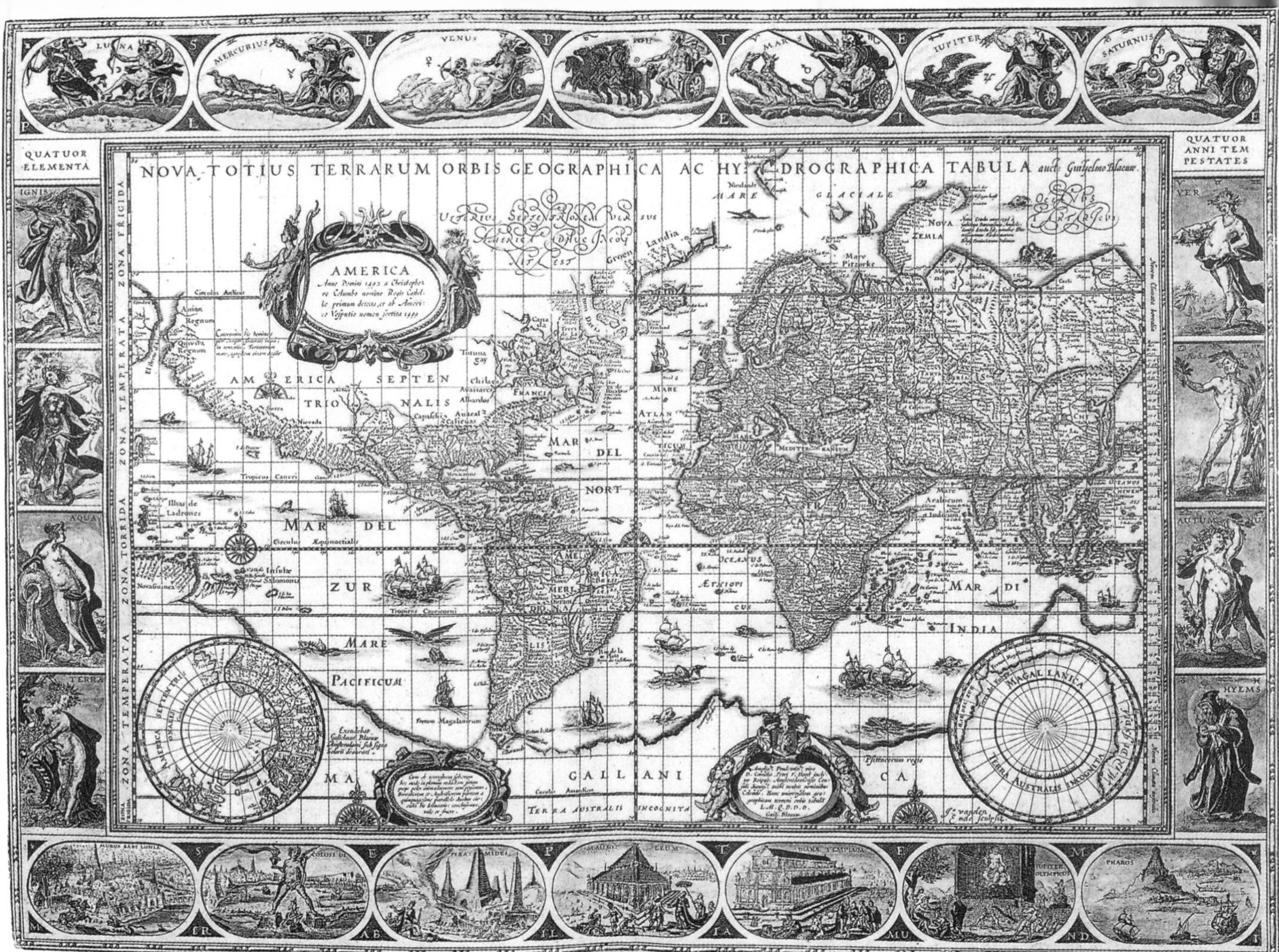

Columbus' map showing the tropics of Cancer and Capricorn (see Tropical Year)

TRIANGULUM AUSTRALE The Southern Triangle. Bright little constellation near **CENTAURUS**.

TRIFID NEBULA **NEBULA** in the zodiac constellation **SAGITTARIUS**.

TRIGON Term sometimes used for the **TRIPLICITIES**.

TRINE Astrological **ASPECT** which occurs when three bodies or signs are 120° apart from each other in the zodiac band.

TRIPLICITIES The four groups of three signs of the zodiac that belong to the same **ELEMENT**. The **FIRE** triplicity consists of **ARIES**, **LEO** and **SAGITTARIUS**; the **EARTH** triplicity is **TAURUS**, **VIRGO** and **CAPRICORN**; the **WATER** triplicity is **CANCER**, **SCORPIO** and **PISCES**; the **AIR** triplicity is **GEMINI**, **LIBRA** and **AQUARIUS**. See also **QUADRUPLICITIES**.

TRIPTELIMUS Alternative name for **POLLUX**.

TRISMEGISTUS See **HERMES TRISMEGISTUS**; **THOTH**

TRITON Larger of **NEPTUNE'S** two originally known moons; orbits very close to its **PRIMARY** in a **RETROGRADE** motion. Photographs taken during the Voyager flyby of 24 August 1989 show it to be smaller than estimated, extremely cold (−186° C/303°F) and bright blue. In Greek mythology, Triton was the son of **POSEIDON** and Amphitrite.

TROJANS Groups of **ASTEROIDS** which have a similar orbit to **JUPITER**; one group are 60° in front of the planet, are named for the Greek heroes who fought the Trojan War; the second group, 60° behind the planet and are named for the Trojan defenders; altogether over 220 are known.

TROPICAL YEAR Interval between spring **EQUINOXES**; the time taken by the Sun to make successive journeys through the **VERNAL POINT**; this amounts to 365 days 5 hours 48 minutes 46 seconds. See also **YEAR, ZODIAC, TROPICAL**.

TROPOPAUSE Interface between the **TROPOSPHERE** and **STRATOSPHERE**.

TROPOSPHERE Layer of atmosphere extending from sea level for about 11 km/7 miles above the Earth's surface.

TRUTINE OF HERMES See **HERMES, THE RULE OF**

TUCANA, the Toucan Southern constellation, one of the **SOUTHERN BIRDS**; contains part of the Small **MAGELLANIC CLOUD** and two fine **GLOBULAR CLUSTERS**.

TUESDAY Second day of the week, named for the god of war, **TIU** in germanic languages, and **MARS** in latin languages.

TUNGUSKA METEORITE **METEORITE** that fell on a remote Siberian forest 30 June 1908; so great was the impact that trees were destroyed in an area about 40 km/25 miles across, possibly the result of part of **ENCKE'S** comet exploding.

TWELFTH HOUSE Astrological **HOUSE** associated with the twelfth sign of the zodiac **PISCES** and ruled by **NEPTUNE**; concerns a need for seclusion, service to others, self-sacrifice and escapism; the house of secrets and the subconscious mind.

TWELFTH SIGN OF THE ZODIAC See **PISCES**

TYCHE OR TUCHE Roman goddess of luck.

TYPHON In Greek mythology, monstrous son of **GAEA** and Tartarus; father, by Echidne, of many other monsters including Cerberus, the Lernean **HYDRA** and the Chimaera; killed by **ZEUS** and buried under Mount Etna.

TYRO Nymph beloved by **POSEIDON**, mother of **PELIAS**, **NELEUS** and Aethra.

ULTRAVIOLET ASTRONOMY Study of ULTRAVIOLET RADIATION emitted by celestial bodies; very useful for the understanding of STELLAR WIND and BINARY STARS. As such radiation does not penetrate the atmosphere, work has to be carried out from satellites; the HUBBLE space telescope will provide much new data.

ULTRAVIOLET RADIATION ELECTROMAGNETIC RADIATION beyond the violet end of the visible spectrum; in the band between visible light and X-RAYS, between 380 and 2 NANOMETRES.

ULUGH BEIGH (or BEG) (1394–1449) Islamic prince and astronomer, ruler of Uzbekistan; built a noted observatory in his capital, Samarkand.

ULYSSES In Greek mythology, a king of Ithaca who wandered the Greek world; also known as odysseus.

UMBRA Shadow; the dark central cone of shadow cast by a satellite or planet; also the dark central region of a SUNSPOT. See also PENUMBRA.

UMBRAL ECLIPSE Term applied to an ECLIPSE of the Moon when it enters the Earth's shadow.

UMBRIEL Third largest satellite of URANUS with a diameter of 1 174 km/730 miles.

UNASPECTED PLANETS Planets which receive no major ASPECTS in a CHART; this is a very rare configuration.

UNDERWORLD See HADES

UNDINA ASTEROID 92, discovered in 1867; one of the largest in the group with a diameter of 250 km/155 miles.

UNICORN Name for the constellation MONOCEROS.

UNITED STATES NAVAL OBSERVATORY Situated at Flagstaff, Arizona, but separate from the LOWELL Observatory; its main TELESCOPE, the 155 cm/61 inch reflector, was used to take the photographs which led to the discovery of PLUTO'S moon, CHARON.

UNIVERSAL TIME See GREENWICH MEAN TIME

UNIVERSE The cosmos and everything in it; theories about its origins have always exercised the minds of men; two of the current theories are the BIG BANG and the STEADY STATE.

UNUKALHAI Alpha Serpentis, in the Caput section of the divided constellation SERPENS.

UPPSALA OBSERVATORY Situated in Uppsala, Sweden, its present building was erected in about 1850; it has a fine collection of old astronomical literature.

URANIA In Greek mythology, one of the MUSES; her name means heavenly, or celestial, and she presides over ASTROLOGY and ASTRONOMY.

URANIENBORG Tycho BRAHE'S castle observatory, completed in 1580; built on the Danish island of Hven (or Ven), a present from Brahe's patron Frederick II of Denmark. The castle featured two tall round towers at the north and south, used as observatory platforms. Brahe filled his castle with precision equipment and made the most accurate observations of his time; in 1584 he added a further observatory, Stjerneborg, which was remarkable because it was built underground and fitted with sliding roof panels to allow telescopes to 'see' the sky.

URANUS Seventh planet from the Sun, discovered in 1781 by William HERSCHEL; Uranus is four times the size of Earth, and orbits the Sun in eighty-four years; unlike any other planet in the Solar System, its axis is so tilted towards its orbital plane (98°) that its poles point towards the Sun during its orbit; it is girdled by a system of eleven main rings and numerous

Telescope at US Naval Observatory

thin ones, and has fifteen known moons (see **URANUS SATELLITES**), all of them rather dark. Astrologically, Uranus rules **AQUARIUS** and the **ELEVENTH HOUSE**, is **EXALTED** in **SCORPIO**, at **DETRIMENT** in **LEO** and at **FALL** in **TAURUS**; Uranus is associated anatomically with the circulatory system; its attributes include freedom, independence, change, originality, unpredictability, electricity, genius, intellect, eccentricity, technology, modern science, aeronautics, radio and TV space travel and the unexpected. In mythology, Uranus was the personification of the sky, son and husband to **GAEA** and father of the **TITANS**; he was castrated by his son **CRONOS** (**SATURN**) with a flint sickle and his children usurped his powers.

URANUS RETURNS See **PLANETARY RETURNS**

UR-NAMMU (fl. 2112–2095 BC) Founder of the Third Ur Dynasty, who presided over the Golden Age of Sumerian art; initiated the building of the great **ZIGGURAT**.

URSA MAJOR, the Great Bear Most conspicuous of the northern constellations, one of **PTOLEMY'S** original forty-eight; it is circumpolar in UK and northern areas of USA; the main star pattern is the Plough, or Big Dipper, consisting of seven stars: the 'handle' is made up of Alkaid (Eta), Mizar (Zeta) and **ALIOTH** (Epsilon); the ploughshare is made up of Megrez (Delta), **PHAD** (Gamma), **MERAK** (Beta) and **DUBHE** (Alpha). Dubhe and Merak are known as 'The Pointers' as they appear to point towards **POLARIS**. Contains many galaxies and the famous **OWL NEBULA**. In Greek mythology, the Great Bear is supposed to represent **CALLISTO**, beautiful daughter of King Lycaon of Arcadia; jealous **HERA** turned her into a bear; Callisto's son Arcas was about to shoot her when **ZEUS** intervened and put Callisto into the heavens as the Great Bear.

Ulysses ignores the Sirens

Background: US Naval Observatory

URSA MINOR, the Little Bear North Polar constellation, one of **PTOLEMY'S** original forty-eight; its **ALPHA** is **POLARIS** the **POLE STAR**; in Greek mythology, it represents Arcas, son of **CALLISTO**, who was turned into the Great Bear by **ZEUS**. See also **URSA MAJOR**.

UTNAPISHTIM Babylonian counterpart of Noah.

Mural from tomb six in the Valley of the Kings

VAGRANCY ACT Act passed in England in 1824 describing astrologers as 'vagabonds and rogues' and banning them from following their profession.

VALENS (fl. fourth century) Roman Emperor whose court astrologer Heliodorus cast **HOROSCOPES** and predicted the future by observing the stars.

VALLEY OF THE KINGS Valley northwest of Thebes, burial site of the Pharoahs.

VAN ALLEN BELTS Two areas in the Earth's **MAGNETOSPHERE** containing trapped electrically charged **PARTICLES**; the lower region (1 000 km/600 miles to 3 000 km/1 875 miles) above the Equator contains **PROTONS** and **ELECTRONS**; the higher region, which curves down towards the magnetic poles, is 15 000 km/ 9 320 miles to 25 000 km/15,500 miles above the Equator, and contains **PROTONS** from the **SOLAR WIND**. Van Allen belts present a hazard to exploratory spacecraft orbiting the Earth as they interfere with the electronic instrumentation; **MERCURY**, **JUPITER**, **SATURN**, **URANUS** and **NEPTUNE** have Van Allen belts; they were named for James Van Allen, who discovered them from observations made in 1958 by the satellite Explorer 1.

VARIABLE STARS Stars whose brightness varies over periods of time. Most are discovered by photography, but early types visible to the naked eye include **ALGOL**, the 'winking star'. In 1786, only twelve variables were recognized; by 1941, there were 8 445; today more than 29 000 are known. Various factors make a star 'wink': eruptive variables are the result of flaring gases in their **CORONA** and **CHROMOSPHERE**; pulsating variables, such as the **MIRA** or **CEPHEID VARIABLES**, regularly contract and expand; rotating stars present different degrees of brightness depending on physical features such as 'starspots', which come round regularly; explosive variables such as **NOVAE** and **SUPERNOVAE** burst into light; and **ECLIPSING BINARIES** vary as they move in and out of **CONJUNCTION** with each other, or if a small hot star is eclipsed by a **SUPERGIANT**, in which case the intense light from the small star shines fiercely through the giant's atmosphere.

VAULT OF THE HEAVENS Old name for the **CELESTIAL SPHERE**, the imaginary spherical dome which surrounds the Earth, around which the celestial bodies appear to move. See also **MUSIC OF THE SPHERES**.

VEDAS Four sacred books of the Brahmin: the Rig Veda (hymns); Samaveda (chants); Yajurveda (sacrificial prayers); Atharvaveda (hymns and spells).

VEGA Alpha Lyrae, brightest star in the constellation **LYRA**, and fifth brightest visible star in the sky; the standard star for zero **MAGNITUDE**; it is surrounded by a mass of dust particles which may be a planetary system in the making.

VEIL NEBULA Remnants of a **SUPERNOVA** which exploded between 20 000 and 30 000 years ago in the constellation **CYGNUS**; also called Cirrhus Nebula and Cygnus Loop. Strong source of **RADIO WAVES**.

VELA, the Sails Constellation formed from the archaic **ARGO**; the brightest star is Regor (Gamma Velis) and **MARKEB** (Kappa Velis) and Delta Velis are two components of the **FALSE CROSS**. See also **CARINA**.

VELA PULSAR Short period **PULSAR** discovered in 1968; possibly a **SUPERNOVA** remnant.

VENATOR, Nicolaus Astronomer whose main claim to fame is his naming of Alpha and Beta Delphini by reversing his name: **ROTANEV** and **SUALOCIN**.

VENUS Second planet from the Sun, nearest planet to Earth, and much the same size (6 051 km/3 760 miles radius), it orbits the Sun in 225 days but rotates very slowly (**RETROGRADE**) on its axis so that one Venusian day (243 Earth days) lasts longer than a Venusian year. No moons. Venus is enshrouded in an unbroken cocoon of creamy cloud which reflects 79 per cent of the sunlight shining on it: therefore, apart from the Sun and Moon, it is the brightest celestial object in the sky, appearing as the Morning Star or Evening Star, depending on the season, and the position of the observer. Astrologically, Venus rules **TAURUS** and **LIBRA**, is at **DETRIMENT** in **ARIES**, and at **FALL** in **VIRGO**. It is associated with the throat, kidneys and back; Venus is considered to influence such traits as adaptability, harmony, friendship, ability to love and artistic creativity. On the negative side, Venus subjects can be over-romantic, weak-willed, clinging, careless and indecisive. In Roman mythology, Venus is the goddess of love, beauty, harmony and fruitfulness; she is identified with the Greek **APHRODITE**.

VENUS TABLET Astrological text on a clay tablet found at **NINEVEH** in 1849/50 by archaeologist Sir Austin Layard (1817–1894); when deciphered in 1911 it proved to list sightings of **VENUS** made by early Babylonian astrologers (1702–1681 BC).

VERNAL EQUINOX See **EQUINOX**

VERNAL POINT Point at which the **GREAT CIRCLES**, the **ECLIPTIC** and the **CELESTIAL EQUATOR** intersect at the **SPRING EQUINOX**; the Sun crosses the equator and its **DECLINATION** is zero. The **OBLIQUITY OF THE**

ECLIPTIC remains very nearly constant, but not entirely because the Earth is not a perfect sphere. As a result, each year when the Sun returns to the Vernal Point, it does not return to the exact place relative to the fixed stars. The Vernal Point recedes each year by about 50″ of **ARC**, about 1° every 72 years. See also **PRECESSION OF THE EQUINOXES**.

VERTEX Point where the **PRIME VERTICAL** intersects the **ECLIPTIC** in the west.

VERTUMNUS Ancient Roman god of the seasons, presiding over orchards and gardens.

VERY LARGE ARRAY The world's largest **RADIO ASTRONOMY INSTRUMENT ARRAY** set up in 1980 near Socorro, New Mexico, USA. Twenty-seven huge dishes (25 m/82 ft across) lie along the arms of a great 'Y'; each arm is 21 km/13 miles long. In effect this produces a gigantic telescope 34 km/21 miles across which can pick up millions of radio wavelengths.

VESPERTINE Setting just after the Sun.

VESPUCCI, Amerigo (1454–1512) Florentine explorer-navigator who used an **ASTROLABE** to plot the Southern Cross (**CRUX AUSTRALIS**).

VESTA **ASTEROID 4**, the brightest of the asteroids, just about visible to the naked eye; discovered by **OLBERS** in 1807. In Roman mythology, Vesta was the goddess of the hearth, the equivalent of the Greek **HESTIA**, keeper of the Sacred Flame of Olympus.

Very large Array radio telescope

VIA LACTEA Latin for **MILKY WAY**.

VIA SOLIS Latin for 'the Way of the Sun', a term sometimes used to describe the **ECLIPTIC**.

VINALIA Roman wine festivals honouring **JUPITER** and associated with **VENUS**.

VINDEMIATRIX Epsilon Virginis in the zodiacal constellation **VIRGO**.

VIRGIN Name and symbol for the zodiacal constellation **VIRGO**.

VIRGO, the Virgin Very large and rich zodiacal constellation, one of **PTOLEMY'S** original forty-eight; crosses the equator. Its brightest star is Spica (Alpha Virginis), the sixteenth brightest star in the sky, and there are eight other stars above the fourth **MAGNITUDE**; Virgo also includes the collection of faint galaxies known as the **VIRGO CLUSTER**. **VIRGO THE ZODIAC SIGN** is the sixth sign of the zodiac, a **NEGATIVE FEMININE MUTABLE EARTH** sign ruled by **MERCURY**; **VENUS** is at **FALL** in Virgo, and **NEPTUNE** at **DETRIMENT**. In Greek mythology, Virgo represents Astraea, the goddess of justice and order, daughter of **ZEUS** and Themis, who found life on sinful Earth too distressing and so was translated to the stars.

VIRGO CLUSTER Very rich and spectacular concentration of **GALAXIES** gathered in the direction of the constellation **VIRGO**.

VISIBLE HORIZON Also called sensible horizon; the boundary beyond which an observer cannot see. Astrologers use the **CELESTIAL HORIZON** for their calculations.

VISUAL MAGNITUDE Apparent brightness of a celestial body as seen by the naked eye.

VOID OF COURSE Term originally concerned with **HORARY ASTROLOGY**, referring to a body which passed through a zodiac sign without forming an **ASPECT** either to or from another body. Also used in **NATAL ASTROLOGY** to describe a planet that does not form an aspect before leaving the sign of its original **RADICAL** placing. The Moon is said to be 'Void of Course' between its last major aspect in one sign and its entry into the next.

VOLANS, the Flying Fish Small constellation that intrudes into **CARINA**.

VON BRAUN, Wernher (1912–1977) German rocket pioneer who assisted in the making of the wartime V2 rockets. Later, he led the American team which in 1958 launched Explorer 1.

VOYAGER Name given to two very successful space probes launched from Cape Canaveral in 1977 to send back data from the remotest members of the Solar System.

VULCAN Name given to a hypothetical planet near the orbit of **MERCURY**, whose existence was postulated in 1859 by **LEVERRIER** to account for discrepancies in Mercury's orbit; Einstein proved the impossibility of its existence in 1915. In Roman mythology, Vulcan was the son of **JUPITER** and **JUNO**, the 'smith-god' of fire and metalwork.

VULPECULA, the Fox Constellation near **CYGNUS**; contains the splendid **PLANETARY NEBULA** known as the **DUMBELL NEBULA**.

VULPECULA ET ANSER Fox and goose; old name for the constellation **VULPECULA**.

Venus by Canova

WANING MOON **PHASE** of the Moon when it is decreasing in brightness after being Full: **VENUS** also wanes.

WATCHERS OF THE HEAVENS See **FOUR WATCHERS OF THE HEAVENS**

WATER BEARER Name given to **AQUARIUS**.

WATER ELEMENT See **ELEMENT**

WATER MONSTER Name for the constellation **HYDRA**.

WATER SIGNS **CANCER**, **SCORPIO** and **PISCES**; also known as Water **TRIPLICITIES**.

WATER SNAKE Name for the constellation **HYDRUS**.

WATER TRIPLICITY See **TRIPLICITIES**

WAXING MOON Phase of the Moon when it is increasing in brightness until it becomes **FULL**; **VENUS** also waxes.

WEDNESDAY Fourth day of the week; named for **WODEN** in germanic languages, and his equivalent **MERCURY** in latin languages.

WEI Epsilon Scorpii in the zodiacal constellation **SCORPIUS**.

WESTERBORK OBSERVATORY **RADIO ASTRONOMY** observatory in northeast Netherlands; boasts twelve 25 m/82 feet reflector dishes spread along a line 1.62 km/1 mile long; two end dishes mounted on rails for extra mobility.

WESTERN ANGLE Astrologically, the **CUSP** of the **SEVENTH HOUSE**, opposite the **ASCENDANT**.

WEST POINT Where the western horizon intersects the **CELESTIAL EQUATOR** and the **PRIME VERTICAL**.

WEST'S COMET Very long period **COMET** visible to the naked eye, last seen March 1976.

WEZEA Delta Canis Majoris; third brightest star in **CANIS MAJOR**.

WHALE Name for the constellation **CETUS**.

WHIRLPOOL GALAXY M51 The first **SPIRAL** to be recognized; seen by Lord **ROSSE** in 1845. Lies in the constellation **CANES VENATICI**.

WHITAKER'S ALMANACK Launched in 1868 by bookseller Joseph Whitaker (1820–1895) and still going strong; tabulates the daily **EQUATION OF TIME** (the difference between **SIDEREAL** and **GREENWICH MEAN TIME**), data essential to the erection of an accurate **BIRTH CHART**.

WHITE DWARFS Elderly, highly compressed stars; one cubic centimetre of white dwarf matter weighs about one tonne, and each square centimetre of surface radiates anything between thirty to eighty times as much heat as the Sun; white dwarfs have spent most of their nuclear energy and are on the cooling-down stage before they become inert. See also **NEUTRON STARS**.

WHITE, Edward Higgins II (1930–1967) First American astronaut to walk in space, from Gemini IV, in 1965.

WILD DUCK CLUSTER M11 An **OPEN CLUSTER** in the constellation **SCUTUM**.

WIND, Solar See **SOLAR WIND**

WINDS In classical mythology the sons of **ASTRAEUS** and **EOS**: **BORREAS**, **NOTUS**, **EURUS** and **ZEPHYRUS**.

WINGED HORSE Alternative name for constellation **PEGASUS**.

WINTER SOLSTICE Point at which the Sun appears to reach its lowest

Yerkes Observatory

DECLINATION south of the **CELESTIAL EQUATOR**; in reality, the point when the Earth reaches the highest point on the **ECLIPTIC** relative to the Sun. The shortest day and longest night of year; in the northern hemisphere, the first point of **CAPRICORN** (around 21 December); in the southern hemisphere, the first point of **CANCER** (around 21 June). The winter solstice is a **CARDINAL POINT** in the zodiac. See also **SUMMER SOLSTICE**.

WODEN Anglo-Saxon name for **ODIN**.

WOHL, Louis de (1903–1961) Berlin-born astrologer who persuaded Winston Churchill to employ him as Official Astrologer to the British War Cabinet after convincing him that Adolf Hitler was basing his campaign on astrological advice given by Karl Ernst **KRAFFT**; this was doubtful, but de Wohl held an honorary commission in the Army and worked on astrological 'disinformation' smuggled into enemy territory to lower morale.

WOLF Name for the constellation **LUPUS**.

WOLF, Maximilian Franz Joseph (1863–1932) German astronomer, first to use photography to observe **ASTEROIDS**; found 232 altogether, the first one being asteroid 323 Brucia (1891).

WONDERS OF THE WORLD See **SEVEN WONDERS OF THE WORLD**

WOOLLEY, Sir Charles Leonard (1880–1960) English archaeologist who excavated pyramids and **ZIGGURATS** at **UR**.

WOOLLEY, Sir Richard (1906–1986) Tenth Astronomer Royal from 1956 to 1971; after retiring from Greenwich he became the first Director of the South African National Observatories.

XANTHIAN MARBLES Collection of ancient sculptures and friezes discovered by Sir Charles Fellows in 1838 at Xanthus, a Greek city of Lycia, Asia Minor; now in the British Museum.

XIPHIAS From the Greek meaning sword; former name for the constellation **DORADO**; also ancient name for a sword-shaped **COMET**.

X-RAY ASTRONOMY Study of the **X-RAY** sources in the Universe, initiated in 1949 when it was discovered that the Sun emitted Xrays; all work carried out by satellites or rockets, as X-rays are absorbed by the Earth's atmosphere. In 1978, it became apparent that most stars emit X-rays, which effectively broadened the base of this branch of astronomy.

X-RAYS Penetrating, high-frequency short-wave **ELECTRO MAGNETIC RADIATION** produced when fast electrons pass through matter; shorter wavelengths than **ULTRAVIOLET RADIATION**; when they.reach extremely short wavelengths they become **GAMMA RAYS**. Discovered in 1895 by Wilhelm Konrad von Röntgen (1845–1923).

XYLOMANCY Divination by rods or twigs.

YANG See YIN/YANG.

YEAR Time taken for the Earth to orbit the Sun once; there are many different ways of expressing this: in the GREGORIAN CALENDAR, used by most people in the west today, the calendar year is normally 365 days, with an extra day every fourth or leap year: the average is 365.2425 days; the TROPICAL (or **Solar**) year is the time interval between successive VERNAL EQUINOXES, 365.249219 days; the SIDEREAL year is the time taken to complete the circuit relative to the FIXED STARS; this is 365.25636 days; a LUNAR YEAR is twelve SYNODIC MONTHS, about 354 days. Astrologers use the Tropical year.

YEAR FOR A DAY See DIRECTIONS'

YED POSTERIOR and **YED PRIOR** Two fixed stars, Epsilon and Delta respectively, of the constellation OPHIUCUS.

YERKES OBSERVATORY Founded in 1897 by millionaire Charles Yerkes at the behest of George HALE; major American observatory at Williams Bay, near Chicago, housing a 101.6 cm/40 in refractor TELESCOPE, still the largest in the world.

YIN/YANG Chinese philosophical concept of the interdependent duality; not mutually exclusive opposites but complementary states both of which contain the seed of the other within them. Western astrology reflects this in the idea of alternating Positive/ Negative signs around the zodiac and the acknowledgement of the influence of the POLAR (that is directly opposite) sign.

The Yin/Yang symbol

YOD The FINGER OF FATE; see also QUINCUNX.

YOUNG, Charles Augustus (1834–1908) American astronomer, among the first to study the Solar CORONA and CHROMOSPHERE by spectroscopy.

ZADKEIL Pseudonym of R.J. Morrison (1795–1874), one of the ANGELIC ASTROLOGERS; became a professional fortune teller in 1930.

ZANIAH Eta Virginis in the zodiac constellation VIRGO.

ZARATHUSTRA See ZOROASTER

ZAVIJAVA Beta Virginis in the zodiac constellation VIRGO.

ZELENCHUKSKAYA ASTROPHYSICAL OBSERVATORY Important Russian observatory situated at Mount Semirodriki in the Caucasus, 3 000 ft above sea level. Home of the largest reflector TELESCOPE in the world, with a diameter of 6 m/236 in.

ZEND-AVESTA Sacred writings of ZOROASTER.

ZENITH Point directly over the observer's head, at the intersection of the two GREAT CIRCLES, the PRIME VERTICAL and the MERIDIAN. See also NADIR.

Zelenchukskaya Observatory

Background: Zeus gives birth to Athene

ZEPHYRUS In Greek mythology, the west wind, son of ASTRAEUS and EOS, brother to BOREAS and NOTUS; identified with the Roman Favonius.

ZERO, Absolute Lowest possible temperature, equivalent to −273° Celsius or Zero Kelvin.

ZETA AQUILAE The star DHENEB.

ZETA AURIGAE ECLIPSING BINARY in the constellation AURIGA; one of the three HAEDI near CAPELLA; sometimes called by its old name Sadatoni.

ZETA LIONIS The star ADHAFERA.

ZETA ORIONIS The star ALNITAK.

ZEUS Greatest of the Greek gods; the youngest son of CRONOS and RHEA; the only child saved from being eaten by his father, Zeus was brought up in the Dictaean cave on Crete suckled by AMALTHEA (either a she-goat or a nymph). When grown, forced his father to disgorge his brothers and sisters, and initiated the war of the TITANS, which he and his fellow Olympians won decisively; established the gods' home on Mount OLYMPUS, married his sister HERA, and ruled the world with the power of his thunderbolts; fathered countless progeny on many different nymphs and goddesses, giving rise to many creation myths. The Romans called him JUPITER.

ZIGGURAT Huge stone stepped pyramid-style monument built by the Babylonians, the best known to us being the Great Ziggurat at Ur, already ancient in 2000 BC. Babylon's 'Tower of Babel' was a ziggurat. The corners of all these huge temple-towers were aligned with the CARDINAL POINTS, and there was always a shrine at the top.

ZODIAC Term based on the Greek word meaning 'image of an animal or living being', used by astrologers and astronomers. Describes a belt of sky around the CELESTIAL SPHERE about 8° to 9° above and below the ECLIPTIC, the pathway along which the Sun, Moon and planets appear to move – apart from PLUTO, which can wander about 17° from the ecliptic. The ecliptic passes through the twelve zodiac constellations ARIES, TAURUS, GEMINI, CANCER, LEO, VIRGO, LIBRA, SCORPIO, SAGITTARIUS, AQUARIUS and PISCES. Offshoots of other constellations (CETUS, ORION, OPHIUCHUS and SEXTANS) appear partially in the zodiac. The zodiacal constellations are of irregular size and do not take up equal parts of the zodiac belt. Astrologically, the zodiac circle is divided into twelve equal sections of 30° each, starting at the FIRST POINT OF ARIES. Although the zodiac signs are named after the constellations, the two no longer coincide. See also ZODIAC SIGNS; ZODIAC, SIDEREAL; ZODIAC, TROPICAL.

ZODIAC, Sidereal Zodiac system mainly used by eastern and Indian astrologers; the planets are observed against the background of the constellations; the problem with this kind of zodiac is establishing a recognizable starting point, as there are no signposts in the sky to indicate where each of the irregular constellations begins or ends. Also known as the fixed zodiac. See also ZODIAC, TROPICAL.

ZODIAC, Tropical Man-made zodiac of twelve equal segments of 30° each. It starts at the VERNAL POINT, the point where the ECLIPTIC and the CELESTIAL EQUATOR intersect and the Sun is at zero DECLINATION (about 21 March). Some 2 000 years ago, when the tropical zodiac was established, this was the FIRST POINT OF ARIES, as the constellation behind the Sun was ARIES; the PRECESSION OF THE EQUINOXES means that the constellation behind the Sun at the vernal point is now AQUARIUS, but Aries is retained as the first sign of the zodiac.

ZODIAC SIGNS Astrologers divide the zodiac into twelve equal 30° segments; they are named after the zodiac constellations, but are not coincident with them. They are also known as Sun-signs. Each sign is allocated a PLANETARY RULER and special characteristics. See also ARIES, TAURUS, GEMINI, CANCER, LEO, VIRGO, LIBRA, SCORPIO, SAGITTARIUS, CAPRICORN, AQUARIUS and PISCES.

ZODIACAL BAND See ZODIACAL LIGHT.

ZODIACAL LIGHT Wedge of faint light which can be seen rising at the western horizon after sunset, or at the eastern horizon before sunrise, best observed in the tropics; elsewhere it can be seen at the EQUINOXES (in northern latitudes, the evening of the SPRING EQUINOX and the morning of the AUTUMNAL EQUINOX; vice versa for southern latitudes). Gegenschein, or counterglow, is the same effect occurring at the antisolar point (directly opposite the Sun), best seen in December and January in northern latitudes and June and July in southern latitudes. Very occasionally, these two are linked by a thin ribbon of light called the Zodiacal Band, that stretches along the ECLIPTIC. Such glows along the zodiac are caused by reflected sunlight scattered Earthwards by interstellar dust PARTICLES surrounding the Sun. Zodiacal light was first discovered by CASSINI in 1683.

ZONE TIME System of time keeping, based on twenty- four MERIDIANS, each 15° apart and starting from the PRIME MERIDIAN at Greenwich. It gives a time difference of one hour between two adjacent zones. Also called Standard Time.

ZOROASTER Founder of an ancient Persian religion, which taught that a person's state after death depended on the amount of good and evil in their life. Also called Zarathustra.

ZOSMA Delta Lionis in the zodiacal constellation LEO.

ZUBENELCHEMALE Beta Librae in the zodiacal constellation LIBRA.

ZUBENELGENUBI Alpha Librae in the zodiacal constellation LIBRA.

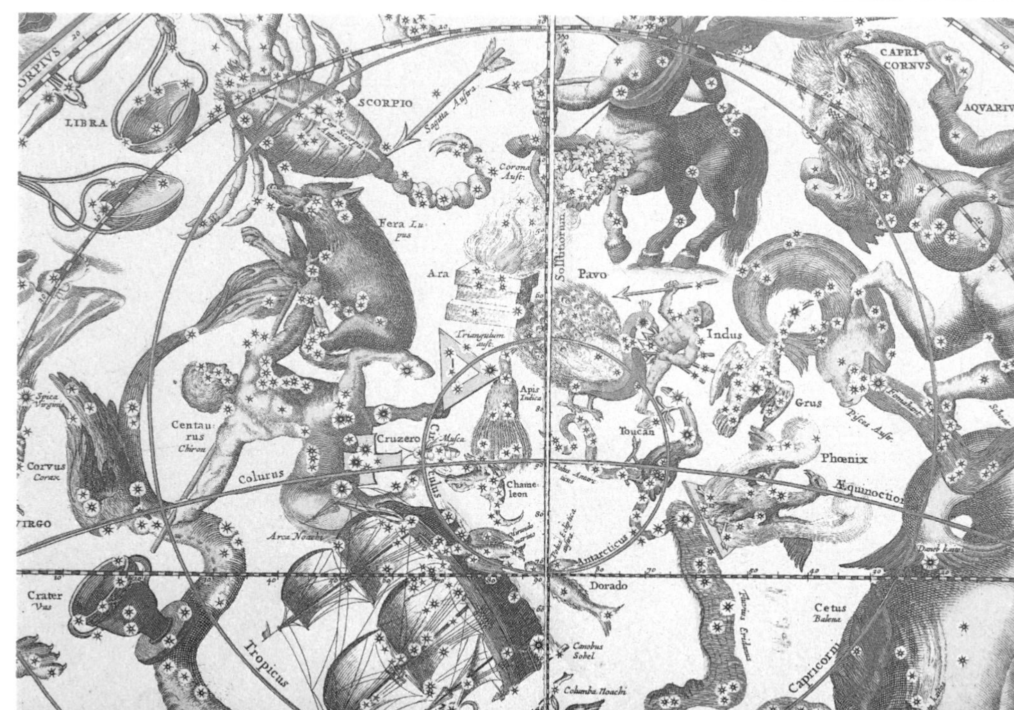

Map of the star groups, including zodiacal constellations

Index

Picture Acknowledgements

KEY: AAA = Ancient Art & Architecture Collection; BL = British Library; BM = British Museum; Barnaby's = Barnaby's Picture Library; Bridgeman = Bridgeman Art Library; M. Holford = Michael Holford; Hulton = Hulton Picture Company; Mansell = The Mansell Collection; MEPL = Mary Evans Picture Library; SI = Syndication International; SPL = Science Photo Library.

BL/Octopus Group Ltd 8. BM/Bridgeman 11. Iraq Museum, Baghdad/Scala 12. AAA 13 (top); BM/C.M. Dixon 13 (bottom). AAA 15. Skyscan 16. Louvre/Bridgeman 18. BM/Bridgeman 19 (left); BM/C.M. Dixon 19 (right). Louvre, Paris 20. Archaeological Museum, Istanbul/C.M. Dixon 21 (top); AAA 21 (bottom). BM/M. Holford 23. Duomo, Siena/Scala 24. AAA 26. ET Archive 27. Biblioteca Apostolica Vaticana/Octopus Group Ltd 29. Bibliothèque Nationale, Paris 30. Zev Radovan, Jerusalem 31. Biblioteca Statale, Lucca/Scala 32. Pinacoteca, Vatican/Scala 33. BM/AAA 34. BL/Bridgeman 35. Science Museum, London/M. Holford 36. Naprstek Museum, Prague/Werner Forman Archive 39, National Maritime Museum/ET Archive 41. Tony Morrison/South American Pictures 42. NASA/SPL 43, Zev Radovan 70-71. ET Archive 96-97. Popperfoto 98. Ann Ronan Picture Library 99. ET Archive 100 (left and right). Hulton 101. Milan Museum/Scala 102. ET Archive 103 (top); Museo Nazionali, Naples/Alinari 103 (bottom). Ann Ronan 104 (left and background). M. Holford 105 (top); BM/ET Archive 105 (bottom). Kunsthistorischen Museum, Vienna/ET Archive 106. Mansell 107 (right and background). NASA/ET Archive 108. SI 109 (top); Mansell 109 (bottom). Musée Condé, Chantilly/ET Archive 110; Hulton 110 (background). Fortean Picture Library 111. Private Collection/Bridgeman 112 (top); Popperfoto 112 (bottom). Sparta Museum, Greece/Sonia Halliday 113. Roy Miles Fine Paintings, London/Bridgeman 114. Museo Nazionali, Naples/Alinari/Mansell 115 (top); Lick Observatory, California/SPL 115 (bottom). BM/M. Holford 116 (top); Ann Ronan 116 (bottom and background). Il Duomo, Florence/Alinari/Mansell 117. Hulton 118. Ann Ronan 119 (top); Hulton 119 (bottom). MEPL 120. Mansell 121 (top); NASA/ET Archive 121 (bottom). Mansell 122 (left); Ann Ronan 122-123 (background). Vatican Museums & Galleries, Rome/Bridgeman 123 (top); ET Archive 123 (bottom). Mansell 124 (top); Anaya Publishers Ltd 124 (bottom). Mansell 125 (top); M. Holford 125 (bottom). Hulton 126 (top); Mansell 126 (bottom). ET Archive 127 (top); Ronald Royer/SPL 127 (bottom). Ann Ronan 128 (top); Mansell 128-129 (background). Martin Dohrn/SPL 129. Popperfoto 130. Mansell 131 (top); Berlin Museum/Giraudon 131 (bottom). Kunsthistorischen Museum, Vienna/ET Archive 132. Ann Ronan 133 (top); Hulton 133 (bottom). Ann Ronan 134 (top); National Gallery of Art, Washington/Bridgeman 134 (bottom). Barnaby's 135. Ann Ronan 136 (top); Uffizi Galleries, Florence/Scala 136 (bottom). MEPL 137 (bottom); ET Archive 137 (right). Scala 138 (left). Fitzwilliam Museum, Cambridge 138 (right). Hulton 139. Popperfoto 140. SI 141 (top)) Kim Naylor 141 (bottom). Bettmann Archive/Hulton 142 (top); Musée Granet, Aix-en-Provence/Bridgeman 142 (bottom). Mansell 143. NASA/The Research House 144. ET Archive 145 (top); Orville Andrews/SPL 145 (bottom). ET Archive 146 (bottom and background). AAA 147. Museo Capitolino, Rome/Alinari/Mansell 148. Mansell 149 (top); Stephanie Colasanti 149 (bottom). Sonia Halliday 150. ET Archive 151 (top); Sonia Halliday 151 (bottom). Popperfoto 152 (top). Ann Ronan 152 (background). Bardo Museum, Tunis/Sonia Halliday 153. Fotomas Index 154. Hassia, Paris/Sonia Halliday 155 (top); Musée Versailles/ET Archive 155 (bottom). Mansell 156 (top); M. Holford 156 (bottom). SI 157 (top); Hulton 157 (bottom). C. M. Dixon 158 (top); Museo Nazionali, Naples/Alinari/Mansell 158 (background). Christie's, London/Bridgeman 159 (top); National Gallery, London 159 (bottom). Museo Borghese, Rome/Alinari/Mansell 160. SI 161 (top); Ann Ronan 161 (bottom). AAA 162. SI 163 (top); Harvard College Observatory/SPL 163 (bottom). ET Archive 164 (top); Barnaby's 164 (bottom). AAA 165. Barnaby's 166. C. M. Dixon 167 (top); Stephanie Colasanti 167 (bottom); Ann Ronan 167 (background). Mansell 168. BM/ET Archive 169 (top); Robin Scagell/SPL 169 (bottom). Lars Thomas/Fortean 170. Barnaby's 171. MEPL 172. ET Archive 173 (top); Mansell 173 (bottom). BM/ET Archive 174. John Sanford/SPL 175 (top); Popperfoto 175 (bottom). ET Archive 176 (top); Mansell 176 (bottom). Musée Condé, Chantilly/Bridgeman 177. Richard Gee/Barnaby's 178 (top); Mansell 178 (bottom). Robert Estall 179 (top); Ann Ronan 179 (background). Popperfoto 180 (bottom); Mansell 180 (background). Mansell 181 (top); Hulton 181 (bottom). Louvre/Mansell 182. Barnaby's 183. ET Archive 184. ET Archive 185 (top and background). Popperfoto 186. Peter Menzel/SPL 187 (bottom); Galleria Pitti, Florence/ Alinari/Mansell 187 (right). Hulton 188. M. Holford 189 (top); SPL 189 (bottom). BL/Bridgeman 190 (bottom); BM/M. Holford 190 (background).

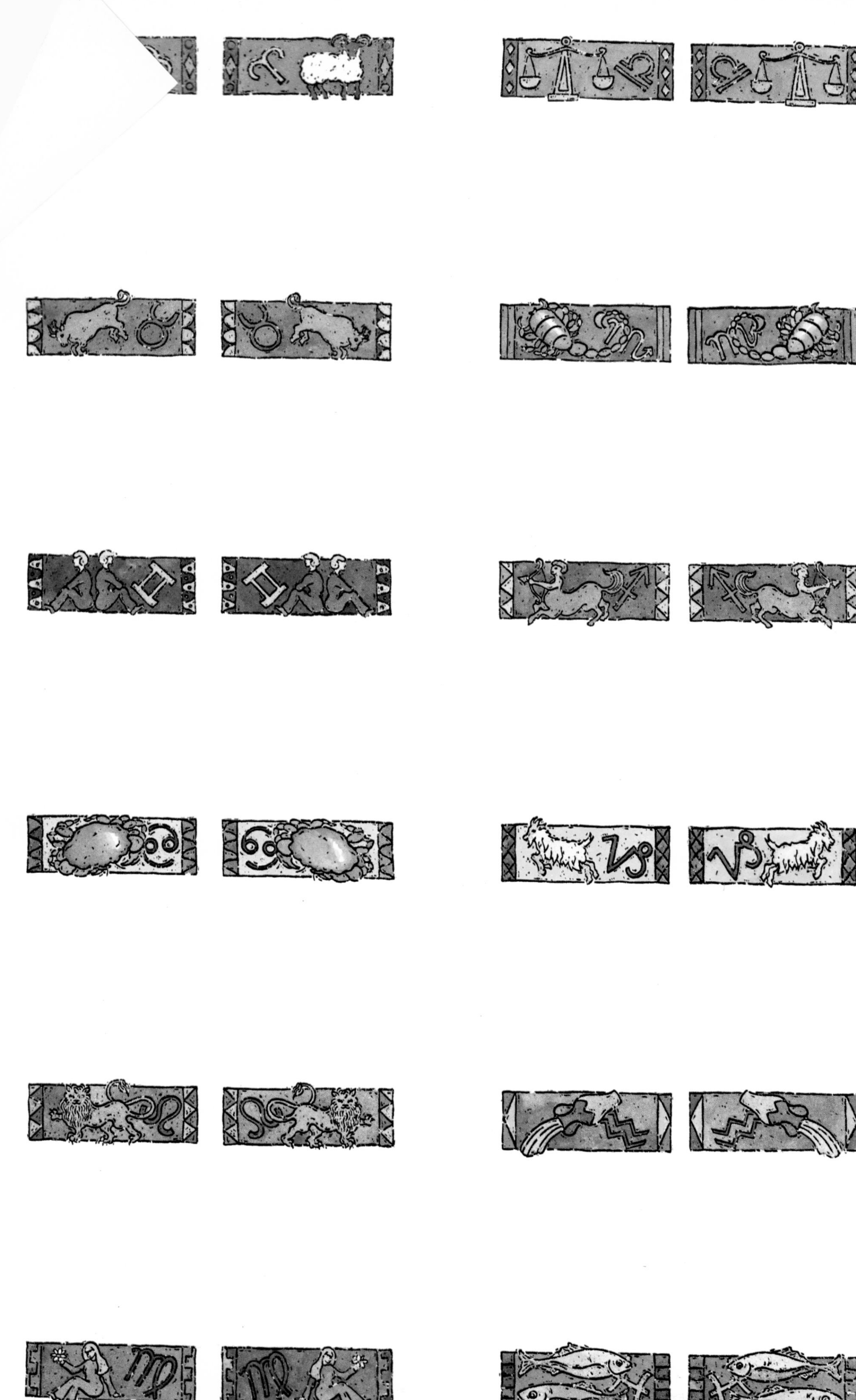